# The Middle East

## Volume 2
IRAN • IRAQ • ISRAEL

Titles in the series

## Volume 1
BAHRAIN • CYPRUS • EGYPT

## Volume 2
IRAN • IRAQ • ISRAEL

## Volume 3
JORDAN • KUWAIT • LEBANON • OMAN

## Volume 4
QATAR • SAUDI ARABIA • SYRIA

## Volume 5
TURKEY • UNITED ARAB EMIRATES • YEMEN

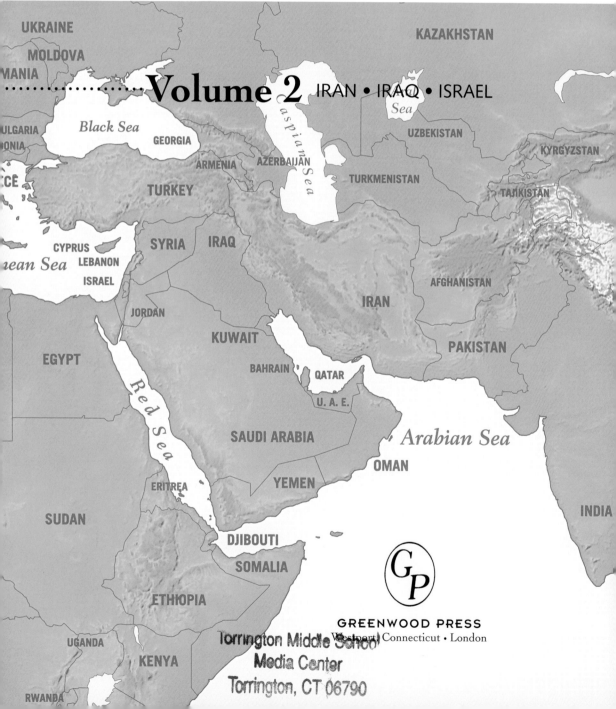

# Discovering
# World Cultures

# The Middle East

## Volume 2   IRAN • IRAQ • ISRAEL

**GREENWOOD PRESS**
Westport, Connecticut • London

Torrington Middle School
Media Center
Torrington, CT 06790

Library of Congress Cataloging-in-Publication Data

Discovering world cultures: the Middle East / by Creative Media Applications.
    p. cm. — (Middle school reference)
      Contents: v. 1. Bahrain, Cyprus, Egypt — v. 2. Iran, Iraq, Israel — v. 3. Jordan, Kuwait, Lebanon,
    Oman — v. 4. Qatar, Saudi Arabia, Syria — v. 5. Turkey, United Arab Emirates, Yemen.
      Includes bibliographical references and index.
      ISBN 0–313–32922–2 (set: alk. paper)—ISBN 0–313–32923–0 (v. : alk.paper)—
    ISBN 0–313–32924–9 (v. 2: alk. paper)—ISBN 0–313–32925–7 (v. 3: alk. paper)—
    ISBN 0–313–32926–5 (v. 4: alk. paper)—ISBN 0–313–32927–3 (v. : alk. paper)
      1. Ethnology — Middle East. 2. Middle East — Social life and customs. I. Creative Media  Applications.
      II. Series.
    GN635.N42D57   2004
    306.'0956 — dc22    2003044263

British Library Cataloguing in Publication Data is available.

Copyright © 2004 by Greenwood Publishing Group, Inc.

Library of Congress Catalog Card Number: 2003044263
ISBN:  0–313–32922–2  (set)
        0–313–32923–0 (vol. 1)
        0–313–32924–9 (vol. 2)
        0–313–32925–7 (vol. 3)
        0–313–32926–5 (vol. 4)
        0–313–32927–3 (vol. 5)

First published in 2004

Greenwood Press, 88 Post Road West, Westport, CT 06881
An imprint of Greenwood Publishing Group, Inc.
www.greenwood.com

Printed in the United States of America

∞

The paper used in this book complies with the Permanent Paper Standard
issued by the National Information Standards Organization (Z39.48–1984).

10   9   8   7   6   5   4   3   2   1

A Creative Media Applications, Inc. Production
WRITER: Sandy Pobst
DESIGN AND PRODUCTION: Alan Barnett, Inc.
EDITOR: Susan Madoff
COPYEDITOR: Laurie Lieb
PROOFREADER: Betty Pessagno
INDEXER: Nara Wood
ASSOCIATED PRESS PHOTO RESEARCHER: Yvette Reyes
CONSULTANT: Abraham Marcus is Associate Professor of Middle Eastern History and
    former Director of the Center for Middle Eastern Studies at the University of Texas at Austin.

PHOTO CREDITS:
AP/Wide World Photographs pages: x, 2, 4, 7, 8, 17, 21, 25, 26, 28, 32, 37, 47, 48, 53, 65, 66, 68, 71, 76, 80, 86, 89, 95,
    101, 102, 104, 107
© Hulton-Deutsch Collection/CORBIS pages: 10, 12, 63
© Diego Lezama Orezzoli/CORBIS page: 11
© Michael Nicholson/CORBIS page: 15
© Bettmann/CORBIS pages: 19, 99
© AFP/CORBIS page: 23
© Reuters NewMedia Inc./CORBIS page: 29
© Faleh Kheiber/Reuters/Landov pages: 42, 51
© Caren Firouz/Reuters/Landov page: 45
© Michael Maslan Historic Photographs/CORBIS page: 55
© Araldo de Luca/CORBIS page: 56
© Christine Osborne/CORBIS page: 60
© Goran Tomasevic/Reuters /Landov page: 73
© ASAP/Landov pages: 84, 92, 109, 116
© Bojan Brecelj/CORBIS page: 96

# Table of Contents

Thanks to Linda Miller Raff, Mary Ann Segalla,
and Amy Snyder for their contributions.

# INTRODUCTION

The Middle East. The name conjures up many different images for most Westerners: fascinating ancient civilizations, the rise and fall of powerful empires, and—most recently—bloody conflicts and suicide bombers. This series introduces the history, customs, and cultures of the people living in the Middle East in the hope of inspiring a fuller understanding of a complex region.

## What Is the Middle East?

"The Middle East" is a rather vague name for such an important region of the world. What is it in the middle of? And how is it different from the Near East and the Far East?

Most of the geographical terms used in the world today, such as the label "Middle East," originated with Europeans and Americans. As Europeans explored the world around them, they first headed east. The lands that bordered the eastern basin of the Mediterranean Sea— Anatolia (Turkey), Syria, Palestine, and Egypt, as well as their immediate neighbors—became known as the "Near East." Countries farther away, such as China and Indonesia, were referred to as the "Far East."

The term "Middle East" has been in use for only the past century. It was first used by an American military officer to describe the geopolitical

## MEASURING TIME

Most of the world today uses the Gregorian calendar, which is based on the solar year. Because it is a Christian calendar, historical dates have traditionally been designated as occurring before the birth of Christ (B.C.) or after the birth of Christ (A.D., an acronym for the Latin phrase *Anno Domini,* meaning "in the year of the Lord"). In recent years, historians have started to use neutral, nonreligious terms to describe these divisions of time. The *Discovering World Cultures: The Middle East* series follows this practice, using B.C.E. (before the Common Era) rather than B.C. and C.E. (Common Era) in place of A.D. (Some people define the terms as "Before the Christian Era" and "Christian Era.") The dating system remains the same: 1000 B.C. is the same as 1000 B.C.E., while 2003 C.E. is the same as A.D. 2003.

region that included the countries between the Mediterranean Sea and India—those countries in the middle of the Eastern Hemisphere that shared a common culture. Today, there are many different definitions of the Middle East. Some scholars include the countries of northern Africa in their definition of the Middle East. Others use a cultural definition that includes all the predominantly Islamic countries in Africa and Asia. This series adopts the definition used by most modern scholars, adding Egypt to the original list of Middle Eastern countries because of its shared history and Arabic culture.

## Birthplace of World Religions

As home to the world's earliest civilizations, the Middle East is also the birthplace of three of the world's major religions: Judaism, Christianity, and Islam. Followers of these three religions worship the same god and share a common early history. Today, about 2 billion people worldwide identify themselves as Christian, while about 1.3 billion follow Islam. Nearly 14 million are Jews. Together, these three groups make up 53 percent of the world's population.

### Judaism

Judaism is the oldest of the three religions, originating nearly 4,000 years ago in the land of Israel (also known as Palestine). Jews believe that Abraham, who was born in Ur in present-day Iraq, was the founder of Judaism. About 1800 B.C.E., he began to teach that the world was created by a single god. God made a covenant, or agreement, with Abraham: if Abraham left his home and followed God's commandments, God would bless Abraham with children and establish a great nation. Moses, a descendant of Abraham's son Isaac, later led the Jewish people out of slavery in Egypt. God made a new covenant with Moses, providing instructions and rules for living a holy life, including the Ten Commandments.

According to Jewish tradition, Abraham's first son, Ishmael, is the ancestor of the Arab people. His second son, Isaac, is the ancestor of the Jewish people.

Jews believe that when they follow the Torah—the first five books of the Hebrew Bible, or holy book—and keep God's laws, the Jewish people and the nation of Israel will be blessed by God. They also believe that God will send a Messiah, a political leader chosen by God to bring the

Jewish *exiles* back to Israel, rebuild Jerusalem and restore the Temple that was destroyed by the Romans in 70 C.E., and put an end to the evil in the world. (For more information about Judaism, please see page 108 in Volume 2.)

## Christianity

Christianity grew out of Judaism about 2,000 years ago in Israel when Jesus Christ, a Jewish man, began teaching about faith and God's love. Christians believe that Jesus Christ is the son of God, the Messiah sent by God to save people from sin and death. They believe that Jesus was resurrected after his death and that, through faith, they too will have life after death. The Christian Bible includes both the Hebrew Bible (Old Testament) and the teachings of Jesus and his disciples (the New Testament). Unlike Jews and Muslims, Christians believe in the Trinity of God—that God exists as the Father, the Son, and the Holy Spirit. (For more information about Christianity, please see pages 56–60 in Volume 1 of *Discovering World Cultures: The Middle East*.)

## Islam

Islam was founded in the seventh century by the Prophet Mohammad, who was a direct descendant of Ishmael. Muslims believe in only one god, Allah, the same god worshiped by Jews and Christians. According to Islamic tradition, Allah's message to humans has been delivered by prophets, such as Abraham, Moses, Jesus, and Mohammad. Holy books, including the Torah, the Christian Gospels, and the Qur'an, preserve the word of Allah. Because the countries in the Middle East are predominantly Islamic, a detailed overview of Islam is provided here.

### *Basic Beliefs*

Muslims believe that the "five pillars of Islam" are the key to salvation:

- *Shahadah:* the acknowledgment that "there is no god but God and that Mohammad is the messenger of God"
- *Salah:* five daily ritual prayers
- *Zakat:* the giving of money to the poor
- *Sawm:* the dawn-to-dusk fast during the month of Ramadan, Islam's most important religious observance
- *Hajj:* the pilgrimage to Mecca, the birthplace of Mohammad

### Forms of Islam

About 85 percent of the Islamic community follows the Sunni tradition (in Arabic, *Sunni* refers to the people who follow the sunna, or example, of the prophet). Sunni Muslims believe that the *caliph,* or spiritual leader, should be chosen by the consensus of the Islamic community. They also believe that following *shari'a,* or Islamic, law is essential in living a life that ends in salvation.

The Shi'a tradition teaches that Mohammad appointed his cousin and son-in-law Ali and his descendants to be the spiritual and worldly leaders of Islam after Mohammad's death. Shi'ite (SHE-ite) Muslims believe that these leaders, called *imams,* are free of sin and infallible. About 15 percent of all Muslims follow Shi'a Islam, but there are several different branches within the Shi'a tradition.

Wahhabism is an Islamic reform movement that originated in the eighteenth century in Saudi Arabia. Its members are the most conservative, fundamentalist group in Islam. Members reject any

*Iraqi Shi'ite Muslims gather at a holy site in the city of Karbala, Iraq, in April 2003, to mourn the death of one of their most important saints. Under the rule of Iraqi leader Saddam Hussein, they had been banned from observing such rituals for decades. With Hussein's fall from power that same month, however, they were free to worship.*

modern interpretations of Islam, including the celebration of Mohammad's birthday or playing music. Muslims who adopt Wahhabi principles label those who don't share their beliefs as infidels or unbelievers, even those who are moderate Sunnis and Shi'ites.

## Sources of Muslim Teachings and Tradition

The Qur'an is the only holy book of the Islam faith. Muslims believe that the Qur'an contains the literal word of Allah, or God, which was revealed to the Prophet Mohammad. Memorizing and reciting these holy words is an important part of daily prayer and worship. (Many Americans refer to this book as the Koran, a Westernized spelling of Qur'an.)

While the Qur'an is the only holy text, there are other important spiritual sources in the Islamic faith. The Sunna is a collection of all the stories, sayings, and actions of Mohammad. Followers of Islam use these examples to determine correct behavior in areas not covered in the Qur'an. They often come up with different explanations, which is why customs and beliefs vary sometimes from group to group. One of the distinct features of Islam is the Shari'a, a comprehensive body of laws covering personal, civil, and criminal matters.

## COURTESY AND CUSTOMS IN THE MIDDLE EAST

Middle Eastern customs and traditions have developed over centuries, influenced by tribal culture and religion. Visitors to the region should be aware of rules and taboos, such as the ones shown here, that apply in most Middle Eastern countries.

- When greeting a man, clasp his hand briefly without shaking it. A man should never move to shake hands with a woman unless she offers her hand first. Inquiries about an acquaintance's health and interests are expected, but you should never ask about a Muslim's female family members.

- Showing the sole of your shoe to another person, such as when you sit with one leg crossed over the other knee, is very rude. The soles of your shoes should always be pointing downward.

- Always offer and receive items with your right hand. If you are served a meal in a traditional manner, use your right hand for eating (the left hand is regarded as unclean).

- When you visit a person's home, compliments about the home are welcome, but avoid admiring or praising an item excessively. The host may feel obligated to give the item to you as a gift.

- Photographing people is viewed with suspicion in some areas. It is important to ask permission before photographing anyone, especially a woman.

### *Major Religious Holidays*

- *Ashura:* The first ten days of the New Year are a period of mourning for Shi'ite Muslims as they remember the assassination of Hussein, grandson of the Prophet Mohammad, in 680 C.E.

- *Ramadan:* Ramadan honors the time when Mohammad received the first of the Qur'an from Allah. It is the ninth and most holy month in the Islamic year. Muslims do not eat or drink from dawn until dusk during Ramadan. Instead, they reflect on their relationship with Allah, asking for forgiveness for their sins.

- *Eid al-Fitr:* As Ramadan ends, Muslims gather with family and friends to celebrate the feast of Eid al-Fitr. Children often get new clothes for the holiday, which usually lasts three days. Gifts are exchanged among friends and family.

- *Eid al-Adha:* Eid al-Adha (the Feast of the Sacrifice) honors the Prophet Abraham and his devotion to God. At the end of the hajj, the pilgrimage to Mecca, an animal is sacrificed, and the meat is divided between family members and the poor.

## A Final Note

Transcribing the Arabic language into English often creates confusion. The two alphabets are very different and there is not a direct correlation of sounds. As a result, Arabic words are often given several different spellings in Western writing. One source may refer to the *emir* of a region, while another labels the ruler an *amir*. The name of the prophet who established Islam appears as Mohammad, Muhammad, and Mohammed. The Islamic holy book is the Qur'an or Koran, and so on. Another source of confusion is the different place names used by Westerners and those who live in the Middle East. For instance, the body of water between Iraq and the Arabian Peninsula has been called the Persian Gulf for centuries by Westerners. People living nearby, however, refer to it as the Arabian Gulf. In this series, the most commonly used spellings and the labels most familiar to Westerners have been used in an effort to avoid confusion. The exception lies in the spelling of *Qur'an,* the Islamic holy book, since scholars as well as many Muslims prefer that spelling over the Westernized *Koran.*

# Iran

ESTONIA
LATVIA
ANIA

UKRAINE
MOLDOVA
MANIA
BULGARIA
DONIA
CE
nean Sea

Black Sea

GEORGIA
ARMENIA
AZERBAIJAN

Caspian Sea

KAZAKHSTAN

Aral
Sea

UZBEKISTAN

KYRGYZSTAN

TURKMENISTAN

TAJIKISTAN

TURKEY

CYPRUS
LEBANON
ISRAEL

SYRIA

IRAQ

IRAN

AFGHANISTAN

JORDAN

KUWAIT

PAKISTAN

EGYPT

BAHRAIN

QATAR

U. A. E.

Arabian Sea

Red Sea

SAUDI ARABIA

OMAN

INDIA

ERITREA

YEMEN

SUDAN

DJIBOUTI

SOMALIA

ETHIOPIA

UGANDA

KENYA

RWANDA

ran, home to one of the world's oldest cultures, sits on a high plateau in southwest Asia. The people of Iran (ih-RAHN) have always called their country by this name, which means the land of the Aryans—people who originally migrated from Central Asia. Europeans and other Westerners called it Persia until 1935, when the government declared that the country's official name was Iran.

Following a revolution in 1979 when the monarchy was overthrown, Iran has been defined by the religion of Islam, which affects all aspects of life. Most Iranians are Shi'ite Muslims. Their beliefs differ from those of Sunni Muslims, the majority group in Islam, which has created tension between Iran and other Islamic countries. Some countries, such as Bahrain, have accused Iran of sponsoring riots and dissent in an attempt to overthrow the existing governments. In turn, Iran has accused countries that have strong relationships with the United States, such as Saudi Arabia and Kuwait, of being puppets of a foreign government. The United States, often referred to by Iranian leaders as the "Great Satan," has named Iran as one of the world's leading sponsors of terrorism.

## FAST FACTS

✔ **Official name:** Islamic Republic of Iran

✔ **Capital:** Tehran

✔ **Location:** Eastern edge of the Middle East; north of the Gulf of Oman and the Persian Gulf; south of Armenia, Azerbaijan, Turkmenistan, and the Caspian Sea; bordered on the east by Afghanistan and Pakistan and on the west by Turkey and Iraq.

✔ **Area:** 636,296 square miles (1,648,000 square kilometers)

✔ **Population:** 66,622,704 (July 2002 estimate)

✔ **Age distribution:**
0–14 years: 31%
15–64 years: 64%
over 65 years: 5%

✔ **Life expectancy:**
Males: 69 years
Females: 72 years

✔ **Ethnic groups:** Persian (including Gilaki and Mazandarani) 59%, Azeri 24%, Kurd 7%, Arab 3%, Lur 2%, Baluchi 2%, Turkmen 2%, other 1%

✔ **Religions:** Shi'a Muslim 89%, Sunni Muslim 10%, Zoroastrian, Jewish, Christian, and Baha'i 1%

✔ **Languages:** Persian (including dialects) 58%, Turkic (including dialects) 26%, Kurdish 9%, Luri 2%, Baluchi 1%, Arabic 1%, Turkish 1%, other 2%

✔ **Currency:**
Iranian rial (IRR)
US$1 = 7,863 IRR (2003)

✔ **Average annual income:** US$1,630

✔ **Major exports:** Petroleum, carpets, agricultural products

Source: CIA, *The World Factbook 2002;*
BBC News Country Profiles.

# The Iranians

Nearly 67 million people live in Iran, making it the third most populous country in the Middle East (behind Egypt and Turkey). Many Westerners think that all people living in the Middle East are Arabs. However, Iranians are a very diverse people and Arabs make up only a small part of Iran's population. Instead, most Iranians are Persians, descendants of the proud, ancient people who settled the region thousands of years ago.

## The Persians

Iranians of Persian descent make up 59 percent of the population. Their ancestors arrived in the seventh century B.C.E., establishing the Persian Empire in the next century. Although Persia was conquered and ruled by many other countries since then, the Persians maintained a strong cultural identity.

Today, most Persians live in Iran's major cities, especially Tehran. Their native language, Persian (sometimes called Farsi), is the official language of Iran. The majority of Persians practice Shi'a Islam, and many of Iran's religious leaders are Persian. A small number follow other religions, including Judaism, Zoroastrianism, and Baha'i.

## The Turkic People

The Azerbaijanis (sometimes called the Azeri Turks) descended from the Turkic tribes who began migrating into northwestern Iran about 1,000 years ago. They make up the second largest ethnic group in modern Iran. For many years, they lived primarily in the Zagros Mountains, but over the past century many settled in Tehran and other major cities. Most Azerbaijanis are Shi'ite Muslims.

The Qashqais, the next largest group of Turkic people, live in the Fars Province, near Shiraz. They still follow a nomadic lifestyle,

## A GROWING PROBLEM

Iran, already home to one of the world's most crowded cities, had one of the fastest growing populations in the world in the 1980s. Following the 1979 revolution, the government halted all family planning programs and encouraged couples to have large families. The rapid increase in population brought with it many problems, including poverty and unemployment. The policy was changed once again, and small families were promoted. By 2003, the growth rate had slowed to 1.1 percent.

herding their flocks of sheep and goats through Zagros Mountain paths as they move between summer and winter pastures. Nearly all of the Qashqais are Shi'ite Muslims.

Turkmen settlements are found along the northeastern border that divides Iran and Turkmenistan. Although the Turkmen have a nomadic heritage, many today are farmers and herders who live in small villages and towns. They are fairly isolated, with limited telephone access. Most are Sunni Muslims.

### Other Ethnic and Religious Groups

Other ethnic groups that have settled in Iran include the Lurs and Bakhtiaris, Kurds, Baluchis, and Arabs. Armenians and Assyrians are religious as well as ethnic minorities.

Two related groups—the Lurs and the Bakhtiaris—live in the Zagros Mountains. They speak Luri, a language that is closely related to Persian.

The Kurds live along the border of Iraq and Turkey, in what was once the southeastern region of Kurdistan. They are distantly related to the Persians, and their language—Kirmanji—is in the same language family as Persian. The Kurds are the third largest ethnic group in Iran. Although some Kurds were nomads in the past, today most live in permanent settlements. Many have migrated from rural Kurdish villages to towns and cities. The Kurds have fought for their independence throughout Iran's history, but with little success. They are primarily Sunni Muslims.

Most of the people living in the province of Sistan va Baluchestan are Baluchis, members of tribes that once roamed across southeastern

## AN ANCIENT LANGUAGE

Iran's official language—Persian, or Farsi—is over 2,500 years old. Native Persian speakers consider it a vital link to their heritage. Persian is more closely related to Latin, Greek, English, and other Indo-European languages than it is to Arabic. However, the flowing, lyrical language is written using Arabic script and includes many words adopted from Arabic.

*An Iranian woman reads a newspaper written in Farsi, the official language of Iran.*

Iran and western Afghanistan and Pakistan. As a result, the Baluchi language is closer to Pashtu, a common language of Afghanistan and Pakistan. Some Baluchis maintain the nomadic lifestyle of their ancestors, but others have settled in towns or on farms. The Baluchis, who live in one of the most desolate areas of Iran, are very poor. As Sunni Muslims, they often oppose the government's policies and receive little support from Tehran.

Most Iranian Arabs live in the western province of Khuzestan and along the Persian Gulf coast. Some of the men work in the oil industry, which is concentrated in Khuzestan, while others fish, farm, or herd livestock. The Arabs speak Arabic, a Semitic language, which belongs to a completely different language family than Persian. The Arabs in Khuzestan are Shi'ite Muslims and often marry into Persian families. Other Arabs are primarily Sunni Muslims.

Armenians and Assyrians are religious as well as ethnic minorities—both groups practice Christianity.

# Land and Resources

Iran's geography and natural resources have had a significant impact on its history and development. The mountains that nearly surround the high plateau in the center of the country have historically protected Iran from invaders, yet isolated the interior from other regions. Extensive oil and gas reserves provide a level of income that enables Iran to remain independent of most foreign aid.

## Geography

Iran is the second-largest country in the Middle East (Saudi Arabia is the largest). Iran's area is 636,296 square miles (1,648,000 square kilometers)—an area nearly equal to Alaska and Washington combined. Mountainous terrain is common in Iran, with two mountain systems that cover much of the country. Earthquakes are common in the mountain regions, and many of the highest peaks are inactive volcanoes.

The largest mountain system, the Zagros, spreads over much of western Iran, gradually declining in elevation from the northwest corner of Iran to the southeast. Many peaks in the Zagros range are over 9,800 feet (3,000 meters) in elevation, while some top 13,000 feet (4,000 meters). Peaks in the southeastern corner of Iran average less than 4,900 feet (1,500 meters). High plateaus, suitable for farming or grazing, are located between the ridges of the Zagros range. Historically, most of Iran's citizens settled in these plateaus, drawn by the fertile soil and abundant groundwater.

The tall, narrow Elburz (el-BURZ) mountain range borders the Caspian Sea in northern Iran. Its highest peak, Mount Damavand (DA-muh-vand), is an active volcano. It stands 18,602 feet (5,670 meters) tall, making it the highest point in Eurasia west of the Hindu Kush (a mountain range in northern Afghanistan). The moisture-laden winds that blow south over the Caspian Sea provide the coastal plain and the northern side of the Elburz Mountains with plentiful rainfall. Little moisture makes it over the Elburz peaks; the region south of the mountains is very dry.

The Caspian Sea is the largest inland lake in the world. With an area of 152,239 square miles (394,299 square kilometers), it is nearly five times larger than the second largest lake, Lake Superior in North America.

Between the Elburz Mountains and the Caspian Sea is a unique region. It is very humid, with lots of rainfall, unlike most of the rest of Iran. Tea and rice are planted in this region, and farmers use water buffalo to help them cultivate and harvest the crops. Silkworms are also grown here; their cocoons are harvested and processed in the region's silk spinning mills. Caviar factories process the roe of the beluga sturgeons that feed in the southern Caspian Sea.

Other mountainous regions help enclose the Central Plateau, the region in the middle of Iran. Mountain ridges reaching 8,000 to 9,000 feet (2,400 to 2,700 meters) high fill the northeastern corner of Iran near Turkmenistan, while the Eastern Highlands border Afghanistan and Pakistan. Along the Gulf of Oman, the Makran Highlands break up the bleak landscape. The Central Plateau has an average elevation of nearly 3,000 feet (900 meters). Two desert basins lie within the Central Plateau.

## Major Cities

Iran's cities experienced great growth over the last century as the Pahlavi Dynasty pushed to modernize the country. Towns and villages that were once isolated from one another gained access to other regions through improved roadways and a new railway system. Forced settlement of nomadic tribes increased the population of many towns, and the concentration of agricultural lands in the hands of a wealthy few drove millions of rural Iranians to the cities looking for work.

## Tehran

Tehran (tay-RAN), the capital of Iran, is the largest city in the country. One of the youngest of Iran's cities, it was established in the southern foothills of the Elburz Mountains following the Mongol invasions of the thirteenth century. The Qajar Dynasty (1795–1925) chose Tehran as its capital city, an honor retained to this day. Today, Tehran functions as Iran's major center of government, commerce, education, finance, and industry.

The city itself is unassuming. Frequent earthquakes make high-rise buildings risky, so most of the city's structures are one- or two-story mud brick buildings. The bazaar (buh-ZAR), a shopping area that dates from Tehran's founding, is located near modern malls, and it is not unusual to see herds of sheep driven through streets that are congested with automobile traffic. The rapid influx of villagers seeking work has contributed to the growth of slums on the southern edge of Tehran.

## Mashhad

Mashhad (muh-SHAD), located in the northeast, is the second largest city in Iran. Mashhad's growth since the mid-twentieth century has made it the primary commercial center in the region. The sugar beets grown north of Mashhad support a booming sugar processing industry. Carpet and textile factories are other major industries.

## IRANIAN BAZAARS

Iran's bazaars, once threatened by the modernization goals of the Pahlavi shahs, regained their importance following the Islamic Revolution. Found in every city and town in Iran, bazaars function as commercial centers. Their narrow, winding pathways are lined with stalls and booths. Items are grouped by type: foods, textiles, clothing, appliances, jewelry, and so forth. In addition to the merchants who offer their wares for sale, restaurants, banks, and public buildings such as mosques and post offices are often located within the bazaar.

*A crowded bazaar in Tehran, Iran's capital.*

While recognized as a major manufacturing and agricultural center, Mashhad is known throughout the Muslim world as a Shi'ite holy city. Imam Reza, one of the twelve *imams* (ih-MAHMS) revered by Shi'ite Muslims, died and was buried in Mashhad in 818 C.E. (The first twelve *imams* were descendants of Mohammad, considered by most Shi'ites to be the rightful successors to the prophet.) Today, over 20 million pilgrims make their way to Imam Reza's shrine each year. His shrine includes reception halls, a restaurant, a library, a hospital, and one of the largest and most beautifully decorated mosques in the world. Some of the leading Shi'ite religious schools are located in Mashhad.

### Esfahan

Esfahan (es-fuh-HAHN), located in the foothills of the Zagros Mountains in west-central Iran, is world-renowned for its exquisite Persian architecture. Mosques, gardens, bridges, and baths—many

*Pilgrims crowd the mausoleum of Imam Reza in the city of Mashhad. The mausoleum is just one part of an elaborate new shrine built in honor of the religious leader. The shrine opened in 2001.*

dating to the Safavid Dynasty (1491–1722)—are found throughout the city. The Imam Mosque (Masjid-i-Shah), built in the first half of the seventeenth century, is a magnificent example. Intricate mosaic tile work, embellished with floral arabesque designs and Qur'anic calligraphy, covers the interior and exterior of the mosque. The dome rises 177 feet (54 meters) above the ground.

### Shiraz

The most important city in southwestern Iran is Shiraz (shih-RAHZ). Although Shiraz is a commercial and manufacturing center, it is best known as Iran's literary capital. Its first library was established around the beginning of the tenth century. Today, lush, fragrant gardens of flowers and orange trees surround the shrines to Hafez and Saadi, celebrated Persian poets of the thirteenth and fourteenth centuries.

## Climate

Iran's climate varies immensely from region to region. Northwestern Iran experiences very cold winters with heavy snowfalls, while winters in the south and along the Caspian Sea are mild. Hot, dry summers are the norm in much of Iran, though temperatures in the interior often top 119° F (48° C) in July. High humidity along the Persian Gulf and Caspian Sea makes those regions especially uncomfortable in the summer.

Rain most often falls in Iran between October and April. The valleys of the Zagros Mountains and the coastal plains bordering the Caspian Sea receive an average of 20 inches (50 centimeters) annually, while most regions measure less than half that amount. The western Caspian coastal plain is the wettest area in Iran. With year-round rainfall, totals exceeding 39 inches (100 centimeters) are not unusual. Parts of the Central Plateau receive less than 4 inches (10 centimeters) per year, making it the driest region.

## Natural Resources

Iran's mineral deposits are its richest natural resources. Not only does Iran have the fourth largest oil reserves in the world, it has the second largest natural gas reserves and one of the largest copper reserves. Minerals such as bauxite (used to produce aluminum), coal, iron, lead, zinc, uranium, and kaolin (used in ceramics and medicines) are also found in abundance. Gold, silver, and semiprecious stones, such as turquoise, are also mined in Iran. Persian Gulf countries import tons of building stone that is quarried in Iran.

## Plants and Animals

Many of Iran's native plants have been destroyed over time by the plowing and cultivation of agricultural fields or the establishment of pastures for livestock. However, many species remain. Thick forests grow on the northern face of the Elburz Mountains, while oak forests flourish in some sections of the Zagros range. Among the native trees growing in both regions are wild pear, pomegranate, almond, and walnut trees. Wild pistachio trees thrive in the desert regions.

With so many different environments, it is no surprise that Iran's animal life is abundant and varied. Mammals such as wolves, bears, rabbits, and mountain goats thrive in the mountains and highlands, while lizards and other reptiles are common in the Central Plateau. Some of the unique animals that live in Iran are threatened by increasing development and the resulting pollution. Wildlife refuges

*The diverse climate of Iran and its many environments support a wide variety of plant and animal life. This peaceful river flows through Kurdistan Province on Iran's border with Turkey. Mount Ararat stands in the background.*

have been established to protect these endangered species, which include the Caspian tiger, Caspian seal, and the desert onager (an Asian wild ass). Unfortunately, their numbers are still declining.

# History

The Persian Empire, one of the greatest of the world's early civilizations, once included present-day Iran, Iraq, Palestine, Syria, and Turkey. Control of the Persian Empire changed hands many times through the years. But even though foreign conquerors introduced new customs and religions to the region, the Persian culture continued to flourish and spread throughout the world. Literature, music, art, rug making, architecture, and science flourished in Persia at a time when some civilizations had no written language or organized government.

## Ancient Days

The earliest civilization in Iran arose in the third millennium B.C.E. in the lowlands, and the surrounding Zagros Mountains, which form the present-day Khuzestan Province. It was called Elam.

## CHOGA ZANBIL

One of the oldest examples of Iranian architecture is Choga Zanbil, the ancient ziggurat built by the Elamites in present-day Khuzestan Province. (A *ziggurat* is a pyramid-like structure with a shrine built into the top layer.) Built in the thirteenth century B.C.E., Choga Zanbil has a square base with five stories, many of which remain largely intact today. Blue and green glazed brick decorated the exterior of the temple, and doors were adorned with animal designs made of mosaics of ivory and glass.

The engineering skill of the Elamites was evident in the water purification site found at Choga Zanbil. Muddy water from the Karkheh River was channeled to the ziggurat by canals and stored in a reservoir. Water from the reservoir was then filtered through gravel, sand, and coal to eliminate sediment and other impurities. This process provided clean drinking water for the Elamites who lived near Choga Zanbil.

*Brick walls rise beyond a courtyard at Choga Zanbil in western Iran.*

# IMPORTANT EVENTS IN IRAN'S HISTORY

**2000 B.C.E.** The Medes and Persians migrate from central Asia to the Iranian plateau.

**2500 B.C.E.** Elamites establish Iran's earliest civilization.

**728 B.C.E.** The Medes establish the Median Empire.

**644 B.C.E.** Assyrians destroy the Elamites.

**550 B.C.E.** Cyrus the Great defeats the Medes and establishes the Persian Achaemenid Empire.

**330 B.C.E.** Alexander the Great conquers the Persian Empire.

**247 B.C.E.** The Parthians push the Greeks from Iran and establish the Parthian Empire.

**224 C.E.** The Sassanids reestablish the Persian Empire.

**635** Arab armies invade the Persian Empire and establish an Islamic Empire.

**1055** Seljuk Turks gain control over much of Iran.

**1219** Genghis Khan and the Mongols invade Iran.

**1501** Safavids conquer Iran and establish Shi'a Islam as the official state religion.

**1722** Iran falls under the control of Afghan tribes.

**1729** Nadir Qoli Beg leads an army that drives the Afghans from Iran, then declares himself *shah*.

**1794** The Qajars come to power after Nadir Shah's assassination.

**1800s** Russia and Great Britain try to influence the Qajars' government in order to gain access to seaports and overland routes to India.

**1906** The shah of Iran agrees to implement a constitutional government.

**1908** The British discover oil in southwestern Iran. They soon begin exporting oil under contracts that provide minimal oil revenue for Iran.

**1914** World War I breaks out, and Iran is used as a staging ground for Allied troops and supplies.

**1926** Reza Khan crowns himself Reza Shah Pahlavi, the first ruler of the Pahlavi Dynasty. The country's name is officially changed to *Iran*.

**1941** During World War II, British and Russian troops invade Iran and take control of oil fields and railroads. Reza Shah abdicates and his son, Mohammad Reza Shah, assumes leadership of Iran, pledging to rule according to the constitution.

**1951** Iranian parliament (the *Majlis*) strips Mohammad Reza Shah of power by appointing Mohammad Mosaddeq prime minister. He moves to nationalize the British-owned oil company.

**1953** The U.S. Central Intelligence Agency, working with the shah's supporters, overthrows Mosaddeq and returns the shah to power.

**1970s** Both Shi'ite religious groups and intellectuals call for an end to the shah's repressive regime.

**1979** Mohammad Reza Shah flees into exile. Ayatollah Khomeini declares Iran an Islamic republic. Iranian students take Americans hostage.

**1980** Iraqi troops invade Iran, starting the Iran-Iraq War.

**1988** The Iran-Iraq War ends.

**1989** Khomeini dies. Ayatollah Khamenei is selected as his replacement. Ali Akbar Hashemi Rafsanjani is elected president.

**1990s** The United States imposes economic *sanctions* against Iran to protest Iranian links to terrorism.

**1997** Mohammad Khatami is elected president on a reform platform.

**2001** Mohammad Khatami wins reelection to the presidency.

Wandering tribes of Aryans moved southward from central Asia and settled the central Iranian plateau around 2000 B.C.E. The Aryans were made up of two main tribes, the Medes and the Persians. The Medes were the first to gain power in the region. Before long, they had conquered Assyria and established the Median Empire (728–533 B.C.E.), which included most of present-day Iran, northern Iraq, and eastern Turkey. By the beginning of the sixth century B.C.E., the Medes ruled over one of the most powerful empires in the Middle East.

Cyrus the Great, a Persian, led his people to a victory over the Medes and became the first leader of the Achaemenid (uh-KEE-muh-nud) Empire (550–330 B.C.E.). Alexander the Great, the Greek conqueror, overthrew the last Achaemenid emperor in 330 B.C.E. When Alexander died, one of his generals ruled over Persia.

Greek rule in Iran ended with an invasion by Parthia, an ancient kingdom bordering the southeastern Caspian Sea, in 247 B.C.E. Parthian rulers extended their empire into Armenia and India. Although they ruled for 500 years, their power was constantly attacked by the Romans and by wandering Afghan tribes.

In 224 C.E., the Persians wrested control over the former Achaemenid Empire, marking the beginning of the Sassanid Empire (224–651 C.E.). Zoroastrianism became the official religion, and its priests gained much power. During the Sassanian period, there was almost constant fighting between the Persians and the Byzantine Empire.

> ### Did You Know?
> Under the direction of Darius the Great, the Iranians constructed the world's first highway. Made of stone, it covered three routes: from Darius's winter capital at Susa to Ephesus on the Mediterranean, from Susa to the Indus Valley (present-day Pakistan), and from Susa to Babylon and Egypt. Relays of horses allowed the royal chariots to cover the 1,679 miles (2,702 kilometers) between Susa and Ephesus in just seven days.

## The Arrival of Islam

The Persian Empire was invaded by Arab armies beginning in 635. Within fifteen years, the empire was completely under the control of the Islamic armies and their religion. Arabic became the official language of Persia, and many Arabic words made their way into the Persian language.

After nearly four centuries of Arab rule, a group of Turkic people called the Seljuk Turks settled in northwestern Iran. In the eleventh century, they overthrew the Arab leaders and ruled much of Iran for two centuries. The Islamic Empire came to an end in the thirteenth century with the crushing attacks of the Mongols. Under the direction of the legendary Genghis Khan, Iran was torn apart, its cities destroyed, and many of its people killed. In 1258, Genghis Khan's grandson completely ended Islamic rule. At its height, the Mongol Empire formed a strip from the eastern coast of China and southern Russia to the Mediterranean Sea.

In 1501, a Turkic-Persian tribe called the Safavids (1501–1736) took over from the weakened Mongols. Shah Abbas is the most famous of the Safavid rulers. His army kept a new threat, the Ottoman Turks, in check. The Safavids established Shi'a Islam as the official religion of Iran.

Afghan tribes invaded Persia in 1719 and defeated the Safavids a few years later. Nadir Qoli Beg, a mercenary who was hired to fight for the Safavids, led an army that pushed the Afghans out of Persia in the late 1720s. After expanding the Persian Empire to include much of Afghanistan, Turkey, and Russia, he declared himself *shah,* or ruler. He invaded India and brought many riches back to Iran, including the famous Koh-i-Noor diamond and the jewel-encrusted Peacock Throne. His harsh rule ended in 1749, when he was assassinated by a group of his army chiefs.

Following a struggle for power after Nadir Shah's assassination, a new dynasty was founded by the Qajars, a Turkmen tribe that lived in the northwest (in present-day Azerbaijan). The Qajar shahs ruled Iran, as it was becoming known to the West, from 1794 until 1921.

## THE KOH-I-NOOR DIAMOND

One of the world's largest diamonds was found in India thousands of years ago. Believed to have been almost 800 carats before it was cut, or about the size of a man's fist, the diamond has a fascinating history of intrigue and thievery.

The Mogul emperors took possession of the diamond when they ruled India in the sixteenth century. Nadir Shah heard stories that the Mogul emperor kept it hidden in his turban. While visiting the emperor in India, Nadir Shah suggested that they wear each other's turbans, a traditional gesture that demonstrated friendship and trust. Later that night, alone in his chambers, Nadir Shah unwrapped the turban and found the diamond. Awed by its size and beauty, he called it Koh-i-Noor, or "mountain of light."

Nadir Shah took the diamond back to Persia, but after his death, it ended up in the hands of Ahmed Shah, an Afghan chief. Because the diamond had belonged only to rulers, the chief used it to prove that he should be king of Afghanistan. The diamond eventually made its way back to India. When the British took over the region, they found the Koh-i-Noor and claimed it as part of the British crown jewels. Today, the stone is on display in the Tower of London with the other royal jewels. Both India and Afghanistan have claimed ownership of the diamond and asked for its return.

During much of the Qajar Dynasty's reign, Russia and Britain tried to influence Iran's politics and economy in order to take advantage of its strategic location. Russia wanted access to Iran's ports on the Caspian Sea. Britain wanted to maintain its overland routes to India, an important part of its empire. By the late 1800s, many Iranians resented the rampant corruption in their government and the control that foreign countries seemed to have over the shah. They demanded a

*Fath Ali Shah was a shah in Iran in the 1800s. By the end of that century, Iranians had become frustrated with corruption in the government and the power that foreign countries had over the shah. As a result, a constitution was established in 1906.*

constitutional government that would limit the power of the shah while giving Iran's citizens a stronger voice in the government. In 1906, the shah approved a *constitution* that outlined the responsibilities of each government group, including an elected legislature called a parliament.

Even with constitutional reform, Russia and Britain continued to influence Iran's government. The British had discovered and developed oil wells in Iran and wanted to protect these valuable assets. The Qajars took money from both Russia and Britain because Iran was deeply in debt. Meanwhile, the average Iranian was suffering from food shortages and a poor economy. The outbreak of World War I in 1914 made the situation worse. Although Iran remained neutral during the war, many battles were fought in the country. Several key supply routes to the Persian Gulf, the Arabian Sea, and the Caspian Sea passed through Iran. British oil reserves were in the region. As the war expanded into Africa, Iran became a staging ground for British troops and supplies. Whole villages in Iran were destroyed, and food became very scarce. Starvation probably killed more Iranians than the war itself.

## Modernizing Iran

In 1921, Reza Khan became the commander of Iran's armed forces and was supported by the British. Over the next five years, he quickly moved up in the government, becoming prime minister in 1923 and the first shah of the Pahlavi Dynasty in 1926. One of his first acts as shah was to officially change the country's name to Iran.

Reza Shah's main goal was to modernize Iran through industrialization and the development of a *secular* (nonreligious) public education system. He needed a powerful, centralized government in order to accomplish this goal. Reza Shah used the military to force nomadic tribes into settlements where they would have to acknowledge his authority. He set about tearing down bazaars in towns and cities across Iran, building new shopping centers in their place.

A national banking system and a cross-country railroad were established. Rules promoting equality for women were instituted, including the right to appear in public without wearing a *chador* (a black veil that covers a woman from head to toe) and equal access to education. Although these changes improved the lives of many Iranians, people grew to resent Reza Shah's repression of opposing viewpoints and his use of the police force to silence his detractors. He had become a dictator who executed anyone who threatened his hold on power. The religious leaders and merchants were especially bitter, because the changes introduced by the shah threatened their authority, power, and way of life.

Not only did the shah's actions anger Iranian citizens, he also offended Britain and the Soviet Union as he took steps to lessen their influence. In 1932, Reza Shah abruptly ended Britain's contract to produce and export oil from Iran. He also promoted trade and commercial agreements with the Germans.

## World War II

World War II interrupted many of Reza Shah's programs. Iran's oil resources and strategic location were too valuable for the Allies to ignore or to let fall into the hands of the Axis powers. Allied British and Soviet troops invaded Iran in 1941, taking control of the railroad and oil reserves. Realizing that he could no longer stay in power, Reza Shah *abdicated,* or gave up his position as shah. His son, Mohammad Reza Shah, was

*Mohammad Reza Shah reads a speech in Tehran in February 1950. Unlike his father, this shah ruled according to the constitution, not as a dictator. Nevertheless, the following year Mohammad Mosaddeq was appointed prime minister and the shah lost all power to run the government until Mosaddeq was overthrown in 1953.*

allowed to rule Iran with the understanding that he would rule according to the constitution, instead of as the dictator his father had been.

Mohammad Reza Shah struggled to maintain control of the government after World War II. Many Iranians wanted the government to take control of the British-owned oil company in southwestern Iran. Mohammad Mosaddeq, a member of the Iranian parliament, became the leader of the movement to nationalize the oil industry. In 1951, the Iranian parliament took control of the oil company and appointed Mosaddeq prime minister. This action stripped the shah of his power to lead the country.

Britain responded to the change in leadership by blocking sales of Iranian oil. The United States negotiated with the two countries but was unable to reach a compromise. The United States worried that the situation in Iran would encourage the Soviet Union to take over Iran. (While the former Soviet Union and the United States had been allies during World War II, they quickly became enemies after the war ended. The Soviets were trying to expand the number of communist countries, while the United States was encouraging the growth of democracy.) The U.S. Central Intelligence Agency worked with the shah's supporters to overthrow Mosaddeq in 1953. Once the shah was back in power, he allowed European and U.S. interests to take over the oil company once again.

Mohammad Reza Shah's rule became increasingly authoritarian after 1953. He created a secret police force to silence any opposition. His government's strong relationship with the United States led many Iranians to distrust the shah. They viewed the shah as an American puppet; that is, they felt he was implementing policies that had been approved or suggested by the United States. Iran also suffered from increasing corruption in the government and a widening gap between rich and poor Iranians.

In the early 1960s, the Islamic clergy, especially Ayatollah Ruholla Khomeini (eye-yuh-TOL-uh ko-MAY-nee), began speaking out against the shah. (*Ayatollah* is a title used by Shi'ite Muslims to refer to the highest-ranking religious leaders.) Khomeini was forced to leave the country, but sent cassette audiotapes of his speeches into Iran to encourage Muslims to overthrow the shah. Intellectuals and other professionals also opposed the shah, both because foreign countries— especially America—played a strong role in the shah's government and because of the shah's harsh repression of political opponents. They wanted the government to be more democratic. By the late 1970s, the conservative religious groups and more liberal professional groups were united in their call for a new government. Protests and riots broke out across Iran in 1978, growing larger and more violent as the year progressed.

## An Islamic Republic

By January 1979, Mohammad Reza Shah knew he had lost control of Iran and fled the country. Ayatollah Khomeini returned to Iran and took control of the country two weeks later. He declared Iran an Islamic republic. Although Mehdi Bazargan acted as prime minister in the months following the shah's departure, Khomeini held all the real power. The result was not the type of government that the professional class had hoped for.

The ayatollah represented those in the country who wanted Iranians to follow the Qur'an in all aspects of their lives and abandon modern Western ideas. Under this new regime, women again had to veil

## AYATOLLAH RUHOLLA KHOMEINI

Sayyid (SIGH-yuhd) Ruholla al-Khomeini, orphaned at age fifteen, later became the best-known Islamic cleric in the world. His dedication to religious studies as a young man led to his earning the title *ayatollah,* literally "gift of God."

When Western influence became prevalent in Iran during Mohammad Reza Shah's reign, Khomeini denounced the shah's programs of secular education and equality for women as immoral and counter to Islamic principles. In response, the shah had Khomeini arrested and, later, *exiled.* Despite his exile, Khomeini continued to spread his message to his followers: overthrow the shah and force the Americans out of Iran.

Riots and protests forced the shah out of Iran in 1979. When Khomeini returned to Iran, millions of supporters welcomed him home. Within the year, Khomeini had been named imam and supreme leader of Iran. He quickly silenced his political enemies by persecuting or executing them.

*Ayatollah Ruholla Khomeini as pictured on a poster during the overthrow of the shah in 1979.*

themselves in the chador and could go out in public only in the company of a male family member. People were punished, persecuted, or executed if they broke strict Islamic laws. Believers of the Baha'i faith were driven out of Iran or killed.

Many people left Iran during this time, especially those in the middle and upper classes. Some had supported the shah. Others were concerned about the growing violence against anything modern. A depressed world economy caused the cost of food and goods to rise. Unemployment went up, too. The Kurds and other small ethnic groups in northwest Iran began rioting and demanding freedom.

In November 1979, Iranian students, protesting against the shah's being allowed to live in the United States, broke into the U.S. embassy in Tehran. They took over 90 Americans hostage, demanding that the United States return the shah to Iran to stand trial for crimes that he may have committed. Tensions between Iran and the United States grew as the days ticked by. The hostages were kept in horrible conditions until their eventual release fifteen months later.

## THE IRAN HOSTAGE CRISIS

Although the shah fled the country early in 1979, many Iranians wanted him to return to Iran and stand trial for corruption. They were frustrated and angry that the shah was in the United States receiving state-of-the-art medical treatment for cancer when many Iranians could not afford food and basic health care. Daily demonstrations were staged outside the American embassy in Tehran.

On November 4, a group of militant students at the demonstration forced their way into the embassy and made captives of the Americans who worked there. The students held the Americans as *hostages,* refusing to release them until the United States government returned the shah to Iran. U.S. president Jimmy Carter thought that giving in to the Iranian kidnappers' demand might encourage other groups to kidnap Americans. Instead, he froze billions of dollars that the Iranian government had placed in American banks. The Iranians would not be able to use their money until all the American hostages were safely home.

After two weeks, the Iranians released thirteen hostages. A secret U.S. military mission to rescue the remaining hostages was launched in April 1980, but failed. Eight American soldiers died when one of the rescue helicopters crashed into an American transport plane.

In 1981, the Iranians started negotiating seriously with the American government. Iraq had invaded Iran three months earlier, and Iran desperately needed the money from its frozen American bank accounts to finance what became known as the Iran-Iraq War (1980–1988). The United States agreed to release $7.9 billion from the accounts after Iran freed the hostages. On January 20, 1981, after 444 days as prisoners, the remaining hostages arrived safely at an American military base in West Germany.

## The Iran-Iraq War

In the midst of ongoing protests and rebellion against Khomeini's government, a border dispute between Iran and Iraq (ih-RAHK) escalated into war in 1980. While Iraqi troops invaded Iran in 1980 in an effort to "protect" Arabs living in Khuzestan Province from the Islamic Revolution, Iraq's president, Saddam Hussein, had another motive for the attack: Iraq worried that the ongoing revolution and establishment of an Islamic government in Iran would encourage Shi'ite Muslims in Iraq to rebel.

Saddam Hussein expected an easy victory over a weakened Iran. But the Iranians fought hard to defend their country. The Iran-Iraq War lasted eight years and led to a loss of over 100,000 lives. Both countries went deeply into debt because of the war's high cost.

Khomeini died in June 1989. He was beloved by many Iranians. Others believed he had taken the country in a wrong direction. While most of Iran grieved, Ayatollah Ali Khamenei (KHAH-meh-neh-EE) was named as the new spiritual leader of Iran.

*In 2002, Iranian troops carried coffins containing the recently discovered remains of soldiers who had died in the Iran-Iraq War. The war, which claimed the lives of 100,000 soldiers, had ended fourteen years before.*

## Iran Today

By 1989, civil unrest was subsiding, and Iran was starting its slow recovery from the Iran-Iraq War. A new president, Ali Akbar Hashemi Rafsanjani (RAHF-sahn-jah-NEE), was elected in 1989. With Ayatollah Khamenei's blessing, Rafsanjani began to soften some of the policies that Ayatollah Khomeini had enforced. He also implemented economic reforms intended to help Iran pay off huge debts incurred during the Iran-Iraq War. Some reforms, such as moving to a market-based economy with prices that rise or fall based on demand, were intended to make Iran's economy competitive with other modern countries. While these reforms helped the country as a whole, they have often created hardships for Iran's poorest citizens, who can't afford the higher prices. Conservative religious leaders often compared Rafsanjani's attempts to modernize Iran's economy and repay foreign debts to the actions of the Pahlavi shahs. They claimed that Rafsanjani was allowing foreigners too much control over Iran's economy.

## IRAN'S GOVERNMENT

Following the 1979 revolution, the Islamic Republic of Iran was established. It is a *theocratic republic,* a form of government in which religious leaders hold the most power.

Iran's most powerful political leader is the *faqih* (fah-KEE), or supreme spiritual leader. The *faqih* makes sure that the country's laws and practices conform to Islamic law, appoints judges and commanders of the armed forces, and approves presidential candidates. Ayatollah Khomeini was the first *faqih.* Following his death, the Assembly of Experts—a group of religious experts elected by the citizens of Iran—met to select the next *faqih.* There was a heated debate about the amount of political experience needed by a *faqih.* The assembly's choice of Ayatollah Khamenei—a man with keen political perception but not the top religious scholar—demonstrated that both elements were necessary.

The president of Iran is elected every four years and must be a Muslim man. All Iranians over age fifteen have the right to vote. Advisers to the president, called the Council of Ministers, are appointed by the president but must be approved by the *Majlis* (MAJ-lis).

The *Majlis,* sometimes called the Islamic Consultative Assembly, is Iran's only elected legislative body. Its 290 members are elected to four-year terms. Although most of the legislators were Muslim clerics immediately following the revolution, there are fewer clerics being elected today. Members of the *Majlis* enact laws and approve economic policies.

Once the *Majlis* passes a bill, it is reviewed by the Council of Guardians—a group of Islamic scholars and judges. If they determine that the proposed law is consistent with Islamic law and the Iranian constitution, it becomes law. Otherwise it is sent back to the *Majlis* to be reworked.

In 1997, Mohammad Khatami (KHAHT-ah-mee), a moderate
Muslim, was elected president by a wide margin. He promised to reform
the government by protecting civil rights, opening the governmental
decision-making process to greater public scrutiny, and concentrating on
social concerns. Khatami also stated his belief that women should—
within the framework of Islam—have an equal role in society. During his
first term, the Iranian press was given far more freedom than it had had in
the past. This drew opposition from religious conservatives in the *Majlis*
(parliament) and court system. Khatami won a close race for reelection in
2001, but he faces increasing resistance from the conservatives as he tries
to move the country toward open, democratic government.

Since the 1980s, the relationship between the United States and Iran
has been one of distrust. Despite opinion polls indicating that Iranian
citizens want a better relationship with the United States, the Iranian
government has refused to restore diplomatic ties with the United States.
In December 2003, following a devastating earthquake that killed more
than 30,000 people, the United States immediately offered humanitarian
aid and assistance to Iran. The Iranian government welcomed the offer of
relief, but emphasized that this would not automatically result in an
improved relationship between the two countries.

Unrest between different ethnic and religious groups still troubles
Iran. Many of the smaller ethnic groups, including the Kurds and Arabs,

*President Mohammad Khatami (second from right, sitting) is shown in the Iranian
parliament with two of the governmental ministers he appointed upon his reelection in 2001.
Khatami has spent much of his time in office pushing for a more democratic Iran.*

hoped the revolution would improve their position in Iran. But, in fact, the opposite has happened. They have even less representation in the current government than they had before. As a result, protests and violence break out frequently in different parts of Iran.

# Economy

Although efforts have been made to diversify Iran's economy since the 1920s, it is still heavily reliant on its oil resources for income. The Iran-Iraq War caused major economic losses when factories and oil transport facilities were bombed. Iran continues to import much of its food, medical supplies, raw goods for its factories, and military supplies.

## Business and Industry

Industrial development has been particularly difficult to achieve in Iran, mainly because of Islamic laws concerning money. (According to Islamic principles, banks cannot charge interest on loans.) Following the nationalization of the oil industry in 1951, the government was able to finance manufacturing facilities and other industrial developments. Today, Iran's government continues to provide incentives for the establishment of new industries and actively seeks investment money from some foreign countries, particularly Russia.

### Petroleum

Iran's oil reserves are the fourth largest in the world, behind Saudi Arabia, Russia, and Kuwait. The oil and gas produced from these reserves have provided the bulk of Iran's national income since the 1920s. Iran is a founding member of the Organization of Petroleum Exporting Countries (OPEC), but it hasn't always followed OPEC policies.

Another important natural resource is Iran's natural gas reserves, the second largest in the world. In 1966, Iran began producing and exporting natural gas through the National Iranian Gas Company. The former Soviet Union was the largest customer until the 1980s, when it refused to pay the price Iran was demanding for the gas.

### Carpets

Persian carpets have always been recognized for their artistry and beauty. Many were sold to foreigners before the 1979 revolution. When the

Islamic government took control, its leaders prohibited the sale of carpets to Western countries. They believed that the carpets were national treasures and that *infidels* (non-Muslims) should not be allowed to own one. By 1984, however, the income that the carpets could produce was greatly needed, and carpets were once again exported to the West.

## Agriculture

At one time, Iranians grew nearly enough food to support the nation's citizens. But by the time of the revolution, over half of the food supply was imported from other countries. As incomes rose in the cities, rural villagers increasingly migrated to urban areas seeking work, decreasing the number of farmers even more. The new government tried to implement land reform laws that would force large landowners to give land to the poor, but the Council of Guardians ruled that Islam protects an owner's right to his land. Today, Iran continues to import much of its food supply despite efforts to increase self-sufficiency.

Spices such as pepper, cardamom, and saffron are one of Iran's main agricultural exports. Fruits, nuts, and caviar are also important exports.

### Did You Know?

Half of the world's caviar is harvested and produced in Iran. Iranian caviar is produced from the roe (eggs) of the beluga sturgeon, a fish that can weigh up to 2,000 pounds (900 kilograms). The southern coast of the Caspian Sea has become known as the "caviar coast."

*These women are planting rice near the Caspian Sea city of Bandar-e-Anzali in Iran. Although various food crops are grown in Iran, the country has to import most of its food from other places.*

## Media and Communications

The Iranian press has continued to publish many viewpoints since the revolution, but its writings are closely monitored by the government. Articles that are judged to be antireligious or against the best interests of the country are forbidden. Publishers of such articles may lose their right to distribute their newspapers or magazines.

While newspapers are readily available to most Iranians, the same cannot be said about telephone service. The shah's push for modernization from the 1940s through the 1970s included a focus on telecommunications *infrastructure,* or foundation. Today, telephone connections are fairly easy for most Iranians to obtain; the problem is the lack of telephones. The rural villages are the least connected.

By the end of 1995, one of every eight Iranian households had a television satellite dish, many of which were produced in a state-run factory. Fearing the spread of Western culture, however, the legislature passed a law forbidding the private ownership of satellite dishes. Despite the heavy fines if they were caught, Iranians continued to watch channels such as MTV and the British Broadcasting Corporation (BBC). The Voice of America channel, which provides Persian-language

*Iranian movie star Ftemeh Motamed Aria (right) and other actors are shown during the filming of a movie in 2000. Since President Khatami's election in 1997, many cultural boundaries imposed by strict religious leaders have been relaxed. This allows much more freedom in the arts, even with a portrait of the ayatollah in the background.*

programming and information on how to immigrate to the United States, quickly gained popularity. Finally, in an effort to stave off Western influence, the government allowed the state-run television station to create and broadcast satellite programs that weren't necessarily Islamic in content.

# Religion and Beliefs

One of the world's earliest monotheistic religions—Zoroastrianism—emerged in Iran over 2,500 years ago. Although Jews and early Christians fleeing persecution sometimes settled in Iran, it has been an Islamic country since the seventh century, when the Persian Empire fell to Arab conquerors. Shi'a traditions flourished in Iran, and in the sixteenth century the Safavid Dynasty declared Shi'a Islam the official state religion. In 1979, the Islamic Revolution created a *theocracy*—a government headed by religious leaders.

## Zoroastrianism

Zoroastrianism (zor-oh-AS-tree-uhn-izm) is an ancient Persian religion, founded in northern Iran by Zoroaster sometime between the sixteenth and eleventh centuries B.C.E. It was the official religion of Persia under the Achaemenids and, later, the Sassanids. Followers of this religion believe in a supreme god—Ahura Mazdah—who is attended by six good spirits representing good thoughts, devotion, righteousness, the divine kingdom, salvation, and immortality. Opposing these forces of good is a host of evil spirits. The struggle in this world between good and evil is represented by fire (light) and darkness. Fire temples play an important role in worship rituals because fire symbolizes the presence of good in the world. Zoroastrians believe that those who are virtuous will be rewarded with life after death.

Zoroastrian traditions were largely abandoned following the Arab invasions in the seventh century. Today, although only a few thousand Iranians practice Zoroastrianism, elements of the religion live on in Iranian culture through celebrations such as No-Ruz.

## Shi'a Islam

Islam arrived in Iran following the Arab defeat of the Sassanid Empire in the middle of the seventh century. Although defeated militarily, most

Iranians considered themselves culturally superior to their Arab conquerors, many of whom were unable to read or write. As a result, most Iranians continued to practice their own religions and speak their own language. The exception was the peasants, who welcomed Islam's message of equality. Early Arab Muslim rulers tolerated the practice of other religions, believing that Islam belonged to the Arabs. Those Iranians who converted to Islam in the early days of Arab rule were not required to pay the taxes levied on the infidels (non-Muslims), but they were not considered equal to the Arab Muslims either.

A deep division appeared in the Islamic community following the Prophet Mohammad's death. Most Muslims believed that the Islamic community should elect Mohammad's successor. This was the process used to select the first four *caliphs,* or Islamic leaders, following Mohammad's death. This group became known as Sunni Muslims (*sunni* comes from the Arabic word *sunna,* meaning "tradition"). Those who believed that the prophet appointed his son-in-law and cousin Ali as his successor—primarily Iranian and Iraqi Muslims—were known as *Shi'a,* or followers of Ali. Iranian Muslims embraced Shi'a Islam for two primary reasons. First, the Iranian culture had always stressed the importance of family, and leadership of the Persian Empire had

*Students pray at the mosque of the Fiziyeh school in Qom, Iran.*
*This school is the world's largest center for the education of Shi'a Muslims.*
*Ayatollah Ruholla Khomeini himself was once a teacher there.*

traditionally passed down from father to son. Second, Ali's son Hussein married a daughter of the last Persian king. In following Shi'a Islam, Iranian Muslims were able to maintain their national identity as well as uphold their religious beliefs.

Shi'ite Muslims believe that Mohammad's spiritual authority is inherited by his direct descendants. The Jafari Shi'ites, sometimes referred to as Twelver Shi'ites, are the main sect in Iran. They believe that there were twelve imams appointed by Allah to succeed Mohammad as religious leaders. These twelve, all direct descendants of Mohammad, were considered *infallible,* or incapable of making a mistake when interpreting the Qur'an. According to Shi'ite tradition, the twelfth imam, Mohammed al-Mahdi, did not die. Rather, he is hidden, waiting for the time when he will return as the *Mahdi,* or Messiah, and restore justice to the world. (A smaller Shi'ite group, the Ismailis, believes that there were only seven imams.)

Until the Mahdi returns, Shi'ite Muslims follow the leadership of *mujtahids* (mooj-TAH-hids), men who have proven their ability to

> ### *Did You Know?*
> A religious leader who wears a black turban and black robes is a *sayyid,* a descendant of the Prophet Mohammad. It has a higher rank than clerics who wear white turbans and brown robes.

## SUFISM

Sufism (SOO-fih-zum), or Tasawouf, is a mystical movement within Islam. It began in the earliest days of Islam, when companions of Mohammad met at the platform in Medina where he prayed to discuss the meaning of Qur'anic verses and disciplines that would lead to inner knowledge. They became known as the Ahl as-Suffa, the people of the platform. Two of the earliest Sufi teaching centers were established in the provinces of Khorasan and Fars in Iran.

Sufis (SOO-fees) dedicate themselves to meditation, purification, and service in order to seek a better understanding of the reality of God and the relationship between God and humans. Because Sufis believe that people cannot achieve oneness with God through language and logic alone, music and dance are often included as part of the meditative service. This is in direct conflict with strict orthodox Muslim beliefs that music should have no role in religious services.

*An Iranian Sufi with traditional symbols of his faith.*

faithfully interpret religious law. The highest level of *mujtahids* are the *ayatollahs*, considered the most learned people in society and the personification of the Mahdi, the hidden imam.

Shi'a Islam differs from Sunni Islam in other ways as well. Shi'ite Muslims follow seven pillars of faith rather than the five outlined by Sunni tradition. The *shahadah*, the recitation of faith, is the same for both Shi'ites and Sunnis. Likewise, both Sunni and Shi'ite Muslims fast during Ramadan, give alms to the poor, and perform the hajj, or pilgrimage to Mecca. However, Shi'ites are summoned to prayer three times a day rather than five times as are Sunnis. The two additional pillars of faith followed by Shi'ites are the pledge to *jihad* (holy war) whenever Islam is threatened, and the promise to engage in good thoughts, words, and deeds. This last pillar reflects ancient Zoroastrian beliefs. (To learn more about Islam, see pages ix–xii in the introduction to this volume.)

## The Baha'i Faith

The Baha'i (bah-HAH-ee) religion grew out of Shi'a Islam in much the same way that Christianity arose from Judaism. In 1844, as people anticipated the end of the century, a young Persian merchant claimed that he was the *Báb* (bab), or "gateway" to the twelfth and hidden imam. He announced that another holy messenger would soon follow, bringing a new age of peace and justice that was promised to Jews, Christians, Muslims, and other religious groups. The established Islamic clergy viewed the Báb's message of a new society that promoted equality for all people—men and women, rich and poor—with alarm. The Báb was executed in 1850, and many of his followers were persecuted and killed as well.

## BASIC BAHA'I BELIEFS

Baha'is work toward the achievement of eight basic principles, which they believe will ultimately result in the formation of a peaceful, international society.

- rejection of all types of prejudice
- equality between men and women
- recognition of one God, whose message has been partially revealed over time to founders of the world's great religions
- elimination of the gap between the wealthy and the poor (economic justice)
- quality education for all
- the independent search for religious truth by each individual
- the creation of a global society
- harmony between science and religion

One of the Báb's followers—Bahaullah (bah-HAH-oo-LAH)—was the son of a wealthy Persian. He was arrested and exiled for his beliefs. While in exile in Palestine, he wrote volumes that he claimed were revelations from God. In 1863, Bahaullah announced that he was the "Promised One" foretold by the Báb. He died in 1892, still exiled from his country. Today, the Baha'i world headquarters are located in Israel (formerly Palestine).

Since its beginning in the mid-nineteenth century, Baha'i has been considered *heretical,* or sacrilegious, by Islamic leaders. Because it arose from Islam but gave equal credence to all religions, Baha'i has faced especially harsh persecution in Iran. Today, most Baha'is follow their traditions in secret.

# Everyday Life

For some Iranians, everyday life is much the same today as it was for their ancestors. However, most modern Iranians' day-to-day lives are vastly different from those of their grandparents or great-grandparents. As more Iranians migrate to cities, they gain access to modern conveniences unavailable in Iran's villages. One thing that has remained constant throughout Iran's history is the importance of family.

## Family Life

The emphasis on family life in Iranian culture stretches back to the ancient Persians. The behavior of family members reflected upon the family and affected its standing in society. As a result, strict codes of morality emerged. Traditionally, extended families shared the same living compound, which reinforced behavioral conventions and ensured the continuation of traditional values. Today, with more and more Iranians moving to urban areas, nuclear family living arrangements (parents and children) are becoming more common. Even so, family members try to locate living quarters near relatives so they can continue to offer support to each other.

Iranians treasure their children, often including them in social outings. While large families were the norm in the not-so-distant past, Iranian families today have an average of two children.

Despite the changes that living in cities has brought about, Iranians continue to value their tradition of hospitality. In Iranian society, extending hospitality to guests is considered both a duty and an honor. While long workdays in urban areas make it more difficult to spend time with family and friends, opportunities to visit and entertain are still treasured.

The role of women in Iran underwent massive changes in the twentieth century. The Pahlavi shahs' efforts to modernize Iran, included improving the lives of women and providing educational and job opportunities. One of the most controversial announcements was the abolishment of *hijab*, the Islamic belief in modesty of dress, which require that a woman should cover her entire body except her face and hands when appearing in public. When the Ayatollah Khomeini came to power after the Islamic Revolution, he reinstated *hijab*. Although women still have access to education and jobs, women are limited in the type of work they can obtain. For instance, women are allowed to serve as assistants to Islamic judges, but not as judges themselves.

> In 1994, about one-third of administrative workers in Iran's government were women. That same year, women represented about two-fifths of all university students.

## Dress

Iranians today follow Islamic tradition of *hijab* in their dress. *Hijab* refers to the Qur'an's requirements of modesty in manners, behavior,

*Family traditions are an important part of life for Iranians. This extended family is observing a New Year's festival in a park north of Tehran. On this last day of the Persian New Year celebration, it is considered bad luck to be indoors.*

speech, and appearance in public. While pictures in Western newspapers of women in head coverings or full-length chadors have introduced non-Muslims to the concept of *hijab* as it applies to women, many are not aware that men must follow *hijab* as well. Men's clothing must be loose-fitting and modest. They may not wear gold or silk.

## Education

Public education was first introduced in Iran in 1906. These primary-level schools were located in cities and often served only the children of the wealthy. In 1925, Reza Shah announced that the public school system would offer free secondary education as well, with an emphasis on math, science, and literature. Although this was a positive step, it failed to provide educational access to many Iranians; by 1979, fewer than half of all adults were literate.

Following the revolution, there was a massive school building campaign. Schools were built throughout the country, and traveling schools were designed to accommodate the children in nomadic tribes. Today, every village and town in Iraq has a primary school, but secondary and high schools are concentrated in urban areas. Adult literacy programs were also established over the past two decades. These efforts have resulted in an overall literacy rate of more than 70 percent. Since the revolution, religious studies are considered as important as other subjects.

Children between the ages of six and fourteen are required to attend primary and secondary school, although many girls do not continue past primary level. Those students who want to continue on to high school must demonstrate their readiness through exams and good behavior. Because education in Iran is valued highly, there is great competition for the openings in high schools and universities. Students must take an entrance exam, and only those with the highest scores are allowed to continue their education. Students who are accepted into certain state university programs must agree to work in Iran's rural areas for a time after graduation to repay the cost of tuition. In addition to the free public institutions, several private Islamic institutes offer classes at the university level.

## Recreation and Leisure

Following the 1979 revolution, religious leaders banned many forms of entertainment, from gambling to nightclubs to pop music. They encouraged family-oriented entertainment, sports, and other recreational activities. Today, hiking and picnicking are favorite family outings, as are excursions to museums, poetry readings, movie theaters, and concerts. Winter vacations are often spent along the Persian Gulf coast, while the cool mountains draw many summer visitors. Religious and historical sites are popular tourist attractions as well.

Iranians enjoy several sports, including horse racing, snow skiing, and table tennis, but soccer is by far the national favorite. Cities boast several teams that play in front of thousands of spectators. Tehran alone supports ten stadiums. In recent years, women have been allowed to attend soccer games, although separate seating for men and women is provided.

*Did You Know?*

There is a special stadium in Tehran for Christian athletes. There, men and women can attend the same sporting events or compete against each other.

Many Iranian women enjoy competing in sports, but—under Islamic law—they face more stringent guidelines for participation. Women athletes must either compete in special stadiums where only female spectators are allowed or they must compete while wearing a chador or long coat and veil. Target shooting, equestrian show jumping, and snow skiing are popular sports for women athletes.

Many Iranian men take part in martial arts exercises in a unique gymnasium called a *zurkhaneh* (ZOOR-khah-nah), or house of strength. Dating back to the Arab invasion in the seventh century, the exercises performed at the *zurkhaneh* were once secret preparations for a Persian overthrow of the new Arab regime. Today, the exercise sessions are a combination of bodybuilding, gymnastics, and wrestling. Each session begins and ends with a prayer to Imam Ali. One man recites verses from the *Shahnameh,* a book that recounts the legends of ancient Persian kings, while the men brandish wooden clubs and shields or swing lengths of chain above their heads in a re-creation of ancient battlefields. Periods of bodybuilding exercises are followed by wrestling matches.

## Food

Like many other cultural innovations, Persian cooking traditions migrated throughout the Middle East as the Persian Empire expanded. Many of these techniques and recipes are still revered by modern Iranians, as are the Iranian customs of hospitality.

Rice and bread are the mainstays of the Iranian diet, supplemented by fresh vegetables and fruit. Many dishes include meat, but in small amounts. Iranians love sweet pastries such as baklava and rice puddings, but desserts like these are generally reserved for special occasions. Nuts and fruit, both fresh and dried, are common snacks. Most Iranians do not consume pork, shellfish, or alcohol, all of which are taboo for Muslims.

Long-grained, fluffy rice called *chelo* is served at almost every meal. It often accompanies stews of fruit, vegetables, and meat that combine the sweet and sour flavors unique to Persian cooking. *Chelo* kebab, the national dish of Iran, features lamb or chicken kebabs served over rice that has been steamed, then cooked with butter and saffron. (Kebabs are small pieces of meat that have been marinated in yogurt and herbs, placed on a skewer, and grilled over charcoal.)

Iran's varied climate enables a wide variety of nuts, fruits, and vegetables to be grown. Persian melons (similar to cantaloupe), pomegranates, apples, plums, peaches, dates, apricots, and sour cherries are among the many fruits produced in Iran. Besides being eaten fresh or dried, some fruits such as pomegranates are cooked into syrups that are used in traditional dishes.

Traditionally, meals are served on a cloth placed on the floor. In urban areas, many families have dining tables as well. Dishes are served on large platters, and people serve themselves. In the past, diners tore

## NAN-O-PANIR-O-GERDU

### (CHEESE AND WALNUT SPREAD)

*All the herbs in this recipe should be fresh. Chop them coarsely before measuring.*

1/4 pound feta cheese
2 cups chopped walnuts
1 clove garlic, peeled and crushed
1/4 cup tarragon
1/4 cup mint
1/4 cup scallions
1/4 cup basil
1/4 cup olive oil
1 tablespoon freshly squeezed lime juice
1/2 teaspoon salt
1/4 teaspoon freshly ground black pepper
*Lavash* or pita bread

In a food processor, mix all the ingredients except the bread to create a grainy paste. Taste and adjust seasoning as desired. Spoon the cheese and herb mixture into a small serving bowl, and place it on a round platter.

To serve, cut the *lavash* or pita bread into 4-inch pieces and place it on the platter. (You can substitute sliced and toasted French or Italian bread if *lavash* or pita bread isn't available).

Source: Adapted from *A Taste of Persia* by Najmieh K. Batmanglij.

off pieces of bread to scoop up their food, but today many families use forks and spoons. (All ingredients are cut into bite-sized pieces, so knives aren't necessary.) Iranian hospitality is legendary, and hosts make sure that their guests get the best pieces of meat or the ripest fruit. It is very rude not to accept the hosts' generosity, although guests are expected to protest before accepting the food being offered.

## Holidays and Festivals

Most of Iran's holiday celebrations are rooted in Islamic tradition, although the No-Ruz (Iranian New Year) festivities are secular in nature. Iranians also observe several days of national importance, such as Revolution Day (February 11), which commemorates the 1979 overthrow of the shah, and Oil Nationalization Day (March 20).

### Ashura

Like all Muslims, Iranians observe the major Islamic holidays such as Eid al-Fitr, a period of celebrating at the end of Ramadan, and Eid al-Adha, the Feast of the Sacrifice that commemorates Abraham's obedience to God. (For more information about these celebrations, please see page xii in the introduction to this volume.) Additionally, many public holidays in Iran honor Shi'ite traditions, including the births, martyrdom, and deaths of the twelve imams.

For Shi'ite Muslims, one of the most important days of the year is Ashura, a day of remembrance. Ashura is a period of mourning that marks the martyrdom and death of the Prophet Mohammad's grandson—Imam Hussein—and his family in 680. Special plays, Taziyeh (tah-ZEE-ya), or "Mournings for Hussein," are performed on stages set up in front of mosques.

### No-Ruz

One of the oldest festivals in Iran is No-Ruz, or "New Day." It marks the beginning of the Iranian New Year and is rooted in Zoroastrian rituals. Although efforts were made to repress the holiday in the early years of the Islamic Revolution, the tradition has continued. Today, No-Ruz is celebrated as a national holiday rather than a religious one.

No-Ruz always starts on March 21, the first day of spring, and lasts thirteen days. In preparation for the holiday, houses are cleaned, and new clothes are bought for the entire family. Wheat or lentil seeds are planted; the green sprouts that appear during No-Ruz represent spring and new growth. Candles burn in each room of the house during the week before No-Ruz, representing the fire of the Zoroastrians.

On the last Tuesday night of the old year, Iranians celebrate Chahar Shanbeh Soori, the Festival of Fire. People gather around bonfires lit in public places and take turns leaping over the flames, the remnants of an ancient purification ritual that wards off illness and bad luck. Feasts of food that bring good luck, such as noodle soup and snacks of dried nuts and fruit, are shared with everyone. In modern times, fireworks have added to the festivity. Like American children on Halloween, Iranian children dress in shrouds or hide under chadors to resemble the spirits of their ancestors who traditionally visit on this night. The children bang pots and pans to frighten away the bad spirits before Wednesday arrives. (In Islamic tradition, Wednesday is considered an unlucky day. This nod to Islamic beliefs has helped preserve No-Ruz as a national holiday.) As they make their way through the streets, the children stop at houses and ask for treats.

On the morning of March 21, each family prepares a Haft Sinn (haft SEEN)—a special cloth set with seven items that begin with the Persian letter *s* (*Sinn*). These items symbolize new growth, resurrection, and blessings for No-Ruz. Things that represent the creation of the world—including water, a goldfish (animals), wheat sprouts (plants), and candles (fire)—are also found on the Haft Sinn. A decorated egg, representing fertility, and a mirror, representing multiple blessings, are often placed on the cloth. Devout Muslim families may place a Qur'an on the Haft Sinn as a blessing for the upcoming year, while more liberal

*For devout Muslim families, the Qur'an plays an important role in the celebration of No-Ruz. It is often one of the seven items included in the Haft Sinn, a special cloth set with items that represent blessings and renewal for the new year.*

families add a copy of Firdawsi's *Shahnameh* (The Epic of Kings), a classic volume that recounts the legends of ancient Persia and symbolizes pride in the Iranian heritage.

No-Ruz is a time for visiting friends and family. Presents are exchanged and feasts are held. On Sizdah-Beder, the thirteenth—and last—day of the celebration, the wheat sprouts are thrown away to get rid of any bad luck. Then, also to avoid misfortune, the family spends most of the day outdoors, at a park or other natural area, picnicking and playing with friends.

## The Arts

The arts flourished in ancient Persia as early emperors employed artisans to record their war triumphs in stone carvings, sculptures, and paintings. Later, the shahs celebrated and honored Islam by constructing mosques and minarets adorned with ceramic tile mosaics, metalwork, and unique architectural elements. Poets and poetry have always occupied a special place in Iranian culture. Even the gardens that grace the shrines throughout Iran have a distinctive artistry about them.

Pride in Iran's artistic heritage remains strong today. Following the Islamic Revolution in 1979, the new Ministry of Culture began sponsoring fine art exhibits that featured calligraphy, painting, photography, pottery, and sculpture.

### Textile Arts

Persian carpets have long been considered the most exquisite carpets in the world. Master weavers make the best carpets out of silk thread,

## AN ANCIENT ART

Discoveries of Persian carpets dating back to the fifth century B.C.E. illustrate how ancient the art of carpet weaving is in Iran. It is an art that requires much skill and hours of labor. A handwoven carpet with an intricate design may require several years to complete. While skilled weavers can tie 12,000 knots each day, 1 square yard (0.8 square meters) of carpet can have 1 million hand-tied knots.

Many Iranian girls learn the art of weaving at a young age. They study Persian designs and learn how to create natural dyes that are rich in symbolism. Rose petals, pistachio and walnut shells, and various leaves are all used to produce carpet dyes. The color red represents happiness and riches, while blue wards off the evil eye (bad spirits). Orange signifies faith. White and green are seldom used; white because it symbolizes grief and green because it is a sacred color that is associated with the Prophet Mohammad.

tying millions of knots as they create their masterpieces. The more knots there are, the finer and more sophisticated are the designs. Persian carpet designs differ depending on which ethnic group makes them. Kurdish carpets are filled with animal designs, while carpets from Sistan va Baluchestan often feature the tree of life in the center. Most Iranian homes, whether rich or poor, are furnished with carpets, which serve as a place of prayer as well as for visiting and sleeping. Carpets also decorate the walls of many homes. Nomadic people often use carpets as saddle blankets for their camels and as doors for their tents.

## Visual Arts

Pottery is one of the earliest art forms of ancient Persia, with artifacts dating back 6,000 years. Much of the early pottery was decorated with animal designs. Sculptures, paintings, and carvings along with colorful glazed bricks decorated Pasargad Palace (c. 550 B.C.E.) and Persepolis (c. 518 B.C.E.), two magnificent buildings of the Achaemenid Empire.

Although early Persian artists depicted human activity in their work, geometric patterns called *arabesque* and calligraphy rose to prominence following the introduction of Islam to Iran. (Islamic beliefs do not allow artists to show the human form.)

During the Safavid Dynasty (1501–1722), artistic expression flourished. The art of miniatures—tiny paintings on glass, paper, or other objects—was refined during this period. Iranian miniatures often feature landscapes filled with gardens and animal life, although some illustrate ancient poems or verses from the Qur'an. The paintings are so small that viewers must use magnifying glasses to see all the details.

## Architecture

Architecture is considered by many experts to be Iran's greatest accomplishment. Its first great period of innovation occurred in the Achaemenid Empire (550–330 B.C.E.). Palaces were built upon great platforms that nestled into the sides of mountains. Gigantic stone columns marked the buildings' exteriors. Wide hallways with marble-paved floors graced the interior. Floral and animal motifs decorated colorful glazed bricks.

The domes that are synonymous with mosques today were first built in Iran during the Sassanian period (224–642 C.E.). The vaults that supported these massive domes were constructed of fired bricks. They were incorporated into religious buildings during the early days of the Islamic Empire.

Another great age of architectural development occurred under the Safavids. Mosques built during this era influenced Islamic buildings throughout central Asia, Afghanistan, Pakistan, and India. The intricate stone and stucco carvings, painting, tile and mirror work combine to create a visual proclamation of God's greatness.

Some architectural innovations were practical. In the deserts, people developed *badgirs,* rectangular structures that towered high above homes and captured breezes to cool the homes. They also built water storage units called *anbars.* Tall minarets served as landmarks for nomadic tribes, marking the location of inns or villages.

## Performing Arts

Iranian music is a vital part of most festivities, although conservative Muslims do not believe it has any role in Islamic worship. Stringed instruments often accompany traditional Iranian songs and dances, which vary from region to region.

The film industry in Iran is burgeoning, especially since the revolution. About sixty films are produced each year in Iran, many of which are shown at international film festivals. In 1997, filmmaker Abbas Kiraostami won the Palme d'Or at the Cannes film festival for *A Taste of Cherry.* Strict censorship keeps filmmakers from showing situations or viewpoints that are in opposition to the government or that illustrate suffering experienced by Iranians. As a result, many films are rich in symbolism.

## Literature

With roots in a rich heritage of storytellers, the literary tradition in Iran is over one thousand years old. Until recently, poetry has been the foremost form of writing. Firdawsi was one of the first great poets in Iran's history. In the eleventh century he wrote the *Shahnameh* (The Epic of Kings), a recitation of ancient Persian history. Another eleventh-century poet, Omar Khayyam, authored the *Rubaiyat,* which is known throughout the world. During the thirteenth and fourteenth centuries, Saadi and Hafez gained recognition for their moral tales and lyric recitations. Shrines to these two great poets remain popular tourist attractions in Shiraz today.

# Iraq

Iraq, located at the center of three continents, was known in ancient days as Mesopotamia—the land between the rivers. Some of the world's earliest civilizations developed in Mesopotamia, earning it the designation "the cradle of civilization." Alternately flourishing and neglected through the centuries, Iraq entered the twentieth century with hopes for developing a modern society. Over the past four decades, however, war and internal upheaval have devastated Iraq's land along with much of its hope.

Iraq shares borders with Turkey, Iran, Kuwait, Saudi Arabia, Jordan, and Syria. Only 36 miles (58 kilometers) of coastline along the Persian Gulf keep Iraq from being completely landlocked. While Iraq has not developed long-standing diplomatic relationships with any of the surrounding countries, boundary disputes with Iran and Kuwait have resulted in wars with those two countries.

Today, Iraq's future is uncertain. In March 2003, troops from the United States and Great Britain led an invasion into Iraq that toppled President Saddam Hussein's government. Hoping to rebuild a democratic Iraq, the two countries set up an interim government that will rule Iraq indefinitely. While many Iraqis are glad to see Hussein's reign ended, few want to live in an occupied country.

## FAST FACTS

- ✔ **Official name:** Republic of Iraq
- ✔ **Capital:** Baghdad
- ✔ **Location:** Center of the Middle East; surrounded by Turkey, Iran, Kuwait, Saudi Arabia, Jordan, and Syria
- ✔ **Area:** 168,754 square miles (437,072 square kilometers)
- ✔ **Population:** 24 million (July 2002 estimate)
- ✔ **Age distribution:**
  0–14 years: 41%
  15–64 years: 56%
  over 65 years: 3%
- ✔ **Life expectancy:**
  Males: 66 years
  Females: 69 years

- ✔ **Ethnic groups:** Arab 75-80%, Kurdish 15-20%; Turkmen, Assyrian, Armenian, and other 5%
- ✔ **Religions:** Muslim 97% (Shi'a 63%, Sunni 34%), Christian and other 3%
- ✔ **Languages:** Arabic, Kurdish, Assyrian, Aramaic, Armenian
- ✔ **Currency:**
  Iraqi dinar (IQD)
  US$1 = 0.31 IQD
- ✔ **Average annual income:** US$593
- ✔ **Major exports:** Crude oil

Source: CIA, *The World Factbook, 2002;* BBC News Country Profiles.

# The Iraqis

An estimated 24 million people live in Iraq today. About three-fourths of Iraqis are Arab, while Kurds make up the largest minority group with 15 to 20 percent of the population. Regardless of ethnicity, most Iraqis live in urban areas. Even in the rural areas, those who farm and raise livestock generally live within a town or village, with their fields and pastures in the outlying areas.

Although numerous ethnic groups are represented in Iraq, the greatest conflict often surfaces between religious groups—in this case, Sunni and Shi'ite Muslims. Although most Iraqis are Shi'ite Muslims (about 63 percent of the population), most members of Saddam Hussein's government were Sunni Muslims. However, there is also a great deal of antagonism between the Kurds and Arabs.

Most people speak Iraqi Arabic, although Kirmanji, a Kurdish-language dialect, is the official language in the Kurdish-dominated north.

## Arabs

Most of the people living in Iraq are Arabs, descendants of seminomadic Semitic tribes. Traditionally farmers, most Iraqi Arabs are more likely to live in urban areas today. Within the Arab population are two distinctive groups—the Marsh Arabs and the Bedouins.

### The Marsh Arabs

The Marsh Arabs, or Ma'dan, get their name from the marshes that cover their homeland in southeastern Iraq. Traditionally, this group made unique homes with arched ceilings from the reeds that grew in the wetlands. The homes floated in clusters of two or three, built upon layers of reeds. Canoes similar to those used by the Sumerians carried the people from one cluster to another. Most of the Ma'dan supported themselves by hunting and fishing, while others lived a seminomadic life herding water buffalo. It was a lifestyle that was relatively unchanged since the ancient Sumerians lived in the area 6,000 years ago.

---

***Did You Know?***

The Arabic language has three basic forms. Classical Arabic is the language of the Qur'an, used in religious services and prayers by Muslims. Modern Standard Arabic developed from the classical version. It is primarily a written language, used in literature. Spoken Arabic has many dialects that vary widely. (A *dialect* is a regional variation in a language. The grammar, vocabulary, and pronunciation are different from those of other regions.) Iraqi Arabic is similar to Arabic dialects spoken in Syria, Lebanon, and parts of Jordan. Most educated Iraqis are fluent in Modern Standard Arabic as well as Iraqi Arabic.

In the late 1980s and early 1990s, Shi'ite rebels in southern Iraq—including some Marsh Arabs—launched guerrilla attacks against the Iraqi government. When the army fought back, many rebels fled to the marshlands seeking safety. At the same time, army deserters used the marshlands as a hiding place.

In retaliation for the rebel attacks, Saddam Hussein ordered bombing campaigns over the marshland. Villages that weren't destroyed by bombs were bulldozed or burned. In all, over seventy villages were demolished, and many villagers were killed. Gangs of army deserters preyed upon the families whose homes had not been destroyed. Over 200,000 Marsh Arabs—about 80 percent of the group—fled to nearby cities or across the border to Iran.

Hussein didn't stop at destroying the villages. He ordered the marshes drained. Canals were built to divert water away from the marshlands. In its place, raw sewage from nearby cities was piped to the region. Today, the once lush wetlands region is a salty, empty expanse. Livestock find little to eat, and rice can no longer be grown in the area. Several species of wildlife that once flourished in the region are endangered or extinct.

The few villagers that remain hope that the canals will be destroyed and the marshlands restored following the victory of the U.S.-led coalition in 2003. They face an uphill battle to resume their traditional way of life, however. If the water is restored, it will take time for reeds to grow and wildlife to replenish itself. The former marshlands sit on top of a large, unexplored oil reserve. While some activists are working to have the region declared a world heritage site by the United Nations (UN), other groups are pushing to open the reserve for drilling. And, most importantly, after a decade or more of living in the cities, many young Marsh Arabs are hesitant to leave the conveniences and job opportunities that urban areas offer.

### The Bedouins

The Bedouins have a proud heritage as nomadic herders with an exceptional knowledge of the desert. Earlier generations of Bedouins migrated between western and southern Iraq, Kuwait, and Saudi Arabia, moving between grazing lands according to the seasons. However, government policies that restricted the nomads' movement and the lure of an easier life in the cities have resulted in a decline in the nomadic population. Today, few Bedouins follow a traditional nomadic lifestyle.

## Kurds

The Kurds, whose name comes from the ancient Persian word for "hero," are the descendants of the ancient Medes of Iran. They live in a region that is often referred to as Kurdistan, although it is not an independent country. Kurdistan stretches over parts of Turkey, Syria, Iran, Iraq, and Azerbaijan. About half of all Kurds live in Turkey, but the Iraqi Kurds are more active in politics. While the Kurds have their own language, Kirmanji, those who live in Iraq generally speak Arabic as well.

*A Kurdish guard in traditional dress stands outside a government building in October 2002. This was the site of a meeting of various Kurdish leaders whose goal was to unite and possibly gain autonomy from the Iraqi government.*

In Iraq, most Kurds live in the foothills and mountains of the north and northeast. Iraq's largest and most valuable oil fields are found in the Kurdish region, prompting Saddam Hussein to impose an "Arabization" program in the region. Many Kurds lost their homes and farms when Hussein moved Arabs into northern cities in the 1980s, hoping to dilute the power of the Kurds.

Traditionally, the Kurds were a seminomadic tribal people who raised goats and sheep in the mountains and foothills. Men skilled in fighting, known as *pesh merga,* were often hired as soldiers. Today, many Kurds live in urban areas. In fact, three of the five largest cities in Iraq—Mosul (moh-SOOL), Irbil (sometimes seen as Erbil), and Sulaymaniyah—are located in the Kurdish region. Political affiliations, such as the Kurdish Democratic Party (KDP) and the Patriotic Union of Kurdistan (PUK), have largely replaced tribal loyalties.

The Kurdish people have been persecuted throughout history. In modern times, both Turkey and Iraq have repressed their Kurdish population. In the 1970s, with the support of the shah of Iran, Mulla Mustafa Barzana and the KDP nearly succeeded in creating an independent Kurdish area in the north. When the shah withdrew his support from the Kurds in return for a favorable end to a border dispute, however, the Kurdish secession effort failed. During the 1980s, most Iraqi Kurds supported Iran in the Iran-Iraq War. The Iraqi government responded by bombing Kurdish villages and farms and attacking Kurdish settlements and cities with chemical weapons. This scorched-earth policy was intended as a warning: if the villagers supported the guerrillas, they would be destroyed. Thousands of Kurds fled their homes. Some took refuge in the Kurdish cities of Irbil and Sulaymaniyah, while others crossed the border into Iran.

In 1991, a Kurdish rebellion following Iraq's forced withdrawal from Kuwait drew the ire of the Iraqi government. The army was sent to crush the rebels, and the UN coalition forces in the region refused to get

## THE YAZIDIS

The Yazidis are a Kurdish people, but they are considered a separate group because of their religious beliefs. Sometimes called devil worshipers, the Yazidis combine beliefs from Zoroastrianism (an ancient Persian religion), Christianity, Islam, and ancient pagan religions. Shunned by most Iraqis, the Yazidis live in poverty-stricken villages in northwestern Iraq.

involved in the conflict. About 1.5 million Kurds tried to escape by crossing into Turkey, but Turkey closed its borders to the refugees. Hundreds of thousands were trapped in the mountains in the bitterly cold winter.

Following a bitter civil war between Kurdish factions in the 1990s, Kurdish leaders Massoud Barzani of the KDP and Jalal Talabani of the PUK began working toward a free and independent Iraq as well as a unified Kurdish state.

## Other Minorities

The Assyrians living in Iraq today are descendants of the ancient Mesopotamians. They speak Aramaic (air-uh-MAY-ik) and Assyrian, the languages of their ancestors, and follow Christian traditions. Most Assyrians live in northeastern Iraq. Those who live in the cities generally work in business or other professional careers, while rural Assyrians are usually farmers.

Most of Iraq's small Armenian population lives in Baghdad and other northern cities. They are part of the Christian minority in Iraq. While some Armenians settled in Iraq as early as the seventeenth century, the majority arrived as refugees during World War I (1914–1918). They were fleeing present-day Turkey, where the Ottoman Empire had

*Making an interesting comparison of old and new, an Iraqi Kurd passes by a wall mural in Sulaymaniyah, a city in the Kurdish region of Iraq. During the Iran-Iraq War in the 1980s, many Kurds fled their settlements in Iraq to avoid being persecuted for supporting Iran. Others found refuge in Kurdish cities like this one.*

ordered the deportation or massacre of entire Armenian villages. In 2003, as the United States and its allies prepared for war in Iraq, many Armenian families became refugees once again as they sought safety in Lebanon, Syria, and other neighboring countries.

Turkmen settled in Iraq at the command of the Ottoman Empire, whose leaders wanted them to help control the Kurdish tribes. The early Turkmen settlements in the foothills of northeastern Iraq are still vital towns and villages today. While the Turkmen minority has kept its own language alive, it has adopted other aspects of Iraqi culture.

## Land and Resources

Iraq is located in the center of the Middle East. Although much of Iraq is desert, it has two very valuable resources—reliable water sources and oil. The region was once known as the Fertile Crescent, because the ready availability of water in the Tigris and Euphrates rivers made it possible to grow enough food that some could be exported. This capability contributed to the rise of early civilizations. In the twentieth century, the extensive oil reserves in Iraq became the center of the economy, providing billions of dollars of income for the Iraqi government despite the economic *sanctions* that have limited the sale of oil since 1990.

*A fisherman casts his net into the Euphrates River near Qurna, Iraq. The Euphrates and Tigris rivers made the land in this region very good for farming. Early civilizations were established in this area, called the Fertile Crescent, because of the abundance of food—so much food that some of it could be exported. Today Iraq's main export is oil.*

## Geography

At 168,754 square miles (437,072 square kilometers), Iraq is about the same size as the states of Washington and Oregon combined. It is the sixth largest country in the Middle East, behind Saudi Arabia, Iran, Egypt, Turkey, and Yemen. Iraq can be divided into four distinct geographical regions: the deserts, the grasslands, the mountains, and the Baghdad Plain.

The desert region in western and southwestern Iraq is part of the larger Syrian Desert, which also extends into Syria, Jordan, and Saudi Arabia. Few people live in this barren region, a dry, rocky plain with few sandy areas. Vegetation is rare. Winter rains often cause flash flooding in the *wadis* (WAH-dees)—desert streambeds that are dry until the rainy season.

North of Samarra and Hit, between the Tigris and Euphrates, are the grasslands. They are sometimes called *al-Jazirah*, the island. With deep valleys formed by rushing water, the region is difficult to irrigate. Much of this area is desert, but plant life grows year-round.

The mountains that rise up near the borders of Turkey and Iran range from 3,000 to 12,000 feet high (914 to 3,657 meters). The abundant rainfall in the region makes agriculture and livestock grazing possible in many of the valleys and highlands. This region is part of Kurdistan, the homeland of the Kurdish people. Over the centuries, much of the vast oak forest that once covered the mountain slopes has been cut for use as firewood and charcoal. Vast oil fields near Mosul and Kirkuk provide much of the oil that is produced in Iraq.

The Baghdad Plain is an alluvial plain, formed when the Tigris and Euphrates rivers overflow their boundaries and leave behind mud and minerals. Through this process, the plain is built up as much as eight inches (20 centimeters) every hundred years. Reaching from just north of Baghdad to the Persian Gulf, the Baghdad Plain supports most of Iraq's population. Historically, it is one of the most productive agricultural regions in the country, although the high level of salts deposited during flooding makes it increasingly difficult to grow crops. Many native plants, including rockroses, sedges (marsh grasses), and date palms, thrive in the alluvial plain.

Until the early 1990s, a large marshy area in southeast Iraq extended from the point where the Tigris and Euphrates meet to the Iranian border. Saddam Hussein ordered that the marshlands be drained in retaliation for rebel activity in the area. The drainage caused widespread environmental damage, destroying a unique habitat for many species of wildlife.

## The Rivers

Two major rivers—the Tigris and the Euphrates—cross Iraq. They helped make Iraq a major trading center of the ancient world and contributed to its prominence in medieval times. Both rivers have their start in Turkey, but the Euphrates flows through Syria before crossing into Iraq.

The Tigris is the fastest-flowing of the two rivers. It carries a great volume of water within its narrow banks. In the spring, sudden showers can raise the level of the water as much as one foot (30 centimeters) in an hour, causing devastating floods. In contrast, the wide and slow-moving Euphrates River meanders through Iraq, collecting runoff from the wadis. It changes course frequently before joining the Tigris near the city of An Nasiriyah. The river formed by the Tigris and Euphrates, the Shatt-al-Arab, continues on to the Persian Gulf.

Floods, once common from March to May, have been controlled somewhat by the construction of canals, dams, and other flood control systems. In addition, both Turkey and Syria have built dams on the upper Tigris and Euphrates, reducing the flow of water and the chance of floods.

## Major Cities

About three-fourths of the Iraqi population live in an urban society. They reside in the many cities and towns that were established near Iraq's rivers and canals. Even farmers live in towns or villages, traveling to their farmland outside the city limits every day. The three largest and most economically productive cities in Iraq are Baghdad, Basra, and Mosul, but the Shi'ite majority treasures Iraq's holy cities, holding them equal to Mecca in religious importance.

### *Baghdad*

Baghdad, the capital of and largest city in Iraq, is located near the center of the country. Although it is a modern city, mixing nightclubs, cinemas, and theaters with traditional bazaars, Baghdad has ancient roots. It was founded in the eighth century by the Abbasids and quickly became known

While Iraq has four geographic regions, it has only two climatic zones—the mountain zone and the lowlands. The mountain zone in northern and northeastern Iraq receives by far the most rain each year. The foothills get 13 to 22 inches (32 to 57 centimeters) of rainfall annually, while the highest elevations regularly total 40 inches (102 centimeters) of precipitation. The lowlands that form the rest of the country average only 4 to 7 inches (10 to 17 centimeters) of rain per year.

The mountain zone has relatively short dry summers that last from June to September. Temperatures may top 85° F (29° C) in July and August. Winters last from October through May. Snow is common in the upper elevations, where temperatures as low as 12° F (−11° C) have been recorded. Average January temperatures range from 24° to 63° F (−4° to 17° C).

Summer in the lowlands lasts from May through October. These are very dry months, with few clouds, low humidity, and scorching temperatures. While temperatures in July and August average 95° F (35° C) in Baghdad, afternoon highs can soar up to 123° F (50° C). Nights, in contrast, are relatively cool. The winter months bring what little rain falls in the lowlands. While temperatures are generally mild, ranging from 35° to 65° F (1° to 18° C), some areas do experience light frosts at night.

*Iraq's desert climate often causes summertime temperatures in Baghdad to climb well above 100° F (38° C). A street vendor in the city capitalizes on the heat by selling fans and wide-brimmed hats made from palm leaves.*

## Natural Resources

Iraq's greatest natural resource is its oil reserves, among the largest in the world. Some petroleum engineers believe that new discoveries of oil in Iraq are likely. In addition to oil, Iraq has large deposits of natural gas. This resource was largely wasted until recently because most of the gas occurs in oil fields, making it difficult to capture the gas economically.

Abundant water is another important resource in Iraq. With two major rivers and a number of smaller ones, there is a steady supply of water for irrigation. This makes cultivation of crops possible in many areas of the country that don't receive enough rain to support agriculture.

## Plants and Animals

Iraq once had a wide variety of wildlife, but a growing human population, combined with disregard for the effect of government policy on the environment, has led to the disappearance of many species in Iraq. Smaller mammals, such as bats, rodents, jackals, and hyenas, are common, while mountain goats and wild boars can sometimes be found in remote areas. Many species of birds remain in Iraq, although their numbers have declined since the marshlands were drained in the early 1990s. Crows, robins, storks, vultures, hawks, and ducks are among the 400 species that live or winter in Iraq. Reptiles and lizards can be found in the western deserts.

# History

## Ancient Civilizations

About 8,000 years ago, people began migrating into Mesopotamia— literally, the "land between the rivers." They came from the north and the east, from present-day Turkey and Iran, drawn by the Tigris and Euphrates rivers that provided an abundance of water and supported a rich variety of wildlife. Over time, these people would establish three of the world's earliest civilizations—Sumer, Assyria, and Babylon.

### *Sumer*

Sumer was the first great civilization to arise in Mesopotamia, about 4000 B.C.E. It was established in the lowlands of southern Mesopotamia (south of present-day Baghdad), where both the Tigris and Euphrates

## IMPORTANT EVENTS IN IRAQ'S HISTORY

**6000 B.C.E.** First settlers arrive in Mesopotamia.

**4000 B.C.E.** Sumer is established.

**2334 B.C.E.** Sargon I, the leader of the city-state of Akkad, rules Sumer.

**2000 B.C.E.** Babylonian Empire gains power after the Sumerian civilization is destroyed.

**1600 B.C.E.** Babylonia is overthrown.

**1100s B.C.E.** Assyria becomes a regional power. Babylonia regains power.

**722 B.C.E.** Sargon II expands Assyria.

**539 B.C.E.** Persians take control over the Sassanid Empire, which includes Iraq. Alexander the Great and his successors rule for two centuries during this period.

**634 C.E.** Arab armies invade Iraq.

**650** The Sassanid Empire falls.

**750** The Abbasid Dynasty is established; the Golden Age of Islam begins.

**1258** Mongol warriors invade Iraq.

**1335** End of Mongol rule; lawlessness and chaos ensue.

**1683** Iraq becomes part of the Ottoman Empire.

**1914** The Ottoman Empire fights on the side of the Axis Powers in World War I. British troops invade Iraq.

**1916** Iraqi Arabs join the British and other Allied forces in fighting against the Ottomans and Germany.

**1918** Britain and France rule the Arab countries of the former Ottoman Empire; Iraqi Arabs rebel against British rule in their country.

**1921** A provisional Iraqi government, led by King Faisal I, is established.

**1925** The Iraq Petroleum Company begins exploration of Iraqi oil fields.

**1933** King Faisal I dies; his son Ghazi becomes the new king.

**1939** King Ghazi is killed in a car crash. His three-year-old son becomes king, but doesn't rule Iraq until he turns eighteen. World War II begins, with Iraq supporting a new, pro-Germany administration.

**1945** At the end of World War II, Iraq is deeply in debt.

**1950s** Economic turnaround finally begins, when the Western automobile and building boom creates an increased demand for oil.

**1953** King Faisal II takes the throne, implementing policies that favor ties with Western countries.

**1958** Iraq and Jordan form the Arab Union of Jordan and Iraq. A military coup leads to the deaths of Faisal II and his family, as well as other government officials.

**1967** The Baath Party, a secular socialist party, comes to power in Iraq.

**1974** The Kurds, supported by Iran, declare war on the Iraqi government.

**1979** Saddam Hussein rises to power in Iraq.

**1980** Hussein orders an invasion of Iran. The Kurds support Iran; Hussein uses chemical weapons against their villages, killing thousands.

**1988** The Iran-Iraq War ends with both countries billions of dollars in debt.

**1990** Iraq invades Kuwait, its neighbor to the south.

**1991** Iraq ignores UN ultimatum to withdraw from Kuwait. Twenty-eight nations participate in the Persian Gulf War, forcing Iraq to withdraw its troops.

**1998** Iraq refuses to allow UN inspectors looking for weapons of mass destruction into the country.

**2002** U.S. president George W. Bush demands that the UN reinstate the inspection program, urging the use of military force if Hussein doesn't cooperate.

**2003** The United States leads a coalition of nations into Iraq and overthrows Hussein and the Baath Party.

frequently flooded during the rainy season, leaving rich silt that supported the cultivation of crops. However, the flooding was devastating to the early people, often wiping out entire villages and destroying food sources. The Sumerian civilization grew as people organized to control the force of the rivers and to produce excess food that could be traded with people in other regions. Because of their ability to grow surpluses of food—the first time in history this had been accomplished—the Sumerians became master traders, sending ships through the Persian Gulf and trading for goods from India and other eastern countries.

The Sumerians invented a writing system called *cuneiform,* irrigation systems, the wheel, astronomy, and literature. They invented a wheeled chariot and discovered how to produce bronze weapons, gaining an advantage in warfare. Religion played an important role in Sumerian life;

*This plaque contains the writing known as* cuneiform, *which was invented by ancient Sumerians.* Cuneiform *is a series of wedge-shaped figures made with a tool called a stylus, usually in clay.*

powerful priests ruled from pyramid-like temples called *ziggurats*. One of the most important city-states was Ur, the birthplace of Abraham, the founder of Judaism and a prophet of Christianity and Islam. (A *city-state* is an independently governed kingdom that consists of a city and the territory surrounding it.)

From 2334 B.C.E. to 2279 B.C.E., Sumer was ruled by Sargon, the king of the city of Akkad. He worked to unify the city-states, with some degree of success. By 2000 B.C.E., however, the Sumerian civilization had been destroyed by the Babylonians, who established the next great empire in the region.

## Babylonia

After conquering Sumer's city-states, the Amorites established a new empire called Babylonia (bab-uh-LOH-nya). The Babylonians lived in a highly advanced civilization that operated an extensive trading network. They refined the writing system developed by the Sumerians and added to the body of scientific knowledge through their study of astronomy.

King Hammurabi is the best-known of the ancient Babylonian rulers. He ruled over most of Mesopotamia, implementing a sophisticated administrative structure. Hammurabi's greatest contribution was the development of a set of laws called the Code of Hammurabi. It outlined the legal principles that society was based upon, including topics such as land ownership, women's roles, marriage and divorce, contracts, inheritance, wages, and working conditions.

Inscriptions found in the ruins of ancient Babylon note that the Code of Hammurabi was designed "to cause justice to prevail in the country, to destroy the wicked and the evil, that the strong may not oppress the weak."

Babylonia was destroyed around 1600 B.C.E. by the Hittites and Kassites, people who had been able to develop iron weapons. The Hittites remained in power until the twelfth century B.C.E. In later years, the Babylonians became a major power once again, until their eventual defeat by the Persians in 539 B.C.E.

## Assyria

The Assyrians settled in upper Mesopotamia, near the northeastern border of present-day Iraq, around 6000 B.C.E. During different periods, Assyria fell under the control of Sumer and Babylonia. As a result, Assyrian culture was very similar to theirs.

During the twelfth century B.C.E., Assyria became a power in its own right as its armies fought against wave after wave of foreign invaders. The cruel, brutal war techniques that the Assyrians employed terrorized their neighbors. When Assyrian armies approached cities looking for loot, the people often fled, hoping to escape the Assyrians' savagery. In the eighth century B.C.E., Assyrian rulers established a permanent army with the goal of establishing a world empire. Defeated peoples were resettled in new regions where they would have difficulty mounting a rebellion. Under Sargon II (722–705 B.C.E.), Assyria reached from southern Anatolia (present-day Turkey) to the Persian Gulf, and from the Mediterranean Sea to Persia's eastern border (present-day Iran). It later reached into Egypt.

Late in the seventh century B.C.E., the Medes (from present-day Iran)—with help from the Chaldeans (sometimes called the Neo-Babylonians)—conquered the last Assyrian king, ending the Assyrian Empire.

## The Persians and Greeks

Following the fall of the early Mesopotamian civilizations, ancient Iraq was ruled by the Persians (Iranians) and the Greeks. These foreign conquerors introduced their rich cultures to the Iraqi people, influencing their art and architecture as well as their language. The Persians ruled the longest—they controlled the region for all but two centuries between 539 B.C.E. and 633 C.E., but the Greeks arguably

## ANCIENT ACCOMPLISHMENTS

The three major civilizations that arose in ancient Iraq still influence our world thousands of years later. Some of their most innovative and far-reaching achievements are listed here.

| | | | |
|---|---|---|---|
| Sumer | Invented the earliest known form of writing *(cuneiform)*; produced bronze; designed weapons, including the chariot; studied mathematics and astronomy; developed standardized measuring systems; invented the wheel; established an education system; built pyramid-like temples called *ziggurats*. | Babylonia | Established the Code of Hammurabi, an early legal system; developed a calendar with twelve lunar months; created cosmetics, perfumes, and paints; practiced surgery. |
| | | Assyria | Cultivated wheat and domesticated many animals; developed weaving and pottery; known for art and architecture, especially monuments and palaces. |

had the longest-lasting influence through their introduction of Western gods and art and the exchange of scientific knowledge.

## Advent of Islam

Following the death of the Prophet Mohammad, the founder of Islam, Arab armies began campaigns to conquer the Byzantine Empire (in present-day Turkey) and the Sassanid Empire (in present-day Iran and Iraq). Arab armies entered Iraq in 634. Although vastly outnumbered, the Arabs defeated the Sassanid armies. The Iraqis, most of them Christians, paid the tax required of non-Muslims, but the Iranian armies continued to fight. Finally, in 650, the Arabs were victorious. The whole of the Sassanid Empire was under their control. They established a system of government and declared Arabic the official language. Over time, many Iraqis married Arabs and converted to Islam.

The Umayyad caliphate was established in 661 and was based in Damascus, Syria. Iraqi Shi'ites, the majority of Muslims in Iraq, were offended that the caliphate was given to a man whom they believed to be an enemy of Mohammad's. As a result, they launched many rebellions against the Umayyads.

In 680, the Umayyad army surrounded Hussein (Mohammad's grandson) and his family at Karbala, Iraq. When he refused to acknowledge the Umayyad leader, Yazid, as the rightful caliph, Hussein and his family were killed. Today, Hussein's burial site at Karbala is one of the most important religious sites for Shi'ite Muslims.

Unhappy with Umayyad rule, many rebels gathered in Khorasan Province in Iran. There, they rallied around Abd al Abbas, a distant

## A DIVISION WITHIN ISLAM

Ali, the son-in-law of Mohammad, was living in Iraq when he became the fourth caliph (Islamic leader). His selection caused a rift in the Muslim community. The Shi'as—literally, the followers of Ali—believed that he had been divinely appointed by Mohammad to lead the Islamic realm. They declared him to be the caliph of Iraq while religious leaders were meeting to consider the claim of Muawiyah, a member of the Umayyad family, who believed he should be caliph. Ali was murdered in 661, and his son Hasan died shortly after that, leaving the caliphate open for Muawiyah. Shi'ite Muslims cite the ascension of Muawiyah, the deaths of Ali and Hasan, and the later assassination of Ali's second son Hussein, as proof that Islamic leaders of the time supported the powerful elite over the righteous. These events also established a pride in martyrdom for righteous causes that still exists among Shi'ites today.

relative of Mohammad's, who vowed to defeat the Umayyads. In 750, after three years of battle, the Umayyads were overthrown and Abbas became the first caliph of the Abbasid Dynasty. His capital was established in Baghdad.

In the early years of the Abbasid Dynasty, Baghdad gained recognition as a center of philosophy, religion, literature, and scientific discovery. It was also a vital trading center linking eastern Asia with the Mediterranean region. Backed by a strong military power, the Abbasids extended the caliphate from China to southern France. Baghdad rapidly grew into a thriving metropolis; only Constantinople, the capital of the Byzantine Empire, was larger.

By the ninth century, the Abbasid caliphate had begun a slow deterioration. One by one, regions outside of Iraq broke away from the caliphate. The Abbasids brought in Turkish warrior-slaves called Mamluks to serve in the army and provide security in the palaces. Before long, the Mamluks had acquired most of the power in the caliphate. The Abbasid caliphs became religious leaders only. Although

*The golden dome of a shrine in Samarra, Iraq, shines in the sun. Samarra was built during the Abbasid Dynasty, when the cities of Iraq, especially Baghdad, were centers of philosophy, religion, literature, and science. Baghdad was also an important city for trade in the Middle East.*

the Mamluks were conquered by Iranian Shi'ites, who were in turn overthrown by the Seljuk Turks, the Abbasids remained as spiritual figureheads until the Mongol invasion of 1258.

## The Mongols

In the thirteenth century, hordes of Mongol warriors from northeastern Asia rampaged westward across the continent, destroying everything in their path. Famed conqueror Genghis Khan led the initial wave of conquests, but it was his grandson Hulagu who conquered the Abbasids in 1258. The intellectuals and scientists were massacred and their skulls piled into giant pyramids. The irrigation systems that supported life between the rivers were destroyed. Development was neglected, and Iraq's cities slowly declined.

In 1335, Mongol rule ended when the last emperor died. Various groups vied for power. Finally, in 1401, another great Mongol conqueror called Tamerlane swept into Iraq. His armies nearly leveled Baghdad, killing most of the people living there. The same scenario happened over and over again throughout Iraq. What had once been a mostly urban civilization became a country of nomadic tribes as people fled the destruction in the cities.

## Ottoman Rule

In the sixteenth century, two powerful rivals—the Safavids of Iran and the Ottoman Turks of Anatolia (present-day Turkey)—fought to control Iraq. The Safavids, who were Shi'ite Muslims, wanted to control the holy cities of An Najaf and Karbala. The Ottoman Turks, on the other hand, wanted to stop the spread of Shi'a Islam by installing a Sunni leader in Baghdad.

As power shifted back and forth between the Safavids and Ottomans, the rift between the Sunnis and Shi'ites grew deeper. Whichever group held power completely excluded the other from political, economic, and educational opportunities. By 1638, the Ottomans had gained control over Iraq, although their rule was weak and often challenged by the Iraqi tribes.

It wasn't until the late nineteenth century, when Britain and Germany vied for influence in Iraq, that the Ottomans took an active interest in Iraq. A modernization program improved transportation, created a *secular* (nonreligious) educational system, and designed a sanitation program that would meet the Iraqis' basic needs. Western school subjects were included in school curricula, and diplomatic ties were established with Western countries. About the same time, Iraqi Arabs' pride in their heritage began to grow. The Pan-Arab movement, a plan to unite all Arab countries, gained popularity in Iraq and other Arab countries.

Britain's and Germany's interest in Iraq was related to the desire to profit from the commercial potential of the Mesopotamian area. Britain wanted access to the Tigris for an overland route to India, while Germany wanted to build a railroad from Baghdad to Basra. At the beginning of the twentieth century, the British had a new interest in Iraq: they had just begun exploring for oil in southwestern Iran, making southern Iraq a strategic defense location.

## World War I

When World War I broke out in 1914, the Ottoman Empire sided with Germany and Austria-Hungary (the Central Powers), fighting against the Allied forces. (The Allies included Britain, France, and the United States.) Britain promptly invaded Iraq and stationed troops near the southern Iranian border in order to protect British oil fields there. British troops also captured the northern cities of Baghdad and Mosul to protect supply lines between Britain, the Middle East, and India. Britain persuaded the Arab tribes in the region to join the fighting against the Turks by promising that independent Arab countries would be established at the end of the war. The Iraqi Arabs, led by Faisal al-Husein (FIE-suhl all-hoo-SAYN) and supported by British officers, rose up against the Central Powers in 1916.

The war ended in 1918, and the Arabs stood ready to establish their independent nations. However, Britain and France decided to maintain their control over the region until they were convinced that the Arabs could govern themselves. The two world powers divided the former Ottoman Empire into several nations, with Britain ruling over Iraq, Jordan, and Palestine and France ruling over Syria (present-day Syria and Lebanon). Although the Kurds had been led to believe that Kurdistan would be one of the new countries, most of the Kurdish lands and people were divided among Iran, Iraq, Syria, and Turkey.

The resentment that Arabs felt about this betrayal was compounded by Britain's support for the Zionist movement, a push to establish a Jewish state in the nation of Palestine. In the minds of most Arabs, the British plan to give Arab land to the Jews at a time when Arabs had been denied the right to govern themselves was the final outrage. They rebelled against British rule. To appease the Arabs and Kurds, the British installed a provisional government in 1921. Al-Husein was named king and became known as King Faisal I. A council of Arab ministers (government leaders) advised the king. Britain maintained some control over the new country until 1932, when Iraq was recognized as an independent country.

## Independence

A split between the Sunni and Shi'ite factions, as well as between Kurds and Arabs, quickly became apparent. Faisal's government, made up of Iraqi-born military officers and Sunni Arab community leaders, supported the ideals of the Pan-Arab movement while the Shi'ite Muslims and Kurds did not. A long-term treaty signed in 1922 allowed the British to serve in the Iraqi government and to advise the king. In 1925, the Iraq Petroleum Company—owned by several international oil companies—began developing Iraqi oil fields.

King Faisal died in 1933, and his son Ghazi became king. He moved quickly to implement radical Pan-Arab policies. Three years later, a

*Faisal al-Husein (above) ruled Iraq as King Faisal I from 1921 until his death in 1933, when his son, Ghazi, was crowned. Ghazi was killed in an automobile accident just six years later, and his son, Faisal II, became king at three years of age. Faisal II officially took the throne on his eighteenth birthday in 1953.*

Kurdish general and a Shi'ite leader overthrew the government. The prime minister and *parliament* (legislative body) were forced to leave office, although Ghazi was allowed to remain as king. This coup marked the first time that the army influenced Iraqi politics. A car accident in 1939 killed Ghazi. His son, three-year-old Faisal II, became king but didn't assume full power until the early 1950s.

As World War II (1939–1945) began, Iraq ended diplomatic contact with Germany. It also instituted a policy of noncooperation with Britain. When the British demanded that the policy be reversed, the Iraqi military helped a pro-German government take power in Iraq. (Britain, America, the Soviet Union, and other Allied forces were fighting against the Axis powers led by Germany.) Britain invaded Iraq, overcoming military resistance to reestablish control over Iraq. Later in the war, Iraq became a strategic supply center for the Allies.

When the war ended in 1945, Iraq faced many problems. The country was deeply in debt. Minority groups, especially the Kurds, struggled to gain political power. Many Iraqis experienced hardships as a result of the widespread shortages of food and goods. The economy slowed further as hundreds of thousands of educated Iraqis emigrated to Israel, the United States, and other Western countries, creating a shortage of experienced professionals in many fields. In the early 1950s, the downward spiral finally ended when the rapid growth of the automotive industry in the West and the postwar reconstruction of Europe brought increased income from Iraq's oil production.

The largest exodus during this postwar period was due to the creation of Israel as an independent state in 1948. The division of the Arab homeland of Palestine necessary to establish Israel infuriated Arabs around the world. In May 1948, soon after Israel announced its independence, Arab countries—including Iraq—declared war on the new nation. Although outnumbered more than forty to one, the Israeli army crushed the Arabs in less than eight months. It was a humiliating defeat, made worse by Israel's seizure of even more Arab land in Palestine.

Many Arabs blamed Western countries, especially the United States, for their defeat, arguing that without Western support Israel would not exist. They turned to the Soviet Union for financial and military support. (Following World War II, the Soviets and Americans became bitter enemies as the Cold War pitted democracy against the spread of communism.)

Iraq's first direct parliamentary election took place in 1953. The legislative body that was in place when King Faisal II took the throne that year favored pro-Western, Pan-Arab policies. In 1958, Jordan and Iraq joined to form the Arab Union of Jordan and Iraq. Iraq's prime minister, Nuri al-Said, became the premier (ruler) of the new union. There was an immediate outcry from anti-Western Arab groups, particularly the United Arab Republic (UAR) (Egypt and Syria). The UAR launched a campaign urging Iraqi citizens to overthrow their government.

## Revolution

In 1958, a military coup led by General Abdul Karim Kassem shook Iraq. Faisal II and his family were murdered, as was Said. The new government acted quickly to disband the Arab Union and establish ties with the UAR. A series of military power struggles rocked the new Iraqi political scene for the next decade. Diplomatic ties with the United States were severed in 1967, shortly before the Baath (bah-AHTH) Party came to power.

The Baath Party, whose name means "renaissance" or "revival," advocated a secular, *socialist* government in which the government

*Members of the Baath Party march past Iraqi soldiers and a portrait of their leader, Saddam Hussein, during military training in early 2003. The Baath Party had been in power in Iraq since 1968.*

controlled large businesses and the economy without influence from religious leaders. Many large, privately owned companies were taken over by the Iraqi government, ending any large-scale free enterprise efforts by Iraqis. The new Revolutionary Command Council (RCC)—the supreme executive, legislative, and judicial body—established a friendly relationship with the Soviets, but remained hostile toward the West.

As the Baath Party leaders struggled to maintain power in the first years, the Kurds in northern Iraq launched attacks against the new government. In 1970, the Baath Party leaders agreed to form an autonomous (independent) Kurdish region and add Kurdish ministers to the cabinet if the fighting stopped. This turned out to be a ruse to buy the government time. The Kurdish region had the most productive oil fields in the country, and the Iraqi government wasn't about to give up the revenue.

Supported by the government of Iran, which at the time was friendly with the United States, the Kurds declared war on the Iraqi government in 1974. The Kurds' early successes worried the Iranians, however; if the Kurds in Iran decided to join the Iraqi Kurds, they could form a very powerful political group. As a result, the shah of Iran was willing to listen when the Iraqi government offered to move the southern boundary between the two countries to the center of the Shatt-al-Arab

*Saddam Hussein rose through the ranks of the Baath Party and came to power in 1979. Although he was called "president," he ruled the country as a dictator. Hussein is shown here giving a television address in March 2003, during which he rejected a demand by the United States that he leave Iraq or face war.*

in return for the Iranians' withdrawal of their support for the Kurds. (The Shatt-al-Arab is the only navigable river in the two countries that empties into the Persian Gulf. Previously, Iraq claimed ownership of the entire river, prohibiting Iran from using it as a shipping channel.) The Iranians, eager to gain river access to the Persian Gulf, agreed.

In 1975, abandoned by the Iranians, the Kurdish army finally gave up. New restrictions were placed on the Kurds, including a ban on studying Kurdish history or language. Arab Iraqis were resettled in the Kurdish region, many forcibly, in an effort to weaken Kurdish political power.

Saddam Hussein, a member of the Baath Party, rose to power in 1979. One of his first acts was to strengthen the national security force, using it to silence political opponents through torture and execution. Hussein soon ruled the country as a dictator.

## The Iran-Iraq War

At the same time that Saddam Hussein came to power, a power shift occurred in Iran when the Shi'ite religious leader Ayatollah Khomeini (eye-yuh-TOL-uh ko-MAY-nee) overthrew the shah of Iran. The resulting Islamic republic, based on a strict interpretation of Islamic laws, threatened Hussein's hold on power. Many Shi'ite Muslims, the majority in Iraq, wanted to see the same kind of religious state in Iraq.

Declaring that the border drawn between Iran and Iraq in 1975 was invalid, Hussein invaded Iran in 1980 and quickly took control of the oil-rich Khuzestan Province. He thought that Iraq would quickly gain control of Iran since its new government was not firmly established. The Iranians fought back, however, and the resulting war lasted eight years.

When the Iraqi Kurds supported the Iranians, the Iraqi army retaliated by destroying many Kurdish villages. In flagrant disregard for international law, Hussein ordered the use of chemical weapons against the Kurds and Iranians. Outrage erupted in the international community when word of the chemical attacks spread. Finally, in 1988, after hundreds of thousands of deaths, Khomeini and Hussein agreed to end the war.

The war devastated the economies of both countries. Billions of dollars had been spent on the war effort, leaving Iraq deeply in debt. Attacks on oil refineries, electrical generating plants, and other vital parts of the *infrastructure* severely hampered the country's efforts to rebuild.

## The Persian Gulf War

Wreckage from ships bombed during the Iran-Iraq War remained in the Shatt-al-Arab, blocking Iraq's only waterway to the Persian Gulf. Kuwait (koo-WAYT), Iraq's tiny neighbor to the south, had much greater access to the Persian Gulf, as well as better oil production. On August 2, 1990, the Iraqi army invaded Kuwait and took control of its oil fields. Iraq's naked aggression toward another Arab country shocked the world. Hussein justified the invasion by arguing that, historically, Kuwait was part of Iraq.

The UN gave the Iraqis an ultimatum—withdraw from Kuwait by January 15, 1991. Economic sanctions were imposed in an effort to solve the problem diplomatically. When Hussein refused to withdraw his troops, twenty-eight nations sent troops to fight against Iraq in what became known as the Persian Gulf War. Among the countries participating in the action were Saudi Arabia, Egypt, and Syria. This marked the first time that Arabs had ever joined forces with foreigners to fight against another Arab country.

*The skies of Baghdad are lit up with antiaircraft fire as U.S. warplanes strike targets in the city at the start of the Persian Gulf War in January 1991. The Gulf War marked the first time in history that Arab countries had sided with Western nations to fight another Arab country.*

After six weeks of fighting, Hussein withdrew his troops from Kuwait. Back in Iraq, Hussein's army faced rebel attacks by the Shi'ites in southern Iraq and the Kurds in the north. The United States encouraged the insurrections, but did not step in to help when the Iraqi army retaliated against the rebels. Villages in both the north and the south were burned and bulldozed. The marshlands in southeastern Iraq were drained. Mass graves holding thousands of bodies, uncovered in southern Iraq in 2003 after the Baathist government was overthrown, attest to the brutality of the army campaign.

Hundreds of thousands of Shi'ites fled to Iran; a million Iraqi Kurds tried to reach the Turkish border. When Turkey refused to allow the Kurds to cross the border, American, British, and French troops established refugee camps within Iraq.

The UN Security Council decided that, rather than use military force to remove Hussein from office, it would impose further economic sanctions on Iraq. Sales of oil were banned until Hussein stepped down. This move had little effect on government officials, but the living conditions of ordinary Iraqis deteriorated rapidly. There were shortages of food and medicines, power outages were common, and unemployment reached high levels. Because the situation was so dire, the UN voted to allow the Iraqi government to sell oil in order to purchase food and other humanitarian supplies. Unfortunately, most of the money from the sale of oil went directly into the pockets of Hussein and his personal security force, the Republican Guard. In addition, some oil was sold on the black market to Syria and other nearby countries.

In addition to the economic sanctions, Iraq had to agree to destroy all chemical and biological weapons and end any nuclear weapons programs. Its actions were to be verified by UN weapons inspectors. A "no-fly" zone, enforced by U.S. and British troops, was established in the north to protect the Kurds from bombing campaigns. In 1998, Iraq, never a willing participant in the weapons inspections, refused to allow any more UN inspectors into the country. When widespread support for continuing the inspections failed to materialize, the UN stopped enforcing the resolutions.

## Iraq Today

The status quo remained until terrorist attacks in the United States in September 2001 refocused American attention on Iraq. In a speech soon after the terrorist attacks, President George W. Bush described Iraq as one of several countries that sponsor international terrorism and disregard human rights. In 2002, Bush pushed the UN to demand the reinstatement of the Iraqi weapons inspection program. Hussein allowed the inspectors to return to Iraq, but U.S. officials pushed for stronger action. Unhappy with the progress of the inspectors, the United States cited evidence gathered by the Central Intelligence Agency that programs to build weapons of mass destruction (chemical, biological, and nuclear weapons) were still active. The United States also attempted to link Hussein with Al Qaeda (the Islamic terrorist group behind the 2001 terrorist attacks in the United States).

The UN Security Council, led by France and Germany, refused to approve military action against Iraq, preferring to give diplomacy and weapons inspections more time to work. The United States and Britain went ahead with plans to overthrow Hussein's government without the support of the UN, citing the immediate threat posed by Iraq. While some nations joined the U.S.-led coalition, the absence of many allies who participated in the Persian Gulf War was glaring. The push for military action against Iraq in defiance of the UN Security Council caused major political rifts between America and its former allies— particularly France, Germany, Canada, and Mexico.

U.S.-led forces invaded Iraq in March 2003 with a goal of overthrowing Saddam Hussein and eradicating any weapons of mass destruction. Within two months, the U.S.-led coalition held all major Iraqi cities. Bush declared the major combat phase of the war over on

## IRAQ'S GOVERNMENT

After the Baathist Party's rise to power in 1968, Iraq officially claimed a socialist republican government. In practice, however, Saddam Hussein ruled as a dictator from 1979, appointing government officials rather than holding open elections. After the fall of Hussein's regime, an interim government headed by American and British civilians began working with the various ethnic and religious factions within Iraq to create a new, democratic Iraqi government.

In light of the continued looting, U.S. troops have been assigned to help Iraqi police officers with security. In May 2003, the UN Security Council almost unanimously approved the U.S. request to lift the sanctions on Iraq. The resolution leaves the United States and Britain in control of Iraq indefinitely, with the power to sell Iraq's oil and use the revenue to rebuild the country. Criticism of the U.S. invasion and occupation remains, however, since no weapons of mass destruction have been found.

May 1, but Iraqi guerrillas have continued to attack coalition troops. To date, no weapons of mass destruction have been found.

In July 2003, the Iraqi Governing Council was founded. Its members, appointed by the U.S. administrator for Iraq, are responsible for the creation of a new Iraqi constitution, among other duties. The council will serve until a new Iraqi government is elected.

Efforts to locate Saddam Hussein were rewarded in December 2003, when a tip led American soldiers to the fallen dictator's hideout. After interrogation by American forces, Hussein is expected to stand trial for war crimes and genocide. It has yet to be determined whether the trial will be held in an Iraqi court or under the supervision of an international group such as the United Nations.

## Economy

Over two decades of war and economic sanctions have taken their toll on Iraq's economy. Before the Iran-Iraq War (1980–1988), Iraq received about 95 percent of its foreign income from oil. The high cost of the

*An Iraqi oil worker at the Kirkuk oil refinery, about 190 miles (304 kilometers) northeast of Baghdad. Before the Iran-Iraq War, the vast majority of Iraq's foreign income had come from oil production. But more than twenty years of war and instability have prevented Iraqi citizens from benefiting from their country's valuable natural resource.*

long-running war forced Iraq to borrow money from other countries to keep the government operating. Oil production facilities were damaged during the war, making it harder to repay the foreign debt. It's estimated that Iraq's economic losses during the war approached $100 billion.

Iraq rapidly began repairing pipelines and factories at the end of the war, but this rebuilding process was brought to a halt when Iraq invaded Kuwait in 1990. The economic sanctions imposed by the United Nations further hampered rebuilding efforts; what money did come into Iraq as a result of legal and illegal oil sales was confiscated by Hussein rather than spent on public works.

In early 2003, the invasion and subsequent victory of the U.S.-led coalition forces in Iraq temporarily brought economic activity to a standstill. Looters stripped equipment and materials from offices, power plants, and nuclear facilities, making it even harder to get businesses running again. At the end of May, the UN Security Council voted to lift the economic sanctions on Iraq. This cleared the way for the immediate resumption of oil sales. The profits will be placed in an account controlled by the United States and Britain and overseen by the UN.

Under Hussein, the media was placed under tight government control. Iraqi citizens heard only the government's side of any event. Opposing views were not heard. Rather, those who spoke out against the government or Hussein were usually imprisoned and sometimes tortured or killed. When the U.S.-led interim government took control of Iraq in 2003, new television and radio stations were launched, providing many Iraqi citizens with their first glimpse of a free media.

## Religion and Beliefs

Ancient Iraq figures prominently in Judaic, Christian, and Islamic history. The lands between the Tigris and Euphrates rivers are thought to be the location of the Garden of Eden. The ancient city of Ur, located 140 miles (225 kilometers) south of Baghdad, was the birthplace of Abraham, the founder of Judaism who is honored by Christians and Muslims as well. The Tower of Babel, Nineveh (the city to which Jonah was sent), and Babylon (where the Jews were *exiled*) were all located in ancient Mesopotamia.

Since the seventh century, Iraq has been a predominantly Islamic country. Most of the Iraqi Muslims are Shi'ites, and many of their holiest cities are located in Iraq. Small groups of Christians also remain in Iraq.

## Islam

Muslims follow the teachings of the Prophet Mohammad, who established Islam in the seventh century. They believe in one God—Allah—who revealed the Qur'an to Mohammad, the last in a series of prophets that includes Abraham and Jesus. The Islamic community is divided between Sunni and Shi'ite Muslims. Worldwide, most Muslims follow Sunni traditions, but in Iraq the majority of Muslims are Shi'ites.

The split between Sunni and Shi'ite Muslims occurred after the death of Mohammad, when his followers argued over how to choose a successor. Shi'ites believed that Ali, the son-in-law and cousin of Mohammad, was the rightful caliph (religious leader). They also believed that the male descendants of Mohammad, called imams, inherited his spiritual authority. (The number of imams varies by Shi'ite sect. The largest Shi'ite sect—the Jafari or Twelver Shi'ites—believes there were twelve imams.) Many of the

*Muslim men pray in front of a Baghdad mosque during the holy month of Ramadan in 2002.*

imams were murdered by Sunni Muslims or died under mysterious circumstances. As a result, a tradition of martyrdom was embraced by Shi'ites. The Imam Ali Mosque in Najaf, where Ali, the son-in-law of Mohammad and the first imam, is reportedly buried, is one of the holiest sites in the Shi'ite world. Another holy shrine, located in Karbala, marks the burial site of Hussein, the third imam and grandson of Mohammad. Most Shi'ite Muslims consider a pilgrimage to one of these cities equal to a pilgrimage to Mecca (the birthplace of Mohammad).

Early Muslims who supported Ali's claim to the Islamic leadership became known as the *Shi'a Ali,* or followers of Ali. Today they are known as Shi'a or Shi'ite Muslims.

Despite the different views on the selection of caliphs, Sunni and Shi'ite Muslims share many of the same beliefs. Both groups observe the five pillars of Islam: professing that "there is no God but God and Mohammad is his messenger," praying five times daily (Shi'ites pray three times daily), fasting during the holy month of Ramadan, giving alms (charity) to the poor, and making a pilgrimage to Mecca, the birthplace of Mohammad. Shi'ites have two additional pillars of faith—a pledge to undertake *jihad* (holy war) whenever Islam is threatened, and the promise to engage in good thoughts, words, and deeds. (To learn more about Islam, see pages ix–xii in the introduction to this volume.)

### Assyrian Christians

About 700,000 Iraqis—3 percent of the population—are Assyrian Christians. They are descendants of some of the earliest Christians in the world. The Christian community lived side by side with Arabs and Kurds for many centuries without conflict. Following the fiasco of the Gulf War, however, some Christians were persecuted because they were associated with the "Christian" West. Appealing to Islamic solidarity, Saddam Hussein required at one point that all children born in Iraq must be given an Islamic or Arabic name.

About 20,000 Armenian Christians live in Iraq. They, too, faced increased persecution in the 1990s and early twenty-first century.

## Everyday Life

For most Iraqi citizens, the past two decades have been years of sorrow and hardship. Nearly constant war and rebellion, along with the sanctions that crippled Iraq's economy, took their toll on ordinary people while government officials grew increasingly wealthy.

## Family Life

Many aspects of Iraqi family life have remained unchanged for centuries. Each family member is expected to behave in such a way that the family's reputation is enhanced, because that reputation helps determine one's status in Iraqi society. An individual's first loyalty lies with the family. Those who are in a position to help others in their family are expected to do so. This reliance on family means that employers are likely to hire their own family members, trusting that they have the family's best interest at heart. This is true even at the highest level of government; Saddam Hussein's closest advisers and government officials were family members.

In traditional Islamic families, the father is the head of the household and makes the final decision on any important matter. Men and women are more likely to share responsibilities and decision making in urban and educated families, especially when the women work outside the home. Both rural and urban Iraqis revere and respect family elders.

Since the early twentieth century, Iraqi leaders have introduced Western ideas and practices into Iraqi society in an effort to modernize the country. This has led to more educational opportunities for women, especially in urban areas, where many women continue their education and graduate from universities with degrees in math, science, law, or medicine. In the rural villages of the south where Shi'ite traditions remain strong, women are less likely to work outside the home. Instead, they take care of their family and the household. In Iraq, women have the right to vote, and some hold national office.

Marriage traditions are still quite strong in Iraq, and most marriages are arranged—often between cousins. Typically, the couple has the final say about whether the marriage will take place. Traditionally, Arab women do not take their husbands' names after marriage. Instead, a woman uses her name and her father's name. For instance, the name Nawal Ali Nasser identifies Nawal as the daughter of Ali of the Nasser family.

For the ceremony, most brides wear a Western-style white wedding dress, while grooms generally wear a black suit. Following the exchange of vows, Iraqis join a high-spirited procession. Leading the way is a taxi crammed full of wedding musicians who play their instruments as the taxi races through town. Behind them, the newly married couple rides in a car decorated with flowers. Buses and vans full of family and friends follow the wedding car through the streets, honking their horns wildly as the occupants cheer and sing.

In recent years, marriage has been very difficult for ordinary Iraqis. The poor economy has made it impossible for some to save enough for a dowry or housing. Many young men have been forced into hiding to avoid serving in Saddam Hussein's army, while others have been imprisoned for speaking out against the government. Now that Hussein's government has been overthrown and exiles are returning home, more marriages are taking place.

## Dress

Most Iraqis wear Western-style clothing, especially in the urban areas. In southern Iraq, Shi'ite women are more likely to wear the traditional *abaya* (uh-BIGH-uh), a loose black robe that covers the body from head to foot. A head scarf and veil are sometimes worn with the *abaya*.

The Kurdish people of northern Iraq are known for their brightly colored clothes that stand in vivid contrast to the black often worn by Shi'ite women. Kurdish women, most of them Muslim, dress modestly but rarely wear the *abaya*.

*An Iraqi family in Baghdad gathers for a meal during the month-long celebration of Ramadan. Many Iraqis in urban areas wear Western-style dress, with some women retaining the traditional head scarves, as they do here.*

## Education

Before the early twentieth century, only the wealthiest Iraqis could afford an education. Today, however, all children between six and twelve are required to attend one of Iraq's many free primary schools. Not everyone continues on to secondary school; of those who do, most are boys. Those who wish to further their education attend universities or other institutions of higher education or technical training. As a result of the increased access to education, Iraq's literacy rate has risen to 58 percent overall. The number of men who can read and write is much higher than the number of women—71 percent of men are literate compared with 45 percent of women.

Immediately after the overthrow of the monarchy in 1968, plans for widespread literacy classes were implemented. Floating schools were built in the marshlands of southeastern Iraq, while portable schools followed nomadic Iraqis from place to place. This early commitment to education helped Iraq win an award from the United Nations Educational, Scientific and Cultural Organization (UNESCO) in 1979.

After Saddam Hussein came to power in 1979, he required schools to teach his version of Iraqi history. "Patriotic education" classes, in which children had to memorize his favorite sayings and learn military songs and marches, soon replaced other subjects. Schools in the Kurdish region were forbidden to teach Kurdish history or language.

In the days following the overthrow of Hussein's government, schools reopened. However, continued looting and violence in the streets have kept many children away from school.

## Recreation and Leisure

With the focus on day-to-day survival, there has been little time for sports or leisure for most Iraqis. However, soccer—known as football in Iraq—has been a very popular sport. In 2003, following the overthrow of Hussein's government, the Olympic football team resumed training and expects to compete in the 2004 Summer Olympics.

## Food

During its long history, Iraq was ruled by many foreign empires. Each of these conquering peoples introduced a unique cuisine, with new spices and methods of preparation. These foreign influences can be seen in the food of Iraq today, which shares many similarities with the cuisines of Iran, Turkey, and Greece.

In Iraq, as in other Middle Eastern countries, a typical meal begins with *meze* (meh-ZAY), or appetizers. These are small dishes such as salads, olives, and yogurt cheese. One very common meze is hummus, a dip made from chickpeas (an Iraqi staple) blended with garlic and oil. Breakfast generally includes some combination of eggs, cheese, bread, and potatoes, while vegetables, eggs, meat, and bread are usually served at lunch. Dinners are the biggest meal of the day, with meze, meat, salad, vegetables, bread, and fruit. Tea and coffee are often served before and after meals, usually with lots of sugar. *Samoon* is a type of flatbread often served with meals.

Favorite dishes in Iraq include kebabs—meat and vegetables grilled on a skewer and served with rice; *quizi*—roasted, stuffed lamb; *kubba*—finely minced meat mixed with nuts, raisins, and spices, then fried; and *masgouf*—grilled fish prepared on the riverbanks in much the same way as the ancient Sumerians cooked it. Lamb is the most common meat, but beef, chicken, and fish are also eaten. The consumption of pork, shellfish, and alcohol is forbidden by the Qur'an.

Unlike the Western tradition of eating sweet desserts at the end of a meal, Iraqis serve desserts only occasionally, usually for company. Fresh fruit generally ends everyday meals. Candied peels of oranges, lemons,

## SHIRINI (KURDISH PUMPKIN PUDDING)

1-1/2 cups sugar
1 cup water
1/2 teaspoon ground ginger
1/2 teaspoon ground cinnamon
3 to 4 cups bite-sized pieces of fresh
   pumpkin, peeled and seeded (squash or
   yams may be substituted)
Finely chopped walnuts
Yogurt or whipped cream

In medium saucepan, combine sugar, water, ginger, and cinnamon. Bring to a boil over high heat, add pumpkin, and stir. Reduce heat to low, cover, and cook for about 20 minutes. Then remove the lid, and cook for an additional 10 minutes, until almost all the syrup is absorbed and the pumpkin is tender. Stir frequently to prevent sticking.

To serve, spoon into individual bowls and sprinkle with chopped walnuts. Garnish with a dollop of yogurt or whipped cream.

Serves 4 to 6.

Source: Adapted from *Holidays of the World Cookbook for Students* by Lois Sinaiko Webb.

or grapefruit are a favorite sweet treat called *g'shur purtaghal.* Another popular candy is *locum,* made of gelatin, sugar, nuts, and fruit juice.

## Special Occasions

Iraq, like other Arab countries, has a strong tradition of hospitality. Visiting is a favorite activity among Iraqi families and friends, and food is typically an important part of the visit. Guests partake in many rituals that have developed over time. Iraqis expect their guests to initially decline offers of food, as their hosts urge them to eat. Hosts serve their guests first and always offer them the best pieces of meat or the ripest fruit. It is considered rude not to accept the host's generosity. Licking one's fingers at the end of a meal is a sign that the meal was enjoyable. Food is generally served communally, and bread is often used in place of utensils to scoop up bites of food. Although families eat most meals together, there is often no talking during the meal in traditional homes.

One of the biggest celebrations in Iraq comes after the holy month of Ramadan. After a month of fasting from dawn until dusk, the feasts of Eid al-Fitr are a joyous affair. Foods from all over the Middle East are served—for example, *koshari,* a dish of lentils and rice from Egypt, and *yalanchi,* stuffed vegetables from Jordan.

Families also host special events following the *Al-khatma,* a ceremony that takes place at the end of a child's Qur'anic studies. During the ceremony, the child recites from the Qur'an from memory. If no mistakes are made, the child earns the title *hafiz.* The children who earn this title receive gifts and money, and their accomplishments are celebrated with a luncheon for boys or a tea for girls. Fresh fruits and sweets are usually served at this celebration.

## Holidays and Festivals

Since Saddam Hussein came to power in 1979, Iraq has celebrated several secular (nonreligious) holidays, such as Army Day and Republic Day. Republic Day commemorates the overthrow of King Faisal II and the establishment of the republic. Saddam Hussein's birthday was also an important occasion in Iraq. He ordered poems and songs to be written about him and parades to be staged in his honor. Following the overthrow of Hussein's government in 2003, however, these holiday celebrations are not likely to continue.

Since Iraq's population is predominantly Muslim, most of the country's holidays are Islamic ones. Two major Islamic holidays are celebrated by both Sunni and Shi'ite Muslims. Eid al-Fitr marks the end of the holy month of Ramadan with three days of feasting and gift-giving. Eid al-Adha, the Feast of the Sacrifice, commemorates Abraham's obedience to God. For the many Shi'ites in Iraq, Ashura is one of the most important holidays of the year.

## *A New Year's Tale*

The story of Tree at the Boundary is told during the Islamic New Year in the month of Muharram. According to legend, on the first night of the new year, an angel shakes a tree at the boundary where heaven and earth meet. Each leaf on the tree represents a person. If a person's leaf falls off the tree when the angel shakes it, that person will die in the coming year.

### Ashura

Ashura is one of the holiest times of the year for Shi'ite Muslims. It honors the martyrdom of Imam Hussein, the grandson of Mohammad, who was murdered by the Umayyad army near Karbala, Iraq. (The Umayyad caliph ruled the Islamic world, but Hussein had refused to recognize his authority, claiming that he was an enemy of Mohammad.) Traditionally, Shi'ite men and boys gathered at the shrine of Imam

*Iraqi women buy flowers near a holy shrine in Baghdad in 2003, during the celebration of Ashura. That year marked the first time in decades that certain Ashura traditions, which Saddam Hussein had outlawed, could be practiced without fear of punishment.*

Hussein during Ashura. They beat themselves with chains or cut themselves with knives to make amends for their ancestors' failure to defend Hussein.

Under Saddam Hussein, these public displays were outlawed. The number of pilgrims that were allowed to visit Karbala during Ashura was strictly limited. In 2003, just weeks after the U.S.-led coalition forces took control of Baghdad, millions of Shi'ite pilgrims flocked to Karbala to participate in their traditional mourning rituals.

# The Arts

The arts have been an important part of Iraqi culture since ancient days. They remain so today, despite years of repression by Saddam Hussein.

## Traditional Crafts

From the pottery techniques of ancient Mesopotamians to weaving and carpet making, traditional crafts are still practiced today. Artisans sell their wares at bazaars.

## Visual Arts

Baghdad has traditionally enjoyed a vibrant arts scene despite the wars and upheavals that marked the past three decades. Artists have continued to produce bold paintings and sculptures despite the repressive government of Saddam Hussein. And Baghdad's forty-five galleries have continued to show artists' work despite the decline in international visitors and art collectors.

Many of Iraq's best artists studied at the Baghdad Institute of Fine Arts. Bright, colorful abstract paintings are favored in Iraq, although there is a growing interest in sculpture. One gallery owner attributes this to the desire to create something permanent in the midst of chaos.

## Performing Arts

Baghdad is also a center for the performing arts. It is home to the Music and Ballet School as well as the National Symphony Orchestra. During the war between Iran and Iraq (1980–1988), the Persian Gulf War (1991), and the U.S.-led invasion, many theaters were destroyed. The spirit of the performers remained high, however. Within weeks, groups had written new plays and were performing them in the bombed-out theaters. The freedom to put on a play that did not have to be approved by the government marked a new era in the arts in Iraq.

Traditional Iraqi music combines musical forms called *maqams,* which are centuries old, with lyrics from classical Arabic poetry. Traditional instruments, including drums, lutes, and fiddles, accompany the singers. There are as many as seventy *maqams,* but each singer masters only two or three forms. Because this music requires years of study with an older, accomplished *maqam* singer, Iraq's traditional *maqam* music is in danger of dying out. Among the most popular *maqam* singers in Iraq today are Hussein al-Adhami, Hamid as-Saadi, and Farida Muhammad Ali.

Increasingly, Arab popular music is gaining popularity in Iraq. Typically, this musical style includes characteristics of American hip-hop music, with synthesizers, drum machines, and horns as instrumental accompaniment. One of the most admired Arab pop artists today is Abdel-Rahim, an Egyptian who grew up in poverty. His songs reflect a distrust of American and Israeli policies.

## Literature

Iraqis have a long history of storytelling and a proud literary heritage. Several stories from the Jewish and Christian holy books are set in Iraq, including stories of Abraham and Daniel.

### Did You Know?

One of the first pieces of literature in the world, the epic of Gilgamesh, was written by the Sumerians of ancient Mesopotamia thousands of years ago.

One of the best-known stories from this region—*The Thousand and One Nights*—tells of a king who was bitter because his first wife had betrayed him. In revenge, he marries a new wife every day and has her killed the next morning. When he marries beautiful Scheherazade, she begins telling him stories about Sinbad and Aladdin and other adventurers. But each night she stops just before the ending. The king is so anxious to hear how each story ends that he doesn't kill her. Finally, after one thousand and one nights, the king falls in love with Scheherazade and they live together happily for the rest of their lives.

Over the past few decades, most writers had to find a way to tell their stories without being thrown in prison for criticizing the government. The use of symbolism, which could be interpreted many ways, became very important. Some writers worked for the government, earning money by writing poems and stories about Saddam Hussein's triumphs that schoolchildren were forced to memorize.

# Israel

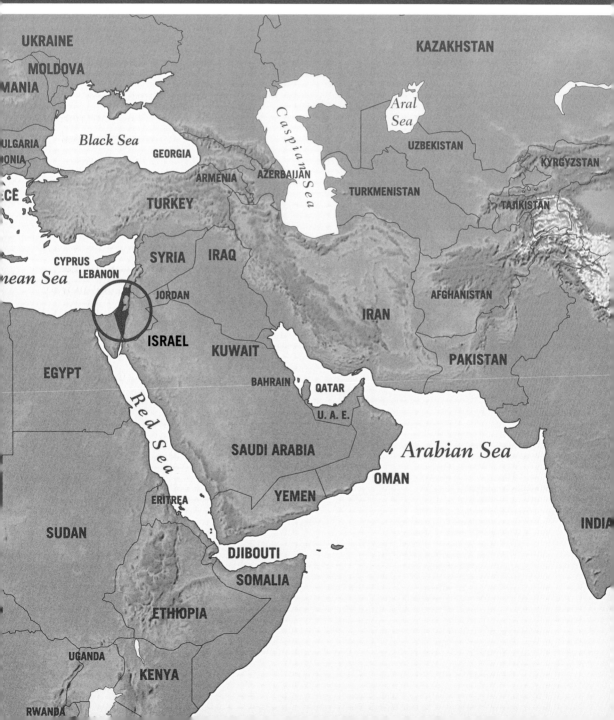

I srael is one of the newest nations in the world. Carved out of Palestine—a predominantly Arab country—as a Jewish state in 1948, Israel has been a center of conflict ever since. It is a homeland for both Jews and Arabs, and religious claims on the city of Jerusalem from both groups have contributed to the clashes.

Although past negotiations have failed to create a lasting peace, a new proposal offered by U.S. president George W. Bush offers hope for a future in which Jews and Arabs can live peacefully in the region.

## The Israelis

For most of Palestine's modern history, Arabs have been the dominant ethnic group. Following the creation of Israel in 1948, however, an influx of Jewish immigrants created a new majority ethnic group.

### Jews

Some 2,000 years ago, the Jews of Israel were *exiled* from their homeland and scattered across Europe, North Africa, and the Middle East. This settlement of Jews outside of Israel is called the Diaspora (digh-AS-pur-uh). During the nineteenth century, exiled Jews began returning to Israel from many different countries. They brought with

## FAST FACTS

✔ **Official name:** State of Israel

✔ **Capital:** Jerusalem

✔ **Location:** Borders the Mediterranean Sea between Egypt and Lebanon

✔ **Area:** 8,019 square miles (20,770 square kilometers)

✔ **Population:** 6,029,529 (July 2002 estimate)

✔ **Age distribution:**
0–14 years: 27%
15–64 years: 63%
over 65 years: 10%

✔ **Life expectancy:**
Males: 77 years
Females: 81 years

✔ **Ethnic groups:** Jewish 80.2% (European-American-born 32%, Israeli-born 21%, African-born 14.6%, Asian-born 12.6%), non-Jewish 19.8% (mostly Arab)

✔ **Religions:** Jewish 80%, Muslim 15% (mostly Sunni), Christian 2%, other 3%

✔ **Languages:** Hebrew (official), Arabic, English

✔ **Currency:**
New Israeli shekel (ILS)
US$1 = 4.45 ILS (2003)

✔ **Average annual income:** US$16,750 (Israeli) US$1,350 (Palestinian)

✔ **Major exports:** Computer software, military equipment, chemicals, agricultural products

Source: CIA, *The World Factbook 2002;* BBC News Country Profiles.

them their own religious practices, histories, and cultures, creating a very diverse Jewish population. Today, 80 percent of Israel's population is Jewish. Two of the major Jewish groups are the Ashkenazim (osh-kuh-NAH-zum) and the Sephardim (suh-FAR-dum).

The word *Ashkenazim* comes from the old Hebrew word for Germany. Ashkenazi (osh-kuh-NAH-zee) Jews are descended from Yiddish-speaking Jews in central and eastern Europe. Ashkenazi Jews give great importance to studying the Hebrew language and following the teachings of the Hebrew Bible and the Torah. Today, Ashkenazim make up approximately 62 percent of the world's Jewish population, with 3.7 million living in Israel.

The Sephardim, also known as Oriental Jews, descended from Jews who settled in Spain, Portugal, and other Mediterranean and Middle Eastern areas. Their name comes from the old Hebrew word for Spain. Generally, Sephardic Jews are less likely to follow religious tradition than the Ashkenazim. Approximately 950,000 Sephardic Jews currently live in Israel.

The first group of Sephardic immigrants arrived in Israel between 1948 and 1952. As a group they were much poorer and less educated than the Ashkenazim, with different cultural traditions. Although they are collectively referred to as Sephardic, each group within this division has its own cultural identity in Israel. Some, like the Iraqi and Yemeni Jews, have a positive image in the eyes of the Ashkenazim, while others are viewed negatively. Over time, many Ashkenazi Jews used the term *Sephardic* as a euphemism for poor or uneducated. As a result, many Sephardic Jews hesitate to label themselves as such. Until recently, the Ashkenazi Jews held most of the political power in Israel, but a Sephardic religious organization known as Shas has recently become one of the most powerful political parties in the country.

A small group of about 300 Samaritans, thought to be descendants of Jews who lived in Israel at the time of the exile to Babylonia, still live

## A LAND OF IMMIGRANTS

When Israel became an independent nation in 1948, the government immediately lifted the restrictions on immigration that the British had established. In 1950, the Israeli government passed the Law of Return, which guaranteed the right of every Jew to immigrate to Israel. Between 1948 and 1960, about 1.2 million Jews from countries around the world settled in Israel.

in Israel today. Their religion is similar to ancient Judaism. Because there are so few Samaritans, some fear that the group will die out within a few generations.

## Arabs

Following Israel's declaration of independence as a Jewish nation in 1948, many Arabs left the country and settled in the West Bank and Gaza Strip, as well as in other Arab countries. These Arabs fully intended to return to Israel following the victory of the Arab armies over Israel. When the Arabs were defeated instead, the exiles formed a Palestinian Diaspora similar to that of the Jews centuries before.

While most Israeli Arabs are Muslims (about 75 percent), there is a small population of Christian Arabs living in Israel as well as a group called the Druze. The Druze religion began in Egypt as an offshoot of Islam. It is a very secretive group; only those born into the Druze community are allowed to practice the religion. The Druze are considered excellent soldiers and often serve in the military.

*The uneasy juxtaposition of Muslims and Jews in Israel makes for very difficult relations at times. An Israeli Jewish woman, right, comforts her friend, an Israeli Arab, who has learned that her son may have aided a Palestinian suicide bomber in his attack against Israelis in 2002.*

A small number of Bedouins, descendants of nomadic Arab tribes who migrated to the region over six centuries ago, live in Israel, mostly in the West Bank area. Known for their desert survival skills, many Bedouins serve in the military guarding the desert borders.

Although Arabs make up less than one-fifth of the Israeli population, they are guaranteed equal rights under Israeli laws. In practice, however, the different Arab religious groups—Christian, Muslim, and Druze—are treated differently. For instance, Christians are allowed to volunteer to serve in the Israeli army, but Druze are drafted.

## Armenians

During the Byzantine era, Palestine (present-day Israel and its occupied territories) was under Christian rule. Religious pilgrims came from many countries to visit holy sites, including the city of Jerusalem. Among these early pilgrims were Armenian monks, who established the Armenian Patriarchate (church headquarters) and St. James Monastery in Jerusalem.

One of the major missions of the monastery was to provide accommodations and hospitality to the thousands of Christian pilgrims who visited the city each year. To accomplish this, the patriarchate purchased land on caravan routes and near holy sites, and built inns to house the pilgrims. By the nineteenth century, the patriarchate had begun to invest in land as a source of income for the monastery. Today, some of the land lies within the walled city of Old Jerusalem and is known as the Armenian Quarter. In New Jerusalem, modern high-rise hotels and shops owned by Armenians line many streets.

During World War I (1914–1918), thousands of Armenian refugees made their way to Jerusalem and other Palestinian cities. By 1925, the Armenian population in Palestine had reached 15,000. The Arab-Israeli War that followed Israel's declaration of independence in 1948 displaced many Armenians. Growing numbers of Armenians emigrated to Lebanon, Syria, the United States, Canada, and Australia. By the end of the twentieth century, fewer than 4,000 Armenians remained in Israel.

## The Baha'is

Another small group, the Baha'is (bah-HAH-ees), follow a religion that incorporates aspects of many world religions. Although it started as an offshoot of Islam, its followers are of many different races and religious backgrounds. The Baha'i world headquarters are located in the city of Haifa.

# Land and Resources

Located along the eastern Mediterranean, Israel is flanked by Lebanon on the north, Syria and Jordan on the east, and Egypt on the southwest.

## Geography

Israel is a small country, stretching only 256 miles (412 kilometers) from its northern border to the southernmost tip. It covers about 8,019 square miles (20,770 square kilometers). At its narrowest point, Israel is only ten miles (16 kilometers) wide. Israel is just slightly smaller than the state of New Jersey.

The West Bank, which lies on the west side of the Jordan River, is twice as wide as Israel and almost a third as long. The Gaza Strip is a 139-square-mile (360-square-kilometer) area of sand and rocks that was not included as part of Israel in the Israel-Egypt treaty of 1949. The Gaza Strip has been the home of Palestinian refugees who fled Palestine when the state of Israel was formed. Both the Gaza Strip and the West Bank, now occupied by Israeli troops, were once Arab territories. Conflicts continue between the Israelis and the Arabs over the control of these areas.

An arrow-shaped desert called the Negev Desert covers the southern portion of Israel. Its southern tip is on the Gulf of Aqaba. The Ramon Crater in the center of the Negev Desert is the world's largest natural crater.

Israel borders four bodies of water: the Sea of Galilee in the north, the Mediterranean Sea on the west, the Dead Sea in the Negev, and the Gulf of Aqaba. The Dead Sea is actually a lake that is so salty no life other than bacteria is able to survive in it. The Dead Sea is seven to eight times as salty as the ocean. It is the lowest sea in the world. Due to evaporation and the diversion of irrigation water from the Jordan River, which feeds into the sea, the Dead Sea is shrinking several feet per year.

The Jordan River flows south through Israel to the Dead Sea from southern Lebanon and Syria. It also feeds into the Sea of Galilee. Although it is only 200 miles (322 kilometers) long, the Jordan River is one of the most famous rivers in the world. According to Christian tradition, Jesus Christ was revealed as the Son of God when he was baptized in the Jordan River at the beginning of his ministry.

The Sea of Galilee, which the Jordan River both feeds and drains, is actually a lake that is about 15 miles (24 kilometers) long. Although the lake is usually calm, cold air from the hills can cause violent storms with high waves. Israel relies on the Sea of Galilee for its water supply. The Sea of Galilee is mentioned in both the Old and New Testaments of the Bible. Much of Jesus Christ's ministry took place near the Sea of Galilee, and Christians believe Jesus performed many miracles there, including calming a storm that threatened to overturn a boat and walking on water.

## Major Cities

### Jerusalem

Jerusalem, Israel's largest city, is the nation's capital. It is a holy place for Jews, Christians, and Muslims. Jerusalem is divided into two parts: Old Jerusalem and New Jerusalem. There is a striking contrast between the two. Old Jerusalem, surrounded by a stone wall that was built in the 1500s, is divided into five quarters, or sections. They are known as the

*The Dome of the Rock mosque in the Temple Mount section of Old Jerusalem can clearly be seen in the center of this aerial photograph.*

Muslim Quarter, the Christian Quarter, the Armenian Quarter, the Jewish Quarter, and the Temple Mount.

The main entrance to the Old City is the Jaffa Gate, in the Muslim Quarter. The *souk,* or Arab market, draws many visitors. The first section of the Via Dolorosa, the path that Jesus walked while carrying the cross, also lies in the Muslim Quarter.

Eleven L-shaped gates were built into the stone wall surrounding Old Jerusalem. The angle of the gates prevented enemy forces from charging through the gates at full speed or using battering rams to gain entrance to the city.

The Via Dolorosa leads to the Christian Quarter and the Church of the Holy Sepulcher. The church was built on the site where Jesus was crucified, buried, and resurrected. Representatives from several Christian denominations—including Greek Orthodox, Roman Catholic, Armenian, and Coptic—supervise different areas of the church. Because there were so many conflicts over which group would keep the key to the church, a Muslim family was appointed as doorkeeper in the twelfth century. Descendants of that family still open and close the doors of the church every day.

The Armenian Quarter is the smallest section of Old Jerusalem. St. James Monastery and Church, built in the twelfth century, are located here. The church is said to be the burial site of Jesus' brother James and St. James, the apostle. There are also many shops featuring Armenian ceramics in the quarter.

### Did You Know?

According to Jewish tradition, when the Messiah returns, he will enter Jerusalem through the Golden Gate that is located in the wall below the Temple Mount. When the Ottomans ruled the city in the sixteenth century, they sealed the gate to prevent its use.

The Jewish Quarter houses the Western Wall, the remains of the outer wall of the Second Temple that was destroyed by the Romans in 70 C.E. Today, this site is one of the holiest places in the world for Jews. Many come to pray at the Wall, often writing prayers on scraps of paper and tucking them into the cracks of the wall. Orthodox Jews, who control access to the Western Wall, have designated a small, separate section of the wall for women's prayers.

The Temple Mount marks the site where the First and Second Temples of the Jewish people once stood. Today, the Dome of the Rock, a Muslim shrine, stands there instead. Under the dome is the historic Moriah Rock, the place where Abraham brought his son to sacrifice him to God. According to Islamic tradition, the rock is also where Mohammad ascended into Paradise.

New Jerusalem stands in sharp contrast to Old Jerusalem. The Knesset, which houses the Israeli government, is found there along with Hebrew University. There are attractive residential streets, busy commercial areas, thriving industrial complexes, and impressive public buildings. The city continues to expand and build modern housing developments to the north.

## Tel Aviv

Tel Aviv on the Mediterranean coast is the second largest city in Israel. Like Jerusalem, it is divided into the old and the new. The old part of the city is known as Jaffa (Yafo). The Tel Aviv-Jaffa area is Israel's second largest metropolitan area, with a population of more than a million. It has a rich business community and abounds with culture.

Tel Aviv is home to many fine shopping areas that offer modern appliances, furniture, and the latest fashions. Local handicrafts, hand-embroidered clothing, and detailed metalwork can also be found there. Sidewalk cafés are scattered among the tall office buildings and contemporary art museums. The Habimah Theater, Zionist Center, and Frederic Mann Auditorium are cultural centers that offer music, dance, and folklore. The United States Embassy stands a block from the Mediterranean Sea.

The city of Jaffa still has a historical atmosphere. There are open markets, art galleries, and restaurants that serve traditional food. The Church of Saint Peter and the Mahmudiye Mosque are two well-known places of interest. The area's busiest marina lies on the eastern shore of the Mediterranean Sea in Jaffa.

## Haifa

Haifa, built on the slopes of Mount Carmel in 1905, is now Israel's third largest city. An industrial boom led to a large increase in the city's population. Haifa is an industrial city with oil refineries, shipyards, and a major seaport, but it is also known for its beautiful Mediterranean coastline.

### Did You Know?

Jerusalem has been settled almost continuously for more than 3,000 years. During that time, it has had more than seventy different names, including Jebus (after the Jebusites who settled the city), Ursalem (after the Canaanite god of peace), Aelia (under Roman and Byzantine rule), and Al Quds al Sharif (under Ottoman rule). It became the capital of Israel in 1950.

## Climate

Largely desert, Israel has hot, dry summers and mild or cool winters. There is little rain during the summer months, but torrential rains pound parts of Israel from October through March. The water must be controlled to keep valuable soil from washing away. This type of rain is typical in the mountains of Galilee, where there can also be snow during the winter. Jerusalem sees snow rarely, perhaps every two or three years.

Temperatures vary from the desert to the coast and the interior valleys. The average temperature in Jerusalem is between 47° F (8° C) and 75° F (24° C). The Negev Desert can be extremely hot. The desert wind can raise the summer temperature as high as 122° F (50° C).

## Natural Resources

Israel is a small country with limited natural resources. Minerals are its best-known resource, but in recent years, natural gas deposits have been discovered off the Mediterranean coast.

*The Dead Sea is an important source of salt and other minerals in Israel. These minerals have been mined for decades, but the mining activity has adversely affected the sea's water levels.*

In the south of Israel, rust-colored sandstone columns formed through centuries of erosion surround the legendary mines of King Solomon. It is thought that the copper from these mines was used to make swords, spears, and shields during the time of King Solomon. More important to Israel than copper are the minerals found in the Dead Sea. Columns of rock salt scattered on the shore produce a wealth of minerals. For decades, Israel has harvested minerals from the Dead Sea to establish a health and skin care industry that is known worldwide. The most well-known of these minerals are magnesium, sodium, calcium, potassium, potash, and bromides. However, there is so much mining in the Dead Sea that the water levels are being affected.

Because of the rise in industry and automobiles, Israel is now facing a larger issue: pollution. Factories and vehicles are the cause of pollution in the groundwater and air. The Jordan River and the Sea of Galilee are the major sources of fresh water for the Israeli people. Low rainfall over the last five years has left Israel's reservoirs badly depleted. In 2002, Israel's water control authority doubled the price of fresh water for private citizens. The Ministry of Environment is responsible for monitoring the quality of the air, water, and land of Israel.

## Plants and Animals

Although Israel is a small country, its varied climate zones support diverse plant and animal life. More than 2,800 species of plants are found in Israel. Some plants became so popular in flower arrangements that they were becoming extinct. The Nature Reserve Authority waged a major campaign to stop people from picking or buying endangered wildflowers.

Centuries of warfare and neglect ravaged the forests that used to cover mountain slopes, but efforts to reforest the land are slowly succeeding. Today, there are over 200 million trees in Israel. Calliprinos oaks cover the upper Galilee and Mount Carmel. Forests of pine, carob, and eucalyptus cover the countryside. In the south there are acacia trees and sabra cactus. In the Negev highlands, date palms grow wherever there is sufficient groundwater.

As in other Western countries, a growing population and increasing industrial development are destroying Israel's natural habitats. Israel has set aside a fifth of its land area as nature reserves.

There are 116 different species of land animals in Israel. Unfortunately, the number of animals within each species is decreasing.

The largest land animals are mountain gazelles, wild boars, foxes, jungle cats, leopards, hyenas, wolves, and Nubian ibex.

In 1969, the Israeli Nature Reserve Authority began a program to breed animals that were known to have lived in Israel during Biblical times and reintroduce them into the wild. A breeding facility known as Hai-Bar was established in Haifa. This program has been successful in reintroducing the fallow deer and white oryx.

## History

### Ancient Days

Around 2000 B.C.E, an ancient people called Canaanites settled in the land now known as Israel. They were a very accomplished culture that developed cities and a government and introduced the use of bronze. The Canaanites worshiped several gods and goddesses. The Canaanite language was the precursor to the Hebrew language used in the Old Testament.

The people of Israel, who have inhabited the land for 3,300 years, trace their roots to a shepherd named Abraham. According to the Bible, God told Abraham to leave the area now known as Iraq and go live in Canaan. There Abraham began a family that included his son Isaac and grandson Jacob. These three are called the *patriarchs* (founding fathers) of the Hebrew people because they helped establish the belief in one God who created the universe.

Jacob had many children whose descendants became known as the Twelve Tribes of Israel, or Israelites. Joseph, one of Jacob's sons, became prime minister to the pharaoh of Egypt. After a terrible famine struck Canaan, Joseph invited the Israelites to come to Egypt, where they lived for many years until a new pharaoh enslaved them. Afraid that the large Hebrew community would overthrow him, the new pharaoh ruled that all Hebrew baby boys should be killed. One mother put her baby in a basket and hid him in the rushes of the Nile River. That baby grew up to be one of the most important people in Israel's history. His name was Moses.

According to the Bible, Moses was commanded by God to lead the Hebrew slaves back to their homeland in Canaan (Israel). This journey is known as the *Exodus*, which most scholars believe to have occurred around 1200 B.C.E.

# IMPORTANT EVENTS IN ISRAEL'S HISTORY

**2000 B.C.E.** Canaanites settle in present-day Israel.

**1300 B.C.E.** Abraham, the founder of Judaism, settles in Canaan.

**1200 B.C.E.** Moses leads the Israelite slaves out of Egypt.

**1020 B.C.E.** Saul becomes the first king of the Israelites.

**1010–970 B.C.E.** Under King David, Israel becomes one of the most powerful countries in western Asia.

**960 B.C.E.** King Solomon builds the First Temple of the Jewish people in Jerusalem.

**928 B.C.E.** Solomon dies and the kingdom is split into two new kingdoms: Israel and Judah (Judea).

**596 B.C.E.** The Babylonians destroy Jerusalem and send the Jews into exile.

**586 B.C.E.** Persia gains control over Babylonian Empire and frees the Jews from slavery. Those who return to Judea rebuild Jerusalem and construct the Second Temple.

**333 B.C.E.** Alexander the Great establishes Greek control over present-day Israel.

**165 B.C.E.** The Jews revolt against Greek rule after altars to Greek gods are placed in the Second Temple.

**ca. 20 C.E.** Jesus Christ begins preaching in Judea.

**63** The Roman army invades Judea.

**70** The Romans conquer the region and rename it Palestine; they destroy the Second Temple and exile most Jews.

**638** The Islamic Empire expands to include Palestine.

**691** Muslims build the Dome of the Rock mosque on the site of the destroyed Jewish temples.

**1096** The Christian Crusades begin.

**1517** The Ottoman Empire begins its 400-year rule over Palestine.

**1800s** European Jews establish the Zionist movement.

**1917** The Balfour Declaration promises British support for independent Arab and Jewish states.

**1922** The League of Nations grants Britain the right to rule Palestine following World War I (1914–1918). Growing numbers of Jewish settlers from Europe and the Middle East immigrate to Palestine.

**1939** Adolf Hitler and the Nazis begin a campaign of genocide against Jews in Europe. This became known as the Holocaust.

**1947** The United Nations (UN) recommends that Palestine be divided into separate Arab and Jewish states.

**1948** Palestine gains its independence from Britain. Israel proclaims its independence the same day. Egypt, Syria, Jordan, Lebanon, and Iraq invade Israel in protest, launching the Arab-Israeli War. Israel wins the war.

**1949** The UN recognizes Israel as an independent nation.

**1956** Israel invades Egypt to gain control of the Sinai Peninsula and the Suez Canal, but relinquishes control to Egypt after international condemnation of its actions.

**1964** Arab Palestinians form the Palestine Liberation Organization (PLO).

**1967** Israel gains control of the Sinai Peninsula, the West Bank, East Jerusalem, and the Golan Heights following the Six-Day War.

**1973** Egypt and Syria attack Israeli forces in the Sinai Peninsula and Golan Heights, starting the Yom Kippur War.

**1979** Egyptian and Israeli leaders sign a peace agreement known as the Camp David Accords.

**1996** Israel announces plans to expand its settlements in Palestinian areas of the West Bank and Jerusalem.

**2002** Israel places PLO leader Yasir Arafat under house arrest.

**2003** U.S. president George W. Bush proposes a "road map" for peace in the region.

## Kingdom of Israel

Around 1020 B.C.E., the Israelites chose Saul as their first king. He was followed by King David. During David's reign, Israel gained many new territories and became one of the most powerful countries in western Asia. David is believed to have written many of the psalms of the Old Testament.

King David died around 965 B.C.E, and his son Solomon became king. In about 960 B.C.E. Solomon built the First Temple of the Jewish people in Jerusalem. This became the center of religious activity in the land. Solomon was known as a wise ruler who established peace along Israel's borderlands. He encouraged trade with other countries and divided Israel into twelve districts, each with its own governor.

After Solomon's death, the tribes of Israel split into two kingdoms. The northern kingdom was still called Israel, while the southern

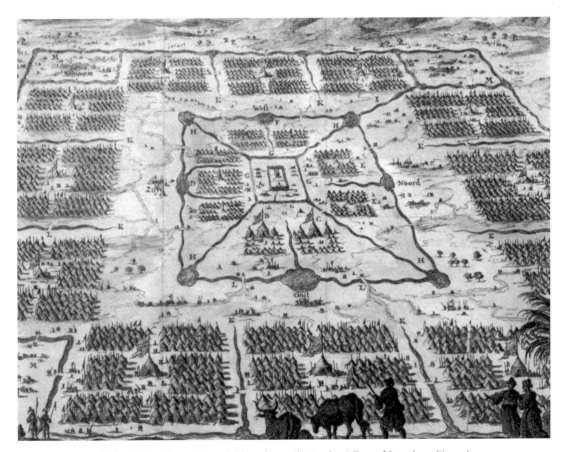

*This eighteenth-century etching shows the twelve tribes of Israel positioned around the First Temple at the center, in what would be Jerusalem.*

kingdom became known as Judea (Judah). In 596 B.C.E., the Babylonian king Nebuchadrezzar invaded Jerusalem and destroyed most of the city, including the Jews' First Temple. Many of the Jews were exiled to Babylonia (now Iraq), where they lived as prisoners for two hundred years.

## Persian and Greek Rule

After 586 B.C.E., Israel was ruled by a series of foreign powers. Persia was the first civilization to rule Israel after the collapse of the Babylonian Empire. King Cyrus of Persia freed the Jews from their slavery and allowed them to return to Judea. There they rebuilt Jerusalem and built a new temple, called the Second Temple. Some Jews chose to stay in Persia or other places rather than return to Israel, and their scattered communities became known as the Diaspora.

In 333 B.C.E., the period of Greek rule began when Alexander the Great invaded the land. The Greeks established colonies around the coastal plain, but generally let the Jews run their own state. However, the Greek ruler Antiochus IV wanted all people in the kingdom to adopt Greek culture and practices. Some Jews did, but some resisted. In anger, Antiochus built an altar to a Greek god in the Second Temple. This infuriated the Jews, who rose up in revolt around 165 B.C.E. They eventually defeated the king's armies and rededicated the Second Temple as a holy place.

## Roman Rule

The long period of Roman rule began when the Roman army invaded Judea in 63 C.E. The Jews revolted three years later and kept the Romans at bay until 70, when the Roman general Titus entered Jerusalem, destroyed the Second Temple, and took many Jews to Rome as

### *The Western Wall*

The Western Wall in Jerusalem, also known as the Wailing Wall, is all that remains of the Second Temple. Today, many Jews consider it a holy place that symbolizes their history. They say prayers at the wall before the Sabbath and on feast days.

## MASADA

Some Jews refused to surrender to the Romans even after Jerusalem fell. Nearly 1,000 men, women, and children fled to a mountain fortress called Masada, where they defended themselves for three years.

When the Roman army was about to enter the fortress in 73 C.E., tradition says that all the Jews inside committed suicide rather than give the Romans the satisfaction of their surrender.

prisoners. Other Jews were expelled from the land and moved south to settle in the country now called Yemen. The Roman emperor Hadrian refused to let any Jews within sight of the city of Jerusalem. He also renamed the country Palestine in order to further erase the Jews' connection to their homeland of Israel.

The Jewish community did not disappear entirely from Israel. Many of the Jewish political leaders, called the Sanhedrin, moved to Galilee in the northern part of Palestine. Some of the most important pieces of Jewish law, such as the Mishnah, Midrash, and the Palestinian Torah, were completed at this time. In addition, scholars believe Jesus Christ conducted his ministry in the Galilee area around 20 C.E. Some Jews followed his teachings and later became known as Christians. They believed Jesus was the Messiah promised by God who would come to save Israel and all humankind from sin and death. King Herod, the Roman ruler of Israel, saw Jesus as a political threat to the Roman government and ordered him to be crucified.

### Arab Rule

By the mid-600s, Arab Muslims had founded an empire that included parts of Asia, northern Africa, and Spain. The Muslims allowed Jews and Christians to practice their own religions, but both had to pay a special tax. In 691, the Arab Muslim *caliph* (ruler) built the Dome of the Rock mosque on the site of the destroyed First and Second Temples. This site remained sacred to the Jews, but Muslims also considered it as the holy place where their prophet Mohammad rose to heaven. Today, Jews and Muslims remain in conflict over this hill.

### The Crusades

Jewish communities had spread throughout the Muslim Middle East, but the largest community flourished in Spain. From the tenth to the twelfth centuries, known as the Golden Age in Jewish history, Jews in Spain prospered in medicine, the arts, business, and government. However, in 1096, Jews in the Holy Land and in Europe were persecuted in Christian military campaigns known as the *Crusades*.

The Crusades began when Pope Urban II of Rome directed his armies to recapture the Holy Land, which was then ruled by Muslims. As non-Christians, Jews were also targeted. Entire Jewish communities were massacred by the Crusaders. Beginning in the 1200s, Jews were expelled from many countries in Europe. Many settled in Poland, where the Jewish community began to thrive once more.

## The Ottoman Period

From 1517 to 1917, Israel was ruled by the Turkish Ottoman Empire. During this time the first *kibbutz,* or communal farm settlement, was founded, as well as the first all-Jewish city, Tel Aviv. During the 1800s, many Jews believed that the establishment of a Jewish national homeland was the only way to escape persecution and the rising tide of *anti-Semitism,* or hatred directed toward them as non-Christians. A movement known as Zionism was established to create a Jewish independent national state.

In 1917, the British foreign minister, Lord Balfour, pledged support for the establishment of a Jewish homeland in Palestine, now the present states of Israel and Jordan. However, the Balfour Declaration also promised the Arabs their own state, which they believed would

*In 1917, British foreign minister Lord Balfour pledged support for both a Jewish and an Arab state in the same general area of Palestine. Here children displaying Zionist banners greet him at the opening of Jewish University in Palestine in 1925.*

include Palestine. This declaration was the beginning of a bitter Arab-Israeli conflict over the land that still continues today.

In 1922, the League of Nations granted Britain the temporary right to rule Palestine. Under British rule, new cities were created, swamps were drained and forests planted, and wave after wave of new Jewish settlers arrived from Poland, Germany, and other parts of the Middle East. The Arabs resented the growing Jewish population, and anti-Jewish riots led by Arab militants broke out from 1936 through 1939.

## Holocaust

In the early 1930s, a man named Adolf Hitler rose to power in Germany. At a young age, Hitler had come to believe that some people, especially Jews, were inferior to the Aryan race. (Hitler used the label of *Aryan Race* to mean non-Jewish Caucasians with blond hair and blue eyes.) This view was strengthened after Germany's defeat in World War I (1914–1918), which Hitler blamed on the Jews. Soon after the war ended, Hitler was named leader of the German Worker's Party, a political party that later became known as the Nazis. He used this position to build support for his plan to rebuild Germany and his extreme racist policies.

In 1932, Hitler was named chancellor (chief of state) of Germany. He began ruling as a dictator, placing Nazi party members in positions of power in the government. Laws stripping German Jews of their citizenship, property, and civil rights were soon implemented. By 1938, Hitler had ordered thousands of Jews to be sent to concentration camps.

In the days leading up to World War II (1939–1945), Hitler ordered the invasion of Austria and made plans for war against France and Britain. It was his invasion of Poland in 1939, however, which launched World War II. As the Nazis conquered large parts of Europe, they began to fulfill Hitler's plans for genocide (systematic destruction) of the Jewish people. Between 1933 and 1945, six million Jews were shot by firing squad or killed in concentration camps. One of the many horrors of the concentration camps was the furnaces in which the bodies of Jews killed in gas chambers were burned. This genocidal campaign, in which nearly two out of every three Jews living in Europe were murdered, has become known as the *Holocaust,* which means "burned sacrifice."

## Independence and Statehood

The devastation the Jews experienced during the Holocaust strengthened their determination to establish their own homeland in Palestine. Thousands of Jewish settlers arrived in Palestine during and immediately after World War II. The Arabs continued to oppose Jewish settlement, which led to many violent conflicts between the two groups.

In 1947, the United Nations (UN) recommended that Palestine be divided into Arab and Jewish states. The Jews agreed to this plan; the Arabs did not. Fighting continued unabated. Britain's temporary rule of Palestine ended on May 14, 1948. That same day, Israel proclaimed its independence and became a state. The next day, armies from the Arab countries of Egypt, Syria, Jordan, Lebanon, and Iraq invaded Israel.

*Statehood did not come to Israel without cost. As soon as Israel announced its independence, it was attacked by a coalition of Arab nations. In this picture, Arab soldiers approach a large opening blasted into the wall of a synagogue in Old Jerusalem.*

### 1948 Arab-Israeli War

Israel won the first Arab-Israeli war of 1948. In addition to defeating the Arab armies, Israel also gained control of about half the land intended for the new Arab state as outlined in the 1947 UN resolution. Egypt was left in control of the Gaza Strip, located between Israel and the Mediterranean Sea, and Jordan controlled the West Bank, an area between Israel and the Jordan River. The city of Jerusalem was divided into Arab and Israeli sections, with Israel controlling the western half of the city and Jordan controlling the eastern half. In 1949, Israel signed a temporary peace agreement with the invading Arab countries, but a permanent peace treaty was never signed because the Arab nations did not recognize Israel as a legitimate state. However, Israel was recognized as a new state by the United Nations in 1949 and admitted as the UN's fifty-ninth member.

### Sinai Invasion

Arab-Israeli clashes continued throughout the 1950s and 1960s. The first of three wars, called the Sinai Invasion, began in 1956. Israel invaded Egypt in order to gain control of the Sinai Peninsula and the Suez Canal. (The Suez Canal is a very important shipping lane that connects the Mediterranean and Red seas, facilitating trade between Europe and Asia.) Many countries in the international community, disapproving of Israel's actions, protested the invasion. As a result, Israel returned control of the Sinai area and the Suez Canal to Egypt.

## THE PALESTINE LIBERATION ORGANIZATION

The Palestine Liberation Organization (PLO) was formed in 1964 as a result of the Six-Day War. The PLO represents the Arab Palestinian views in the continuing conflicts over an independent Palestinian state. Beginning in the 1960s and continuing to the present, PLO military forces have carried out terrorist attacks against Israeli military and civilian targets. Since 1969, Yasir Arafat has been the leader of the PLO.

*PLO leader Yasir Arafat (right), pictured in February 2000.*

## Six-Day War

After the Sinai Invasion, the United Nations sent peacekeeping troops into the area. In 1967, Egyptian President Gamal Abdel Nasser demanded the withdrawal of those troops. When the UN troops left, Nasser sent his Egyptian troops back into the Sinai region to close shipping lanes to the Israelis. Israel responded by launching a surprise air attack that destroyed almost all of the Arab air forces within hours. By the end of the war, which lasted only six days, Israel controlled even more Arab land, including the Sinai Peninsula, the West Bank, the eastern section of Jerusalem, and the Golan Heights, an area bordering Israel. Israel announced that it would return those territories if the Arab nations would recognize the state of Israel. They did not, and the conflicts continued.

## Yom Kippur War and Camp David Accords

In 1973, Egypt and Syria launched massive attacks against the Israelis in the Sinai Peninsula and the Golan Heights. This time, it was the Israelis who were caught unprepared because the attacks began on Yom Kippur, the holiest day in the Jewish religion. The Egyptian army reclaimed much of the Jewish-held territory early in the war. However, with the help of military aid from the United States, the Israeli forces eventually defeated the Egyptians and reclaimed nearly all the territories they had won during the Six-Day War.

In 1978, the leaders of Egypt, Israel, and the United States met to work out a peace agreement to end the Arab-Israeli conflicts. Under the leadership of U.S. president Jimmy Carter, Egyptian president Anwar el-Sadat and Israeli prime minister Menachem Begin signed the Camp David Accords in 1979. These agreements included Egypt's recognition of Israel's right to exist as a state, Israel's return of Jewish-occupied parts of the Sinai to Egypt, and a joint agreement for national independence for the Palestinians. Many Arab nations opposed the treaty. The PLO continued to attack Israel, and in 1981, Sadat was assassinated by an Egyptian religious group that opposed the Camp David Accords.

## Israel Today

Despite peace agreements, Jews and Arabs continue to fight over each group's right to the area known as Palestine. In 1996, newly elected Israeli president Benjamin Netanyahu announced plans for expanding Israeli communities in the Palestinian-held areas of the West Bank and eastern sections of Jerusalem. The Palestinians protested violently, which led to another Arab-Israeli peace agreement, called the Wye River Memorandum. This 1998 agreement stated that Israel would return areas of the West Bank to the Palestinians, and the PLO would stop calling for the destruction of Israel. Only one Israeli withdrawal from the West Bank took place, however, before Palestinian attacks stopped the peace process.

A new prime minister, Ehud Barak, took office in 1999. He met with U.S. president Bill Clinton later that year and in 2000, hoping to reach a peace agreement with the Palestinians. Negotiations stalled, however, when neither side could agree on a process for transferring occupied territory in the West Bank back to Palestinian control. When the 2000 talks ended in failure, violent conflicts between Israel and Palestinians broke out once more.

*An Israeli army colonel unfolds a map of an area in the Gaza Strip as he speaks to Palestinian officials in June 2003. Israel was to begin withdrawing its forces from the area as part of the implementation of the "road map" to peace.*

Jews and Arabs continue to hold periodic peace talks, but no agreement for settling the Palestinian issue has held. Palestinian armies and suicide bombers continue to attack Israelis, and Israeli military forces continue to bomb Palestinians and occupy Palestinian territory. In 2002, Israel launched Operation Defensive Shield in response to Palestinian attacks. Israeli prime minister Ariel Sharon called PLO leader Yasir Arafat an "enemy of the people" and put him under house arrest.

In 2003, U.S. president George W. Bush presented his "road map" to peace, a proposal for achieving an independent Palestinian state that can exist peacefully with Israel. Both Ariel Sharon and Palestinian prime minister Mahmoud Abbas agreed to the general terms of the plan, which involves an end to Palestinian violence and a withdrawal of Israeli troops and illegal settlers from the West Bank, but both leaders expect the other to act first. Israel charges that the Palestinian leader is doing little to crack down on terrorist groups, while Palestinians point to newly established Jewish settlements in the West Bank as proof that Israel is not fulfilling its part of the agreement.

Both leaders have had difficulty achieving these goals. Abbas has not cracked down on militant Palestinian groups, fearing that would result in a civil war. Sharon has ordered Jewish settlers to dismantle illegal settlements in the West Bank, but new ones are established almost as quickly to replace those that are removed.

## Economy

Israel's economy is as diverse as its culture. It includes a wide range of products and services. Tourism is a major source of income. Every year about 2 million visitors travel to Israel. In recent years, however, because of the increasing conflict between the Israelis and the Palestinians, Israel's tourist trade has dramatically declined.

Agriculture is also very important to the Israeli economy. Throughout the years, Israelis have used their land wisely. They irrigated dry land and drained swamps for farming. They built the National Water Carrier, a complex system that brings water from the Sea of Galilee to the desert. The Israelis import foods that would need a lot of water to grow and cultivate crops that need less water.

Israel is nearly self-sufficient in its food production. Poultry, dairy, beef, vegetables, fruits, and cotton are the main crops. Israel exports citrus fruits around the world. Roses, carnations, and other flowers are grown year-round in greenhouses and sold in Europe.

Although there are not many fish along the coast of Israel, fishing is a major industry. Fishing boats that travel to the Ethiopian coast and fish farming in the north of the country and in inland ponds supply fish for the Israeli people and also for export. Fishing ranks with agriculture as a major source of income.

Food products are not all that is exported from Israel. Minerals found in the Dead Sea are exported around the world. These include sodium, calcium, potassium, and magnesium. The desert provides Israel with phosphates and granite. Materials to make glass, ceramics, tile, and fine porcelain are also taken from the desert.

## Business and Industry

The General Federation of Labor, or Histadrut, is a special labor union in Israel. It owns many Israeli businesses. Eighty percent of Israeli adults belong to this union, and so do all of the Israeli cabinet members. This organization has been instrumental in guiding Israel's progress in manufacturing.

The aircraft industry is growing rapidly. Vulcan Steel Foundries produces steel for aircraft. The manufacturing of military and transport equipment has been very successful.

Textiles are one of the largest industries in Israel. Thousands of Israelis work in the mills producing some of the finest fabrics in the world. Swimwear and leather clothing are designed and made in villages. Each garment is a unique work of art.

The Israeli diamond market is one of the largest in the world. Although diamonds are not mined in Israel, cutting, polishing, and trading diamonds is an important occupation. About half of the diamonds sold today are cut in Israel.

Israel is continuously improving its methods of production. Since there is little oil and coal in Israel, solar energy has become an important source of power for homes and factories. An influx of Russian Jews between 1989 and 1999 provided many qualified scientists and professional experts who are energizing Israel's economy. However, the outbreak of Palestinian unrest in 2000 has caused a slowdown in Israel's tourism and high-tech economy.

# Religion and Beliefs

### Judaism

Jews have been persecuted throughout history. They were forced to move from their homes, live in ghettos, convert to other religions, or live as slaves. Many were killed. The most tragic instance of this anti-Semitism in modern times was the Holocaust, the systematic murder of six million European Jews by Nazi Germany between 1933 and 1945.

Today there are about 14 million Jews worldwide. Most live in the United States and Israel.

### *Basic Beliefs*

Jews believe that there is one God, all-knowing and all-powerful, but also just and merciful. The instruction and commandments that God gave to

*Jewish men, one draped in an Israeli flag, pray at the Western Wall in Old Jerusalem during the Passover holiday. The Western Wall is one of the holiest sites in all of Judaism. It is all that remains of the Second Temple, which was destroyed by the Romans in 70 C.E.*

Moses and the Israelites at Mount Sinai are known collectively as the Torah. Jews believe that when they follow the Torah and keep God's laws, the Jewish people and the nation of Israel will be blessed by God. Prayer, the study of the Torah, and acts of charity are three components of a holy life according to Jewish tradition. (For more information on Judaism, see pages viii–ix in the introduction to this volume.)

### Judaism in Israel

Although there are many forms of Judaism worldwide, only the Orthodox movement is officially recognized in Israel. Orthodox Jews believe that the entire Torah, including the oral tradition that interprets the written Torah (the first five books of the Bible's Old Testament), is a direct and unerring record of God's word. They believe that the Torah is true and that it exists today untouched by human interpretations over the centuries. Orthodoxy also dismisses the assertion by more liberal movements that Jewish law should adapt to fit modern culture. Traditional Orthodox groups, such as the Hasidim (hah-SID-im), live apart from modern society and maintain traditional dress and language. Modern Orthodox Jews live within modern society, yet observe Jewish law. In Israel, Orthodox Jewish law applies in matters such as marriage, divorce, and religious conversion.

Jews in Israel identify themselves by their acceptance of Orthodoxy. Those who follow Orthodox tradition call themselves *dati,* or religiously observant. They follow Jewish law faithfully. A subset of this group is the *haredi,* or ultra-Orthodox. About 15 to 20 percent of Israeli Jews consider themselves *dati.* Those who don't strictly follow Jewish law are called *lo dati.* This group includes Jews who consider themselves traditionalists— people who believe in the principles of Judaism although they do not strictly observe all the Jewish laws—as well as *secular* (non-religious) Jews. Even those Israeli Jews who consider themselves secular often observe some Jewish traditions, such as limiting activities on the Sabbath and avoiding pork and other nonkosher foods.

### Islam

Muslims follow the teachings of the Prophet Mohammad, who established Islam in the seventh century. They believe in one God— Allah—who revealed the Qur'an to Mohammad, the last in a series of prophets that includes Abraham and Jesus. Devout Muslims observe the five pillars of Islam: professing that "there is no God but God and

Mohammad is his messenger," praying five times daily, fasting during the holy month of Ramadan, giving alms (charity) to the poor, and making a pilgrimage to Mecca, the birthplace of Mohammad. Most Israeli and Palestinian Muslims follow the Sunni traditions. (To learn more about Islam, see pages ix–xii in the introduction to this volume.)

## Christianity

Christianity developed as an offshoot of Judaism. Followers of Jesus Christ believe him to be the son of God and the Messiah that was promised to the Jewish people. About 10 percent of the Israeli population is Christian, mostly of Arab descent. There are several Christian denominations in Israel; the largest are the Eastern Orthodox Church and the Eastern Catholic Church. (To learn more about Christianity, please see pages 56–60 in Volume 1 of this series.)

## Druze

The Druze comprise less than 2 percent of the non-Jewish ethnic groups in Israel. The Druze religion, which began in Egypt in 1017 as an offshoot of Shi'a Islam, teaches that God has appeared on earth in

*Lighting the candles for the Jewish Sabbath table.*

human form throughout history, including incarnations as Jesus Christ and al-Hakim (the Islamic leader who established the Druze religion). Little else is known, since the Druze do not allow converts or marriage outside of their religious community.

## Everyday Life

More than 70 percent of Israelis live in cities and towns. Most of them live in cities in the northern half of Israel, crowded into apartment buildings. Some have their own homes in cities like Jerusalem, Tel Aviv, and Haifa. Others live in smaller cities like Dan or Eilat.

A minority of people in Israel participate in cooperative living arrangements. The kibbutz system is unique to Israel. Everyone living in a certain village shares everything that is owned, produced, or earned equally. Originally, all kibbutzim (the plural of kibbutz) were communal farms. Today, the people who live on a kibbutz might blow glass or make toys, furniture, shoes, electronic equipment, or work in other kibbutz-owned businesses. They eat their meals together in a large dining hall. Kibbutz members are not paid money for their work, but are given food, clothing, medical services, education, and housing. Kibbutz children attend schools run by their kibbutz. Although the kibbutz system is successful, less than 4 percent of the people of Israel live in kibbutzim.

A moshav is another type of settlement, in which families farm their own land and own their own homes. These families have more independence than the members of a kibbutz, although they may market their goods and buy products as a group.

Resistance to Israel's compulsory military service among Israeli youth is growing. In 2002, 300 teens signed a letter to Prime Minister Ariel Sharon, stating that they would not serve in the army because its actions oppressed the Palestinian people. Those who refuse to serve are generally court-martialed and sentenced to prison.

### Dress

Some Israeli Jews wear clothing that displays their religious beliefs. Orthodox and Conservative Jewish men wear yarmulkes (YAH-muh-kuhs), or small caps, during prayer. Some men wear yarmulkes at all times, even though religious law does not require it. Orthodox men wear a black coat, long sideburns, and a black, brimmed hat. Conservative and Orthodox women always keep their heads covered.

## Education

The Jewish culture has always had a firm belief in
education. In Israel elementary education is offered free
to children. There are state, independent, and state
religious schools. About 70 percent of Israeli children
attend nonreligious schools. There are separate schools
for Jewish children and Muslim children. They are
required to go to school until they are sixteen. Most
children go on to secondary school unless they are
needed to help their families financially. Some students
go on to college or go into a trade or industry.

Israeli boys are required to serve three years in the army once they
finish high school, while unmarried girls must serve two years. Arabs are
not required to serve in the army, although most Druze do. Some
extremely religious Jews study in a religious school instead of serving in
the army.

There are seven universities and technical institutes in Israel.
Hebrew University is the most revered. It offers two campuses, one in
West Jerusalem and the other on Mount Scopus. The Hadassah
Medical Center was built in 1961 when Jordan denied Jews the use of
the hospital on Mount Scopus. It is one of the most modern facilities in
the Middle East. It offers studies in medicine, nursing, dentistry, and
pharmacology. It also houses a cancer research center.

## Recreation and Leisure

Israelis play sports of all kinds: they bowl, swim, climb mountains, ride
horses, fish. White-water rafting on the Jordan River and rock climbing
in the Negev Desert are also popular. The major team sports are soccer
and basketball. Israel has a national soccer team that is one of the best
in the Middle East.

## Food

In Israel, as in many other Middle Eastern countries, the food has
origins in many different areas of the world. Because the majority of
Israel's population is Jewish, they must follow the Jewish laws
concerning food, called *kashrut*. According to these laws, pork, rabbit,
and shellfish are forbidden. Dishes containing dairy products must be

cooked and eaten at a different meal from those containing meat. Even the dishes used to cook and serve dairy and meats must be kept separate. Foods that are neither meat nor dairy, such as vegetables, fruits, eggs, and fish, are known as *pareve* foods. They can be eaten with either group.

Because no cooking is allowed on the Sabbath, traditional foods that can be prepared the day before and simmered all night are usually served. *Cholent,* a hearty stew, and *kugel,* a pudding made of vegetables and noodles, are popular for this reason.

Breakfast is typically a hearty meal. It is not unusual to be served salads, cheeses, olives, bread, juice, and coffee. This tradition developed on the kibbutz, whose members had to get up very early and work many hours before breakfast was served. The main meal is served at noon when children come home from school. At night, a light meal, such as salads, eggs, and cheese is generally served. Popular foods in Israel include *falafel*—fried balls of mashed chickpeas and spices, and *blintzes*—thin pancakes with fillings of cheese, meat, or fruit.

## OFF MEMOOLEH BETAPOOZIM

### (CHICKEN STUFFED WITH ORANGES)

1 2-1/2- to 3-pound chicken
1 lemon
2 teaspoons salt
1 teaspoon garlic powder
2 teaspoons paprika
1 teaspoon chili powder
1 teaspoon ground coriander
2 oranges
1 cup water
2 onions, peeled and halved

Preheat oven to 425 degrees.

Rinse the chicken inside and out under cold running water, then pat dry with paper towels. Place the chicken in a roasting pan. Cut the lemon in half, and rub one half over the surface of the chicken.

Mix the spices together in a small bowl, then sprinkle the mixture over the chicken.

Squeeze the juice from the remaining lemon half and from one of the oranges into the roasting pan and add water. Place the remaining orange, whole and unpeeled, into the cavity of the chicken. Add the onions to the pan.

Cook the chicken for 15 minutes, then baste with the pan juices and lower heat to 350 degrees. Cook for 1 hour, basting after 30 minutes.

Remove the orange from the cavity of the chicken. Cut the orange and onions into small pieces and serve with the chicken. This dish is delicious with rice or pasta.

Serves 4 to 6.

Source: Adapted from *Cooking the Israeli Way* by Josephine Bacon.

As in many other countries, traditional foods are prepared for holidays. Passover is a Jewish holiday that honors the flight of the Jews from slavery in Egypt thousands of years ago. At the *seder,* or celebratory meal, roast lamb represents the sacrifice of the lamb, bitter herbs the bitterness of slavery. *Charoset,* a dish made of apples, nuts, sugar, and spices, symbolizes the mortar used by the Hebrew slaves to make bricks in Egypt. Parsley and eggs represent greenery and the renewal of life in springtime, while saltwater represents the tears of Israeli slaves. Matzo replicates the flat, unleavened bread that the Jews baked without letting it rise, because there was no time to wait as they fled Egypt. There is a particular order in which each guest tastes food from the seder plate as the story of the Exodus is told.

## Holidays and Festivals

Most of the public holidays celebrated in Israel are Jewish religious holidays. They include Rosh Hashanah, Yom Kippur, Sukkoth, Hanukkah, and Pesach (Passover).

### Rosh Hashanah

Rosh Hashanah (rohsh ha-SHAH-nah) is celebrated on the first and second day of the year according to the Jewish calendar. It occurs in September or October of the Gregorian calendar (the "modern" calendar used in America and most of the world). On Rosh Hashanah, Jews look back at the past year's mistakes and plan how they can improve during the coming year. Rosh Hashanah and Yom Kippur are the two most important holidays in the Jewish year.

### Yom Kippur

Yom Kippur (YOHM kih-POOR), or the Day of Atonement, is the holiest and most personal holiday in the Jewish tradition. In the days between Rosh Hashanah and Yom Kippur, Jews make amends to those whom they have wronged and forgive those who have caused them pain. Then, on Yom Kippur, individuals attend services in the synagogue and seek forgiveness from God for their sins. A day-long fast is observed.

### Sukkoth (Feast of the Booths)

Sukkoth (SOO-kuhs) begins five days after Yom Kippur. It is a holiday of thanksgiving and rejoicing. The holiday gets its name from the temporary booths or shelters *(sukkahs)* that Moses and the people of Israel lived in while wandering in the desert for forty years. As part of the eight-day festival, each family builds a sukkah and uses it as much as possible. Meals are eaten there and family members may sleep in it.

### Hanukkah

The Festival of Lights, or Hanukkah (HAH-nah-kah), celebrates the rededication of the Temple in Jerusalem in 165 B.C. Under the Syrian ruler Antiochus IV, the practice of Judaism was prohibited throughout Palestine (present-day Israel) and the Temple was used for pagan rituals. The Maccabees, a group of Jewish rebels, fought against the forces of Antiochus and finally pushed them out of Jerusalem. After cleaning the Temple, the Jews found only a small amount of oil to use in the holy lamps that illuminated the Torah. Miraculously, the flames stayed lit for eight days, until more oil could be obtained.

At Hanukkah, Jews light the candles on the menorah (a candelabrum) each night for eight nights to celebrate the miracle of the oil lasting for eight nights.

### Pesach (Passover)

Pesach (PAY-sakh), or Passover, is the most widely celebrated holiday in the Jewish calendar. It honors the flight, or Exodus, of the Israelites from Egypt following years of slavery. Because the Israelites did not have time to let their bread rise when they fled Egypt, no leavening (yeast or other substance that makes bread rise) is allowed to be present in Jewish homes during the eight days of Pesach. The holiday begins with a seder (SAY-dur), a festive meal with special prayers and symbolic foods that help Jews remember the Exodus.

## The Arts

Israel is rich in art and culture. It has many museums and theaters. Many Israeli writers, painters, and sculptors have become well known throughout the world. Quite often, Jewish themes are evident in the works of Israeli artists. In addition to the visual arts, Jewish heritage is celebrated through folktales, folk dances, and traditional songs.

## Visual Arts

Works of art can be found in many places in Israel. From the museums to the street bazaars, the Israeli people display their fine embroidery, paintings, and sculptures. In Mount Zion, shops and studios surround a continuous street fair. Jaffa is home to an art colony and many studios along the winding streets.

The Museum of Contemporary Art in Tel Aviv and the Israel Museum in Jerusalem have some of the most extensive art collections in the world. The Haifa Museum of Ancient Art offers a display of ancient art that tells of the archaeological discoveries made in Israel. The Bet Gavriel in Tiberius is a theater complex that often hosts high-level Israeli-Palestinian peace talks.

A unique set of fine stained-glass windows is found in the synagogue at the Hadassah Medical Center. These twelve windows depict the twelve sons of Jacob and the tribes they founded. Marc Chagall, a Jewish artist who was born in a small town in Russia, was seventy-two when he was commissioned to create them.

## Performing Arts

Music is an important part of Israel's heritage. The Israel Philharmonic Orchestra is respected throughout the world for its sweeping sounds and impressive presentations. The orchestra plays in the Mann Auditorium in Tel Aviv, the largest performance hall in the country.

Each year the Israeli arts groups host the Leonard Bernstein International Music Competition in Jerusalem. To honor the memory of Bernstein, a well-known New York conductor, the competition promotes the artistic causes that he supported.

Tel Aviv is the home of the Golda Meir Performing Arts Center. Built in 1994, it hosts such operas as Kurt Weill's *Seven Deadly Sins.* Rock music is popular with the younger crowd, who listen to local artists as well as international stars. Nightclubs in Tel Aviv stay open until the early hours of the morning.

There are many dance troupes in Israel. The Professional Israeli dancers are known for their style and creativity. The most popular modern dance troupes are Inbal, Batsheeva, and Bat Dor. Many kibbutzim have their own dance companies, which give young dancers their first performance opportunities. The *hora,* a well-known folk dance, is enjoyed by Israelis of all ages.

Some consider Israel the "paradise of theater." The Arab Theater, Haifa Repertory Theater, and others are always crowded. Because of the harsh political reality that surrounds the Israelis, theater often serves as an escape.

The Jerusalem Film Center brings together Israelis of various backgrounds. The center features more than 150 films annually. Israeli filmmakers are proficient in producing documentaries that portray the incidents of Israeli life.

## Literature

Since Hebrew is not widely spoken outside of Israel, many Israeli writers are not known outside of the country. But some writers and poets have had their works translated into other languages to reach a wider audience. To spread the word about Israel's great writers, the government started *Ariel*, a literary magazine. It is published in six different languages and showcases essays, poems, and personality profiles of the Israeli literary community.

## ITZHAK PERLMAN

Itzhak Perlman is one of the best-loved violinists in the world. Born in Tel Aviv in 1945, Perlman studied at the Tel Aviv Academy of Music. At the age of ten, he performed his first solo recital. Perlman later studied at the Juilliard School of Music in New York. As a child, Perlman was stricken with polio. He walked with the aid of braces and crutches. For many, Itzhak Perlman symbolizes the devotion, skill, and pride that Israel puts into its music and culture.

# GLOSSARY

**ayatollah** a title used by Shi'ite Muslims to refer to the highest-ranking religious leaders

**caliph** an Islamic spiritual leader, the successor to the Prophet Mohammad

**caliphate** Islamic realm, ruled by a religious and political leader called a caliph

**constitution** a written statement that describes a country's laws and how its people will be governed

**Diaspora** the scattered settlements of Jews outside of Israel

**exile** to force people to leave their homeland for political or religious reasons; a person who is forced to leave his or her country

**imam** a Shi'ite religious leader; one of up to twelve recognized descendants of Mohammad, considered by Shi'ite Muslims to be the only divinely appointed successors to the Prophet.

**infrastructure** the public works that support a country or region, such as power plants, transportation, and communications

**sanctions** punishments, usually economic in nature, that one nation imposes on another in an attempt to influence policy. Economic sanctions often include a ban on imports from the sanctioned country, refusal to export goods to that country, or blocking access to bank accounts.

**secular** nonreligious

**ziggurat** ancient Sumerian temples built in the shape of a pyramid

# BIBLIOGRAPHY

Akrami, Jamsheed. "Sixty-six Years of Film Production in Iran." Zeitgeist Films. http://www.zeitgeistfilm.com/current/closeup/ closeuphistory.html>

Arab.net. "Iraq: The Marshes." <http://www.arab.net/iraq/ iq_marshes.htm>

Armenian National Institute. <http://www.armenian-genocide.org/>

Bacon, Josephine. *Cooking the Israeli Way.* Minneapolis: Lerner, 1986.

Baha'i World. <http://www.bahai.org/>

Bartletti, Don. "Longing for a Lost Paradise." *Austin American-Statesman.* 5/18/03.

Batmanglij, Najmieh K. *A Taste of Persia.* Hong Kong: Mage Publishers, 1999.

BBC News.com. "Country Profile: Israel." <http://news.bbc.co.uk/ 1/hi/world/middle_east/country_profiles/803257.stm>

Bible Resource Center. "Biblical Hebrew." <http://www. bibleresourcecenter.org/vsItemDisplay.dsp&objectID= B5B38E8B-3499-4287-86913AC5447A9915&method=display>

Collier, Robert. "Religious Frenzy and Anger on Once-Banned Pilgrimage." *San Francisco Chronicle.* 4/23/03.

<http://sfgate.com/cgi-bin/article.cgi?f=/c/a/2003/04/23/
MN296904.DTL>

Dixon, Robyn. "Hopes for Happily Ever After." SunSpot.net.
<http://www.sunspot.net/news/nationworld/bal-te.
journal12may12,0,987920.column>

Flora and Fauna in Israel. <http://www.israel-mfa.gov.il/mfa/
go.asp?MFAH0ddk0>

Fox, Mary Virginia. *Iran.* Chicago: Children's Press, 1991.

Gee, Robert W. "Lunch Links Marsh Arabs to Another Era." *Austin
American-Statesman.* 5/18/03.

Grossman, Laurie M. *Children of Israel.* Minneapolis, MN: Carolrhoda
Books, 2001.

Hintlian, George. "Fact File: Armenians of Jerusalem." *Jerusalem
Quarterly File.* Issue 2, 1998. < http://www.jqf-jerusalem.org/
1998/jqf2/armenians.html>

Hintz, Martin and Stephen. *Israel.* Chicago: Children's Press, 1999.

Hiro, Dilip. *Neighbors, Not Friends: Iraq and Iran after the Gulf Wars.*
London: Routledge, 2001.

International Association of Sufism. "Articles on Sufism."
<http://www.ias.org/articles.html>

Jones, Helen Hinckley. *Israel.* Chicago: Children's Press, 1986.

Judaism 101. <http://www.jewfaq.org/>

Landau, Elaine. *The True Book of Israel.* Grolier Publishing Chicago: Children's Press, 1999.

Metz, Helen Chapin, ed. *Iran: A Country Study.* Federal Research Division, Library of Congress. 1987. <http://lcweb2.loc.gov/frd/cs/irtoc.html>

———. *Iraq: A Country Study.* Federal Research Division, Library of Congress. 1988. <http://lcweb2.loc.gov/frd/cs/iqtoc.html>

*Microsoft Encarta Online Encyclopedia.* <http://encarta.msn.com>

Nardo, Don. *The Persian Gulf War.* San Diego: Lucent, 1991.

O'Shea, Maria. *Iran.* Milwaukee, WI: Gareth Stevens, 2000.

Radio Free Europe/Radio Liberty. "Armenians Said Fleeing Iraq." 3/26/03. <http://www.reliefweb.int/w/rwb.nsf/0/5c42a86ef4364446c1256cf5005c69c1?OpenDocument>

Reuters. "Analysis: Distant Prospect of U.S.–Iran Thaw." *New York Times.* 5/13/03. <http://www.nytimes.com/reuters/international/international-iran-usa.html>

Stein, R. Conrad. *The Iran Hostage Crisis.* Chicago: Children's Press, 1994.

Virtual Israel Experience. "Jerusalem—The Old City." <http://www.us-israel.org/jsource/vie/Jerusalem2.html>

Webb, Lois Sinaiko. *Holidays of the World Cookbook for Students.* Phoenix: Oryx Press, 1995.

Young, Caroline. *The Usborne 'Round the World Cookbook*. London: Usborne, 1993.

Zuhur, Sherifa, ed. *Colors of Enchantment: Theater, Dance, Music, and the Visual Arts of the Middle East*. Cairo: The American University in Cairo Press, 2001.

# CUMULATIVE INDEX

Note: Page numbers in *italics* indicate illustrations and captions.

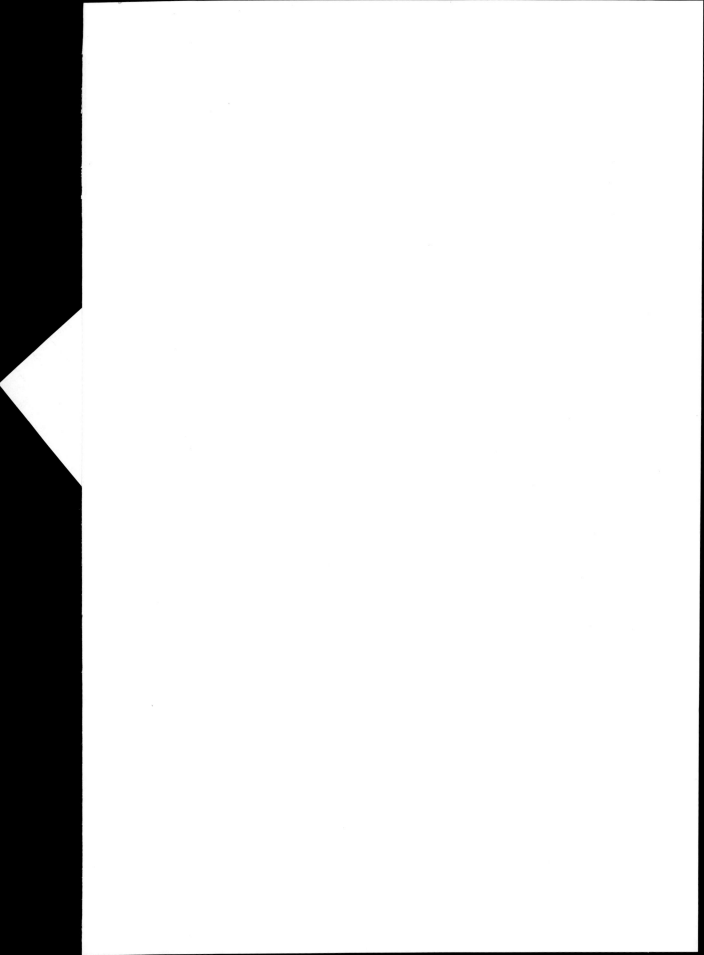

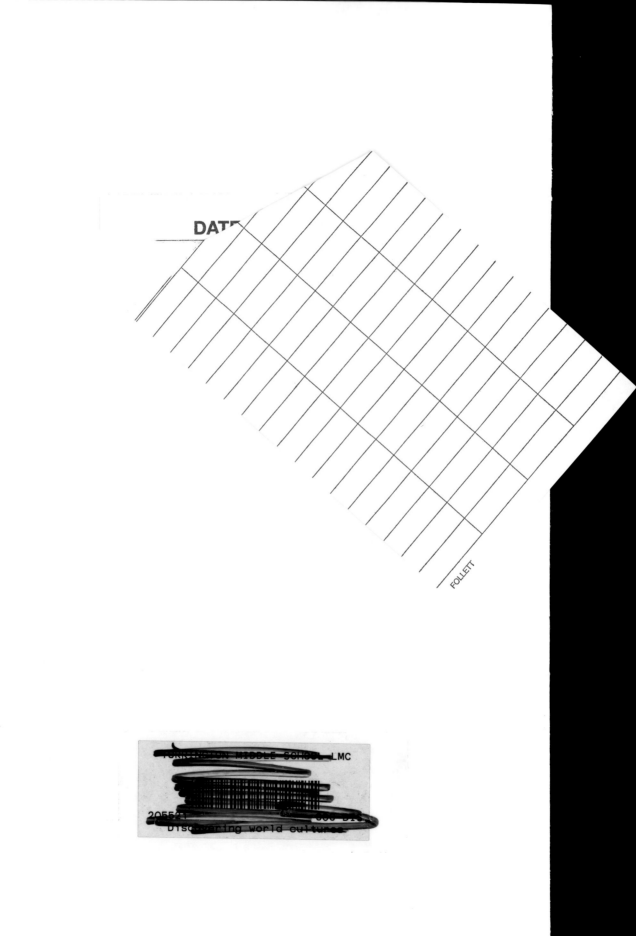

DATE

FOLLETT

# INTERIOR DESIGN
## ILLUSTRATED

# INTERIOR DESIGN
## ILLUSTRATED

### FRANCIS D.K. CHING

 VAN NOSTRAND REINHOLD
NEW YORK

Library of Congress Catalog Card Number 87-10512
ISBN 0-442-21537-1

I$\widehat{T}$P   Van Nostrand Reinhold is an International Thomson Publishing company.
ITP logo is a trademark under license.

Printed in the United States of America
Designed by Francis D.K. Ching

Van Nostrand Reinhold
115 Fifth Avenue
New York, NY 10003

International Thomson Publishing GmbH
Königswinterer Str. 418
53227 Bonn 3
Germany

International Thomson Publishing
Berkshire House,168-173
High Holborn, London WC1V 7AA
England

International Thomson Publishing Asia
38 Kim Tian Rd., #0105
Kim Tian Plaza
Singapore 0316

Thomas Nelson Australia
102 Dodds Street
South Melbourne 3205
Victoria, Australia

International Thomson Publishing Japan
Kyowa Building, 3F
2-2-1 Hirakawacho
Chiyada-Ku, Tokyo 102
Japan

Nelson Canada
1120 Birchmount Road
Scarborough, Ontario
M1K 5G4, Canada

16 15 14 13 12 11 10 9 8 7

**Library of Congress Cataloging-in-Publication Data**

Ching, Francis D.K., 1943-
      Interior design illustrated.
      Includes index.
      1. Interior architecture.  2.  Space (Architecture)
   3.  Interior decoration—History—20th century.  I.  Title.
      NA2850.C45   1987        729         87-10512
   ISBN 0-442-21537-1 (pbk.)

# CONTENTS

# INTRODUCTION

We spend the majority of our lives indoors, in the interior spaces created by the structures and shells of buildings. These spaces provide the physical context for much of what we do, and give substance and life to the architecture which houses them. This introductory text is a visual study of the nature and design of these interior settings.

The purpose of this primer is to introduce to students of interior design those fundamental elements which make up our interior environments. It outlines the characteristics of each element and presents the choices we have in selecting and arranging them into design patterns. In making these choices, emphasis is placed on basic design principles and how design relationships determine the functional, structural, and aesthetic qualities of interior spaces.

This exploration of the ways and means of developing interior spaces begins with space itself, for it is the prime material with which the interior designer must work.

- The first chapter - Interior SPACE - proceeds from a general discussion of architectural space to the particular characteristics of interior space in three dimensions.

- The second chapter - Interior DESIGN - outlines a method for translating programmatic needs and requirements into three-dimensional design decisions.

- The third chapter - A Design VOCABULARY - explores the fundamental elements and principles of visual design and applies each of them to the unique field of interior design.

- The fourth chapter - Interior Design ELEMENTS - describes the major categories of interior elements and discusses how each affects the functional and aesthetic development of interior spaces.

- The fifth chapter - Interior Environmental SYSTEMS - provides an outline of the environmental control systems which must be integrated into a building's interior.

Since interior design is to a great extent a visual art, drawings are used extensively to convey information, express ideas, and outline possibilities. Some of the illustrations are quite abstract; others are more specific and particular. All of them, however, should be viewed essentially as diagrams which serve to demonstrate design principles or to clarify the relationships existing between the elements of a design.

The limits of interior design are difficult to define precisely since it lies in the continuum between architecture and product design. It encompasses both visual and functional design as well as aspects of materials, construction, and technology. This introduction to interior design is therefore broad in scope. The intent, nevertheless, is to treat the subject with clarity, make it as accessible as possible, and stimulate further in-depth study and research.

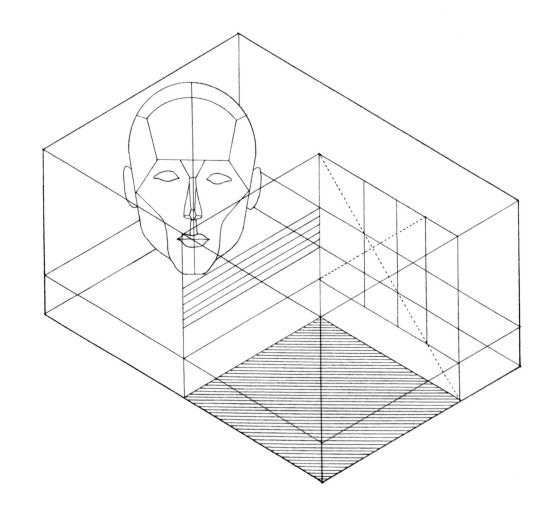

8

# 1

# INTERIOR SPACE

# SPACE

Space is the prime material in the designer's palette and the essential element in interior design. Through the volume of space we not only move... we see forms, hear sounds, feel gentle breezes and the warmth of the sun, smell the fragrances of flowers in bloom. Space inherits the sensual and aesthetic characteristics of those elements in its field.

Space is a material substance like stone and wood. Yet it is inherently formless and diffuse. Universal space has no definition. Once an element is placed in its field, however, a visual relationship is established. As other elements are introduced into the field, multiple relationships are established between the space and the elements as well as among the elements themselves. Space is thus formed by these relationships and we who perceive them.

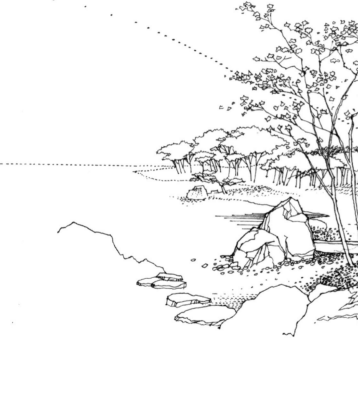

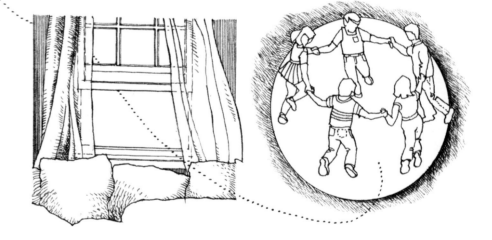

The geometric elements of point, line, plane, and volume can be arranged to articulate and define space. At the scale of architecture, these fundamental elements become linear columns and beams, and planar walls, floors, and roofs.

- A column marks a point in space and makes it visible.

- Two columns define a spatial membrane through which we can pass.

- Supporting a beam, the columns delineate the edges of a transparent plane.

- A wall, an opaque plane, marks off a portion of amorphous space and separates here from there.

- A floor defines a field of space with territorial boundaries.

- A roof provides shelter for the volume of space beneath it.

In architectural design, these elements are organized to give a building form, differentiate between inside and outside, and define the boundaries of interior space.

DEFINING SPACE

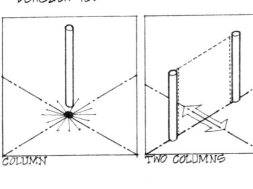

COLUMN

TWO COLUMNS

COLUMNS AND BEAM

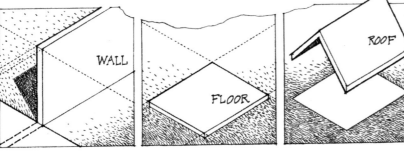

WALL

FLOOR

ROOF

# EXTERIOR SPACE

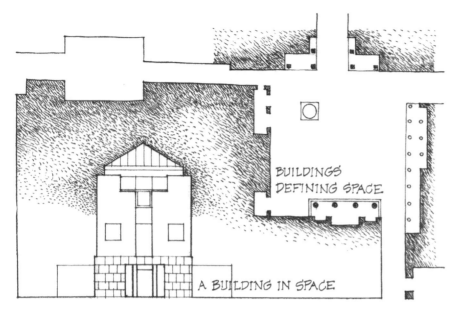

BUILDINGS DEFINING SPACE

A BUILDING IN SPACE

A building's form, scale, and spatial organization are the designer's response to a number of conditions - functional planning requirements, technological aspects of structure and construction, economic realities of cost, expressive qualities of image and style. In addition, the architecture of a building must address the physical context of its site and the issue of exterior space.

A building can be related to its site in several ways. It can merge with its setting or attempt to dominate it. It can surround and capture a portion of exterior space. One of its faces can be made special to address a feature of its site or define an edge of exterior space. In each case, due consideration should be given to the potential relationship, as defined by a building's exterior walls, between interior and exterior space.

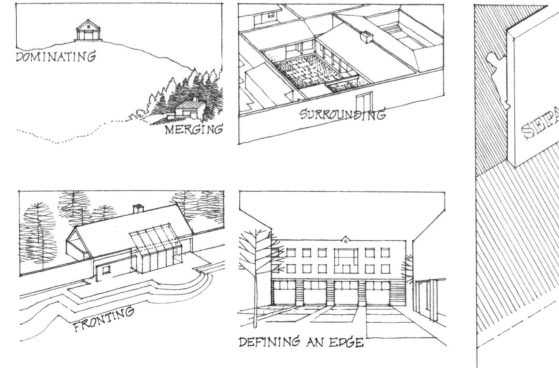

DOMINATING

MERGING

SURROUNDING

FRONTING

DEFINING AN EDGE

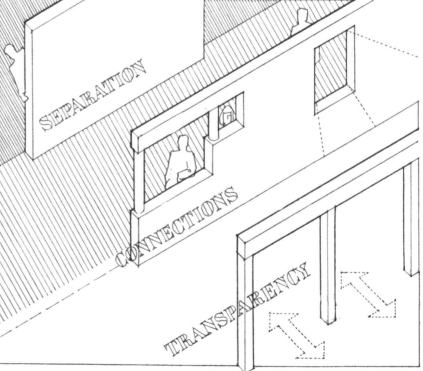

SEPARATION

CONNECTIONS

TRANSPARENCY

A building's exterior walls constitute the interface between our interior and exterior environments. In defining both interior and exterior space, they determine the character of each. They may be thick and heavy, and express a clear distinction between a controlled interior environment and the exterior space from which it is isolated. They may be thin, or even transparent, and attempt to merge inside and outside.

Windows and doorways, the openings which penetrate a building's exterior walls, are the spatial transitions between exterior and interior space. Their scale, character, and composition often tell us something about the nature of the interior spaces which lie behind them.

Special transitional spaces, belonging to both the outside world and the inside, can be used to mediate between the two environments. A familiar example in residential architecture is the porch. Cultural and climatic variations of this theme include the verandah, lanai, and arcaded gallery.

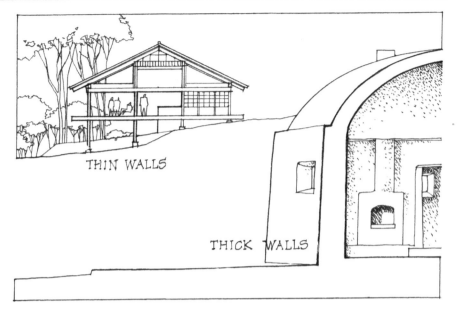

THIN WALLS

THICK WALLS

**SPATIAL TRANSITIONS**

# INTERIOR SPACE

Upon entering a building, we sense shelter and enclosure. This perception is due to the surrounding floor, wall, and ceiling planes of interior space. These are the architectural elements that define the physical limits of rooms. They enclose space, articulate its boundaries, and separate it from surrounding interior spaces and the outside.

Floors, walls, and ceilings do more than mark off a simple quantity of space. Their form, configuration, and pattern of window and door openings also imbue the defined space with certain spatial or architectural qualities. We use terms such as grand hall, loft space, sun room, and alcove to describe not simply how large or small a space is, but also to characterize its scale and proportion, its quality of light, the nature of its enclosing surfaces, and how it relates to adjacent spaces.

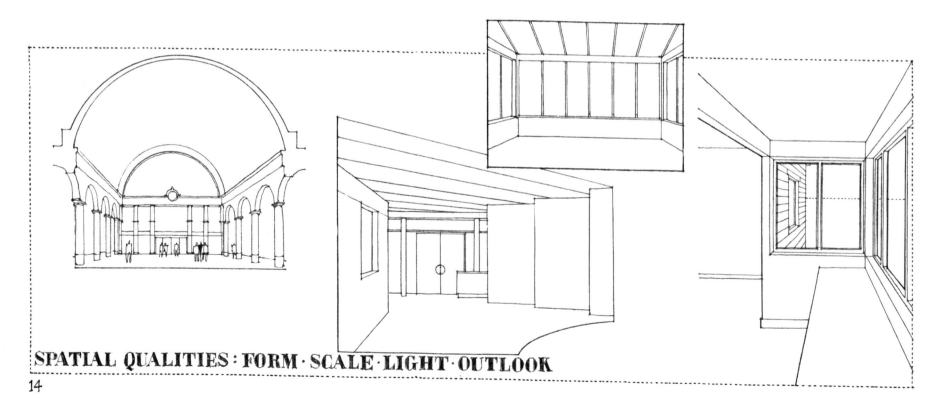

## SPATIAL QUALITIES : FORM · SCALE · LIGHT · OUTLOOK

Interior design necessarily goes beyond the architectural definition of space. In planning the layout, furnishing, and enrichment of a space, the interior designer should be acutely aware of its architectural character as well as its potential for modification and enhancement. The design of interior spaces requires, therefore, an understanding of how they are formed by the building systems of structure and enclosure. With this understanding, the interior designer can effectively elect to work with, continue, or even offer a counterpoint to the essential qualities of an architectural space.

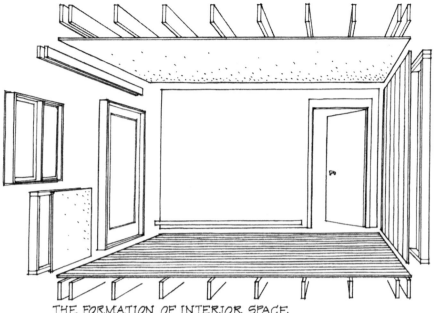

THE FORMATION OF INTERIOR SPACE

CONTINUATION

COUNTERPOINT

CONTRAST

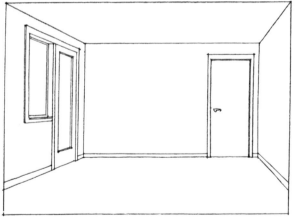

THE BASIC SHELL

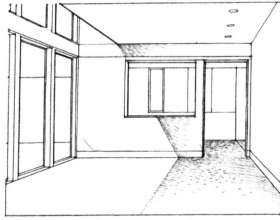

MODIFIED ARCHITECTURALLY

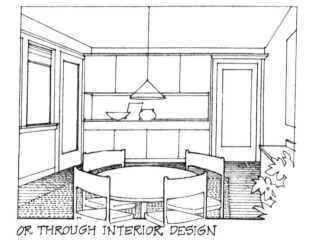

OR THROUGH INTERIOR DESIGN

# STRUCTURING SPACE

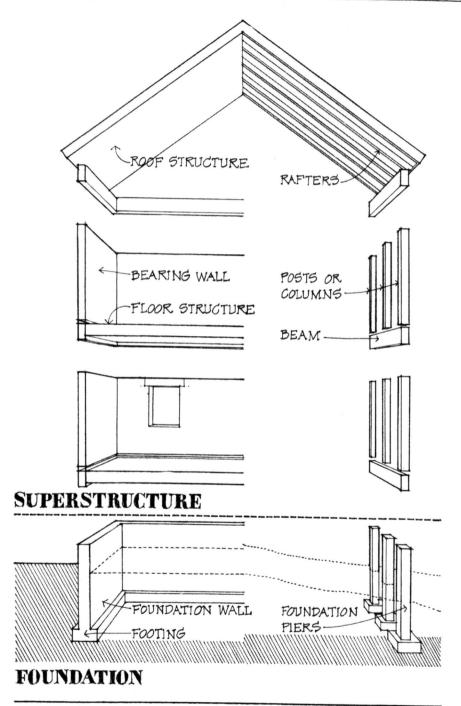

**SUPERSTRUCTURE**

- ROOF STRUCTURE
- RAFTERS
- BEARING WALL
- FLOOR STRUCTURE
- POSTS OR COLUMNS
- BEAM

**FOUNDATION**

- FOUNDATION WALL
- FOOTING
- FOUNDATION PIERS

Most buildings consist of the following constituent elements and systems.

The foundation system forms the base of a building, anchors it firmly to the ground, and supports the building elements and spaces above.

The building superstructure consists of structural floor, wall, column, and roof systems. These systems must work together to support the following types of loads.

- Dead Loads: How a building is constructed determines its dead load, which is the weight of its structural and nonstructural components, including any fixed equipment.

- Live Loads: How a building is used determines its live load, which is the weight of its occupants and any movable equipment and furnishings. In cold climates, snow imposes an additional live load on a building.

- Dynamic Loads: Where a building is located determines its potential load from the dynamic forces of wind and earthquakes.

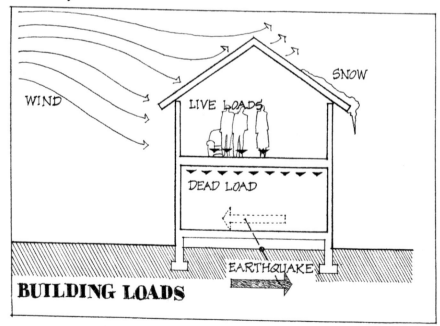

**BUILDING LOADS**

- WIND
- SNOW
- LIVE LOADS
- DEAD LOAD
- EARTHQUAKE

The building envelope consists of exterior walls, windows, doors, and roof, which protect and shelter interior spaces from the exterior environment.

Nonstructural walls, partitions, and ceilings subdivide and define interior space. They generally carry no loads other than their own weight.

Mechanical and electrical systems provide the necessary environmental conditioning of interior spaces and help make them habitable. They provide heat, ventilation, air conditioning, fresh water supply, sanitary waste facilities, electrical power, and lighting.

While the nature of a building's structural system can manifest itself in its interior spaces, the often complex networks of its mechanical and electrical systems are normally hidden from view. Interior designers, however, should be aware of those items which are visible and which directly affect the interior environment - light fixtures, electrical outlets, air supply registers and return grills, and plumbing fixtures. Also of interest are the space requirements for horizontal and vertical runs of electrical and plumbing lines, and air ducts.

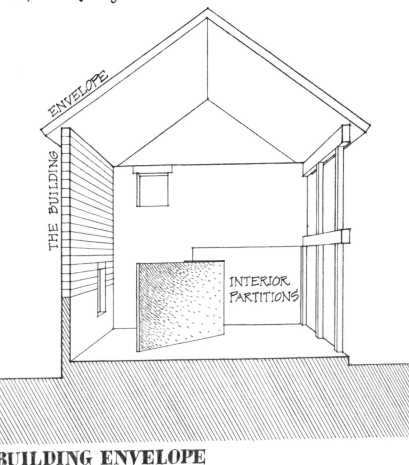

# BUILDING ENVELOPE

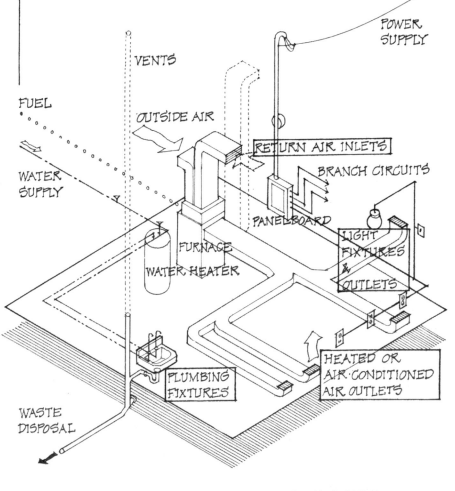

# ELECTRICAL · MECHANICAL SYSTEMS

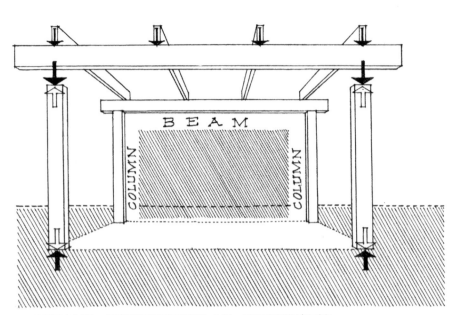

# LINEAR STRUCTURAL SYSTEMS

A building's structural system is formed according to the geometry of its materials and how they react to the forces applied to them. This structural form and geometry, in turn, influence the dimensions, proportion, and arrangement of the interior spaces within the building volume.

The two basic linear structural elements are the column and the beam. A column is a vertical support which transmits compressive forces downward along its shaft. The thicker a column is in relation to its height, the greater its load-bearing capacity and its ability to resist buckling due to off-center loading or lateral forces.

A beam is a horizontal member which transmits forces perpendicular to itself along its length to its supports. It is subject to bending which results in a combination of compressive and tensile stresses. These stresses are proportionally greater at the upper and lower edges of a beam. Increasing depth and placing material where stresses are greatest optimizes a beam's performance.

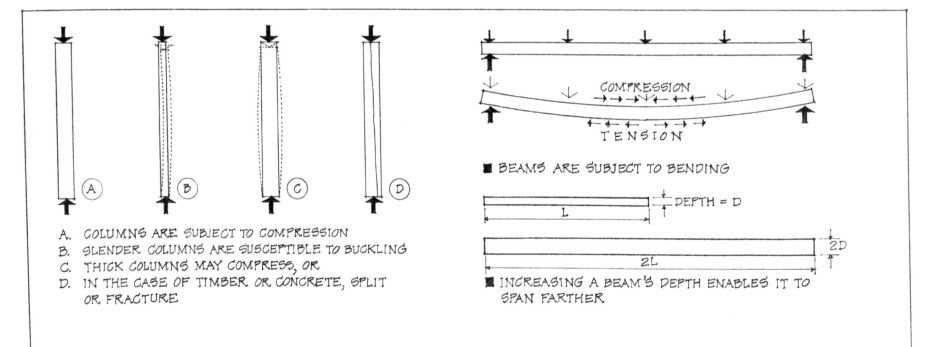

A. COLUMNS ARE SUBJECT TO COMPRESSION
B. SLENDER COLUMNS ARE SUSCEPTIBLE TO BUCKLING
C. THICK COLUMNS MAY COMPRESS, OR
D. IN THE CASE OF TIMBER OR CONCRETE, SPLIT OR FRACTURE

COMPRESSION

TENSION

■ BEAMS ARE SUBJECT TO BENDING

DEPTH = D
L

2D
2L

■ INCREASING A BEAM'S DEPTH ENABLES IT TO SPAN FARTHER

Columns mark points in space and provide a measure for its horizontal divisions. Beams make structural and visual connections across space, between their supports. Together, columns and beams form a skeletal framework around interconnected volumes of space.

While a linear structural system may suggest a grid layout of repetitive spaces, floor, wall, and ceiling planes are necessary for the support and enclosure of interior space. Girders, beams, and joists support floor and ceiling planes, which define the vertical limits of space. Wall planes need not be load bearing and do not have to be aligned with the columns of a structural frame. They are free to define the horizontal dimensions of space according to need, desire, or circumstance.

Linear structural systems are cumulative by nature and eminently flexible. They allow for growth, change, and the adaptation of individual spaces to their specific uses.

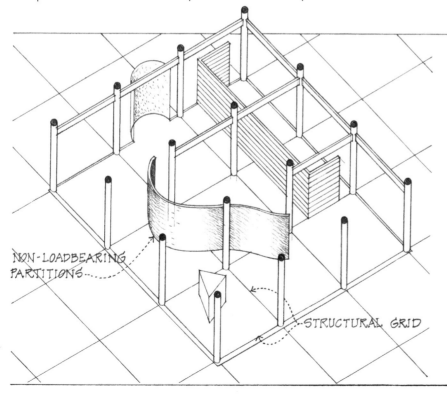

NON-LOADBEARING PARTITIONS

STRUCTURAL GRID

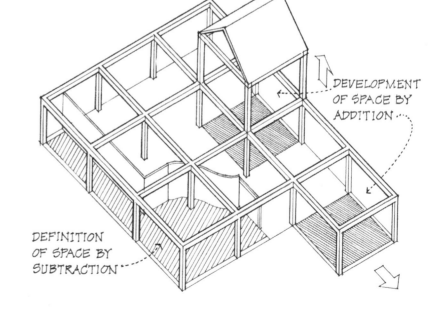

DEVELOPMENT OF SPACE BY ADDITION

DEFINITION OF SPACE BY SUBTRACTION

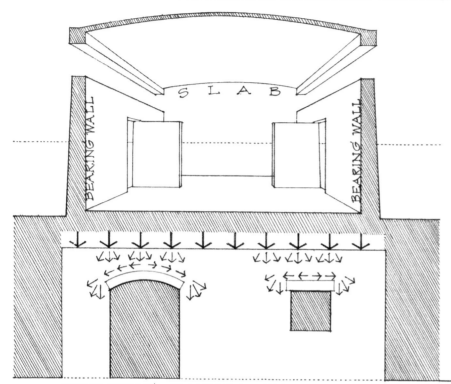

The two principal types of planar structural elements are the load-bearing wall and the horizontal slab. A bearing wall transmits compressive forces, applied along its top edge, to the ground. An exterior wall must also be able to resist lateral forces, such as wind above ground and water and earth pressures below.

A common pattern for bearing walls is a parallel layout spanned by floor joists and roof rafters, or by horizontal slabs. For lateral stability, cross walls are often used to help brace bearing walls.

Window and door openings within a bearing wall tend to weaken its structural integrity. Any opening must be spanned by a short beam called a lintel to support the wall load above.

While linear structural elements outline the edges of spatial volumes, planar elements such as the bearing wall define the physical limits of space. They provide a real sense of enclosure and privacy as well as serve as barriers against the elements.

SMALL BEAMS OR LINTELS ARE REQUIRED TO SPAN OPENINGS IN BEARING WALLS

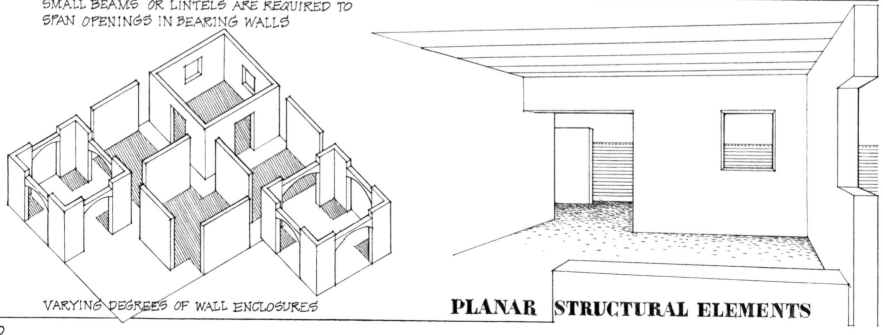

VARYING DEGREES OF WALL ENCLOSURES

# PLANAR STRUCTURAL ELEMENTS

A slab is a horizontal structural plane of reinforced concrete. It is able to support both concentrated and distributed loads well since the resulting stresses can fan out across the plane of the slab and take various paths to the slab supports.

When supported along two edges, a slab can be considered to be a wide, shallow beam extending in one direction. Supported along four sides, a slab becomes a two-way structural element. For greater efficiency and reduced weight, a slab can be modified in section to incorporate ribs.

When integrally connected with reinforced concrete columns, flat slabs can be supported without beams. They form horizontal layers of space punctuated only by the shafts of the supporting columns.

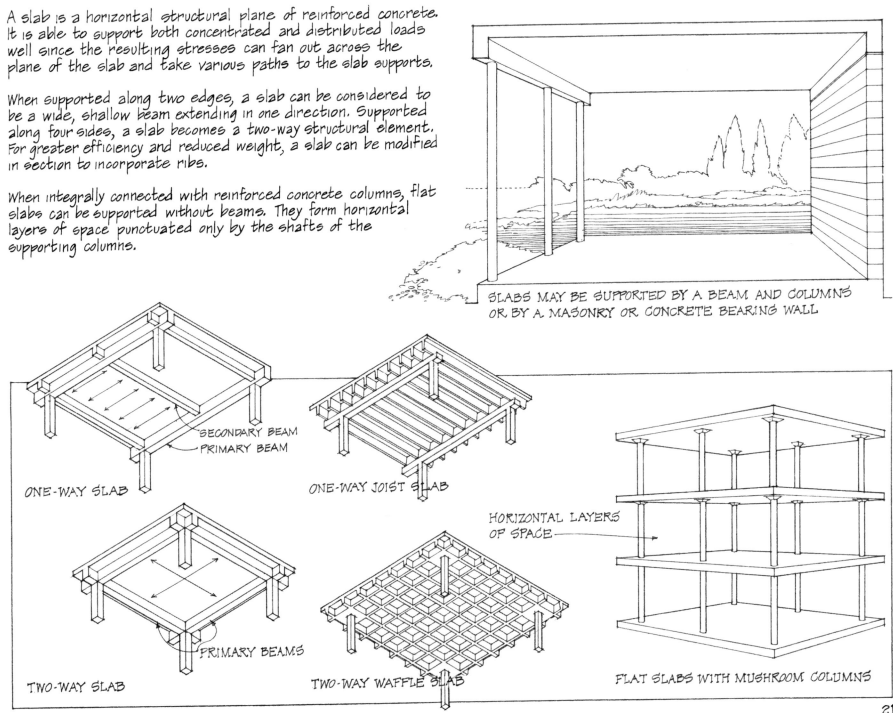

SLABS MAY BE SUPPORTED BY A BEAM AND COLUMNS OR BY A MASONRY OR CONCRETE BEARING WALL

SECONDARY BEAM
PRIMARY BEAM

ONE-WAY SLAB

ONE-WAY JOIST SLAB

PRIMARY BEAMS

TWO-WAY SLAB

TWO-WAY WAFFLE SLAB

HORIZONTAL LAYERS OF SPACE

FLAT SLABS WITH MUSHROOM COLUMNS

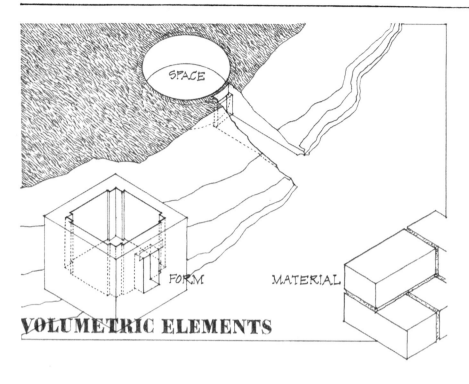

**VOLUMETRIC ELEMENTS**

SPACE

FORM          MATERIAL

A volumetric structural system consists of three-dimensional mass. The mass of the material used fills the void of space. Out of the mass is carved the volume of interior space.

Because of the efficiency of engineering methods and the strength of modern building materials, pure volumetric systems are quite rare today. At a small scale, however, stone and clay masonry units can be seen to be volumetric structural elements. At a larger scale, any building that encloses interior space can be viewed as a three-dimensional structure which must have strength in width, length, and depth.

Most structural systems are in fact composites of linear, planar, and volumetric elements. No one system is superior to all others in all situations. For the structural designer, each presents advantages and disadvantages, depending on the size, location, and intended use of a building. In interior design, we should be aware of the character of the interior spaces each system defines.

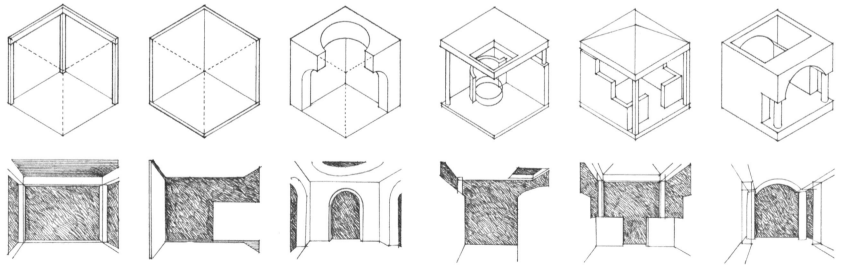

**COMPOSITE SYSTEMS**   COMBINING LINEAR, PLANAR, AND VOLUMETRIC ELEMENTS INTO COMPOSITIONS OF FORMS AND SPACE

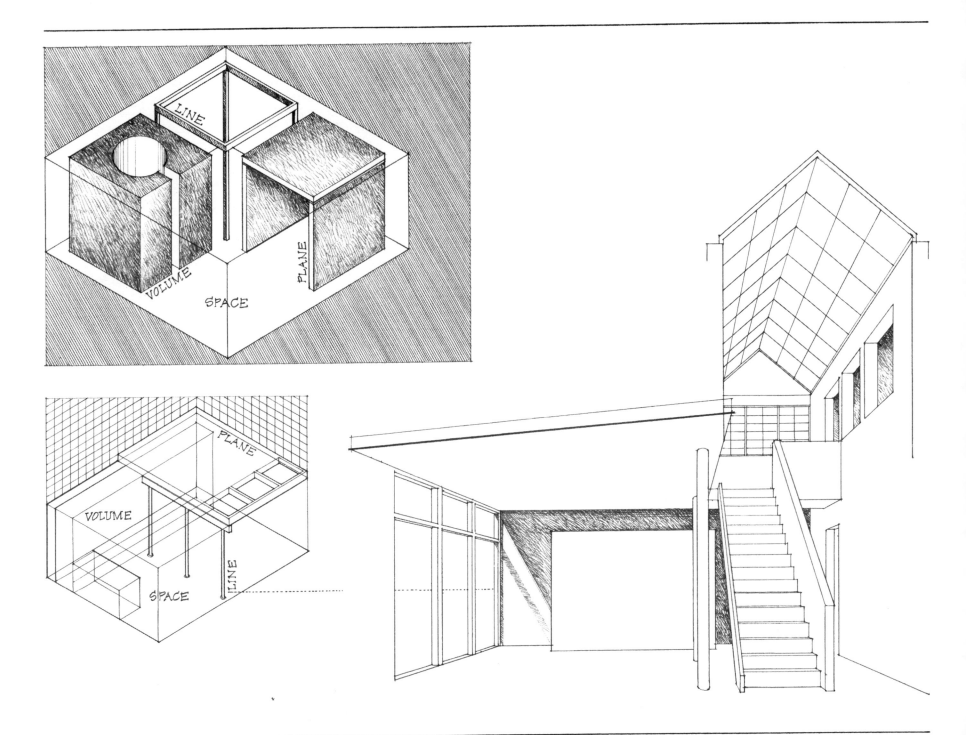

LINE

VOLUME

SPACE

PLANE

PLANE

VOLUME

SPACE

LINE

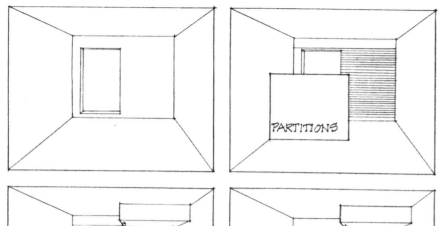

A building's structural system sets up the basic form and pattern of its interior spaces. These spaces, however, are ultimately structured by the elements of interior design. The term structure is not used here in the sense of physical support. It refers to the selection and arrangement of interior elements such that their visual relationships define and organize the interior space of a room.

Non-loadbearing walls and suspended ceilings are often used to define or modify space within the structural framework or shell of a building.

Within a large space, the form and arrangement of furnishings can also function as walls, provide a sense of enclosure, and define spatial patterns. Even a single element, by its form, scale, or style, can dominate a room and organize a field of space about itself.

Light, and the patterns of light and dark it creates, can call our attention to one area of a room, de-emphasize others, and thereby create divisions of space.

# STRUCTURING SPACE    WITH

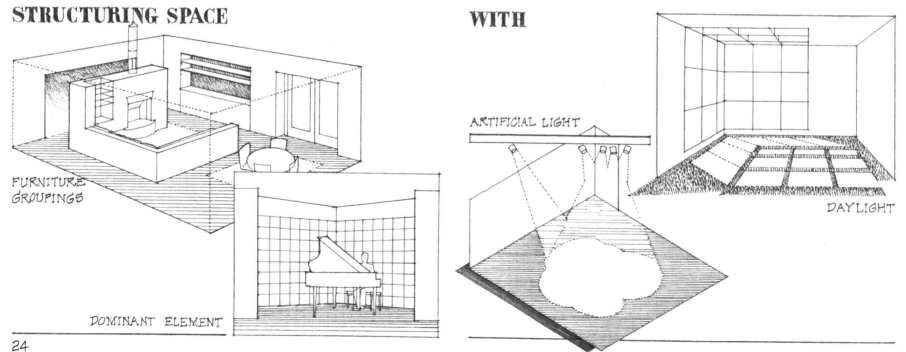

FURNITURE GROUPINGS

DOMINANT ELEMENT

ARTIFICIAL LIGHT

DAYLIGHT

The surface treatment of wall, floor, and ceiling planes can articulate the spatial boundaries of a room. Their color, texture, and pattern affect our perception of their relative positions in space and, therefore, our awareness of the room's dimensions, scale, and proportion.

Even the acoustic nature of a room's surfaces can affect the apparent boundaries of the space. Soft, absorbent surfaces muffle sounds and can expand the acoustical boundaries of a room. Hard surfaces that reflect sounds within a room can emphasize the physical boundaries of the space.

Finally, space is structured by how we use it. The nature of our activities and the rituals we develop in performing them influence how we plan, arrange, and organize interior space.

# INTERIOR DESIGN ELEMENTS

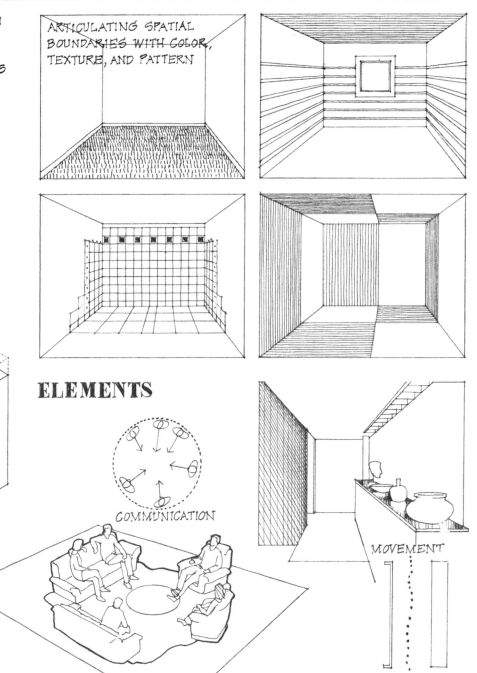

ARTICULATING SPATIAL BOUNDARIES WITH COLOR, TEXTURE, AND PATTERN

INDIVIDUAL OR GROUP ACTIVITIES

COMMUNICATION

MOVEMENT

# SPATIAL FORM

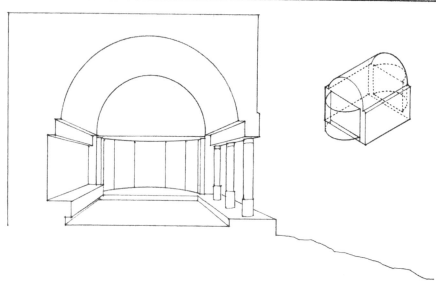

Interior spaces are formed first by a building's structural system, further defined by wall and ceiling planes, and related to other spaces by windows and doorways. Every building has a recognizable pattern of these elements and systems. Each pattern has an inherent geometry which molds or carves out a volume of space into its likeness.

It is useful to be able to read this figure-ground relationship between the form of space-defining elements and that of the space defined. Either the structure or the space can dominate this relationship. Whichever appears to dominate, we should be able to perceive the other as an equal partner in the relationship.

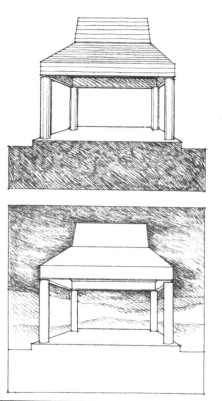

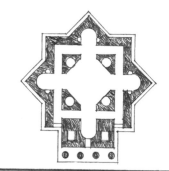

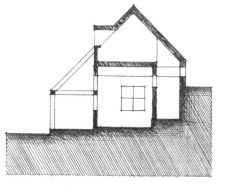

It is equally useful to see this alternating figure-ground relationship occurring as interior design elements, such as tables and chairs, are introduced and arranged within an interior space.

When a chair is placed in a room, it not only occupies space. It also creates a spatial relationship between itself and the surrounding enclosure. We should see more than the form of the chair. We should also recognize the form of the space surrounding the chair after it has filled some of the void.

As more elements are introduced into the pattern, the spatial relationships multiply. The elements begin to organize into sets or groups, each of which not only occupies space but also defines and articulates the spatial form.

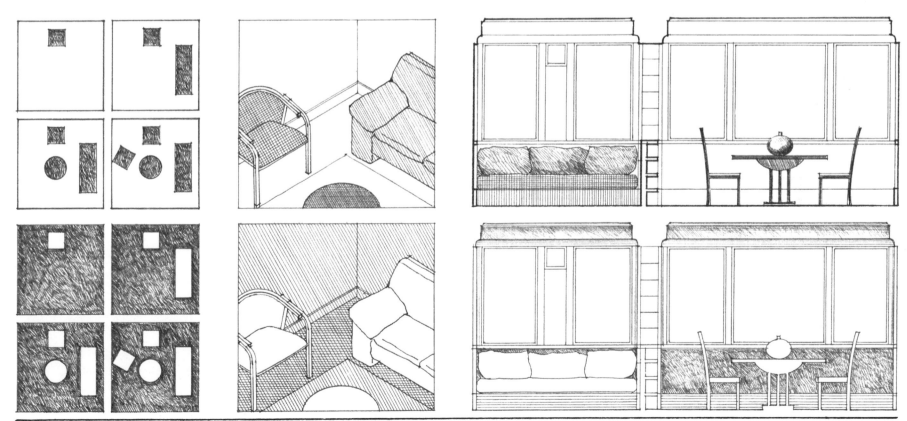

# SPATIAL DIMENSIONS

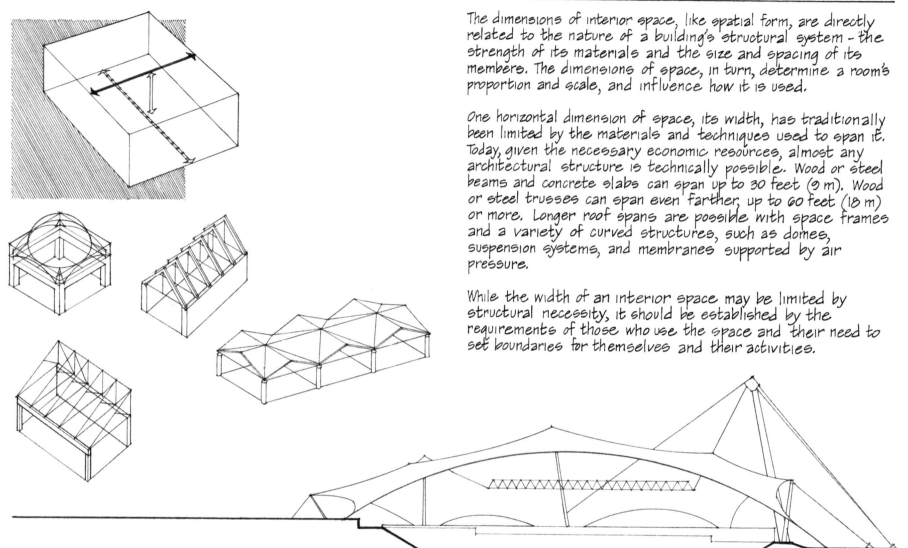

The dimensions of interior space, like spatial form, are directly related to the nature of a building's structural system - the strength of its materials and the size and spacing of its members. The dimensions of space, in turn, determine a room's proportion and scale, and influence how it is used.

One horizontal dimension of space, its width, has traditionally been limited by the materials and techniques used to span it. Today, given the necessary economic resources, almost any architectural structure is technically possible. Wood or steel beams and concrete slabs can span up to 30 feet (9 m). Wood or steel trusses can span even farther, up to 60 feet (18 m) or more. Longer roof spans are possible with space frames and a variety of curved structures, such as domes, suspension systems, and membranes supported by air pressure.

While the width of an interior space may be limited by structural necessity, it should be established by the requirements of those who use the space and their need to set boundaries for themselves and their activities.

The other horizontal dimension of space, its length, is limited by desire and circumstance. Together with width, the length of a space determines the proportion of a room's plan shape.

A square room, where the length of the space equals its width, is static in quality and often formal in character. The equality of the four sides focuses in on the room's center. This centrality can be enhanced or emphasized by covering the space with a pyramidal or dome structure.

To de-emphasize the centrality of a square room, the form of the ceiling can be made asymmetrical, or one or more of the wall planes can be treated differently from the others.

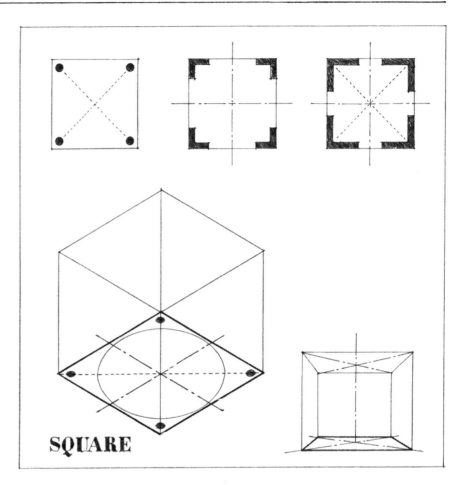

SQUARE

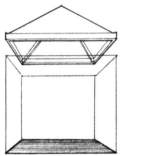 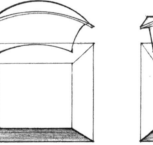

ROOF FORMS EMPHASIZING THE CENTRALITY OF SQUARE ROOMS

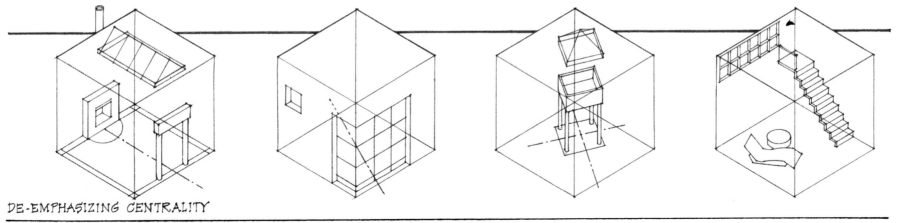

DE-EMPHASIZING CENTRALITY

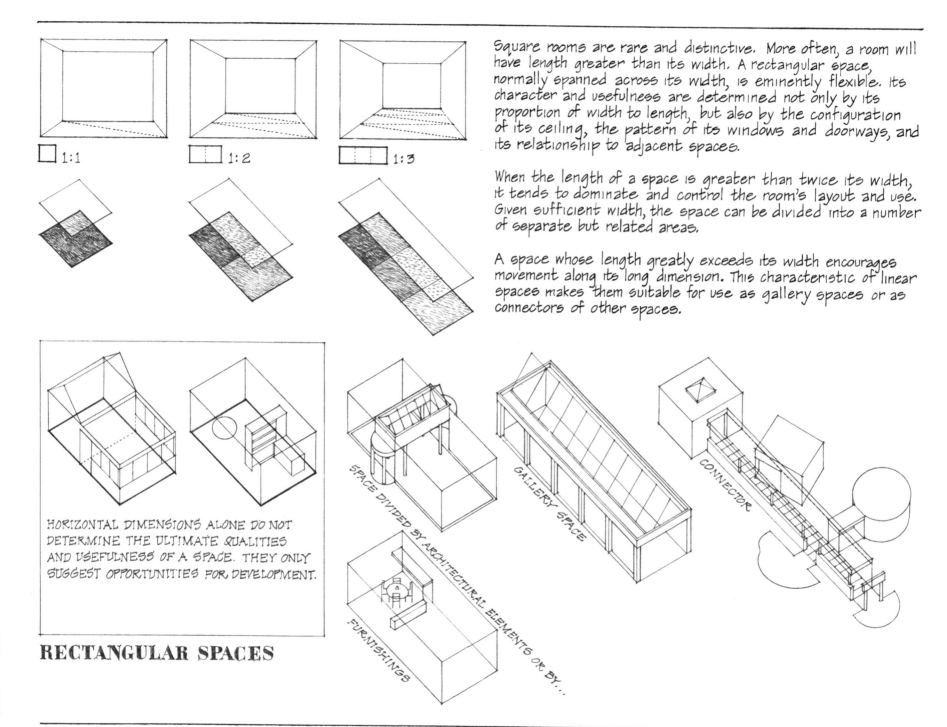

Square rooms are rare and distinctive. More often, a room will have length greater than its width. A rectangular space, normally spanned across its width, is eminently flexible. Its character and usefulness are determined not only by its proportion of width to length, but also by the configuration of its ceiling, the pattern of its windows and doorways, and its relationship to adjacent spaces.

When the length of a space is greater than twice its width, it tends to dominate and control the room's layout and use. Given sufficient width, the space can be divided into a number of separate but related areas.

A space whose length greatly exceeds its width encourages movement along its long dimension. This characteristic of linear spaces makes them suitable for use as gallery spaces or as connectors of other spaces.

1:1  1:2  1:3

HORIZONTAL DIMENSIONS ALONE DO NOT DETERMINE THE ULTIMATE QUALITIES AND USEFULNESS OF A SPACE. THEY ONLY SUGGEST OPPORTUNITIES FOR DEVELOPMENT.

# RECTANGULAR SPACES

SPACE DIVIDED BY ARCHITECTURAL ELEMENTS OR BY...

FURNISHINGS

GALLERY SPACE

CONNECTOR

Both square and rectangular spaces can be altered by addition
or subtraction, or by merging with adjacent spaces. These
modifications can be used to create an alcove space or to reflect
an adjoining circumstance or site feature.

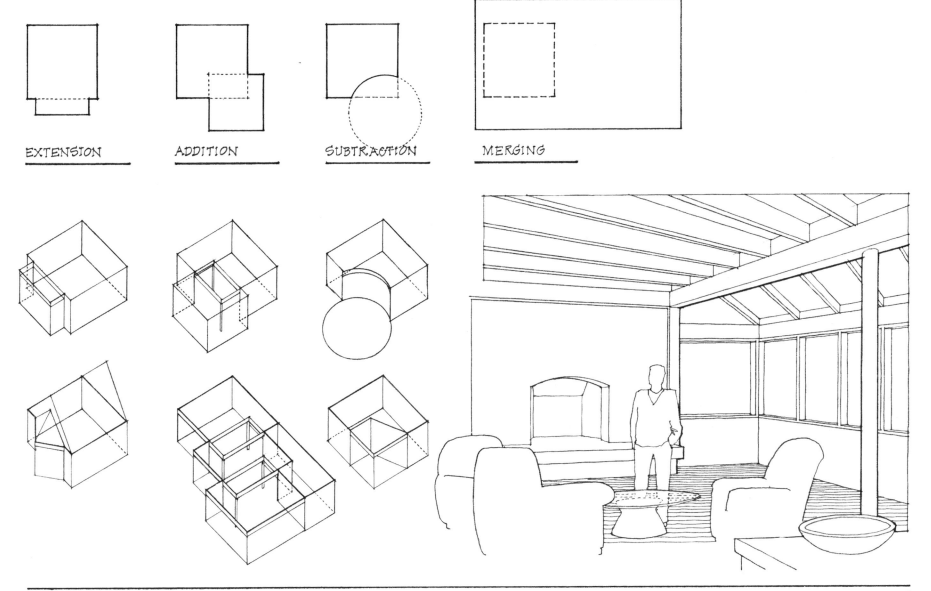

EXTENSION          ADDITION          SUBTRACTION          MERGING

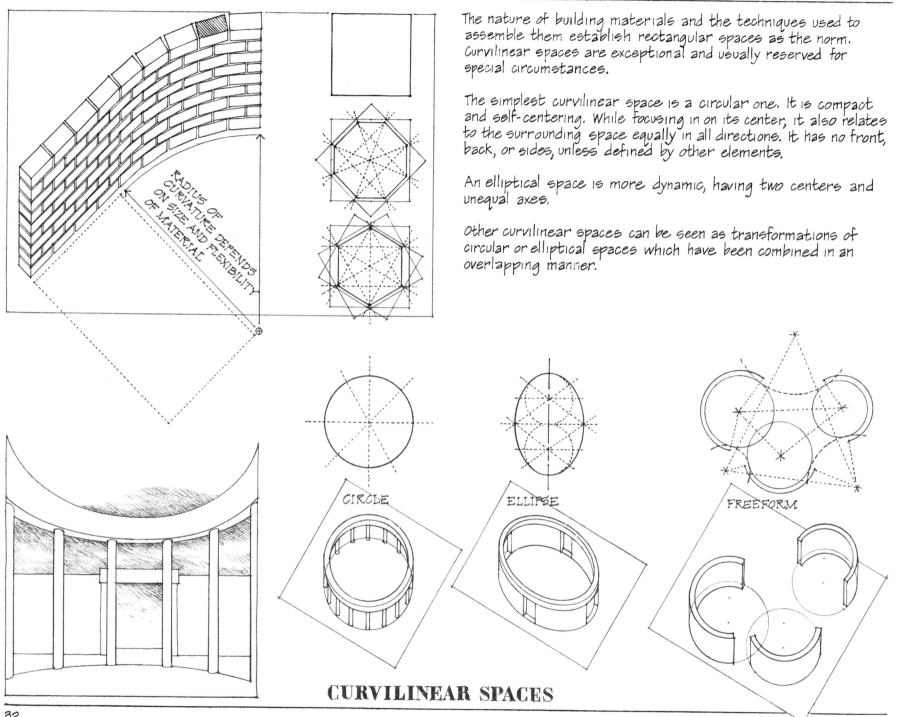

The nature of building materials and the techniques used to assemble them establish rectangular spaces as the norm. Curvilinear spaces are exceptional and usually reserved for special circumstances.

The simplest curvilinear space is a circular one. It is compact and self-centering. While focusing in on its center, it also relates to the surrounding space equally in all directions. It has no front, back, or sides, unless defined by other elements.

An elliptical space is more dynamic, having two centers and unequal axes.

Other curvilinear spaces can be seen as transformations of circular or elliptical spaces which have been combined in an overlapping manner.

RADIUS OF CURVATURE DEPENDS ON SIZE AND FLEXIBILITY OF MATERIAL

CIRCLE

ELLIPSE

FREEFORM

**CURVILINEAR SPACES**

Within a rectilinear context, a curvilinear space is highly visible. Its contrasting geometry can be used to express the importance or uniqueness of its function. It can define a freestanding volume within a larger space. It can serve as a central space about which other rooms are gathered. It can articulate the edge of a space and reflect an exterior condition of the building site.

Curved walls are dynamic and visually active, leading our eyes along their curvature. The concave aspect of a curved wall encloses and focuses inward on space, while its convex aspect pushes space outward.

An important consideration when dealing with a curvilinear space is the integration of furniture and other interior elements into its volume. One way of resolving conflicting geometries is to arrange interior forms as freestanding objects within the curvilinear space. Another is to integrate the form of built-in furniture and fixtures with the curved boundaries of the space.

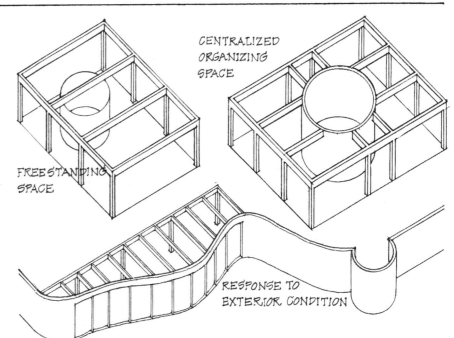

CENTRALIZED ORGANIZING SPACE

FREESTANDING SPACE

RESPONSE TO EXTERIOR CONDITION

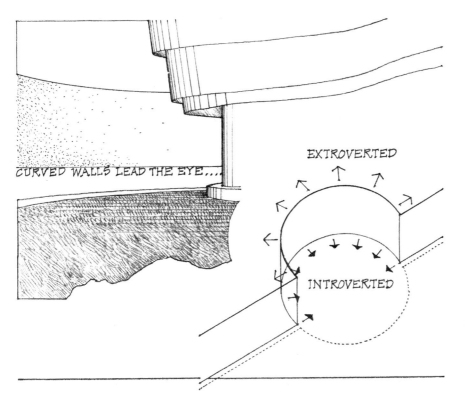

CURVED WALLS LEAD THE EYE.....

EXTROVERTED

INTROVERTED

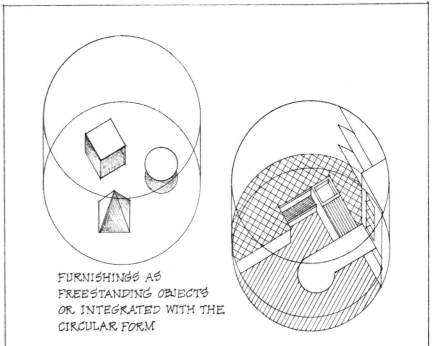

FURNISHINGS AS FREESTANDING OBJECTS OR INTEGRATED WITH THE CIRCULAR FORM

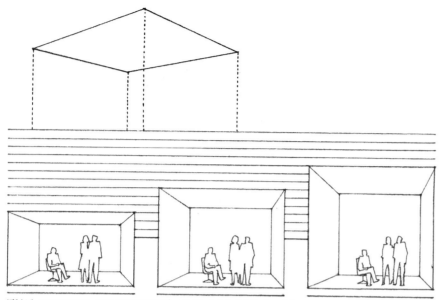

THE EFFECT OF VARYING CEILING HEIGHTS

The third dimension of interior space, its height, is established by the ceiling plane. This vertical dimension is as influential as the horizontal dimensions of space in forming the spatial quality of a room.

While our perception of a room's horizontal dimensions is often distorted by the foreshortening of perspective, we can more accurately sense the relationship between the height of a space and our own body height. A measurable change in the height of a ceiling seems to have a greater effect on our impression of a space than a similar change in its width or length.

High ceilings are often associated with feelings of loftiness or grandeur. Low ceilings often have connotations of cave-like coziness and intimacy. Our perception of the scale of a space, however, is affected not by the height of the ceiling alone, but by its relationship to the width and length of the space.

# THE HEIGHT OF A SPACE

A ceiling defined by a floor plane above is typically flat. A ceiling created by a roof structure can reflect its form and the manner in which it spans the space. Shed, gable, and vaulted ceiling forms give direction to space, while domed and pyramidal ceilings emphasize the center of a space.

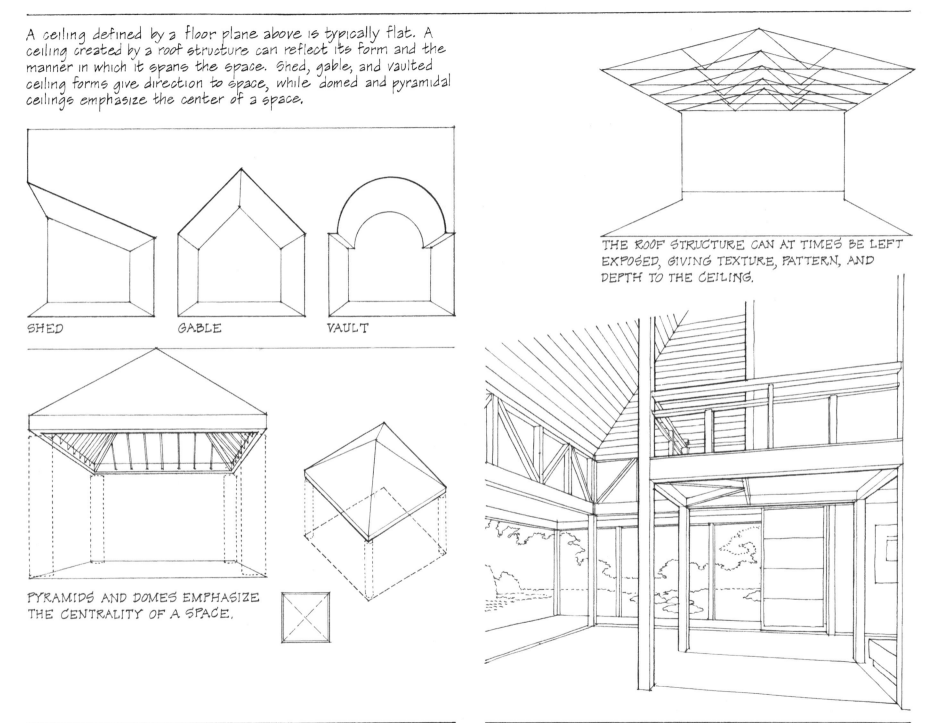

SHED      GABLE      VAULT

PYRAMIDS AND DOMES EMPHASIZE THE CENTRALITY OF A SPACE.

THE ROOF STRUCTURE CAN AT TIMES BE LEFT EXPOSED, GIVING TEXTURE, PATTERN, AND DEPTH TO THE CEILING.

# SPATIAL TRANSITIONS

Although individual spaces may be designed and formed for a certain purpose or to house certain activities, they are gathered together within a building's enclosure because they are functionally related to one another, they are used by a common group of people, or they share a common purpose. How interior spaces are related to one another is determined not only by their relative position in a building's spatial pattern, but also by the nature of the spaces which connect them and the boundaries which they have in common.

Floor, wall, and ceiling planes serve to define and isolate a portion of space. Of these, the wall plane, being perpendicular to our normal line of sight, has the greatest effect as a spatial boundary. It limits our visual field and serves as a barrier to our movement. Openings within the wall plane, windows and doorways, re-establish contact with the surrounding spaces from which the room was originally cut off.

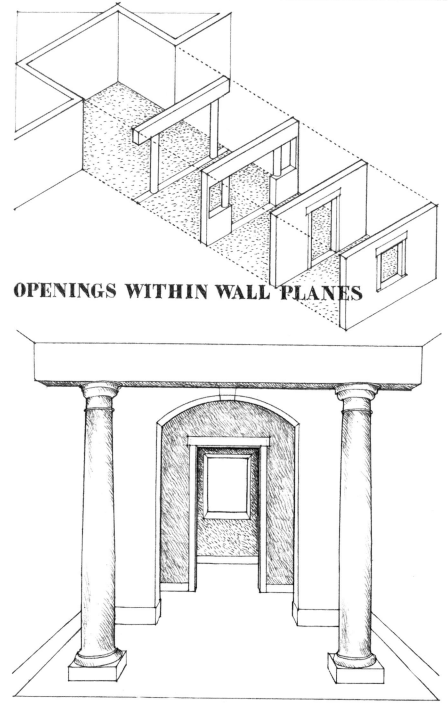

## OPENINGS WITHIN WALL PLANES

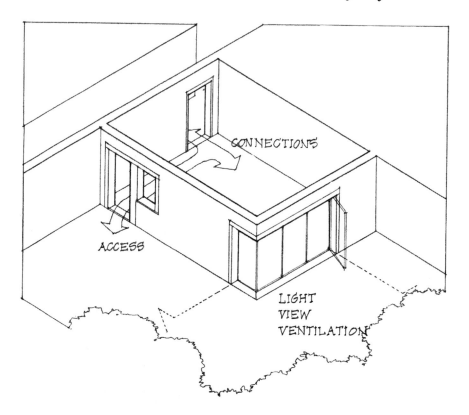

CONNECTIONS

ACCESS

LIGHT
VIEW
VENTILATION

Doorways provide physical access from one space to another. When closed, they shut a room off from adjacent spaces. When open, they establish visual, spatial, and acoustical links between spaces. Large open doorways erode the integrity of a room's enclosure and strengthen its connection with adjacent spaces or the outdoors.

The thickness of the wall separating two spaces is exposed at a doorway. This depth determines the degree of separation we sense as we pass through the doorway from one space to another. The scale and treatment of the doorway itself can also provide a visual clue to the nature of the space being entered.

The number and location of doorways along a room's perimeter affects our pattern of movement within the space, and how we may arrange its furnishings and organize our activities.

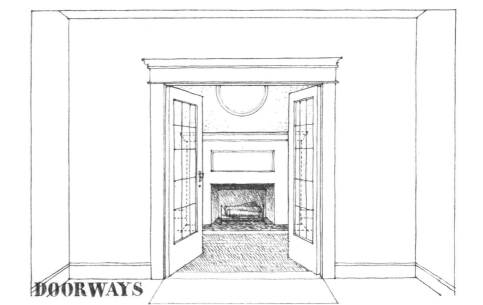

**DOORWAYS**

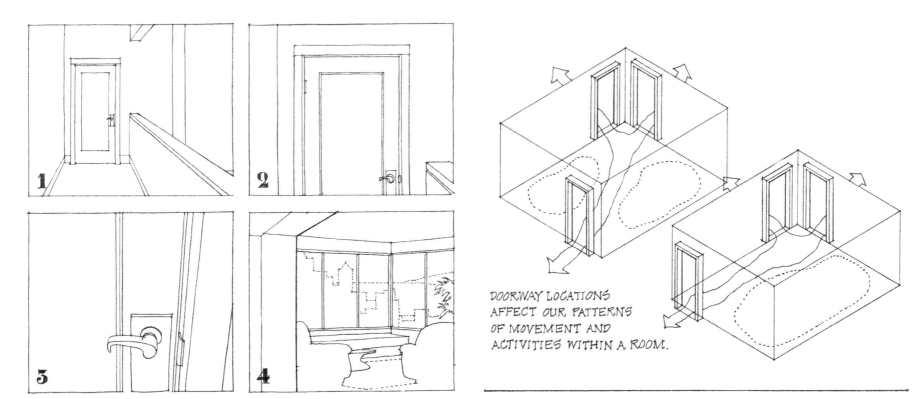

1

2

3

4

DOORWAY LOCATIONS AFFECT OUR PATTERNS OF MOVEMENT AND ACTIVITIES WITHIN A ROOM.

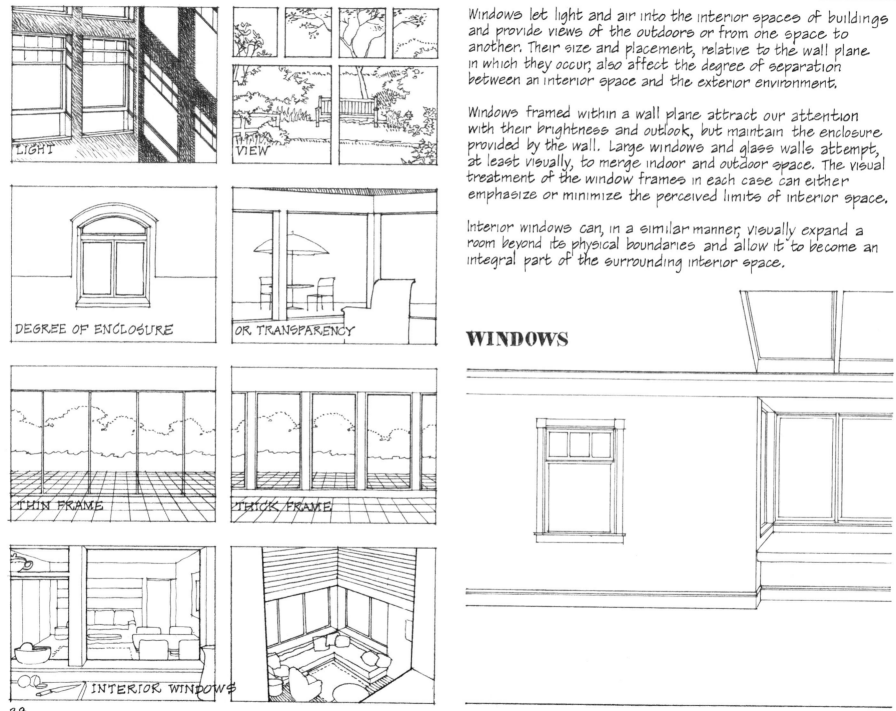

LIGHT

VIEW

DEGREE OF ENCLOSURE

OR TRANSPARENCY

THIN FRAME

THICK FRAME

INTERIOR WINDOWS

Windows let light and air into the interior spaces of buildings and provide views of the outdoors or from one space to another. Their size and placement, relative to the wall plane in which they occur, also affect the degree of separation between an interior space and the exterior environment.

Windows framed within a wall plane attract our attention with their brightness and outlook, but maintain the enclosure provided by the wall. Large windows and glass walls attempt, at least visually, to merge indoor and outdoor space. The visual treatment of the window frames in each case can either emphasize or minimize the perceived limits of interior space.

Interior windows can, in a similar manner, visually expand a room beyond its physical boundaries and allow it to become an integral part of the surrounding interior space.

# WINDOWS

Stairways are also important forms of spatial transitions between rooms. An exterior set of steps leading to a building's entrance can serve to separate private domain from public passage and enhance the act of entry into a transitional space, like a porch or terrace.

Interior stairways connect the various levels of a building. The manner in which they perform this function shapes our movement in space – how we approach a stairway, the pace and style of our ascent and descent, and what we have an opportunity to do along the way. Wide, shallow steps can serve as an invitation, while a narrow, steep stairway can lead to more private places. Landings which interrupt a flight of steps can allow a stairway to change direction and give us room for pause, rest, and outlook.

The space a stairway occupies can be great, but its form can be fit into an interior in several ways. It can fill and provide a focus for a space, run along one of its edges, or wrap around a room. It can be woven into the boundaries of a space, or be extended into a series of terraces.

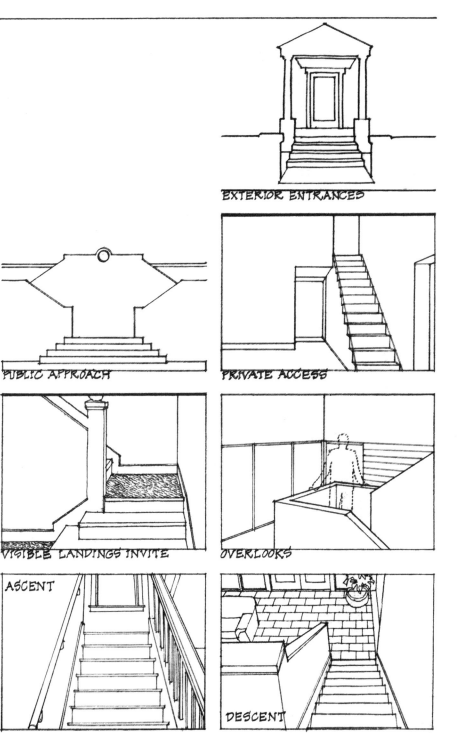

EXTERIOR ENTRANCES

PUBLIC APPROACH

PRIVATE ACCESS

VISIBLE LANDINGS INVITE

OVERLOOKS

ASCENT

DESCENT

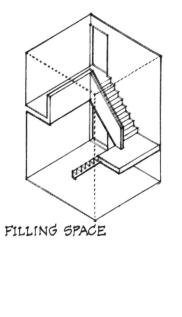

FILLING SPACE

## STAIRWAYS

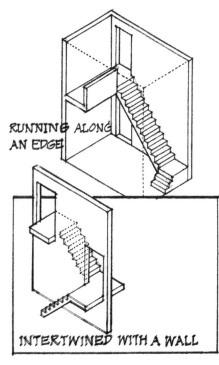

RUNNING ALONG AN EDGE

INTERTWINED WITH A WALL

# MODIFYING SPACE

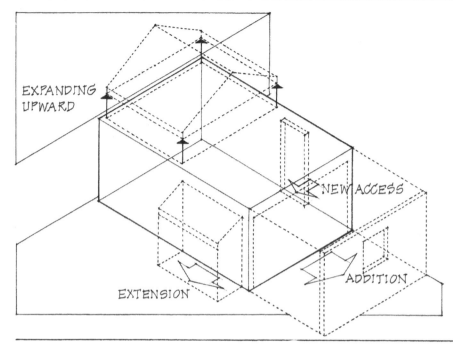

EXPANDING UPWARD

NEW ACCESS

EXTENSION

ADDITION

The architectural planning and design for a new building takes into account the nature of the activities to be housed, the spatial requirements for form, scale, and light, and the desired relationships among the various interior spaces. When an existing building is to be used for activities other than those for which it was originally intended, however, activity requirements must be matched with the existing conditions. Where a misfit occurs, a modification of the existing spaces may be required.

Two major types of alteration can be considered. The first involves structural changes in the boundaries of interior space and is of a more permanent nature than the second, which involves nonstructural modifications and enhancement accomplished through interior design.

A structural change usually involves removing or adding walls in order to alter the shape and rearrange the pattern of existing spaces, or add on new space.

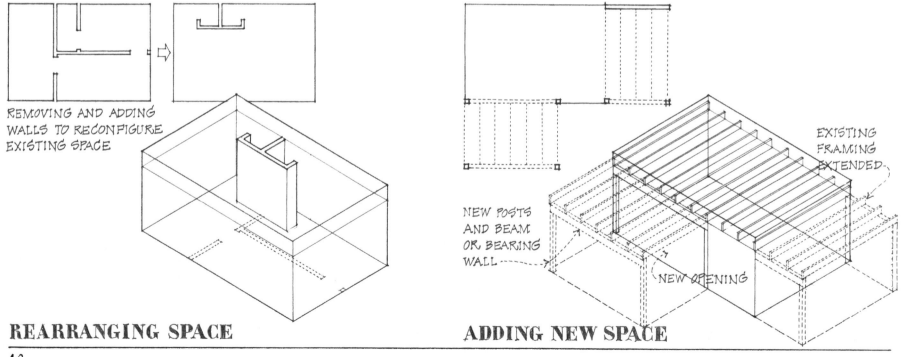

REMOVING AND ADDING WALLS TO RECONFIGURE EXISTING SPACE

**REARRANGING SPACE**

EXISTING FRAMING EXTENDED

NEW POSTS AND BEAM OR BEARING WALL

NEW OPENING

**ADDING NEW SPACE**

Within the boundaries of space, the existing pattern of openings can also be altered. Windows may be enlarged or added for better daylighting or to take advantage of a view. A doorway may be moved or added for better access to a space or to improve the paths of movement within the room. A large doorway may be created to merge two adjacent spaces.

Any changes in the physical boundaries of a space must be carefully planned so that the structural integrity of a building is not adversely disturbed. A portion of a load-bearing wall can be removed if a post-and-beam system is substituted, and the support system below is able to bear the concentrated loads of the new posts. Similarly, new openings in a bearing wall can be created if adequate lintels are installed to carry the wall loads above the openings.

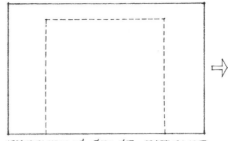
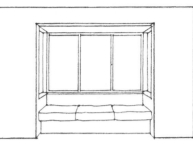

EXTENDING SPACE OUTWARD

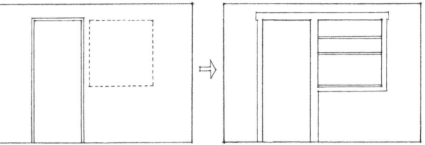

ENLARGING AN EXISTING OPENING

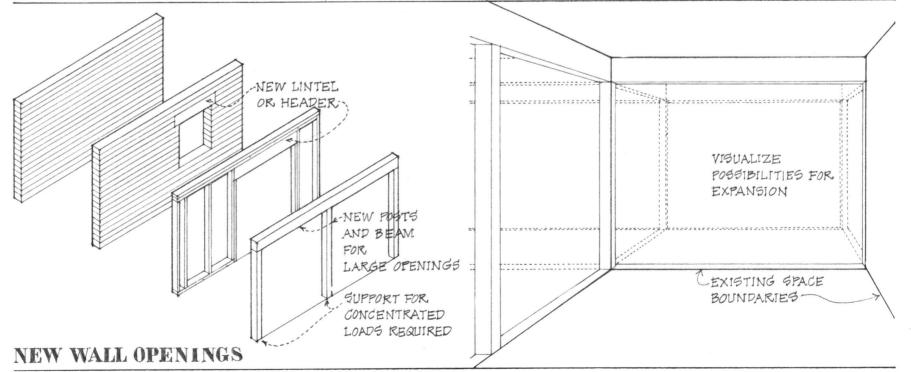

NEW LINTEL OR HEADER

NEW POSTS AND BEAM FOR LARGE OPENINGS

SUPPORT FOR CONCENTRATED LOADS REQUIRED

VISUALIZE POSSIBILITIES FOR EXPANSION

EXISTING SPACE BOUNDARIES

# NEW WALL OPENINGS

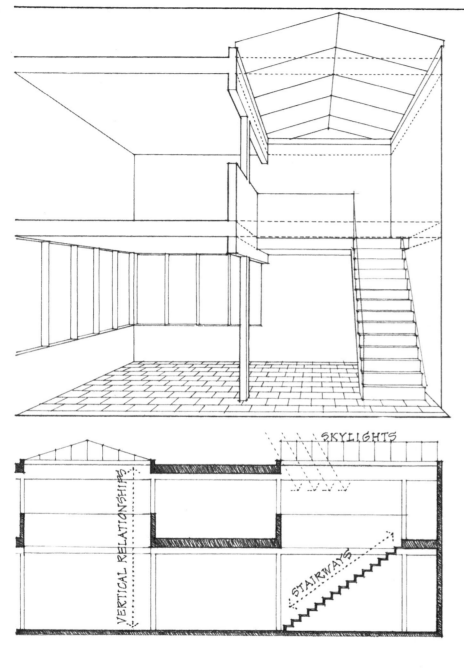

To add a stairway, daylight a space with skylights, or create a vertical relationship between two levels of space, structural changes in the floor or ceiling plane are required. Alterations in these horizontal structures of a building require that the edges of any new openings be reinforced and supported by beams which, in turn, must be supported by posts or bearing walls.

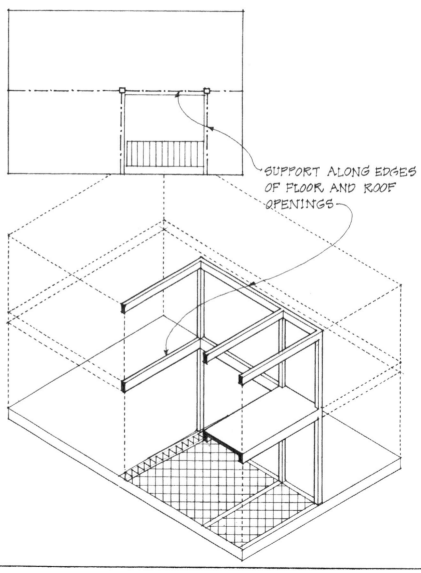

SUPPORT ALONG EDGES OF FLOOR AND ROOF OPENINGS

SKYLIGHTS

VERTICAL RELATIONSHIPS

STAIRWAYS

# VERTICAL EXPANSION

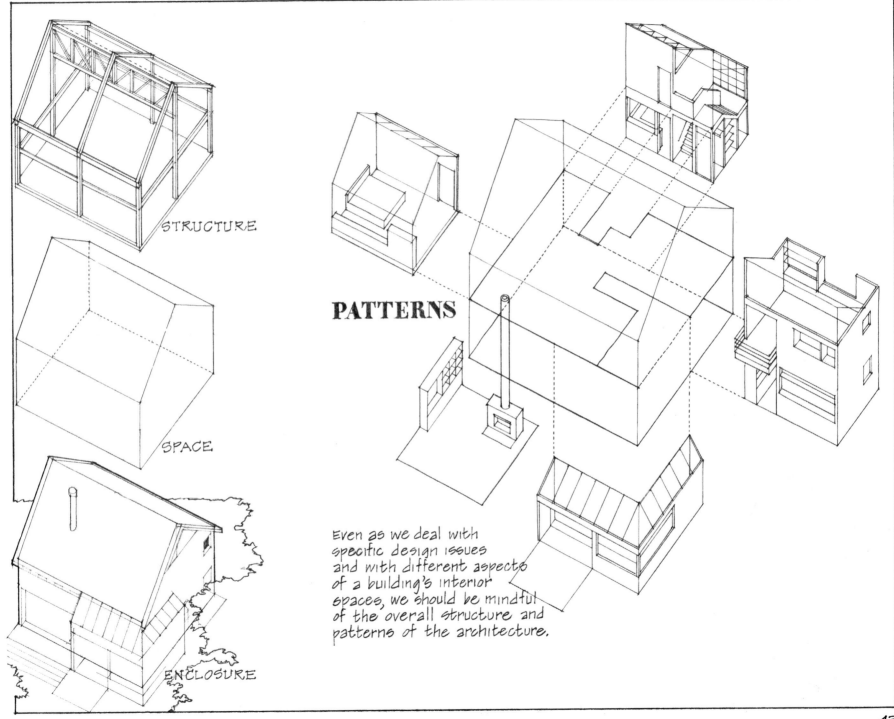

STRUCTURE

SPACE

ENCLOSURE

**PATTERNS**

Even as we deal with specific design issues and with different aspects of a building's interior spaces, we should be mindful of the overall structure and patterns of the architecture.

Major structural changes in a space require the assistance of a professional engineer, architect, or builder. Interior spaces can, however, also be modified and enhanced with nonstructural alterations. While structural changes alter the physical boundaries of space, nonstructural alterations are based on how we perceive, use, and inhabit space. This is the point where we enter the realm of interior design.

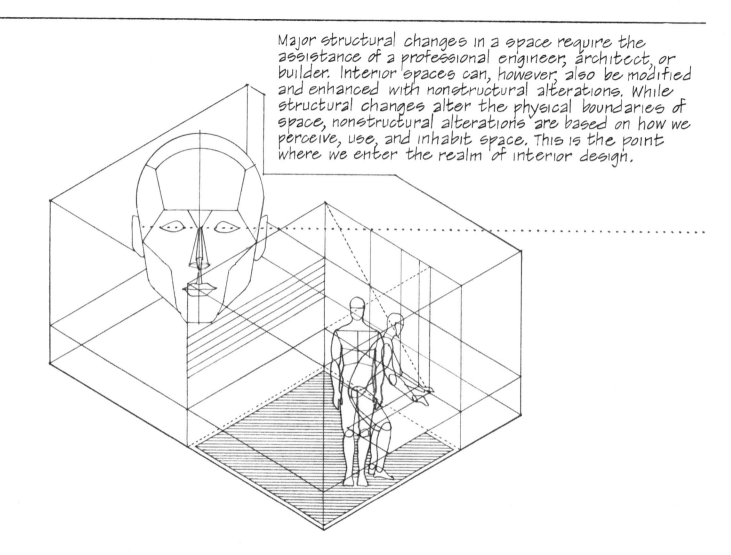

# INTERIOR DESIGN

# INTERIOR DESIGN

Interior design is the planning, layout, and design of the interior spaces within buildings. These physical settings satisfy our basic need for shelter and protection; they set the stage for and influence the shape of our activities; they nurture our aspirations and express the ideas which accompany our actions; they affect our outlook, mood, and personality. The purpose of interior design, therefore, is the functional improvement, aesthetic enrichment, and psychological enhancement of interior space.

The purpose of any design is to organize its parts into a coherent whole in order to achieve certain goals. In interior design, selected elements are arranged into three-dimensional patterns according to functional, aesthetic, and behavioral guidelines. The relationships among the elements established by these patterns ultimately determine the visual qualities and functional fitness of an interior space, and influence how we perceive and use it.

## PLANNING LAYOUT DESIGN OF THE PARTS

### THE ARCHITECTURAL CONTEXT

### INTERIOR ELEMENTS

INTENTIONS

PERCEPTION

USE

INTO A WHOLE

THE INTERIOR ENVIRONMENT

# DESIGN PROCESS

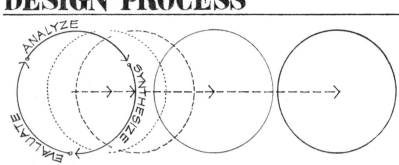

We determine which elements to use and how to arrange them into patterns through the process of design. Although presented as a linear series of steps, the design process is more often a cyclical one in which a sequence of careful analysis, synthesis, and evaluation of available information, insights, and possible solutions is repeated until a successful fit between what exists and what is desired is achieved.

## ANALYSIS:

THE ABILITY TO DEFINE AND UNDERSTAND THE NATURE OF THE DESIGN PROBLEM ADEQUATELY IS AN ESSENTIAL PART OF THE SOLUTION.

### WHAT EXISTS ?

☐ DOCUMENT PHYSICAL/CULTURAL CONTEXT
☐ DESCRIBE EXISTING ELEMENTS
☐ WHAT CAN CHANGE...WHAT CANNOT ?

### WHAT'S DESIRED ?

☐ IDENTIFY USER NEEDS AND PREFERENCES
☐ SET GOALS:
o FUNCTIONAL REQUIREMENTS
o AESTHETIC IMAGE AND STYLE
o PSYCHOLOGICAL STIMULUS AND MEANING

### WHAT'S POSSIBLE ?

☐ WHAT CAN BE ALTERED...WHAT CANNOT ?
☐ WHAT CAN BE CONTROLLED...WHAT CANNOT ?
☐ WHAT IS ALLOWED...WHAT IS PROHIBITED ?
☐ DEFINE LIMITS: TIME, ECONOMIC, LEGAL, TECHNICAL

The design problem is first defined. This definition should include a specification of how the design solution should perform. Goals and objectives should be set.

An analysis of the problem requires that it be broken down into parts, issues clarified, and values assigned to the various aspects of the problem. Analysis also involves gathering relevant information that would help us understand the nature of the problem and develop appropriate responses. From the outset, it is worthwhile knowing what limitations will help shape the design solution. Any givens - what can change and what cannot be altered - should be determined. Any constraints - financial, legal, or technical - which will impinge on the design solution should be noted.

As we cycle through the design process, a clearer understanding of the problem should emerge. New information may be uncovered or be required which could alter our perception of the problem and its solution. The analysis of a problem, therefore, often continues throughout the design process.

### DEVELOP HYPOTHESES
. . . . . . . . . . . . . . . . . . . . . . . . . . . . . . . . >

### MAKE PROJECTIONS
. . . . . . . . . . . . . . . . . . . . . . . . . . . . . . . . >

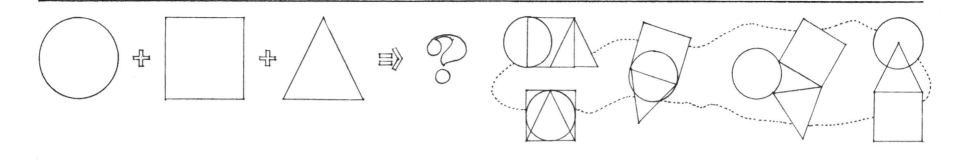

From the analysis of the problem and its parts, we can begin to formulate possible solutions. This requires synthesizing - bringing together and integrating - responses to the various issues and aspects of the problem into coherent solutions.

There are several approaches one can take to generate ideas and synthesize possible solutions to a problem:

- Isolate one or two key issues which have value or importance assigned to them, and develop solutions around them.

- Study analogous situations and use them as models for developing possible solutions to the problem at hand.

- Develop ideal solutions for parts of the problem which can then be integrated into whole solutions and be tempered by the reality of what exists.

It is difficult to develop a good idea without having many to begin with.

# SYNTHESIS:

DESIGN REQUIRES RATIONAL THOUGHT BASED ON KNOWLEDGE AND UNDERSTANDING GAINED THROUGH EXPERIENCE AND RESEARCH. ALSO PLAYING EQUAL ROLES ARE INTUITION AND IMAGINATION, WHICH ADD THE CREATIVE DIMENSION TO THE RATIONAL DESIGN PROCESS.

## SELECT THE PARTS

☐ SELECT AND ASSIGN VALUES TO KEY ISSUES OR ELEMENTS
☐ STUDY THE NATURE OF THE PARTS
☐ VISUALIZE THE WAYS THE PARTS CAN FIT TOGETHER

## GENERATE IDEAS

☐ LOOK AT THE SITUATION FROM DIFFERENT POINTS OF VIEW
☐ MANIPULATE THE PARTS TO SEE HOW A CHANGE MIGHT AFFECT THE WHOLE
☐ SEARCH FOR WAYS TO COMBINE SEVERAL GOOD IDEAS INTO A BETTER ONE

## INTEGRATE INTO A WHOLE
☐

## SIMULATE POSSIBILITIES

## TEST & REFINE IDEAS

# EVALUATION:

DESIGN REQUIRES A CRITICAL REVIEW OF ALTERNATIVES
AND CAREFUL WEIGHING OF THE STRENGTHS AND
WEAKNESSES OF EACH PROPOSAL UNTIL THE BEST POSSIBLE
FIT BETWEEN PROBLEM AND SOLUTION IS ACHIEVED.

## COMPARE ALTERNATIVES

☐ COMPARE EACH ALTERNATIVE WITH DESIGN GOALS
   AND CRITERIA.
☐ WEIGH THE BENEFITS AND STRENGTHS AGAINST THE
   COSTS AND LIABILITIES OF EACH ALTERNATIVE.
☐ RANK ALTERNATIVES IN TERMS OF SUITABILITY AND
   EFFECTIVENESS

## MAKE DESIGN DECISIONS
☐

## DEVELOP & REFINE DESIGN
☐

## IMPLEMENT DESIGN
☐

## RE·EVALUATE COMPLETED DESIGN ·············· >

Given a range of possible solutions, each must be
evaluated according to the criteria set forth in the
problem statement and further clarified in the
problem analysis.

Successive explorations of the problem and the
evaluation of alternative solutions should help narrow
down the choices for design development. While the
initial stages of the design process encourage divergent
thinking about the problem, this latter phase requires a
convergent focus on a specific design solution.

Once a final decision has been made, the design
proposal is developed, refined, and prepared for
implementation. This includes the production of working
drawings and specifications, and other services related
to purchasing, construction, and supervision.

No design process is complete until a design solution
which has been implemented is evaluated for its
effectiveness in solving a given problem. This critical
appraisal of a completed design can build up our
knowledge base, sharpen our intuition, and provide
valuable lessons that may be applied in future work.

One of the idiosyncrasies of the design process is that it does not always lead simply and inevitably to a single, obvious, correct answer. In fact, there is often more than one valid solution to a design problem. How then can we judge whether a design is good or bad?

A design may be good, in the judgment of the designer, the client, or the people who experience and use the design, for any of several reasons:

- A design may be good because it functions well - it works.

- A design may be good because it is affordable - it is economical, efficient, and durable.

- A design may be good because it looks good - it is aesthetically pleasing.

- A design may be good because it recreates a feeling remembered from another time and place - it carries meaning.

- At times, we may judge a design to be good because we feel it follows current design trends - it is in fashion - or because of the impression it will make on others - it enhances our status.

As the foregoing suggests, there are several kinds of meaning which can be conveyed by a design. Some operate at a level generally understood and accepted by the general public. Others are more readily discerned by specific groups of people. Successful designs usually operate at more than one level of meaning and thus appeal to a wide range of people.

A good design, therefore, should be understandable. Knowing why something was done helps to make a design comprehensible. If a design does not express an idea, communicate a meaning, or elicit a response, either it will be ignored or it will appear to be a bad design.

# DESIGN CRITERIA

In defining and analyzing a design problem, one also develops goals and criteria by which the effectiveness of a solution can be measured. Regardless of the nature of the interior design problem being addressed, there are several criteria with which we should be concerned.

## • FUNCTION & PURPOSE

First, the intended function of the design must be satisfied and its purpose fulfilled.

## • UTILITY & ECONOMY

Second, a design should exhibit utility, honesty, and economy in its selection and use of materials.

## • FORM & STYLE

Third, the design should be aesthetically pleasing to the eye and our other body senses.

## • IMAGE & MEANING

Fourth, the design should project an image and promote associations which carry meaning for the people who use and experience it.

A prime criterion for judging the success of an interior design is whether it is functional. Function is the most fundamental level of design. We design to improve the functioning of interior spaces and make our tasks and activities within them more convenient, comfortable, and pleasurable. The proper functioning of a design is, of course, directly related to the purposes of those who inhabit and use it.

To help understand, and ultimately to fulfill, the function and purpose of an interior space, it is necessary to carefully analyze the users' and activity requirements for that space. The following outline can help the designer program these requirements, translate these needs into forms and patterns, and integrate them into the spatial context.

OUTLINE

· ANALYSIS
· SYNTHESIS
· EVALUATION

## 1. USER REQUIREMENTS

IDENTIFY USERS

☐ Individual or group
☐ If group, how many?
☐ Specific or anonymous
☐ Age group
☐
☐

IDENTIFY NEEDS

☐ Group needs
☐ Specific individual needs

TERRITORIAL REQUIREMENTS:
☐ Personal space
☐ Privacy
☐ Interaction
☐ Access

☐ Favored objects
☐ Favorite colors
☐ Special places
☐ Special interests
☐
☐

# 2. ACTIVITY REQUIREMENTS

IDENTIFY PRIMARY & SECONDARY ACTIVITIES

☐ Name and function of primary activity
☐ Names and functions of secondary or related activities

. . . . . . . . . . . . . . . . . . . . . . . . . . . . . . . . . . . . . . . . . .
. . . . . . . . . . . . . . . . . . . . . . . . . . . . . . . . . . . . . . . . . .
. . . . . . . . . . . . . . . . . . . . . . . . . . . . . . . . . . . . . . . . . .

ANALYZE NATURE OF THE ACTIVITIES

☐ Active or passive
☐ Noisy or quiet
☐ Public, small group, or private

☐ If space is to be used for more than one activity, how compatible are the activities?

☐ How often is the space to be used?
☐ What times of day or night?

REQUIREMENTS FOR:
☐ Privacy and enclosure
☐ Access
☐ Flexibility
☐ Light
☐ Acoustic quality
☐ . . . . . . . . . . . . . . . . .
☐ . . . . . . . . . . . . . . . .

# 3. FURNISHING REQUIREMENTS

DETERMINE FURNISHING & EQUIPMENT
REQUIREMENTS FOR EACH ACTIVITY

☐ Number, type, and style of:
☐ Seating
☐ Tables
☐ Work surfaces
☐ Storage and display units
☐ Accessories

☐ Other special equipment required:
☐ Lighting
☐ Electrical
☐ Mechanical

DETERMINE DESIRED QUALITIES OF PIECES

☐ Requirements for:
☐ Comfort
☐ Safety
☐ Variety
☐ Flexibility
☐ Style
☐ Durability
☐ Maintenance

DETERMINE POSSIBLE ARRANGEMENTS

☐ Functional groupings
☐ Tailored arrangements
☐ Flexible arrangements

## 4. SPACE ANALYSIS

DOCUMENT EXISTING OR PROPOSED SPACE

☐ Measure and draw plan, sections, and interior elevations

ANALYZE SPACE

☐ Form, scale, and proportion of the space
☐ Doorway locations, points of access, and the circulation paths they suggest
☐ Windows, and the light, views, and ventilation they afford
☐ Wall, floor, and ceiling materials
☐ Significant architectural details

☐ Location of electrical and mechanical fixtures and outlets

☐ What modifications would be feasible, if necessary?

☐ . . . . . . . . . . . . . . . . . . . . . . . . . . . . .
☐ . . . . . . . . . . . . . . . . . . . . . . . . . . . . .

## 5. DIMENSIONAL REQUIREMENTS

DETERMINE REQUIRED DIMENSIONS FOR SPACE AND FURNITURE GROUPINGS

☐ Area required for each functional grouping of furniture

☐ Space required for:
☐ Access to and movement within and between activity areas
☐ Number of people served
☐ Appropriate social distances and interaction

DETERMINE FIT BETWEEN ACTIVITY & DIMENSIONS OF SPACE

☐ Study ways activity groupings can be accommodated within the shape and proportion of the floor area and the vertical dimension of the space.

# 6. DESIRED QUALITIES

DETERMINE QUALITIES APPROPRIATE TO SPATIAL CONTEXT AND COMPATIBLE WITH CLIENT'S OR USERS' NEEDS OR WISHES

☐ Feeling, mood, or atmosphere
☐ Image and style

☐ Degree of spatial enclosure
☐ Comfort and security

☐ Quality of light
☐ Focus and orientation of space
☐ Color and tone

☐ Acoustical environment
☐ Thermal environment

☐ Flexibility

# 7. DESIRED RELATIONSHIPS

DESIRED RELATIONSHIPS BETWEEN:

☐ Related activity areas
☐ Activity areas and space for movement
☐ Room and adjacent spaces
☐ Room and the outside

DESIRED ZONING OF ACTIVITIES

☐ Organization of activities into groups or sets according to compatibility and use

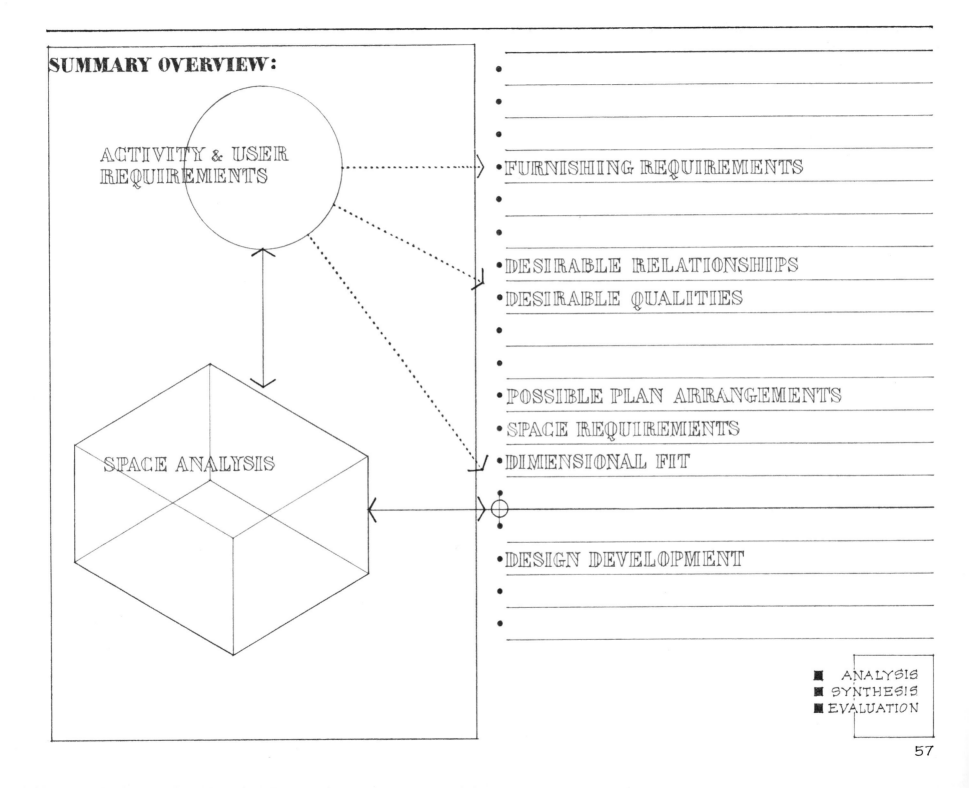

**SUMMARY OVERVIEW:**

ACTIVITY & USER
REQUIREMENTS

SPACE ANALYSIS

- •
- •
- •
- •FURNISHING REQUIREMENTS
- •
- •
- •DESIRABLE RELATIONSHIPS
- •DESIRABLE QUALITIES
- •
- •
- •POSSIBLE PLAN ARRANGEMENTS
- •SPACE REQUIREMENTS
- •DIMENSIONAL FIT
- •
- •DESIGN DEVELOPMENT
- •
- •

■ ANALYSIS
■ SYNTHESIS
■ EVALUATION

# HUMAN FACTORS

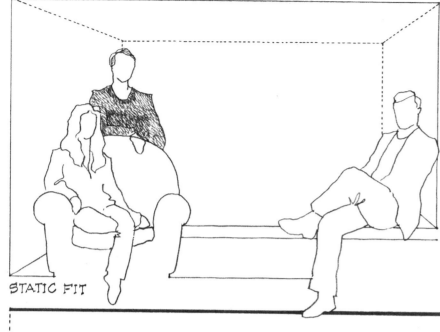

STATIC FIT

The interior spaces of buildings are designed as places for human movement, activity, and repose. There should be, therefore, a fit between the form and dimensions of interior space and our own body dimensions. This fit can be a static one as when we sit in a chair, lean against a railing, or nestle within an alcove space.

There can also be a dynamic fit as when we enter a building's foyer, walk up a stairway, or move through the rooms and halls of a building.

A third type of fit is how a space accommodates our need to maintain appropriate social distances and to have control over our personal space.

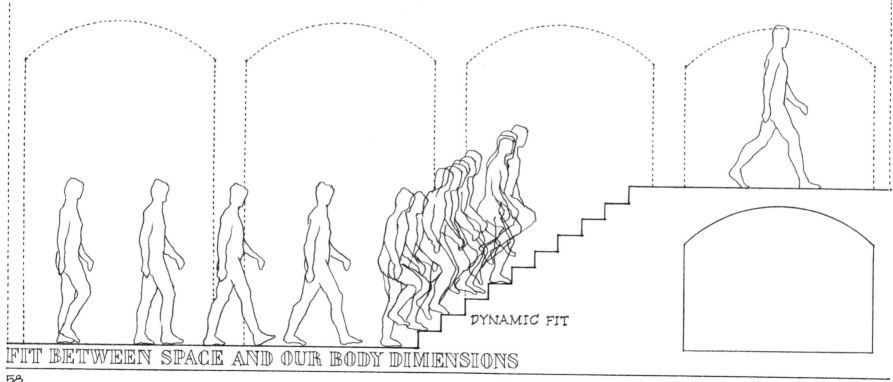

DYNAMIC FIT

FIT BETWEEN SPACE AND OUR BODY DIMENSIONS

In addition to these physical and psychological dimensions, space also has tactile, auditory, olfactory, and thermal characteristics that influence how we feel and what we do within it.

TACTILE

AUDITORY

OLFACTORY

THERMAL

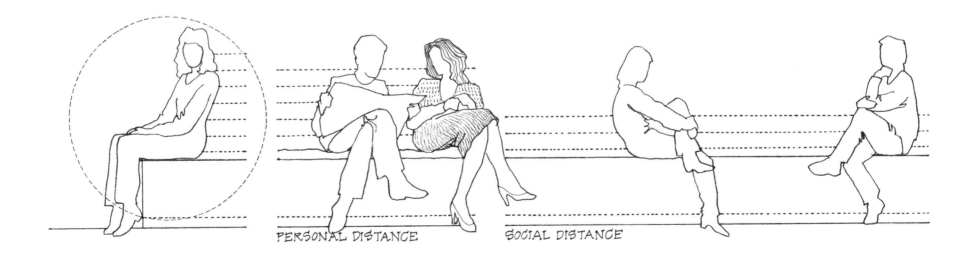

PERSONAL DISTANCE

SOCIAL DISTANCE

PERSONAL SPACE

# HUMAN DIMENSIONS

Our body dimensions, and the way we move through and perceive space, are prime determinants of architectural and interior design. In the following section, basic human dimensions are illustrated for standing, walking, sitting, ascending or descending stairs, lying down, reaching, and viewing. Dimensional guidelines are also given for group activities, such as dining or conversing.

It should be noted there is a difference between the structural dimensions of our bodies and those dimensional requirements which result from how we reach for something on a shelf, sit down at a table, walk down a set of stairs, or interact with other people. These are functional dimensions and will vary according to the nature of the activity engaged in and the social situation.

STRUCTURAL        VS.        FUNCTIONAL DIMENSIONS

Caution should always be exercised whenever you use any set of dimensional tables or illustrations such as these. These are based on typical or average measurements which may have to be modified to satisfy specific user needs. Variations from the norm will always exist due to the differences between men and women, among various age and racial groups, even from one individual to the next.

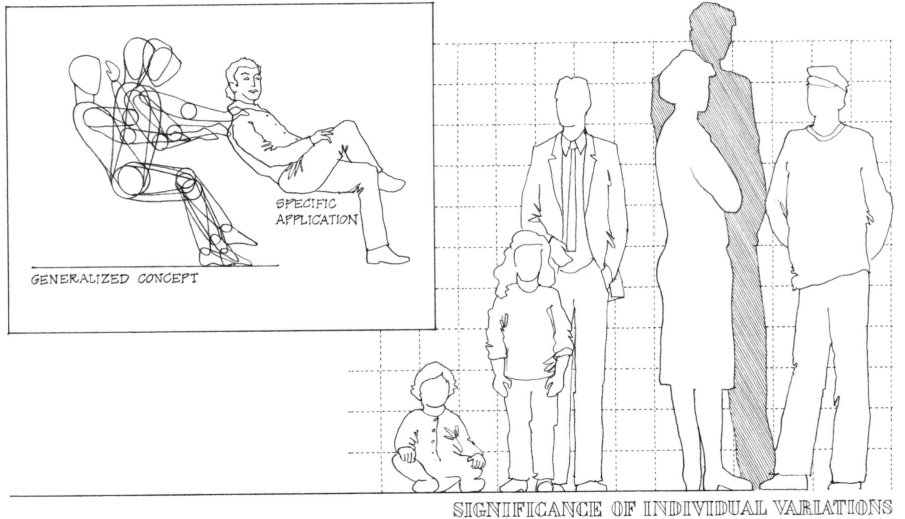

GENERALIZED CONCEPT

SPECIFIC APPLICATION

SIGNIFICANCE OF INDIVIDUAL VARIATIONS

# BASIC HUMAN DIMENSIONS

NOTE ON DIMENSIONS:
Unless otherwise specified, dimensions are in inches, with their metric equivalents in millimeters (shown in parentheses).

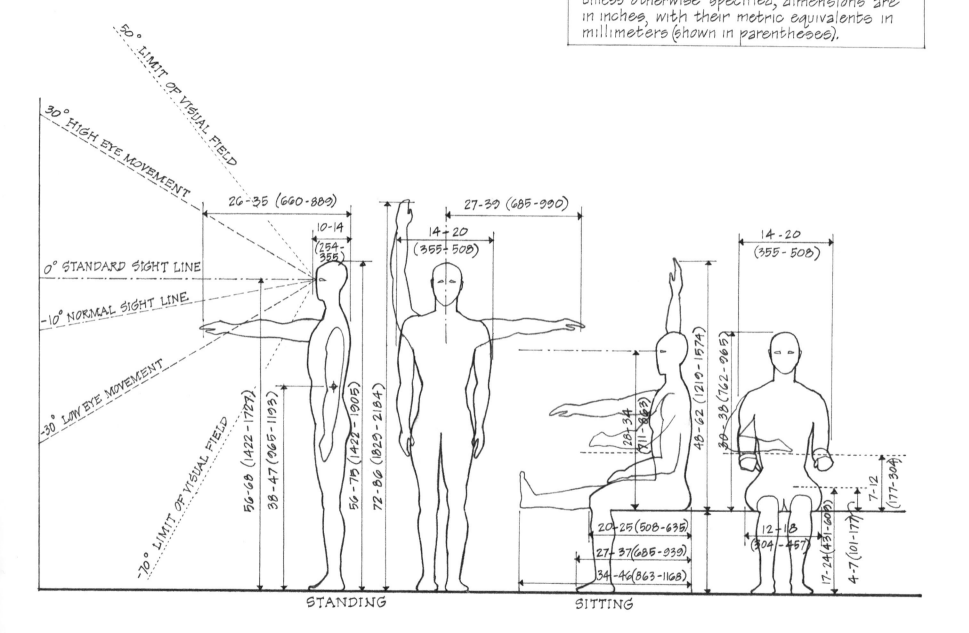

50° LIMIT OF VISUAL FIELD

30° HIGH EYE MOVEMENT

0° STANDARD SIGHT LINE

-10° NORMAL SIGHT LINE

-30° LOW EYE MOVEMENT

-70° LIMIT OF VISUAL FIELD

26-35 (660-889)

10-14 (254-355)

27-39 (685-990)

14-20 (355-508)

14-20 (355-508)

48-62 (1219-1574)

30-38 (762-965)

56-68 (1422-1727)

38-47 (965-1193)

56-75 (1422-1905)

72-86 (1829-2184)

28-34 (711-863)

20-25 (508-635)

27-37 (685-939)

34-46 (863-1168)

12-18 (304-457)

17-24 (431-606)

4-7 (101-177)

7-12 (177-304)

STANDING

SITTING

# DISTANCE ZONES

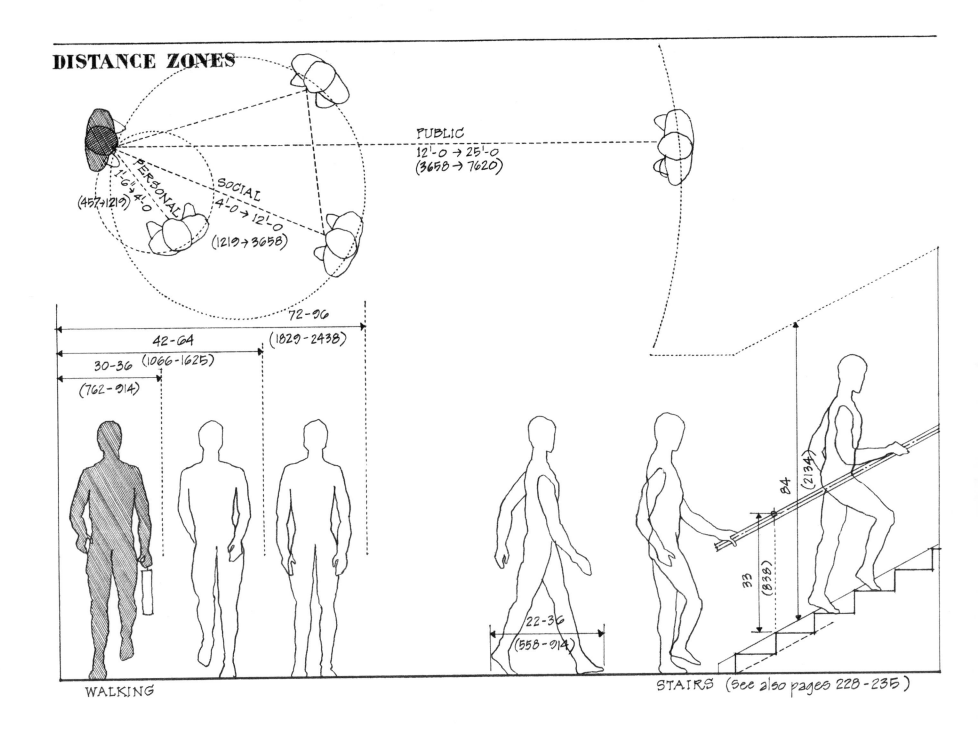

PUBLIC
12'-0 → 25'-0
(3658 → 7620)

PERSONAL
1'-6" → 4'-0
(457 → 1219)

SOCIAL
4'-0 → 12'-0
(1219 → 3658)

72-96
(1829-2438)

42-64
(1066-1625)

30-36
(762-914)

WALKING

22-36
(558-914)

84
(2134)

33
(838)

STAIRS (see also pages 228-235)

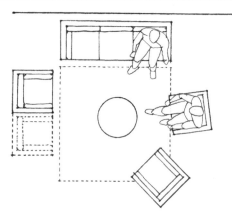

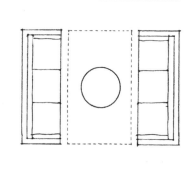

PLAN VIEW

26-28
(660-711)

24-30
(600-762)

3 (76)

PLAN ARRANGEMENTS

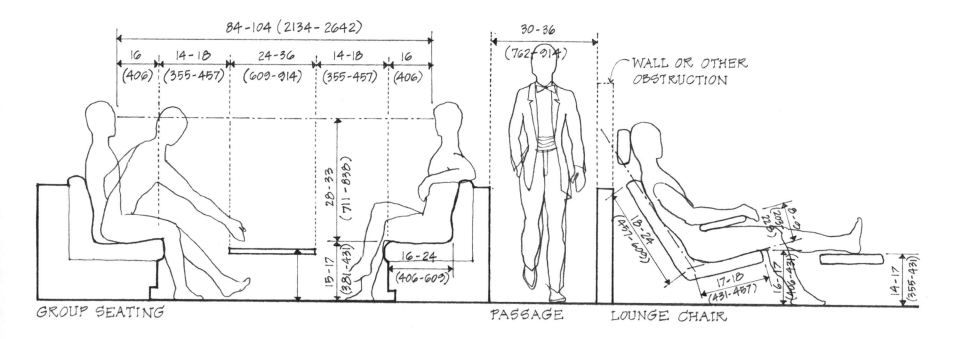

84-104 (2134-2642)

16
(406)

14-18
(355-457)

24-36
(609-914)

14-18
(355-457)

16
(406)

28-33
(711-838)

15-17
(381-431)

16-24
(406-609)

GROUP SEATING

30-36
(762-914)

WALL OR OTHER
OBSTRUCTION

PASSAGE

18-24
(457-609)

17-18
(431-457)

16-17
(406-431)

2-8
(203)

14-17
(355-431)

LOUNGE CHAIR

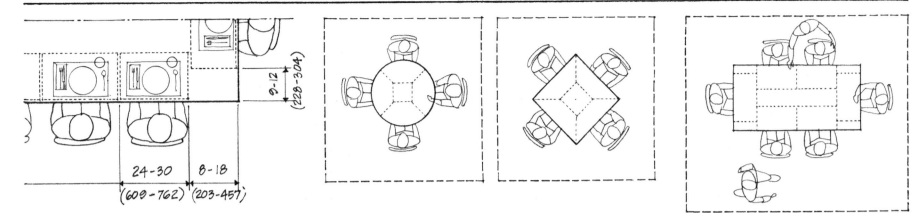

PLAN VIEW

24-30
(609-762)

8-18
(203-457)

9-12

(228-304)

PLAN ARRANGEMENTS

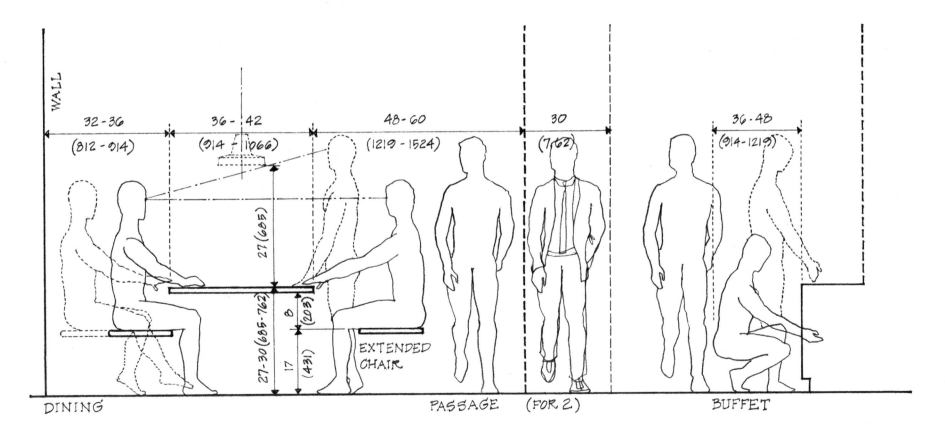

WALL

32-36
(812-914)

36-42
(914-1066)

48-60
(1219-1524)

30
(762)

36-48
(914-1219)

27 (685)

8
(203)

27-30 (685-762)

17
(431)

EXTENDED
CHAIR

DINING

PASSAGE   (FOR 2)

BUFFET

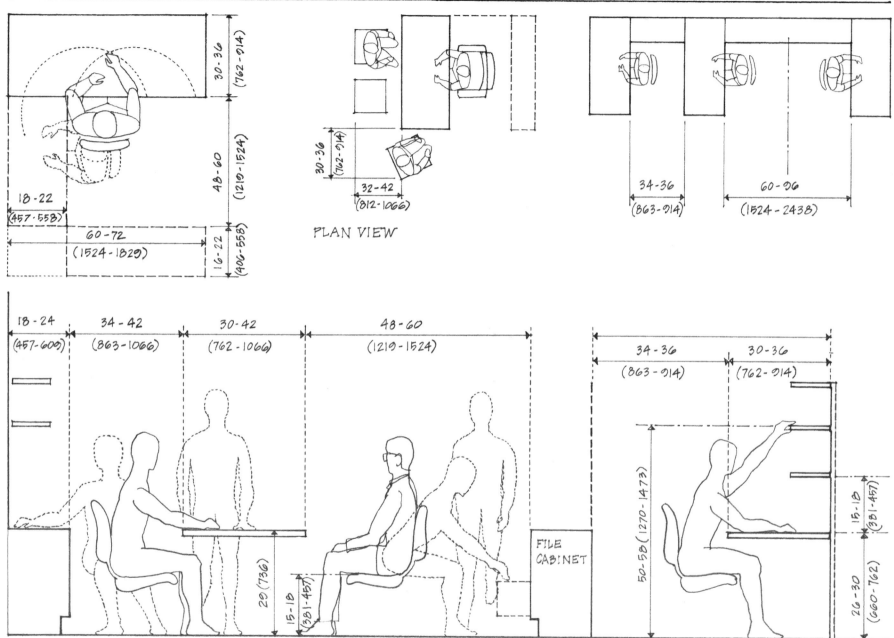

PLAN VIEW

18-22
(457-558)

60-72
(1524-1829)

30-36
(762-914)

48-60
(1219-1524)

16-22
(406-558)

30-36
(762-914)

32-42
(812-1066)

34-36
(863-914)

60-96
(1524-2438)

WORK STATIONS

18-24
(457-609)

34-42
(863-1066)

30-42
(762-1066)

48-60
(1219-1524)

29 (736)

15-18
(381-457)

FILE CABINET

34-36
(863-914)

30-36
(762-914)

50-58 (1270-1473)

15-18
(381-457)

26-30
(660-762)

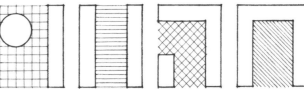

COUNTERTOP CONFIGURATIONS

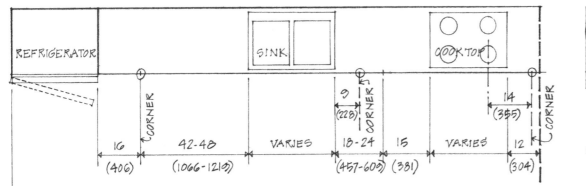

REFRIGERATOR

SINK

COOKTOP

CORNER

9
(228)

CORNER

14
(355)

CORNER

16
(406)

42-48
(1066-1219)

VARIES

18-24
(457-609)

15
(381)

VARIES

12
(304)

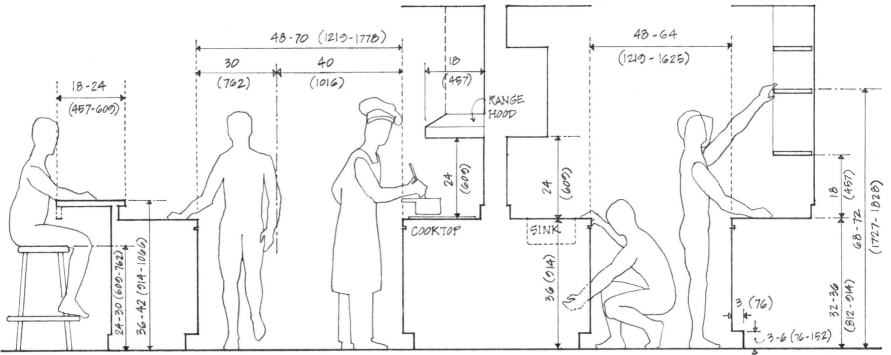

18-24
(457-609)

48-70 (1219-1778)

30
(762)

40
(1016)

18
(457)

RANGE
HOOD

48-64
(1219-1625)

24
(609)

24
(609)

COOKTOP

SINK

36 (914)

24-30 (609-762)

36-42 (914-1066)

18
(457)

68-72
(1727-1828)

32-36
(812-914)

3 (76)

3-6 (76-152)

COOKING

67

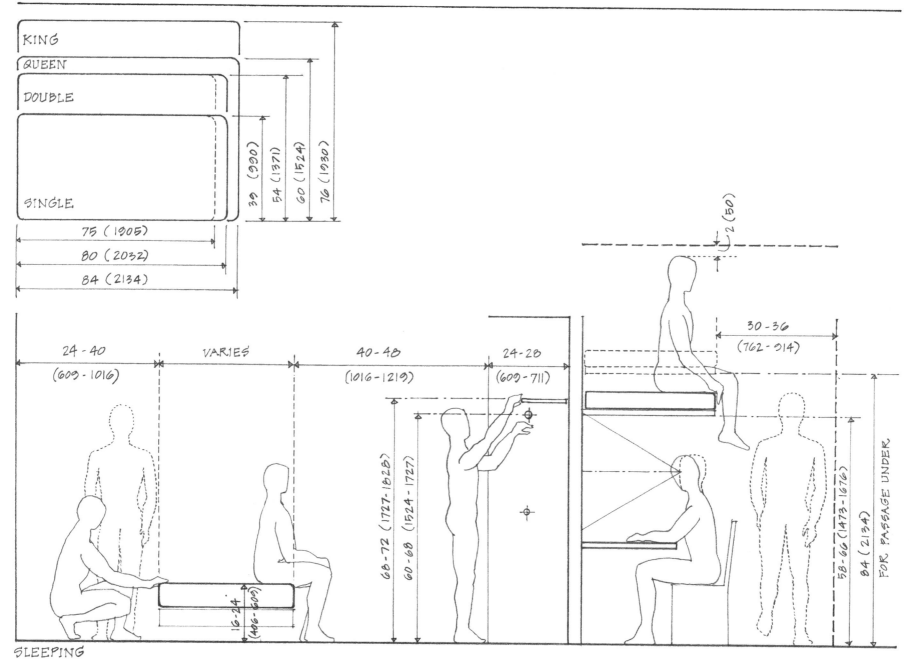

KING

QUEEN

DOUBLE

SINGLE

39 (990)
54 (1371)
60 (1524)
76 (1930)

75 (1905)
80 (2032)
84 (2134)

2 (50)

24-40
(609-1016)

VARIES

40-48
(1016-1219)

24-28
(609-711)

30-36
(762-914)

68-72 (1727-1828)

60-68 (1524-1727)

16-24
(406-609)

58-66 (1473-1676)

84 (2134) FOR PASSAGE UNDER

SLEEPING

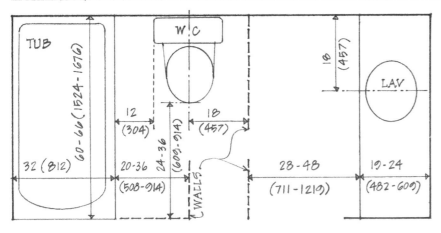

TUB

60-66 (1524-1676)

32 (812)

12 (304)

20-36 (508-914)

24-36 (609-914)

W.C

18 (457)

18 (457)

← WALLS

LAV

28-48 (711-1219)

19-24 (482-609)

PLAN VIEW

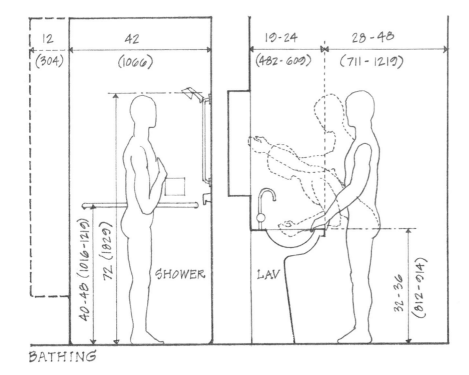

12 (304)

42 (1066)

19-24 (482-609)

28-48 (711-1219)

40-48 (1016-1219)

72 (1829)

SHOWER

LAV

32-36 (812-914)

BATHING

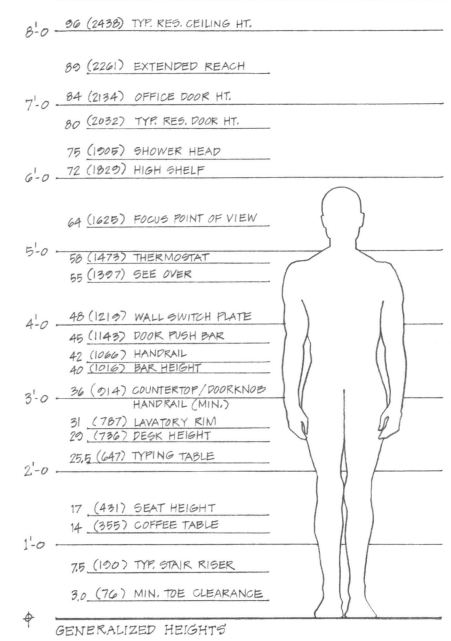

| | | |
|---|---|---|
| 8'-0 | 96 (2438) | TYP. RES. CEILING HT. |
| | 89 (2261) | EXTENDED REACH |
| 7'-0 | 84 (2134) | OFFICE DOOR HT. |
| | 80 (2032) | TYP. RES. DOOR HT. |
| | 75 (1905) | SHOWER HEAD |
| 6'-0 | 72 (1829) | HIGH SHELF |
| | 64 (1625) | FOCUS POINT OF VIEW |
| 5'-0 | 58 (1473) | THERMOSTAT |
| | 55 (1397) | SEE OVER |
| 4'-0 | 48 (1219) | WALL SWITCH PLATE |
| | 45 (1143) | DOOR PUSH BAR |
| | 42 (1066) | HANDRAIL |
| | 40 (1016) | BAR HEIGHT |
| 3'-0 | 36 (914) | COUNTERTOP / DOORKNOB HANDRAIL (MIN.) |
| | 31 (787) | LAVATORY RIM |
| | 29 (736) | DESK HEIGHT |
| | 25.5 (647) | TYPING TABLE |
| 2'-0 | | |
| | 17 (431) | SEAT HEIGHT |
| | 14 (355) | COFFEE TABLE |
| 1'-0 | | |
| | 7.5 (190) | TYP. STAIR RISER |
| | 3.0 (76) | MIN. TOE CLEARANCE |

GENERALIZED HEIGHTS

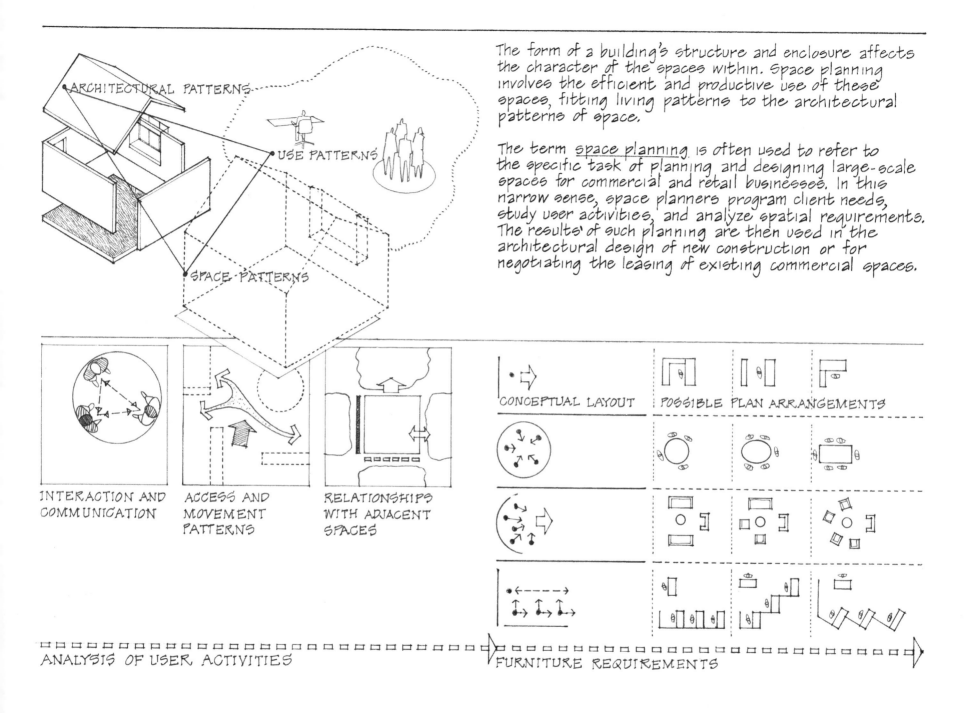

The form of a building's structure and enclosure affects the character of the spaces within. Space planning involves the efficient and productive use of these spaces, fitting living patterns to the architectural patterns of space.

The term space planning is often used to refer to the specific task of planning and designing large-scale spaces for commercial and retail businesses. In this narrow sense, space planners program client needs, study user activities, and analyze spatial requirements. The results of such planning are then used in the architectural design of new construction or for negotiating the leasing of existing commercial spaces.

ARCHITECTURAL PATTERNS

USE PATTERNS

SPACE PATTERNS

INTERACTION AND COMMUNICATION

ACCESS AND MOVEMENT PATTERNS

RELATIONSHIPS WITH ADJACENT SPACES

CONCEPTUAL LAYOUT   POSSIBLE PLAN ARRANGEMENTS

ANALYSIS OF USER ACTIVITIES

FURNITURE REQUIREMENTS

In a broader sense, all interior designers are involved in the planning and layout of interior spaces, whether small or large, residential or commercial. Once a design program has been outlined and developed from an analysis of the client's or users' needs, the design task is to properly allocate the available or desired interior spaces for the various required activities.

Area requirements can be estimated from an analysis of the number of people served, the furnishings and equipment they require, and the nature of the activity that will go on in each space. These area requirements can then be translated into rough blocks of space, and related to each other and to the architectural context in a functional and aesthetic manner.

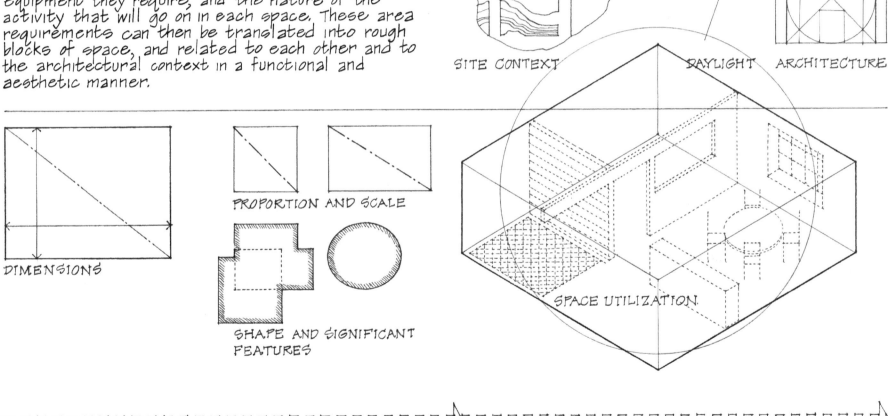

SITE CONTEXT  DAYLIGHT ARCHITECTURE

DIMENSIONS

PROPORTION AND SCALE

SHAPE AND SIGNIFICANT FEATURES

SPACE UTILIZATION

ANALYSIS OF EXISTING OR PROPOSED SPACE  INTEGRATION

# ACTIVITY RELATIONSHIPS

Whether collaborating on the design of a new building or planning the remodeling of an existing structure, the interior designer strives for a proper fit between the demands of activities and the architectural nature of the spaces that house them.

Certain activities may need to be closely related or adjacent to each other, while others may be more distant or isolated for privacy. Some activities may require easy accessibility, while others may need controlled entries and exits. Some activities may require daylighting or natural ventilation, while others may not need to be located near exterior windows. Some activities may have specific spatial requirements, while others may be more flexible or be able to share a common space.

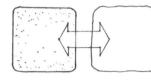

WHICH ACTIVITIES SHOULD BE CLOSELY RELATED?

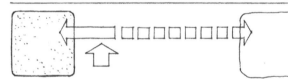

WHICH ACTIVITIES CAN BE ISOLATED BY ENCLOSURE OR DISTANCE?

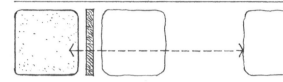

WHAT DEGREE OF ACCESSIBILITY IS REQUIRED?

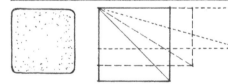

ARE THERE SPECIFIC PROPORTIONAL REQUIREMENTS?

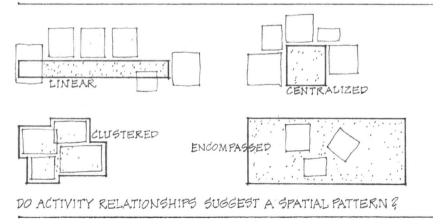

LINEAR

CENTRALIZED

CLUSTERED

ENCOMPASSED

DO ACTIVITY RELATIONSHIPS SUGGEST A SPATIAL PATTERN?

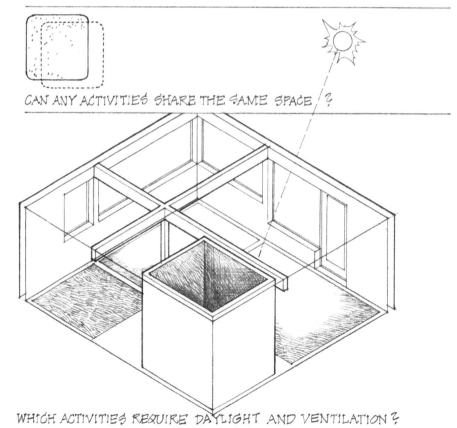

CAN ANY ACTIVITIES SHARE THE SAME SPACE?

WHICH ACTIVITIES REQUIRE DAYLIGHT AND VENTILATION?

As interior areas are organized on the basis of these considerations, along with considerations of the building site and adjacent structures, the shape and form of a new building will begin to develop.

When dealing with an existing structure, the available spaces usually provide clues as to how they can best be utilized. The entries into a space may define a pattern of movement that divides the area into certain zones. Some zones may be more readily accessible than others. Some may be clearly large enough to accommodate group activities, while others are not. Some may have access to exterior windows or skylights for daylighting or ventilation; others may be internalized. Some may include a natural center of interest, such as a view window or a fireplace.

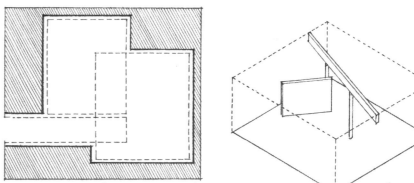

DIVISION SUGGESTED BY ROOM SHAPE OR BY ARCHITECTURE ?

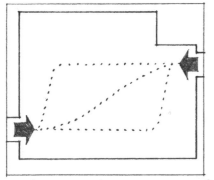

POSSIBLE PATHS OF MOVEMENT?

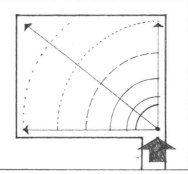

ACCESSIBILITY OF ZONES ?

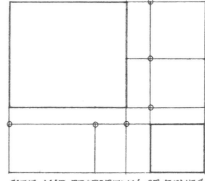

SIZE AND PROPORTION OF ZONES ?

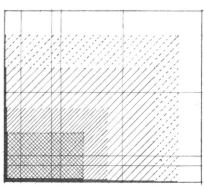

DAYLIGHT AVAILABLE ?

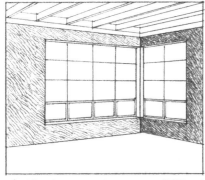

IS THERE AN EXTERNAL OUTLOOK?

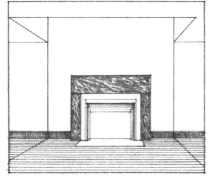

AN INTERNAL FOCUS ?

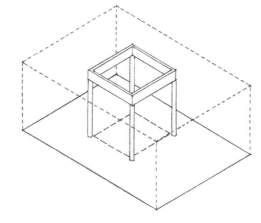

# PLAN ARRANGEMENTS

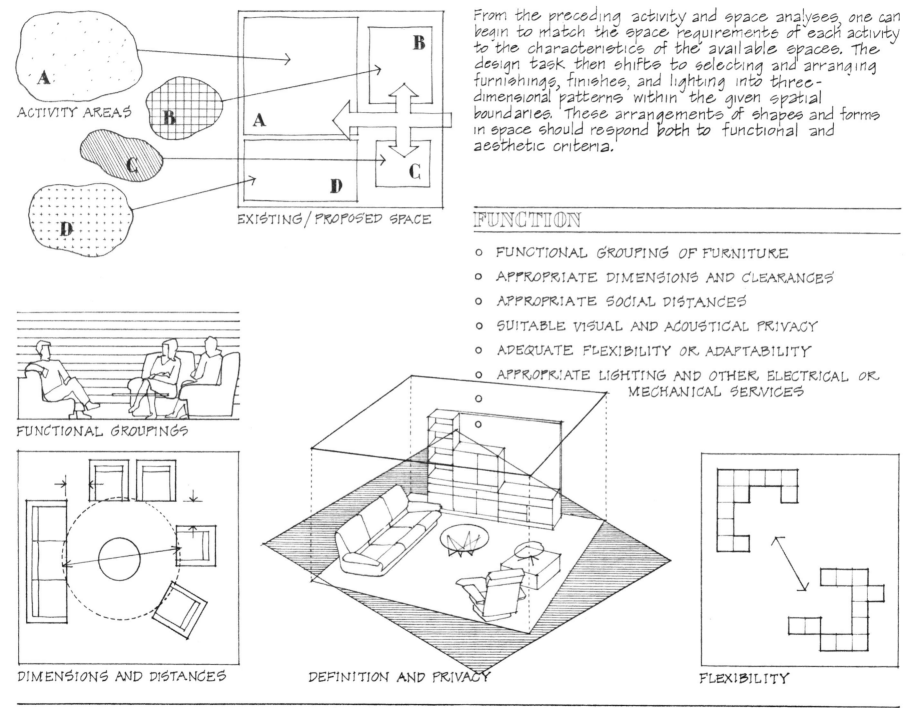

ACTIVITY AREAS

EXISTING/PROPOSED SPACE

From the preceding activity and space analyses, one can begin to match the space requirements of each activity to the characteristics of the available spaces. The design task then shifts to selecting and arranging furnishings, finishes, and lighting into three-dimensional patterns within the given spatial boundaries. These arrangements of shapes and forms in space should respond both to functional and aesthetic criteria.

## FUNCTION

o FUNCTIONAL GROUPING OF FURNITURE

o APPROPRIATE DIMENSIONS AND CLEARANCES

o APPROPRIATE SOCIAL DISTANCES

o SUITABLE VISUAL AND ACOUSTICAL PRIVACY

o ADEQUATE FLEXIBILITY OR ADAPTABILITY

o APPROPRIATE LIGHTING AND OTHER ELECTRICAL OR MECHANICAL SERVICES

FUNCTIONAL GROUPINGS

DIMENSIONS AND DISTANCES

DEFINITION AND PRIVACY

FLEXIBILITY

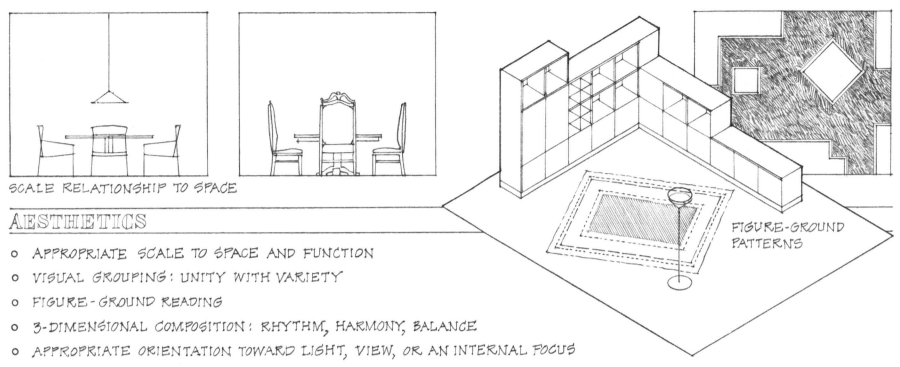

SCALE RELATIONSHIP TO SPACE

FIGURE-GROUND PATTERNS

# AESTHETICS

- o APPROPRIATE SCALE TO SPACE AND FUNCTION
- o VISUAL GROUPING: UNITY WITH VARIETY
- o FIGURE-GROUND READING
- o 3-DIMENSIONAL COMPOSITION: RHYTHM, HARMONY, BALANCE
- o APPROPRIATE ORIENTATION TOWARD LIGHT, VIEW, OR AN INTERNAL FOCUS
- o SHAPE, COLOR, TEXTURE, AND PATTERN
- o
- o

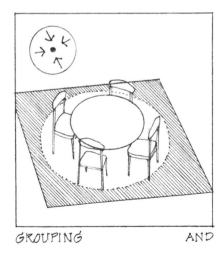

GROUPING          AND

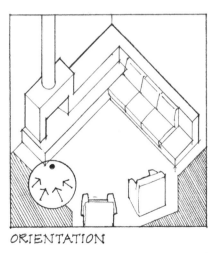

ORIENTATION

OBJECTS IN SPACE          OR

MERGING WITH SPACE

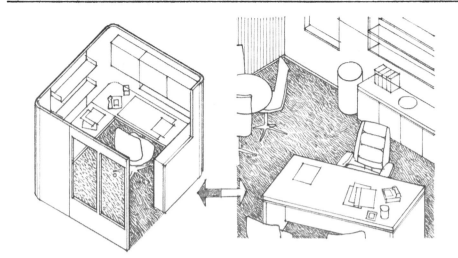

Plan arrangements can be generally classified into two broad categories, according to how each uses the available space. The first exhibits a tight fit between the nature of the activity and the arrangement of furniture and equipment. This may be particularly appropriate when space is at a premium, or when functional efficiency is important. Because a tight fit arrangement may not be readily adaptable to other uses, it is important that it be laid out with great care for its intended use.

## TIGHT FIT

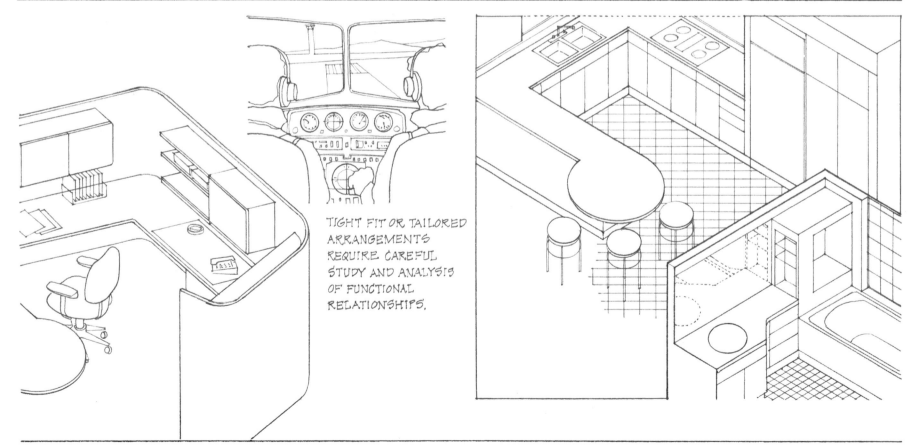

TIGHT FIT OR TAILORED ARRANGEMENTS REQUIRE CAREFUL STUDY AND ANALYSIS OF FUNCTIONAL RELATIONSHIPS.

A tight fit arrangement usually employs modular or unit furniture components which can be combined in a number of ways to form integrated, often multifunctional, structures. Such structures utilize space efficiently and leave a maximum amount of floor area around them. A tailored arrangement of modular furniture can also be used to define a space within a larger volume for greater privacy or intimacy.

Carried to an extreme, a tight fit arrangement can be built in place and become a permanent extension of a room's architecture. Like modular and unit arrangements, built-in furniture utilizes space efficiently, conveys an orderly, unified appearance, and can help mitigate visual clutter in a space.

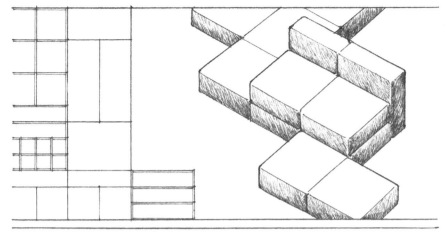

MODULAR FURNISHINGS ARE FLEXIBLE AND SPACE-EFFICIENT

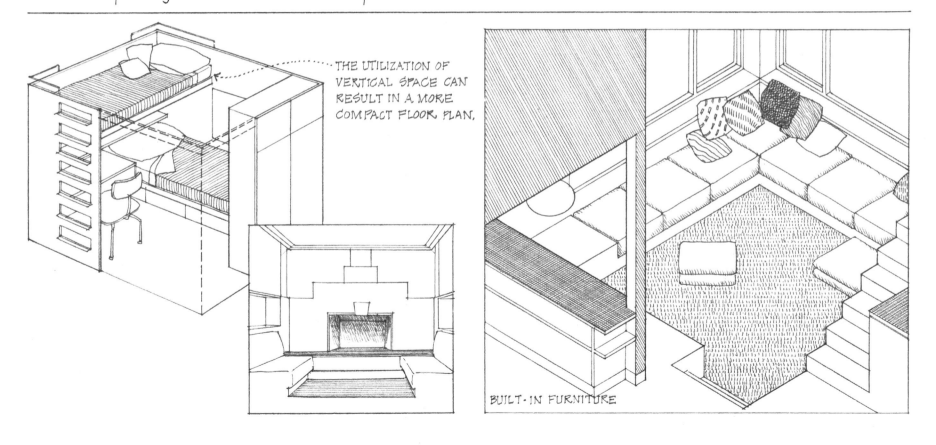

THE UTILIZATION OF VERTICAL SPACE CAN RESULT IN A MORE COMPACT FLOOR PLAN.

BUILT-IN FURNITURE

A second, more common type of plan arrangement exhibits a looser fit between function and space. Loose fit arrangements are desirable for the flexibility and diversity they afford.

Most rooms with a loose fit arrangement can accommodate a variety of uses, especially if the furniture used can be easily moved and rearranged. This inherent flexibility in adapting to changes in use or circumstance makes a loose fit arrangement the more common method for laying out furniture in a space. It also offers the opportunity for a greater mix of furniture types, sizes, and styles to be selected over time to suit almost any design situation.

LOOSE FIT

TIGHT FIT

## LOOSE FIT

LOOSE FIT ARRANGEMENTS REQUIRE THOUGHTFUL COMPOSITION OF THREE-DIMENSIONAL FORMS IN SPACE.

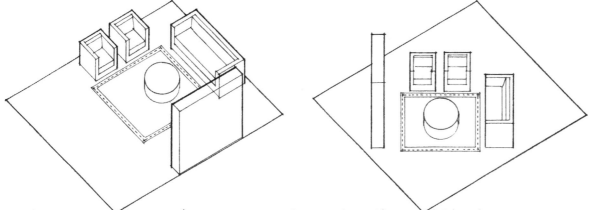

LOOSE FIT ARRANGEMENTS CAN REFLECT CHANGES IN USE OR CIRCUMSTANCE

• THIS CAN REPRESENT A SQUARE FOOT OR
  OTHER CONVENIENT UNIT OF MEASUREMENT

• DRAW OUTLINE OF SPACE

• INDICATE SIZES & LOCATIONS OF WINDOWS & DOORWAYS

• DRAW MAJOR ELEMENTS, THEN SECONDARY ONES

• SKETCHING PLAN VIEWS OF PEOPLE
  HELPS IN ESTABLISHING SCALE

PLAN DRAWINGS ARE VIEWS LOOKING DOWN INTO AN INTERIOR SPACE AFTER A HORIZONTAL CUT IS MADE.

Drawings are valuable aids in visualizing design ideas, exploring possibilities, and communicating proposals to others. These grids represent the major types of drawings used by designers. They can be used as base drawings by laying tracing paper over them and sketching the possibilities you envision. Analyze your ideas, synthesize the good ones, and evaluate the results.

- DRAW PROFILES OF FLOOR & CEILING PLANES
- DRAW ELEVATIONS OF INTERIOR ELEMENTS
- DRAW PEOPLE TO SCALE

SECTION DRAWINGS REPRESENT WHAT IS SEEN AFTER A VERTICAL CUT IS MADE THROUGH AN INTERIOR SPACE.

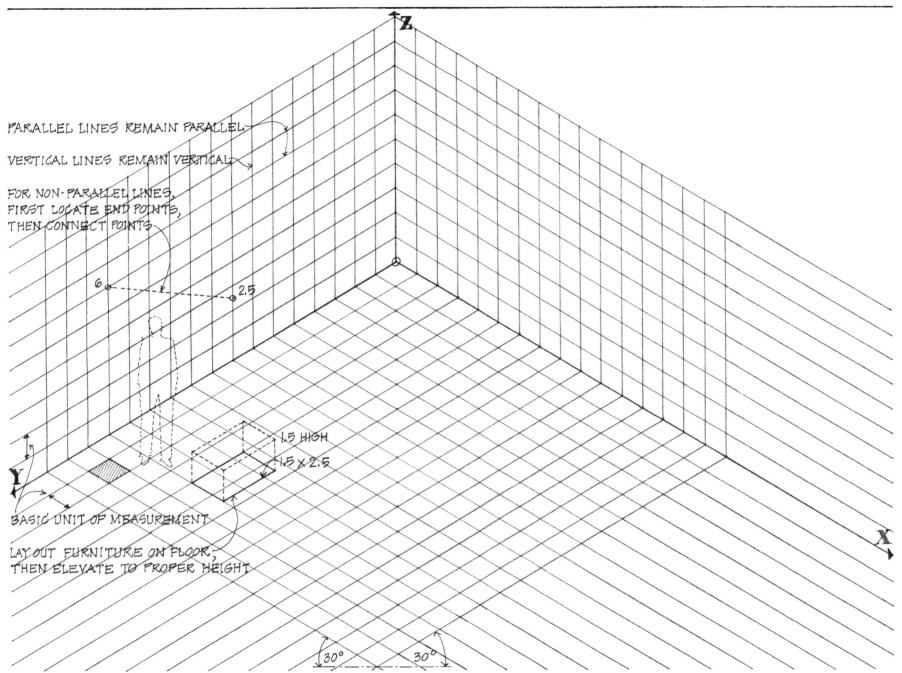

PARALLEL LINES REMAIN PARALLEL

VERTICAL LINES REMAIN VERTICAL

FOR NON-PARALLEL LINES,
FIRST LOCATE END POINTS,
THEN CONNECT POINTS

6          2.5

Z

1.5 HIGH

1.5 X 2.5

Y

BASIC UNIT OF MEASUREMENT

LAYOUT FURNITURE ON FLOOR,
THEN ELEVATE TO PROPER HEIGHT

X

30°      30°

ISOMETRIC DRAWINGS ARE 3-DIMENSIONAL VIEWS LOOKING DOWNWARD INTO A SPACE.

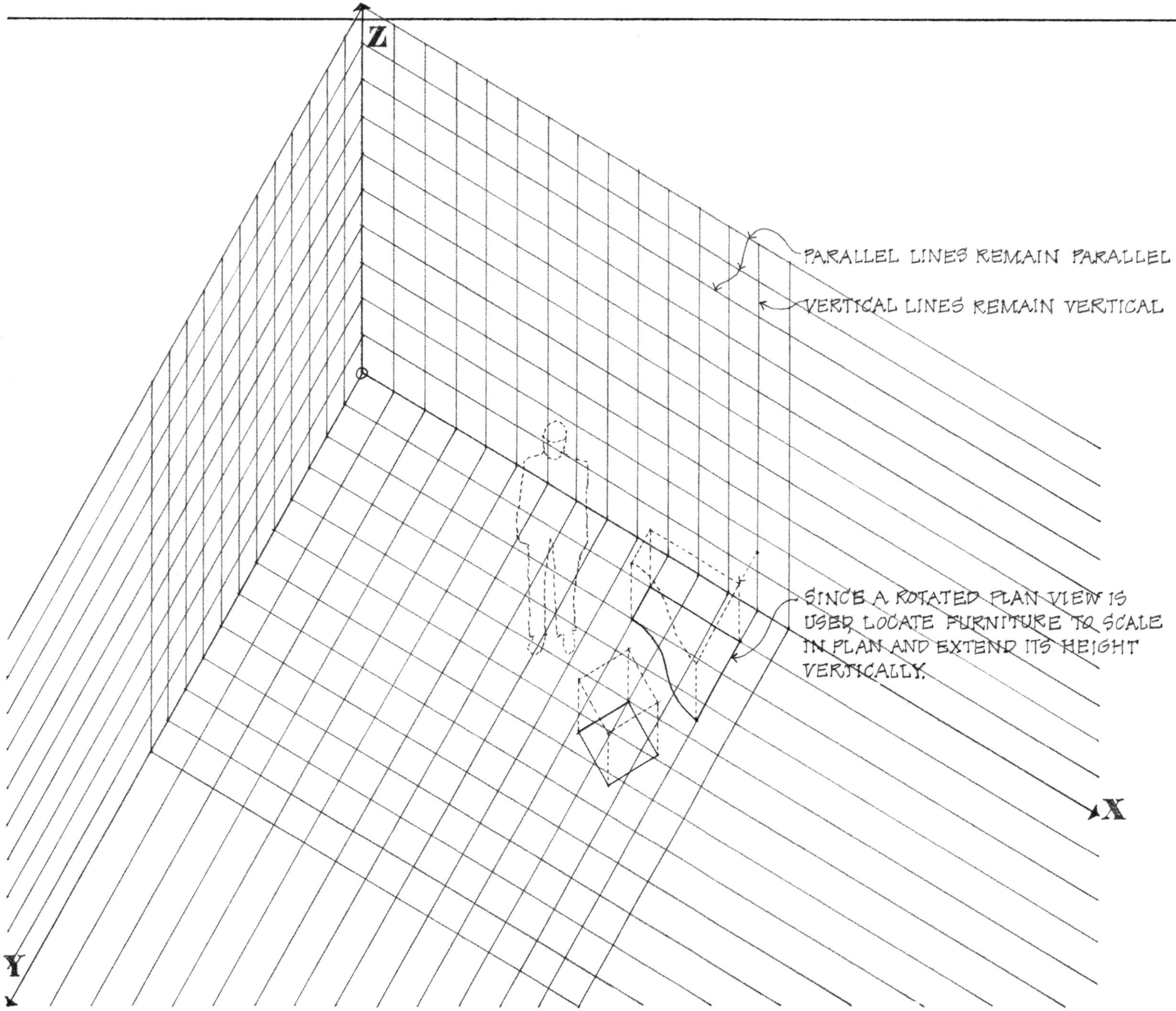

Z

PARALLEL LINES REMAIN PARALLEL

VERTICAL LINES REMAIN VERTICAL

SINCE A ROTATED PLAN VIEW IS
USED LOCATE FURNITURE TO SCALE
IN PLAN AND EXTEND ITS HEIGHT
VERTICALLY.

X

Y

PLAN OBLIQUE DRAWINGS ARE ALSO 3-DIMENSIONAL VIEWS, BUT FROM A HIGHER VANTAGE POINT.

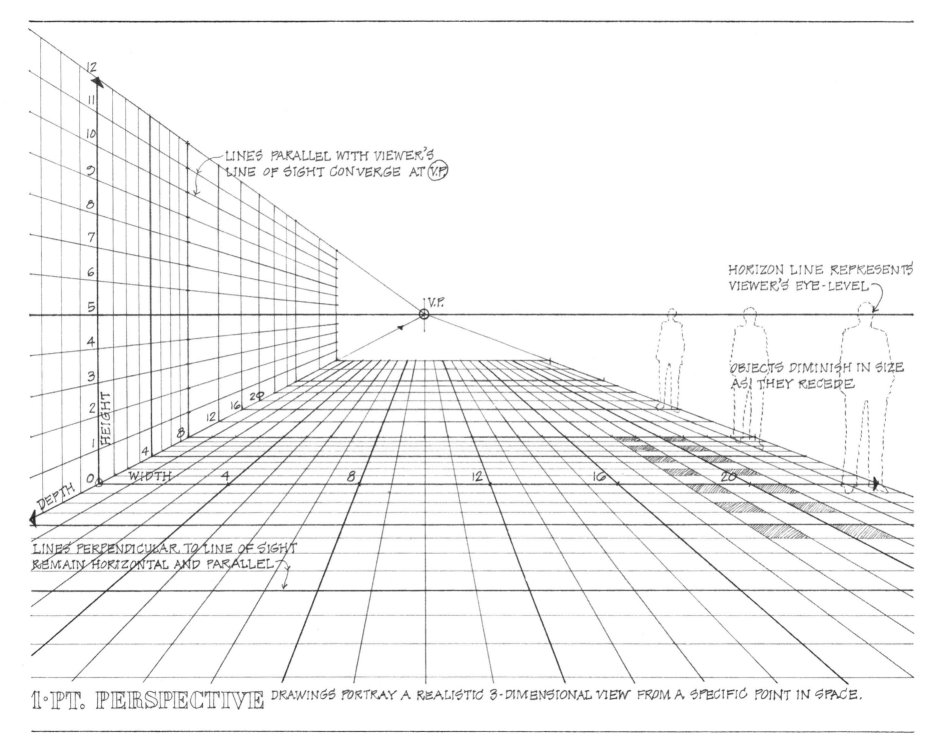

LINES PARALLEL WITH VIEWER'S LINE OF SIGHT CONVERGE AT (V.P.)

HORIZON LINE REPRESENTS VIEWER'S EYE-LEVEL

V.P.

OBJECTS DIMINISH IN SIZE AS THEY RECEDE

HEIGHT

DEPTH

WIDTH

LINES PERPENDICULAR TO LINE OF SIGHT REMAIN HORIZONTAL AND PARALLEL

1·PT. PERSPECTIVE DRAWINGS PORTRAY A REALISTIC 3-DIMENSIONAL VIEW FROM A SPECIFIC POINT IN SPACE.

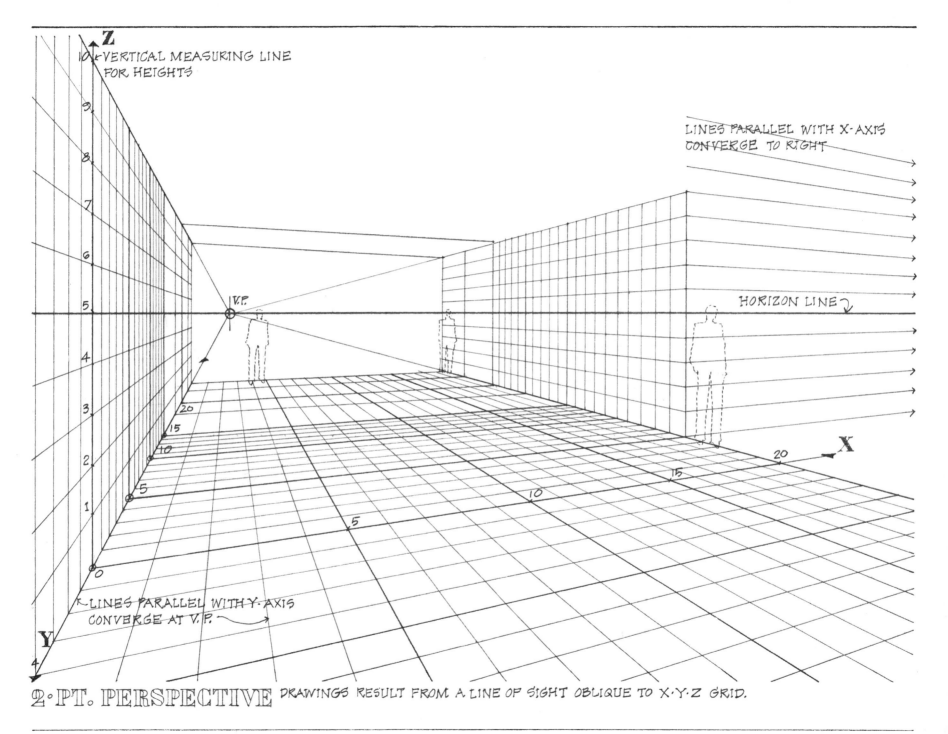

**Z** ← VERTICAL MEASURING LINE FOR HEIGHTS

LINES PARALLEL WITH X·AXIS CONVERGE TO RIGHT

V.P.

HORIZON LINE

**X**

← LINES PARALLEL WITH Y·AXIS CONVERGE AT V.P. →

**Y**

2·PT. PERSPECTIVE DRAWINGS RESULT FROM A LINE OF SIGHT OBLIQUE TO X·Y·Z GRID.

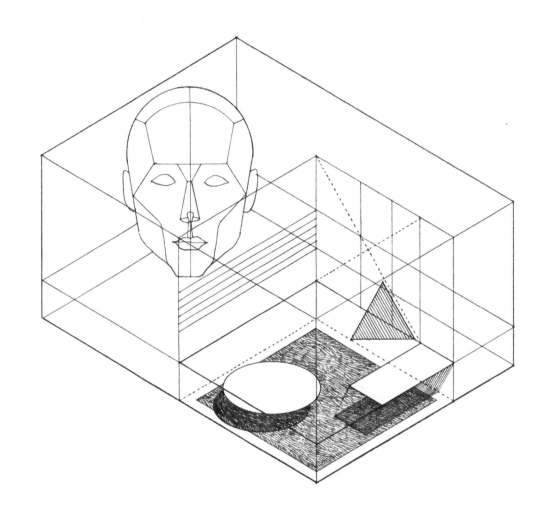

# A DESIGN
# VOCABULARY

# VISUAL PERCEPTION

Our perception of the visual shape, size, color, and texture of things is affected by the optical environment in which we see them and the relationships we can discern between them and their visual setting. If our visual field were undifferentiated we would see nothingness. As a perceptible change in tonal value, color, and texture occurred, however, we would begin to discern an object or figure as differentiated from its background. In order to read the lines, shapes, and forms of objects in our field of vision, therefore, we must first perceive contrast between them and their background.

Those elements which appear to stand out from or in front of their background are called figures. In addition to tonal value contrast, what distinguish a figure from its background are its shape and size relative to that of its field. While a figure shares a common border with its background, it has a more distinct and recognizable shape which makes it appear as an object. Figures are sometimes referred to as positive elements - having a positive shape - while backgrounds are described as negative or neutral elements - lacking a clear or discernible shape.

VISUAL CONTRAST

FIGURE-GROUND RELATIONSHIPS

Figures are most discernible when surrounded by a generous amount of space or background. When the size of a figure is such that it crowds its background, the background can develop its own distinct shape and interact with the shape of the figure. At times, an ambiguous figure-ground relationship can occur wherein elements in a composition can be seen alternately, but not simultaneously, as both figure and ground.

Our visual world is, in reality, a composite image constructed from a continuous array of figure-ground relationships. In interior design, these relationships can be seen to exist at several scales, depending on one's point of view.

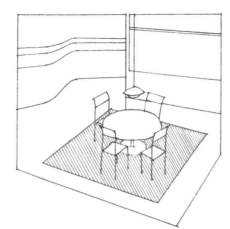

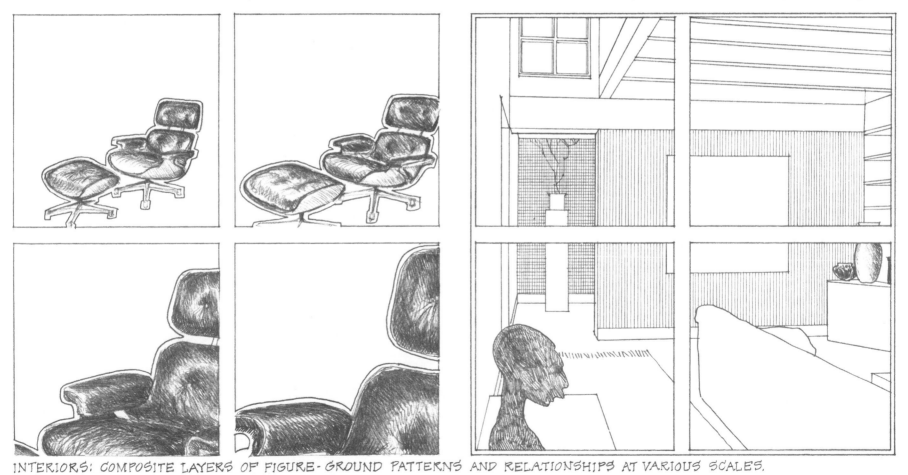

INTERIORS: COMPOSITE LAYERS OF FIGURE-GROUND PATTERNS AND RELATIONSHIPS AT VARIOUS SCALES.

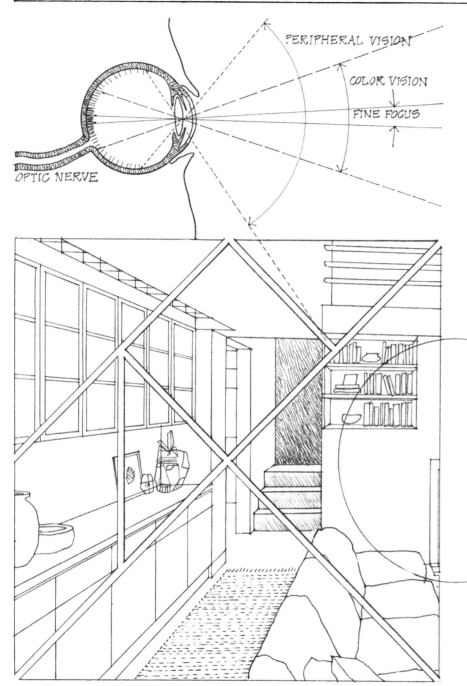

PERIPHERAL VISION

COLOR VISION

FINE FOCUS

OPTIC NERVE

Our ability to focus on and perceive detail is restricted to a fairly narrow cone of vision. In surveying our visual field, our eyes continually move, scan, focus, and refocus to discover visual information. In order to make sense of what we see, the brain interprets the visual data gathered by our eyes and assembles the information into visual patterns that we can recognize and understand.

The normal process of perception is utilitarian and geared toward recognition. When we see a chair, we recognize it to be a chair if its form and configuration fit a pattern established by chairs we have seen and used in the past. If we look carefully, however, we would also be able to perceive the chair's specific shape, size, proportion, color, texture, and material. This ability to see beyond recognition and utility is extremely important to designers. We must continually strive to see and be conscious of the specific visual characteristics of things and how they relate and interact to form the aesthetic quality of our visual environments.

VISUAL CHARACTERISTICS:

## ☐ A DESIGN VOCABULARY

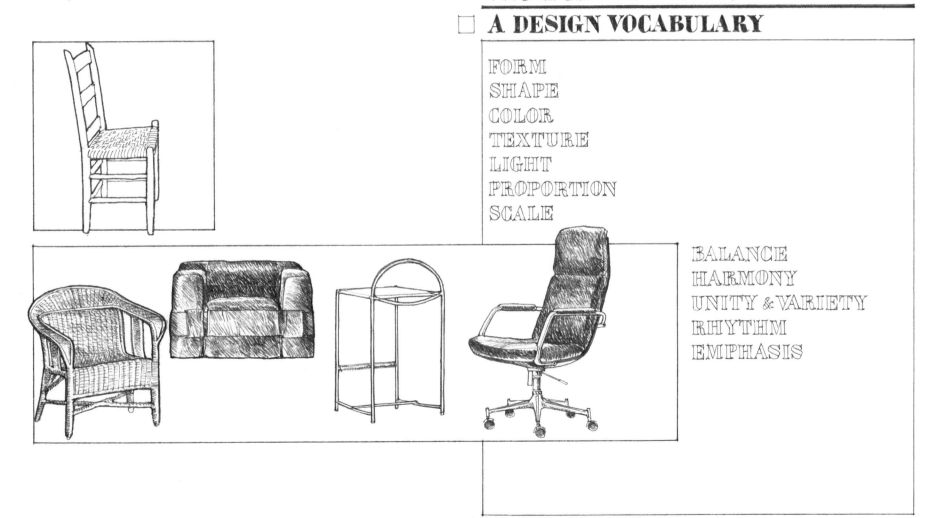

FORM
SHAPE
COLOR
TEXTURE
LIGHT
PROPORTION
SCALE

BALANCE
HARMONY
UNITY & VARIETY
RHYTHM
EMPHASIS

# FORM

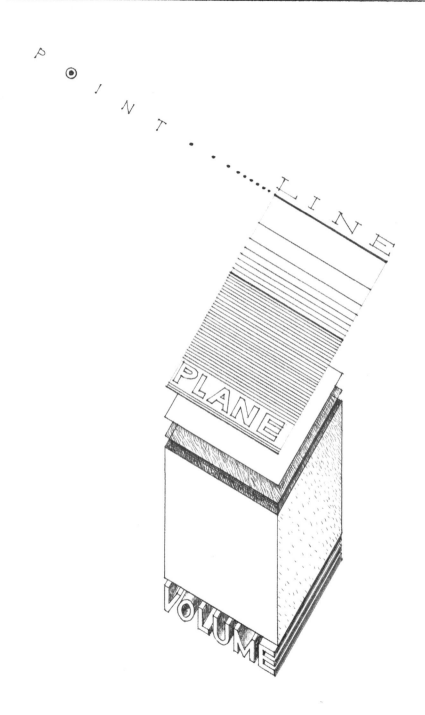

The point is the generator of all form. As a point moves, it leaves a trace of a line - the first dimension. As the line shifts in a direction other than its own, it defines a plane - a two-dimensional element. The plane, extended in a direction oblique or perpendicular to its surface, forms a three-dimensional volume.

Point, line, plane, and volume. These are the primary elements of form. All visible forms are, in reality, three-dimensional. In describing form, these primary elements differ according to their relative dimensions of length, width, and depth - a matter of proportion and scale.

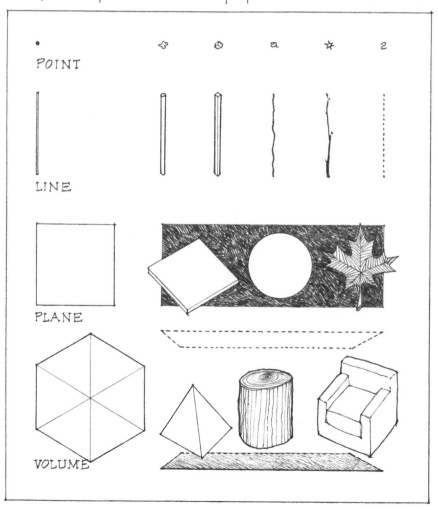

POINT

LINE

PLANE

VOLUME

A point marks a location in space. Conceptually, it has no length, width, or depth. It is, therefore, static and directionless. As the prime generator of form, a point can mark the ends of a line, the intersection of two lines, or the corner where the lines of a plane or volume meet.

As a visible form, a point is most commonly manifested as a dot, a circular shape that is small relative to its field. Other shapes can also be seen as point-forms if sufficiently small, compact, and nondirectional.

When at the center of a field or space, a point is stable and at rest, and capable of organizing other elements about itself. When moved off-center, it retains its self-centering quality but becomes more dynamic. Visual tension is created between the point and its field. Point-generated forms, such as the circle and the sphere, share this self-centering quality of the point.

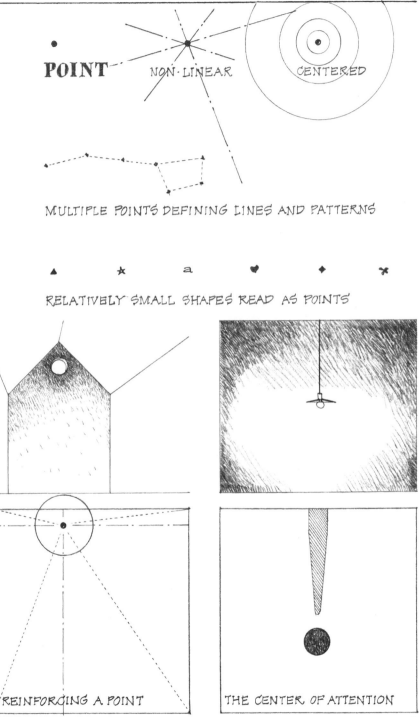

**POINT**    NON-LINEAR    CENTERED

MULTIPLE POINTS DEFINING LINES AND PATTERNS

RELATIVELY SMALL SHAPES READ AS POINTS

POINT-GENERATED FORMS—THE CIRCLE AND THE SPHERE—ARE SELF-CENTERING.

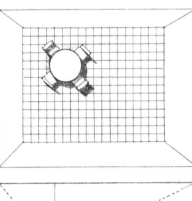

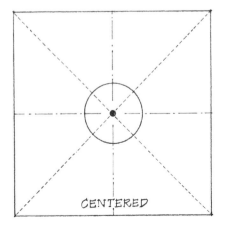

CENTERED      OFF-CENTER      REINFORCING A POINT      THE CENTER OF ATTENTION

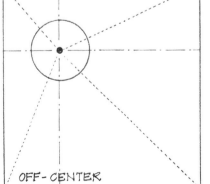

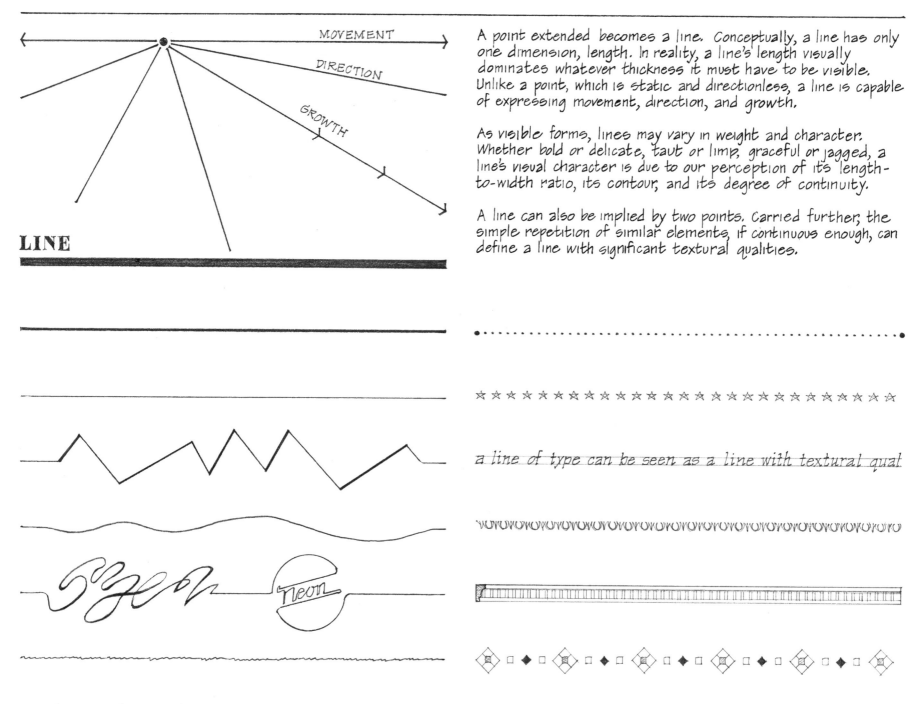

## LINE

A point extended becomes a line. Conceptually, a line has only one dimension, length. In reality, a line's length visually dominates whatever thickness it must have to be visible. Unlike a point, which is static and directionless, a line is capable of expressing movement, direction, and growth.

As visible forms, lines may vary in weight and character. Whether bold or delicate, taut or limp, graceful or jagged, a line's visual character is due to our perception of its length-to-width ratio, its contour, and its degree of continuity.

A line can also be implied by two points. Carried further, the simple repetition of similar elements, if continuous enough, can define a line with significant textural qualities.

a line of type can be seen as a line with textural qual

LINES VARYING IN WEIGHT, CONTOUR, AND TEXTURE

A straight line represents the tension that exists between two points. An important characteristic of a straight line is its direction. A horizontal line can represent stability, repose, or the plane upon which we stand or move. In contrast to this, a vertical line can express a state of equilibrium with the force of gravity.

Diagonal lines, deviations from the horizontal and the vertical, can be seen as rising or falling. In either case, they imply movement and are visually active and dynamic.

A curved line represents movement deflected by lateral forces. Curved lines tend to express gentle movement. Depending on their orientation, they can be uplifting or represent solidity and attachment to the earth. Small curves can express playfulness, energy, or the patterns of biological growth.

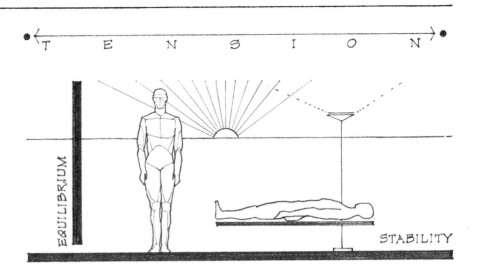

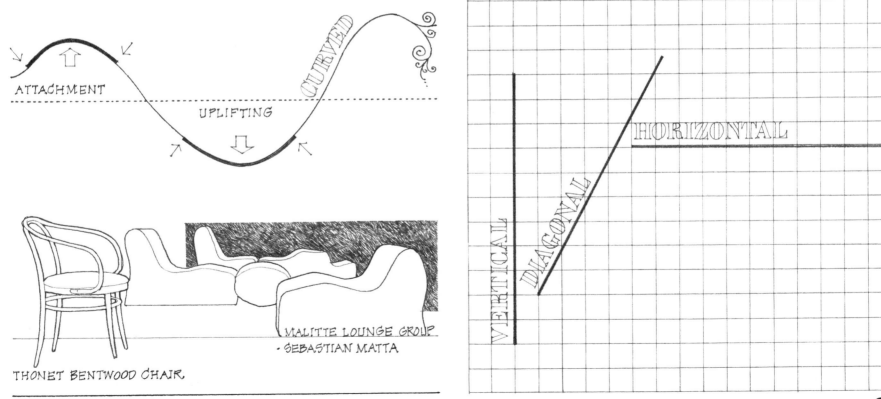

ATTACHMENT

UPLIFTING

CURVED

THONET BENTWOOD CHAIR

MALITTE LOUNGE GROUP
· SEBASTIAN MATTA

VERTICAL   DIAGONAL   HORIZONTAL

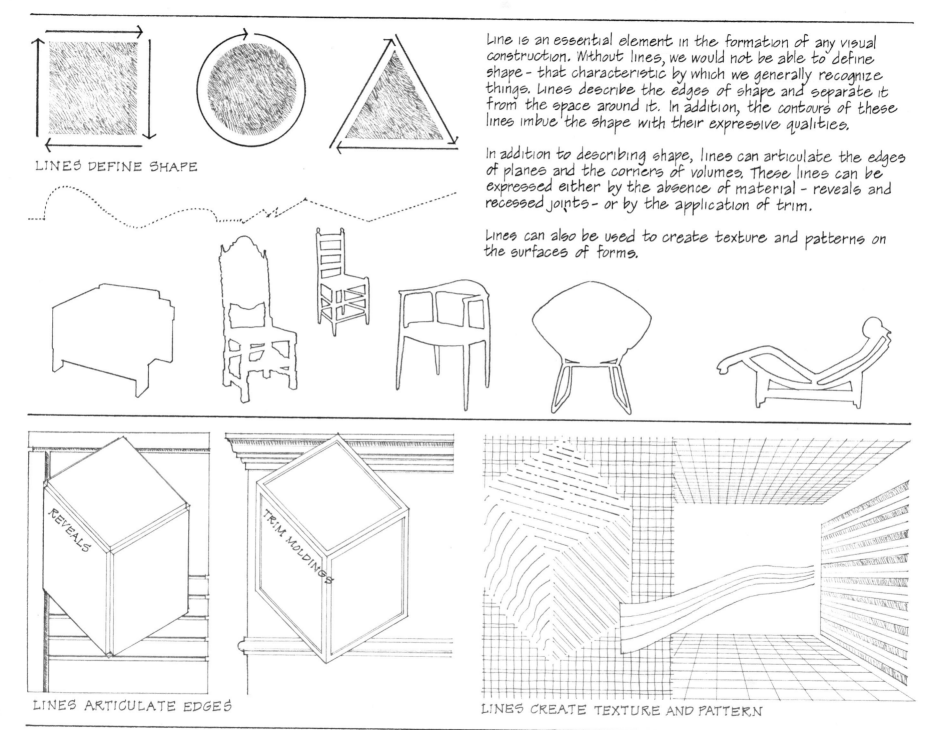

LINES DEFINE SHAPE

Line is an essential element in the formation of any visual construction. Without lines, we would not be able to define shape - that characteristic by which we generally recognize things. Lines describe the edges of shape and separate it from the space around it. In addition, the contours of these lines imbue the shape with their expressive qualities.

In addition to describing shape, lines can articulate the edges of planes and the corners of volumes. These lines can be expressed either by the absence of material - reveals and recessed joints - or by the application of trim.

Lines can also be used to create texture and patterns on the surfaces of forms.

LINES ARTICULATE EDGES

REVEALS

TRIM MOLDINGS

LINES CREATE TEXTURE AND PATTERN

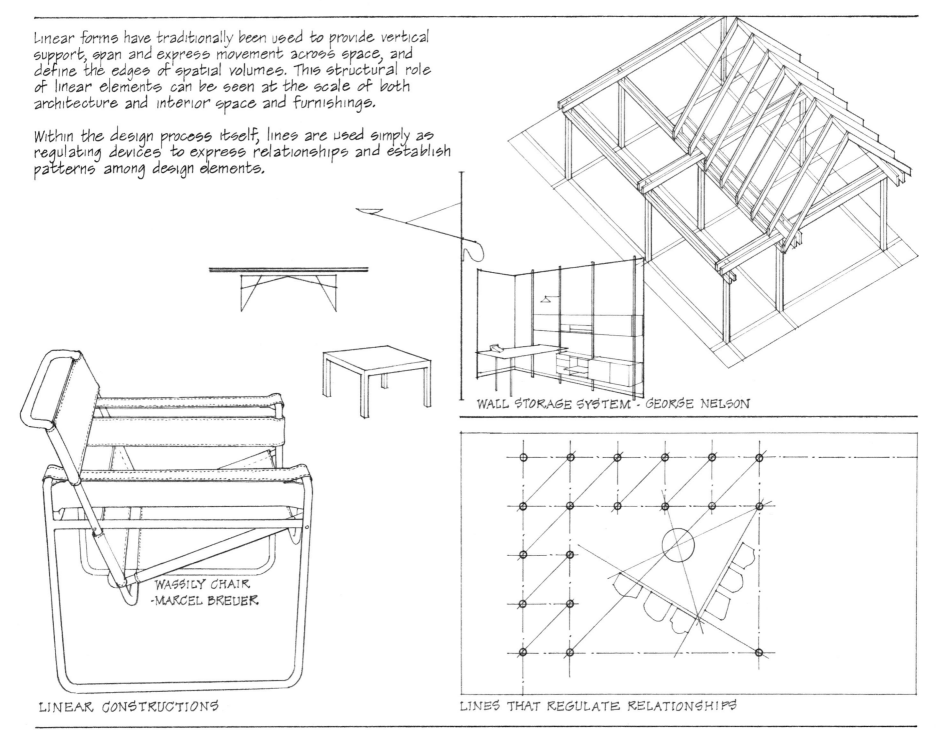

Linear forms have traditionally been used to provide vertical support, span and express movement across space, and define the edges of spatial volumes. This structural role of linear elements can be seen at the scale of both architecture and interior space and furnishings.

Within the design process itself, lines are used simply as regulating devices to express relationships and establish patterns among design elements.

WALL STORAGE SYSTEM - GEORGE NELSON

WASSILY CHAIR
-MARCEL BREUER.

LINEAR CONSTRUCTIONS

LINES THAT REGULATE RELATIONSHIPS

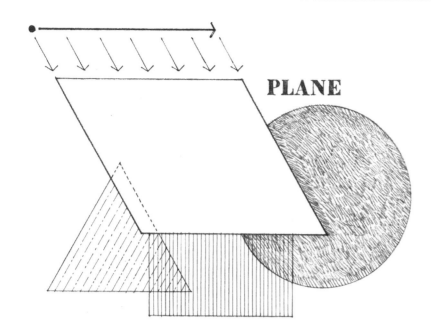

## PLANE

A line shifted in a direction other than its intrinsic direction defines a plane. Conceptually, a plane has two dimensions, width and length, but no depth. In reality, a plane's width and length dominate whatever thickness it must have to be visible.

Shape is the primary characteristic of a plane. It is described by the contour of the lines defining the edges of the plane. Since our perception of a plane's shape can be distorted by perspective, we see the true shape of a plane only when we view it frontally.

In addition to shape, planar forms have significant surface qualities of material, color, texture, and pattern. These visual characteristics affect a plane's:

- Visual weight and stability
- Perceived size, proportion, and position in space
- Light reflectivity
- Tactile qualities
- Acoustic properties

SHAPE IS A PLANE'S DOMINANT CHARACTERISTIC.

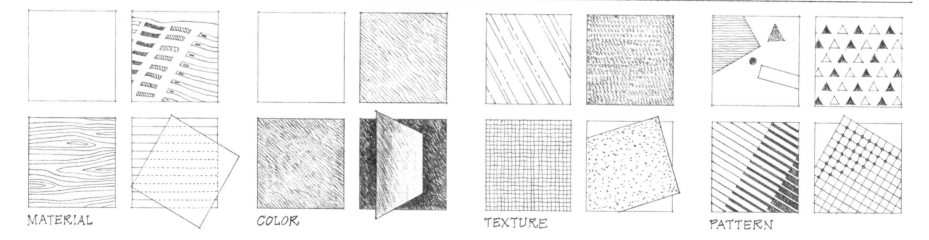

MATERIAL      COLOR      TEXTURE      PATTERN

SURFACE CHARACTERISTICS OF PLANAR ELEMENTS

Planar forms are fundamental elements of architectural and interior design. Floor, wall, and ceiling or roof planes serve to enclose and define three-dimensional volumes of space. Their specific visual characteristics and their relationships in space determine the form and character of the spaces they define. Within these spaces, furnishings and other interior design elements can also be seen to consist of planar forms.

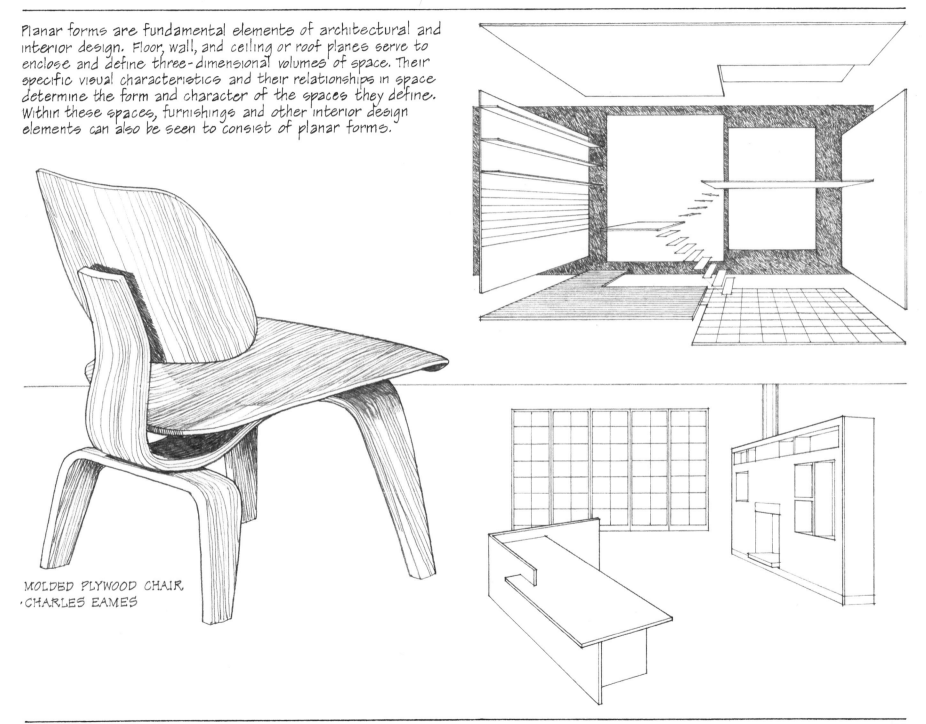

MOLDED PLYWOOD CHAIR
·CHARLES EAMES

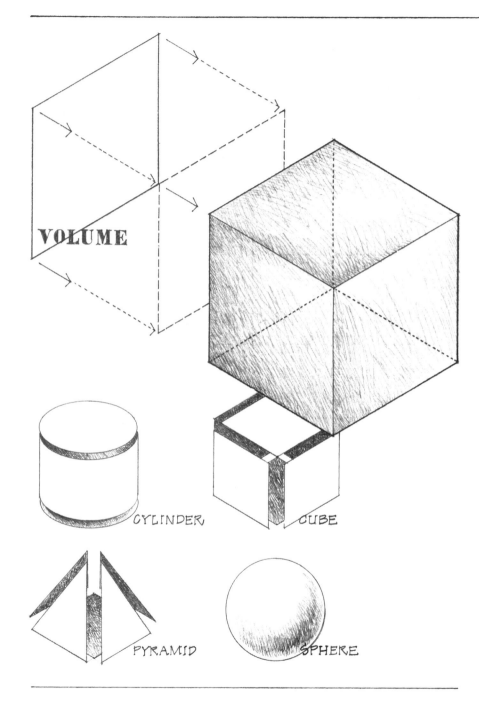

# VOLUME

CYLINDER

CUBE

PYRAMID

SPHERE

A plane extended in a direction other than along its surface forms a volume. Conceptually and in reality a volume exists in three dimensions.

Form is the term we use to describe the contour and overall structure of a volume. The specific form of a volume is determined by the shapes and interrelationships of the lines and planes that describe the boundaries of the volume.

As the three-dimensional element of architectural and interior design, a volume can be either solid (space displaced by mass) or a void (space enclosed by planar forms).

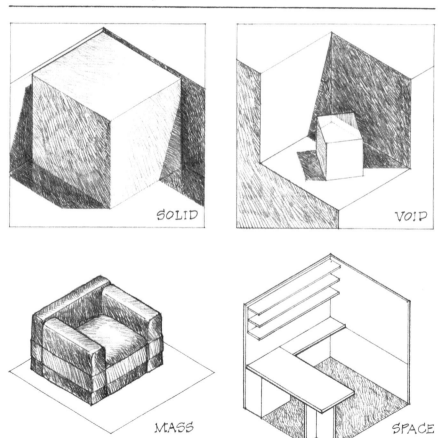

SOLID

VOID

MASS

SPACE

Solid forms and spatial voids. . .This duality represents the essential unity of opposites which shapes the reality of architecture and interior design. Visible forms give space dimension, scale, color, and texture, while space reveals the forms. This symbiotic relationship between form and space can be seen at several scales in interior design.

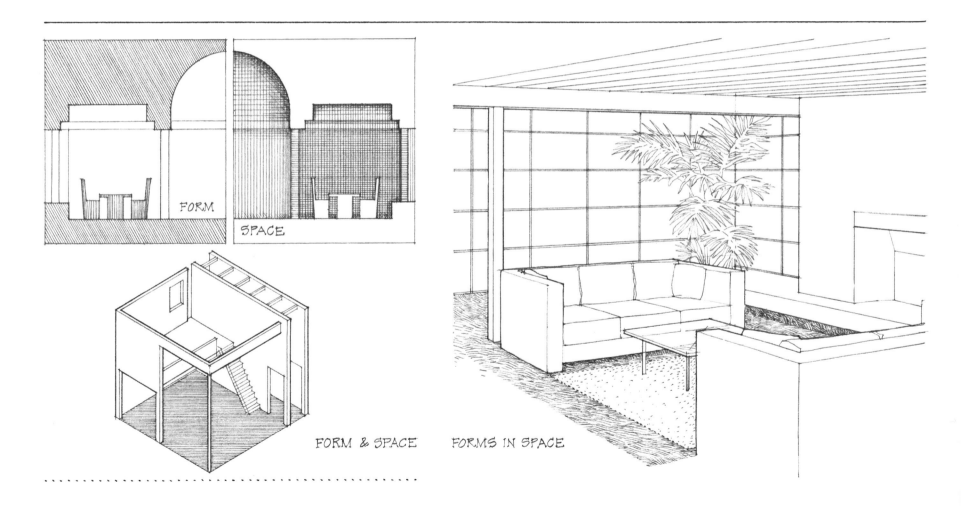

FORM

SPACE

FORM & SPACE

FORMS IN SPACE

# SHAPE

NATURAL SHAPES

NON-OBJECTIVE SHAPES

GEOMETRIC SHAPES

Shape is the primary means by which we distinguish one form from another. It may refer to the contour of a line, the outline of a plane, or the boundary of a three-dimensional mass. In each case, shape is defined by the specific configuration of the lines or planes which separate a form from its background or surrounding space.

There are several broad categories of shapes. Natural shapes represent the images and forms of our natural world. These shapes may be abstracted, usually through a process of simplification, and still retain the essential characteristics of their natural sources.

Non-objective shapes make no obvious reference to a specific object or to a particular subject matter. Some non-objective shapes may result from a process, such as calligraphy, and carry meaning as symbols. Others may be geometric and elicit responses based on their purely visual qualities.

Geometric shapes dominate the built environment of both architecture and interior design. There are two separate and distinct types of geometric shapes – rectilinear and curvilinear. In their most regular form, curvilinear shapes are circular while rectilinear shapes include the series of polygons which can be inscribed within a circle. Of these, the most significant geometric shapes are the circle, the triangle, and the square. Extended into the third dimension, these primary shapes generate the sphere, the cylinder, the cone, the pyramid, and the cube.

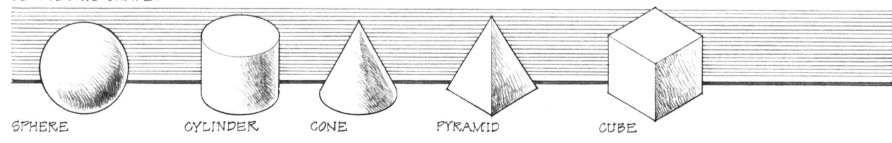

SPHERE          CYLINDER          CONE          PYRAMID          CUBE

The circle is a compact, introverted shape which has as its natural focus its centerpoint. It represents unity, continuity, and economy of form.

A circular shape is normally stable and self-centering in its environment. When associated with other lines and shapes, however, a circle can appear to have apparent motion.

Other curvilinear lines and shapes can be seen to be fragments or combinations of circular shapes. Whether regular or irregular, curvilinear shapes are capable of expressing softness of form, fluidity of movement, or the nature of biological growth.

**CIRCLE**

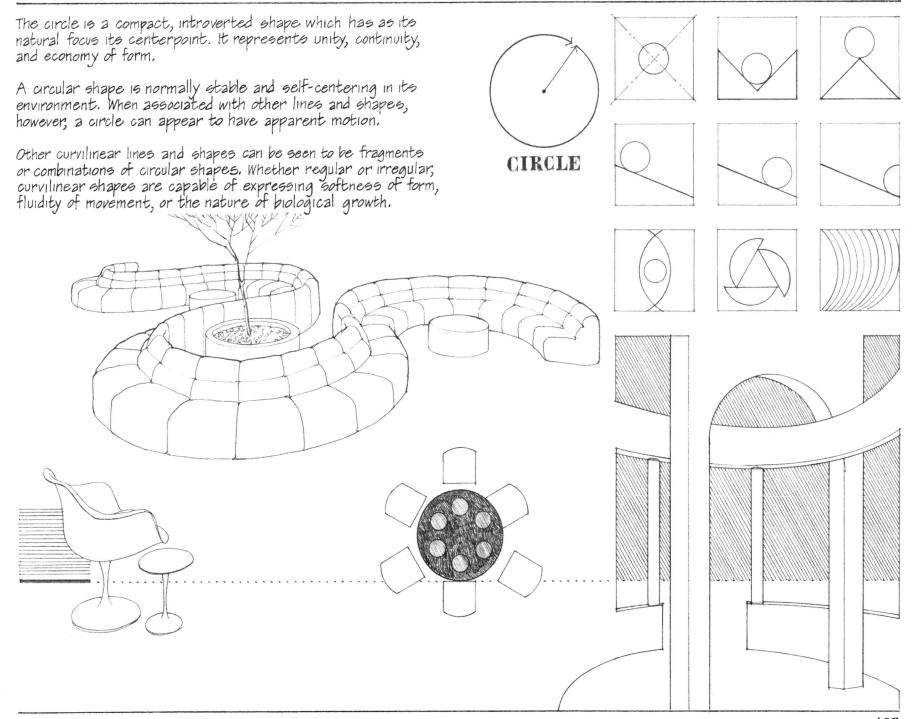

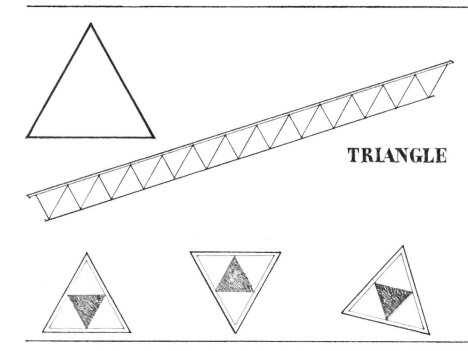

# TRIANGLE

The triangle represents stability. Triangular shapes and patterns are often used in structural systems since their configuration cannot be altered without bending or breaking one of their sides.

From a purely visual point of view, a triangular shape is also stable when resting on one of its sides. When tipped to stand on one of its points, however, the triangular shape becomes dynamic. It can exist in a precarious state of balance or imply motion as it tends to fall over onto one of its sides.

The dynamic quality of a triangular shape is also due to the angular relationships of its three sides. Because these angles can vary, triangles are more flexible than squares and rectangles. In addition, triangles can be conveniently combined to form any number of square, rectangular, and other polygonal shapes.

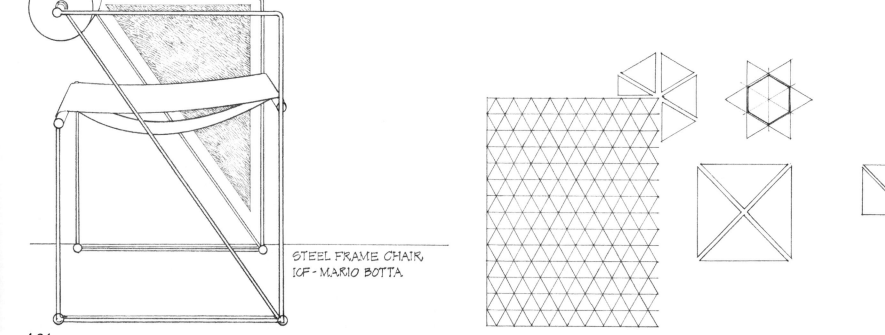

STEEL FRAME CHAIR,
ICF - MARIO BOTTA

The square represents the pure and the rational. The equality of its four sides and its four right angles contributes to its regularity and visual clarity.

A square shape has no preferred or dominant direction. Like the triangle, the square is a stable, tranquil figure when resting on one of its sides, but becomes dynamic when standing on one of its corners.

All other rectangles can be considered to be variations of the square with the addition of width or length. While the clarity and stability of rectangular shapes can lead to visual monotony, variety can be introduced by varying their size, proportion, color, texture, placement, or orientation.

Rectangular shapes are clearly the norm in architectural and interior design. They are easily measured, drawn, and manufactured, and they fit together readily and snugly in construction.

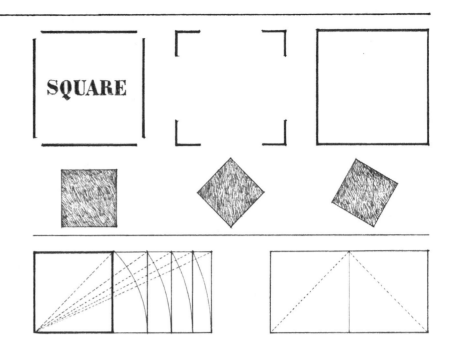

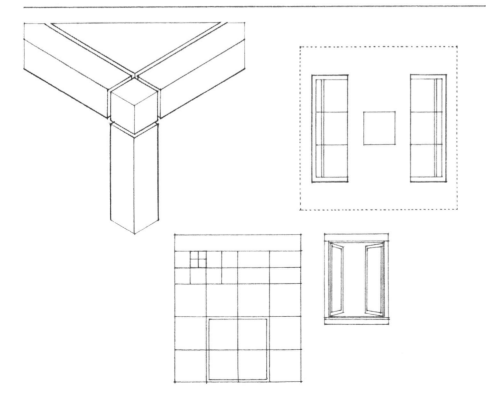

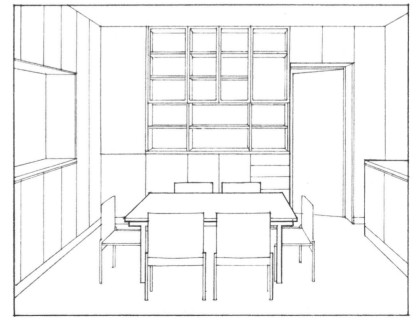

# COLOR

Color is, like shape and texture, an inherent visual property of all form. We are surrounded by color in our environmental settings. The colors we attribute to objects, however, find their source in the light that illuminates and reveals form and space. Without light, color does not exist.

The science of physics deals with color as a property of light. Within the visible spectrum of light, color is determined by wavelength; starting at the longest wavelength with red, we proceed through the spectrum of orange, yellow, green, blue, and violet to arrive at the shortest visible wavelengths. When these colored lights are present in a light source in approximately equal quantities, they combine to produce white light —light that is apparently colorless.

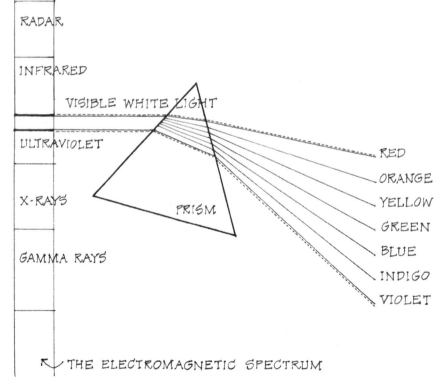

RADAR

INFRARED

VISIBLE WHITE LIGHT

ULTRAVIOLET

X-RAYS

PRISM

GAMMA RAYS

RED
ORANGE
YELLOW
GREEN
BLUE
INDIGO
VIOLET

THE ELECTROMAGNETIC SPECTRUM

When white light falls on an opaque object, selective absorption occurs. The surface of the object absorbs certain wavelengths of light and reflects others. Our eyes apprehend the color of the reflected light as the color of the object.

White light, such as noon sunlight, is composed of the entire spectrum of colored lights. Some light sources, such as fluorescent lamps or light reflected off of a colored wall, may not be well balanced and lack part of the spectrum. This lack of certain colors would make a surface illuminated by such light appear to also lack those colors.

Which wavelengths or bands of light are absorbed and which are reflected as object color is determined by the pigmentation of a surface. A red surface appears red because it absorbs most of the blue and green light falling on it and reflects the red part of the spectrum; a blue surface absorbs the reds. Similarly, a black surface absorbs the entire spectrum; a white surface reflects all of it.

A surface has the natural pigmentation of its material. This coloration can be altered with the application of paints, stains, or dyes which contain color pigments. While colored light is additive in nature, color pigments are subtractive. Each pigment absorbs certain proportions of white light. When pigments are mixed, their absorptions combine to subtract various colors of the spectrum. The colors that remain determine the hue, value, and intensity of the mixed pigment.

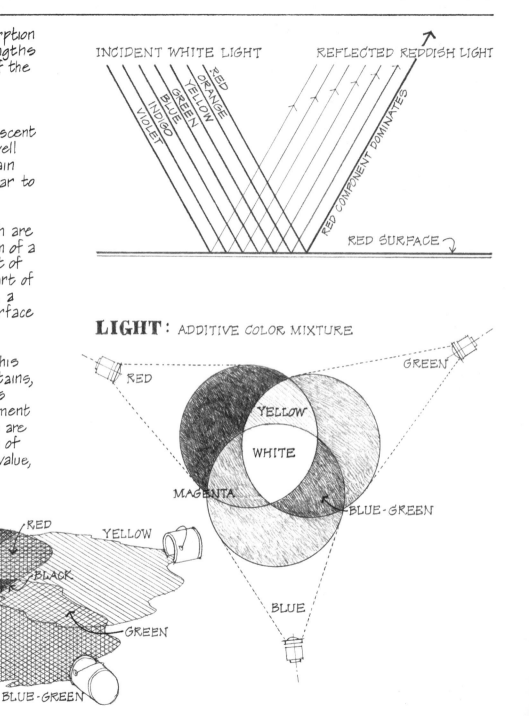

INCIDENT WHITE LIGHT    REFLECTED REDDISH LIGHT

RED
ORANGE
YELLOW
GREEN
BLUE
INDIGO
VIOLET

RED COMPONENT DOMINATES

RED SURFACE

**LIGHT**: ADDITIVE COLOR MIXTURE

RED        GREEN
YELLOW
WHITE
MAGENTA        BLUE-GREEN
BLUE

**PIGMENTS**:
SUBTRACTIVE COLOR MIXTURE

MAGENTA        RED        YELLOW
BLACK
GREEN
PURPLE-BLUE
BLUE-GREEN

Color has three dimensions:

**1. HUE** — The attribute by which we recognize and describe a color, such as red or yellow.

**2. VALUE** — The degree of lightness or darkness of a color in relation to white and black.

**3. INTENSITY** — The degree of purity or saturation of a color when compared to a gray of the same value.

---

All of these attributes of color are necessarily interrelated. Each principal hue has a normal value. Pure yellow, for example, is lighter in value than pure blue. If white, black, or a complementary hue is added to a color to lighten or darken its value, its intensity will also be diminished. It is difficult to adjust one attribute of a color without simultaneously altering the other two.

A number of color systems attempt to organize colors and their attributes into a visible order. The simplest type, such as the Brewster or Prang color wheel, organizes color pigments into primary, secondary, and tertiary hues.

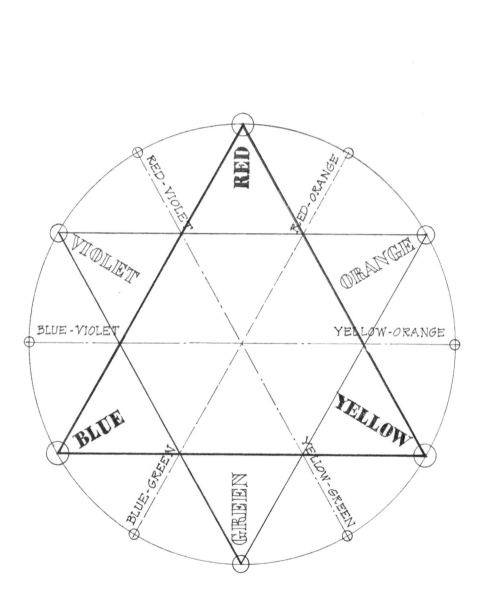

A more comprehensive system for the accurate specification and description of color is the Munsell system, developed by Albert H. Munsell. The system arranges colors into three orderly scales of uniform visual steps according to their attributes of hue, value, and chroma (intensity).

The Munsell system is based on five principal hues and five intermediate hues. These ten major hues are positioned ten hue steps apart and arranged horizontally in a circle.

Extending vertically through the center of the hue circle is a scale of neutral gray values, graded in ten equal visual steps from black to white.

Radiating out from the vertical scale of values are equal steps of chroma or intensity. The number of steps will vary according to the attainable saturation of each color's hue and value.

With this system, a specific color can be identified with the following notation: Hue Value/Chroma, or H V/c. For example, 5R 5/14 would indicate a pure red at middle value and maximum chroma.

While the ability to accurately communicate the hue, value, and intensity of a specific color without an actual sample is important in science, commerce, and industry, color names and notations cannot adequately describe the visual sensation of color. Actual color samples, seen in the color of light, is essential in the design of color schemes.

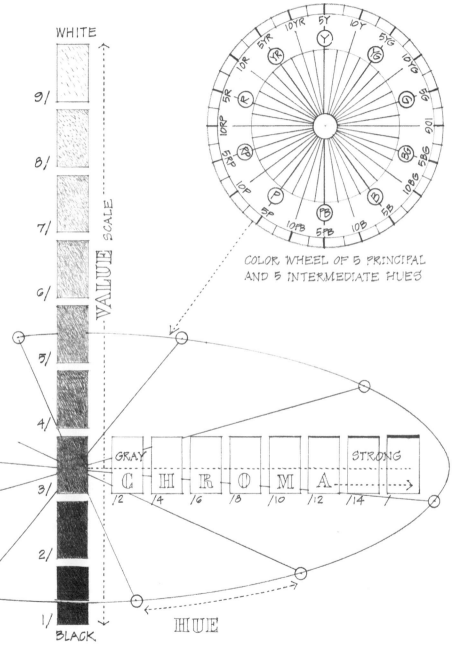

COLOR WHEEL OF 5 PRINCIPAL AND 5 INTERMEDIATE HUES

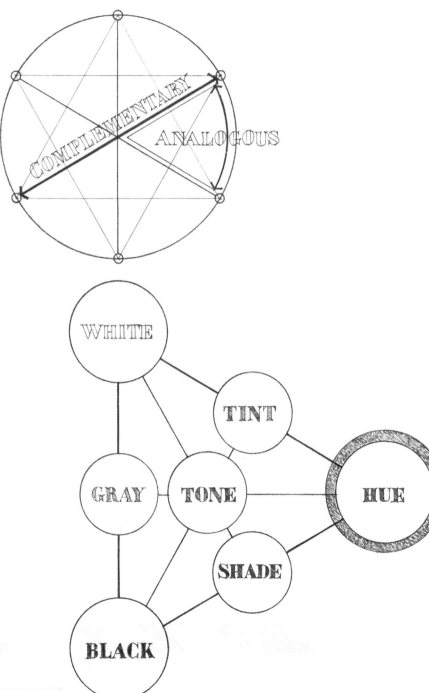

Object colorants, such as paints and dyes, are means to modify the color of the illuminating light, which we interpret to be the color of the object. In mixing the pigments of paints and dyes, each of the attributes of color can be altered.

The hue of a color can be changed by mixing it with other hues. When neighboring or analogous hues on the color wheel are mixed, harmonious and closely related hues are created. In contrast to this, mixing complementary hues, hues directly opposite of each other on the color wheel, produces neutral hues.

The value of a color can be raised by adding white and lowered by adding black. Lightening a hue's normal value by adding white creates a tint of that hue; darkening the hue's normal value with black creates a shade of the hue. A normally high-value color, such as yellow, is capable of more shades than tints, while a low-value color, such as red, is able to have more tints than shades.

The intensity of a color can be strengthened by adding more of the dominant hue. It can be lowered by mixing gray with the color or by adding to the color its complementary hue. Hues that are grayed or neutralized in this manner are often called tones.

**ALTERING COLORS: WITH PIGMENTS....**

Apparent changes in an object's color can also result from the effects of light and from the juxtaposition of surrounding or background colors. These factors are especially important to the interior designer, who must carefully consider how the colors of elements in an interior space interact and how they are rendered by the light illuminating them.

Light of a particular hue, other than white, is rarely used for general illumination. Not all sources of white light, however, are spectrally well balanced. Incandescent bulbs cast a warm glow, while many fluorescents cast a cool light. Daylight, too, can be warm or cool, depending on the time of day and the direction from which it comes. Even the color of a large reflecting surface can tint the light within an interior space.

Warm light tends to accentuate warm colors and neutralize cool hues, while cool light intensifies cool colors and weakens warm hues. If light is tinted with a particular hue, it will raise the intensity of colors of that hue, and neutralize colors of a complementary hue.

The apparent value of a color can also be altered by the amount of light used to illuminate it. Lowering the amount of illumination will darken a color's value and neutralize its hue. Raising the lighting level will lighten the color's value and enhance its intensity. High levels of illumination, however, can also tend to make colors appear less saturated or washed out.

Since the natural fluctuations of light in an interior setting alter colors in often subtle ways, it is always best to test colors in the environment in which they are to be viewed, under both daylight and nighttime conditions.

## ...OR WITH LIGHT

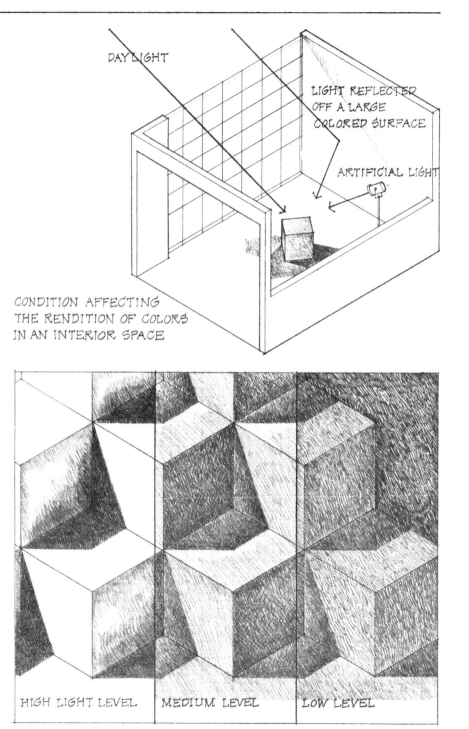

DAYLIGHT

LIGHT REFLECTED OFF A LARGE COLORED SURFACE

ARTIFICIAL LIGHT

CONDITION AFFECTING THE RENDITION OF COLORS IN AN INTERIOR SPACE

HIGH LIGHT LEVEL    MEDIUM LEVEL    LOW LEVEL

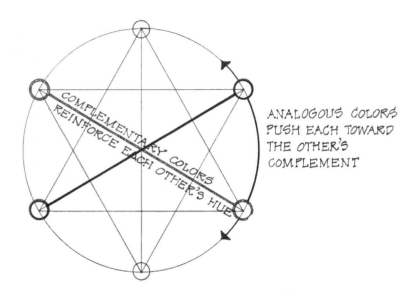

ANALOGOUS COLORS PUSH EACH TOWARD THE OTHER'S COMPLEMENT

While mixing two complementary color pigments results in a neutralized or grayed hue, placing them next to each other can produce the opposite effect. In the phenomenon known as simultaneous contrast, the eye tends to generate a color's complementary hue and project it as an afterimage on adjacent colors. Thus two complementary colors placed side by side tend to heighten each other's saturation and brilliance without an apparent change in hue.

When the two colors are not complementary, each will tint the other with its own complement and shift it towards that hue. The result is that the two colors are pushed farther apart in hue.

Simultaneous contrast in hue is most easily perceived when two colors are fairly uniform in value. If one color is much lighter or darker than the other, the effects of contrasting values become more noticeable.

## THE EFFECTS OF ADJACENT COLORS:      SIMULTANANEOUS CONTRAST

USE THE SUPERIMPOSED SQUARES BELOW AS TEMPLATES TO STUDY THE EFFECT OF SIMULTANEOUS CONTRAST ON THE HUES OF ADJACENT COLORS.

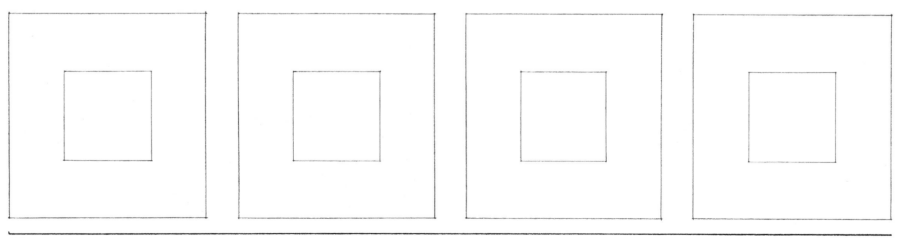

Simultaneous contrast also affects the apparent value of a color, which can be made to appear lighter or darker according to the value of its background color. A light color will tend to deepen a dark color while a dark color will tend to brighten a light color.

Both black and white have a visible effect on colors when brought into contact with them. Surrounding colors with black tends to make them richer and more vibrant, while outlining with white often has the opposite effect. A large area of white will reflect light onto adjacent colors, while thin white lines tend to spread and tint the hues they separate.

The effects of contrasting hues and values depend on areas large enough to be perceived as separate colors. If the areas are small and closely spaced, the eye does not have enough time to adjust to their differences and mixes the colors optically. The effects of optical mixing are often used in the weaving of textiles to create an impression of many hues and values with a limited number of colored yarns or threads.

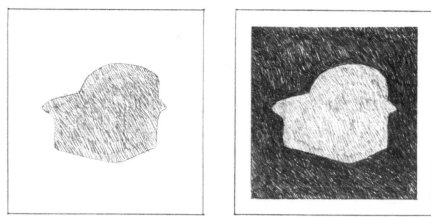

SIMULTANEOUS CONTRAST OF VALUE

USE THESE SUPERIMPOSED SQUARES AS TEMPLATES TO STUDY THE EFFECT OF SIMULTANEOUS CONTRAST ON THE VALUES OF ADJACENT COLORS.

SURROUNDING WITH WHITE........OR BLACK

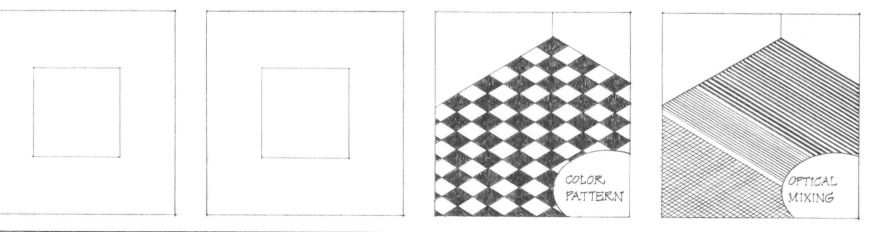

COLOR PATTERN

OPTICAL MIXING

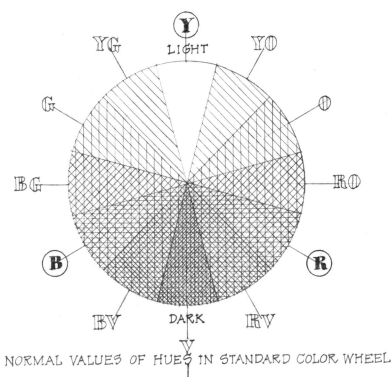

NORMAL VALUES OF HUES IN STANDARD COLOR WHEEL

In addition to how colors interact and alter one another's attributes, it is important to note how color might affect our perception of form and the dimensions and qualities of interior space.

The warmth or coolness of a color's hue, along with its relative value and degree of saturation, determines the visual force with which it attracts our attention, brings an object into focus, and creates space. The following generalizations summarize some of these effects of color.

Warm hues and high intensities are said to be visually active and stimulating, while cool hues and low intensities are more subdued and relaxing. Light values tend to be cheerful, middle values undemanding, and dark values somber.

Bright, saturated colors and any strong contrasts attract our attention; grayed hues and middle values are less forceful. Contrasting values in particular make us aware of shapes and forms. Contrasting hues and saturations can also define shape, but if they are too similar in value, the definition they afford will be less distinct.

VALUE CONTRAST AIDS IN OUR PERCEPTION OF SHAPE

Deep, cool colors appear to contract. Light, warm colors tend to expand and increase the apparent size of an object, especially when seen against a dark background.

When used on an enclosing plane of a space, light values, cool hues, and grayed colors appear to recede and increase apparent distance. They can therefore be used to enhance the spaciousness of a room, and increase its apparent width, length, or ceiling height.

Warm hues appear to advance; dark values and saturated colors suggest nearness. These traits can be used to diminish the scale of a space or, in an illusionary way, shorten one of a room's dimensions.

LIGHT ON LIGHT          DARK ON LIGHT          LIGHT ON DARK

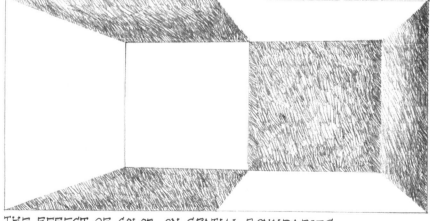

THE EFFECT OF COLOR ON SPATIAL BOUNDARIES

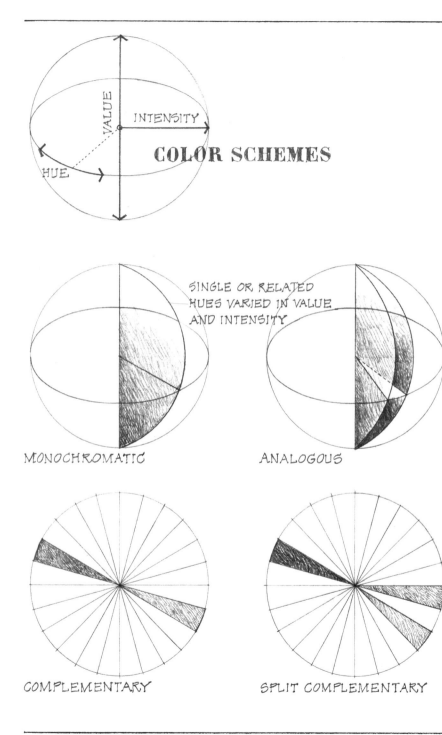

VALUE

INTENSITY

HUE

# COLOR SCHEMES

SINGLE OR RELATED HUES VARIED IN VALUE AND INTENSITY

MONOCHROMATIC

ANALOGOUS

Although each of us may have favorite colors and a distinct dislike of others, there is no such thing as a good or bad color. Some colors are simply in or out of fashion at a given time; others may be appropriate or inappropriate given a specific color scheme. The suitability of a color depends ultimately on how and where it is used, and how it fits into the palette of a color scheme.

If colors are like the notes of a musical scale, then color schemes are like musical chords, structuring color groups according to certain visual relationships among their attributes of hue, value, and intensity. The following color schemes are based on the hue relationships within a color group.

There are two broad categories of hue schemes, related and contrasting. Related hue schemes, based on either a single hue or a series of analogous hues, promote harmony and unity. Variety can be introduced by varying value and intensity, including small amounts of other hues as accents, or bringing shape, form, and texture into play.

Contrasting hue schemes, based on complementary or triadic color combinations, are inherently more rich and varied since they always include both warm and cool hues.

COMPLEMENTARY

SPLIT COMPLEMENTARY

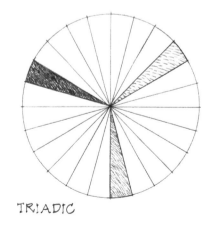

TRIADIC

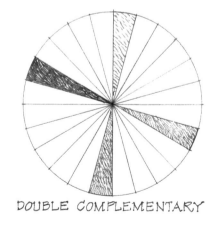

DOUBLE COMPLEMENTARY

Hue schemes merely outline the approaches one can take in organizing a combination of hues. In designing a color scheme, other color relationships must also be considered.

The color triangle developed by Faber Birren illustrates how modified colors - tints, tones, and shades - might be related in a harmonious sequence. The triangle is based on the three basic elements, pure color, white, and black. They combine to create the secondary forms of tint, shade, gray, and tone. Any of the straight-line paths defines a harmonious sequence since each involves a series of visually related elements.

Ultimately, whether a color scheme is lively and exuberant or restful and quiet will depend on the chromatic and tonal values of the hues chosen. Large intervals between the colors and values will create lively contrasts and dramatic effects. Small intervals will result in more subtle contrasts and patterns.

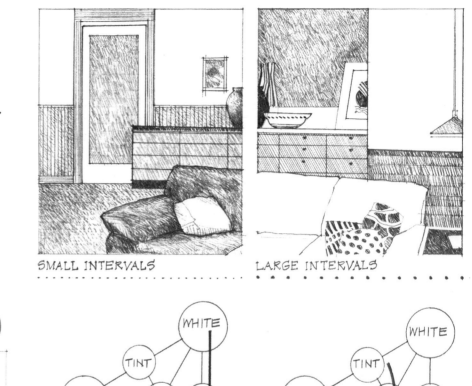

SMALL INTERVALS          LARGE INTERVALS

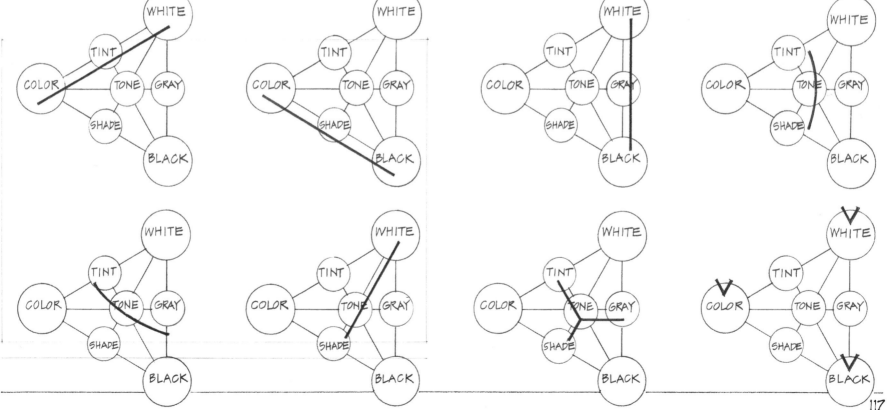

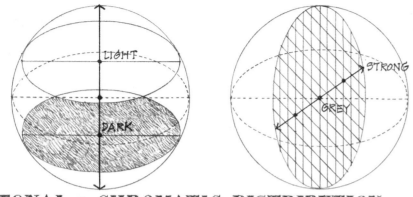

# TONAL & CHROMATIC DISTRIBUTION

In developing a color scheme for an interior space, one must consider carefully the chromatic and tonal key to be established and the distribution of the colors. The scheme must not only satisfy the purpose and use of the space but also take into account its architectural character.

Decisions must be made regarding the major planes of an interior space and how color might be used to modify their apparent size, shape, scale, and distance. Which elements are to form the background, middleground, and foreground? Are there architectural or structural features which should be accentuated, or undesirable elements to be minimized?

Traditionally, the largest surfaces of a room, its floor, walls, and ceiling, have the most neutralized values. Against this background, secondary elements such as large pieces of furniture or area rugs can have greater chromatic intensity. Finally, accent pieces, accessories, and other small-scale elements can have the strongest chroma for balance and to create interest.

Neutralized color schemes are the most flexible. For a more dramatic effect, the main areas of a room can be given the more intense values while secondary elements have lesser intensity. Large areas of intense color should be used with caution, particularly in a small room. They reduce apparent distance and can be visually demanding.

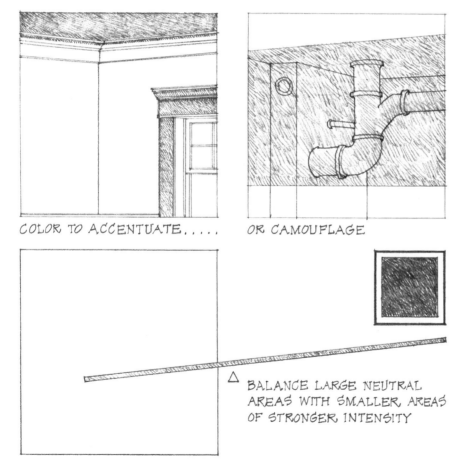

COLOR TO ACCENTUATE......     OR CAMOUFLAGE

BALANCE LARGE NEUTRAL AREAS WITH SMALLER AREAS OF STRONGER INTENSITY

LARGE AREAS OF INTENSE COLOR CAN BE BOTH DRAMATIC AND VISUALLY DEMANDING

Of equal importance to chromatic distribution is tonal distribution, the pattern of lights and darks in a space. It is generally best to use varying amounts of light and dark values with a range of middle values to serve as transitional tones. Avoid using equal amounts of light and dark unless a fragmented effect is desired.

Typically, large areas of light value are offset by smaller areas ........ ⟩ of medium and dark values. This use of light values is particularly appropriate when the efficient use of available light is important. Dark color schemes can absorb much of the light within a space, resulting in a significant loss of illumination.

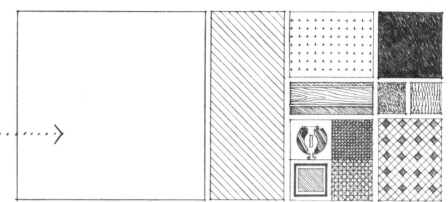

Another way of distributing values is to follow the pattern of nature. In this tonal sequence, the floor plane has the darkest value, surrounding walls are in the middle to light range, and the ceiling above is fairly light. Of course, the distribution of values and their degree of contrast will also depend on the size, shape, and scale of the space. Since light values tend to recede while dark values advance, their placement can modify our perception of these spatial dimensions.

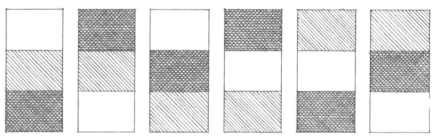

VERTICAL DISTRIBUTION PATTERNS OF TONAL VALUES

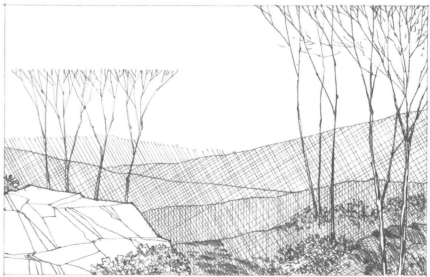

# TEXTURE

TEXTURE: THE 3-DIMENSIONAL STRUCTURE OF A SURFACE

Texture is that specific quality of a surface which results from its three-dimensional structure. Texture is most often used to describe the relative smoothness or roughness of a surface. It can also be used to describe the characteristic surface qualities of familiar materials, such as the roughness of stone, the grain of wood, and the weave of a fabric.

There are two basic types of texture. Tactile texture is real and can be felt by touch; visual texture is seen by the eye. All tactile textures provide visual texture as well. Visual texture, on the other hand, may be illusory or real.

Our senses of sight and touch are closely intertwined. As our eyes read the visual texture of a surface, we often respond to its apparent tactile quality without actually touching it. We base these physical reactions to the textural qualities of surfaces on previous associations with similar materials.

PHYSICAL TEXTURE

VISUAL TEXTURE

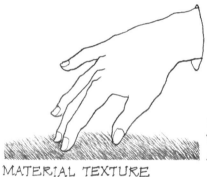

MATERIAL TEXTURE

TEXTURE IS INTERTWINED WITH OUR SENSES OF TOUCH AND SIGHT.

Scale, viewing distance, and light are important modifying factors in our perception of texture and the surfaces they articulate.

All materials have some degree of texture. But the finer the scale of a textural pattern, the smoother it will appear to be. Even coarse textures, when seen from a distance, can appear to be relatively smooth. Only upon closer viewing would the texture's coarseness become evident.

The relative scale of a texture can affect the apparent shape and position of a plane in space. Textures with a directional grain can accentuate a plane's length or width. Coarse textures can make a plane appear closer, reduce its scale, and increase its visual weight. In general, textures tend to visually fill the space in which they exist.

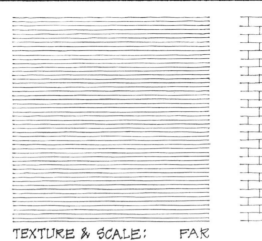

TEXTURE & SCALE:     FAR

NEAR

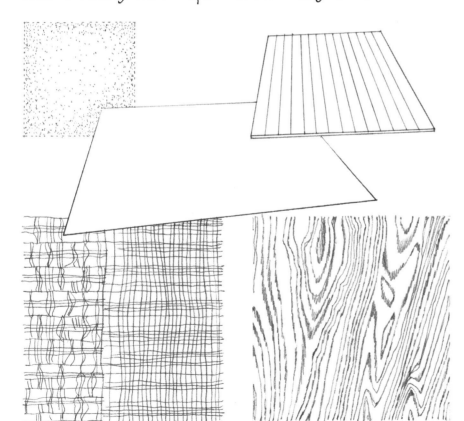

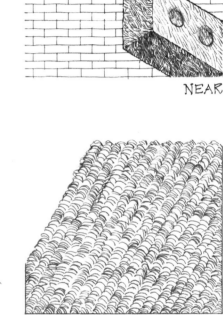

FAR     NEAR

# TEXTURE & LIGHT

Light influences our perception of texture and, in turn, is affected by the texture it illuminates. Direct light falling across a surface with physical texture will enhance its visual texture. Diffused lighting de-emphasizes physical texture and can even obscure its three-dimensional structure.

Smooth, shiny surfaces reflect light brilliantly, appear sharply in focus, and attract our attention. Surfaces with a matte or medium-rough texture absorb and diffuse light unevenly and therefore appear less bright than a similarly colored but smoother surface. Very rough surfaces, when illuminated with direct lighting, cast distinct shadow patterns of light and dark.

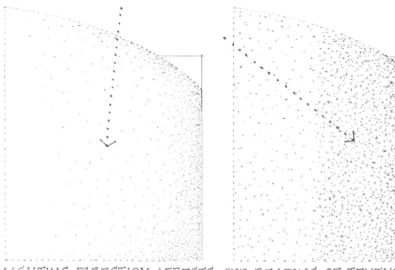

LIGHTING DIRECTION AFFECTS OUR READING OF TEXTURE

SHINY SURFACES REFLECT

MATTE SURFACES DIFFUSE

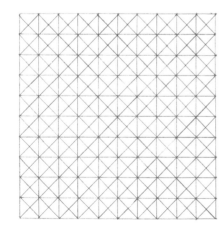

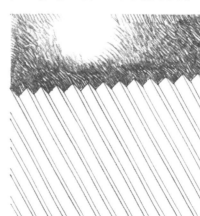

Contrast influences how strong or subtle a texture will appear to be. A texture seen against a uniformly smooth background will appear more obvious than when placed in juxtaposition with a similar texture. When seen against a coarser background, the texture will appear to be finer and reduced in scale.

Finally, texture is a factor in the maintenance of the materials and surfaces of a space. Smooth surfaces show dirt and wear but are relatively easy to clean, while rough surfaces may conceal dirt but are difficult to maintain.

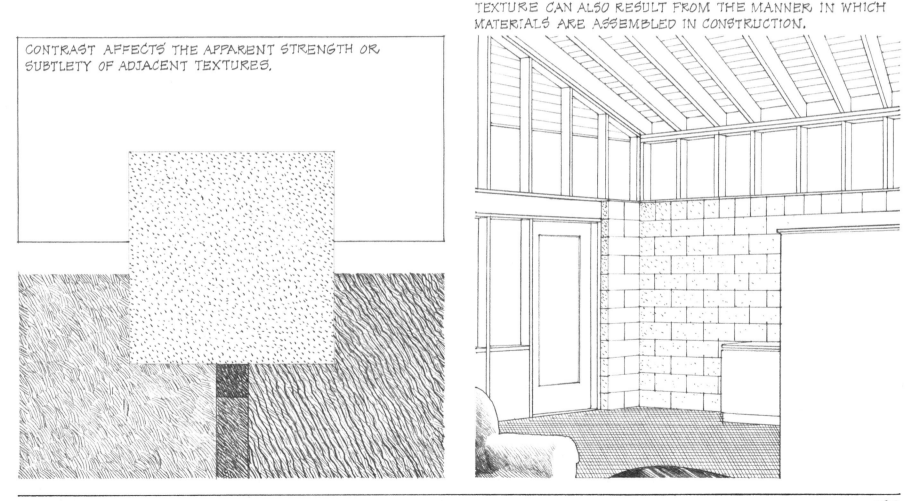

CONTRAST AFFECTS THE APPARENT STRENGTH OR SUBTLETY OF ADJACENT TEXTURES.

TEXTURE CAN ALSO RESULT FROM THE MANNER IN WHICH MATERIALS ARE ASSEMBLED IN CONSTRUCTION.

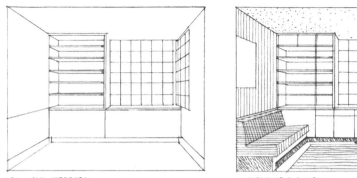

NO TEXTURE.................WITH TEXTURE

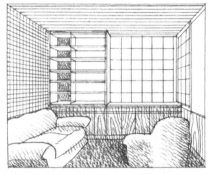

TEXTURE FILLING SPACE

COMPETING TEXTURES

Texture is an intrinsic characteristic of the materials we use to define, furnish, and embellish interior space. How we combine and compose differing textures is just as important as the composition of color and light, and should suit the desired character and use of a space.

The scale of a textural pattern should be related to the scale of a space and its major surfaces, as well as to the size of secondary elements within the space. Since texture tends to visually fill space, any textures used in a small room should be subtle or used sparingly. In a large room, texture can be used to reduce the scale of the space or to define a more intimate area within it.

A room with little textural variation can be bland. Combinations of hard and soft, even and uneven, and shiny and dull textures can be used to create variety and interest. In the selection and distribution of textures, moderation should be exercised and attention paid to their ordering and sequence. Harmony among contrasting textures can be sustained if they share a common trait, such as degree of light reflectance or visual weight.

Texture and pattern are closely related design elements. Pattern is the decorative design or ornamentation of a surface which is almost always based on the repetition of a design motif. The repetitive design of a pattern often gives the ornamented surface a textural quality as well. When the elements that create a pattern become so small that they lose their individual identity and blend into a tone, they become more texture than pattern.

A pattern may be structural or applied. A structural pattern results from the intrinsic nature of a material and the way it is processed, fabricated, or assembled. An applied pattern is added to a surface after it is structurally complete.

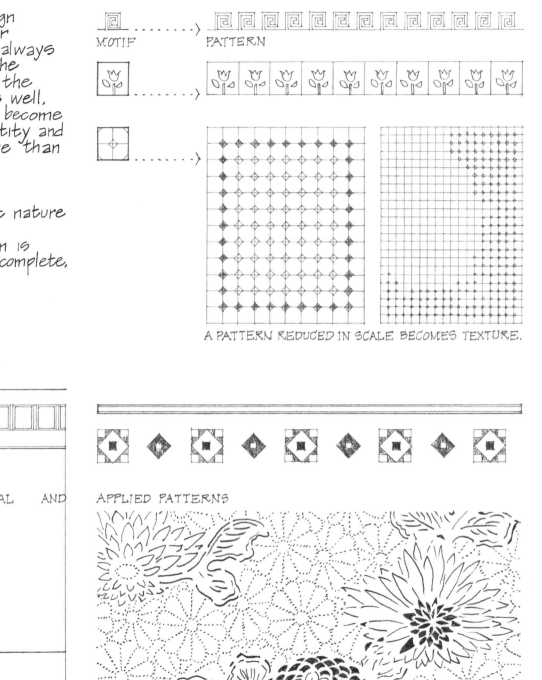

MOTIF     PATTERN

A PATTERN REDUCED IN SCALE BECOMES TEXTURE.

APPLIED PATTERNS

# TEXTURE & PATTERN

STRUCTURAL    AND

# LIGHT

LIGHT ANIMATES SPACE AND REVEALS FORMS AND TEXTURES

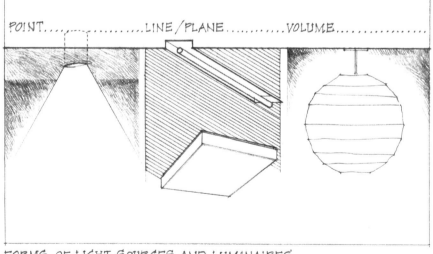

FORMS OF LIGHT SOURCES AND LUMINAIRES

Light is the prime animator of interior space. Without light, there would be no visible form, color, or texture, nor any visible enclosure of interior space. The first function of lighting design, therefore, is to illuminate the forms and space of an interior environment, and allow users to undertake activities and perform tasks with appropriate speed, accuracy, and comfort.

The Zonal Cavity Method (see pages 301-305) for calculating the number of luminaires required to provide a specified level of illumination is a useful technique, especially when one designs general lighting for uniformly lit spaces. Note, however, that a specific level of illumination can be supplied by various combinations of luminaires. The choice of what types of luminaires are used and how they are laid out should be based not only on visibility requirements but also on the nature of the space being illuminated and the activities of its users. The lighting design should address not only the quantity of light required but also its quality.

The layout of luminaires and the pattern of light they radiate should be coordinated with the architectural features of a space and the pattern of its use. Since our eyes seek the brightest objects and the strongest tonal contrasts in their field of vision, this coordination is particularly important in the planning of localized or task lighting.

For the purpose of planning the visual composition of a lighting design, a light source can be considered to have the form of a point, a line, a plane, or a volume. If the light source is shielded from view, then the form of its light and the shape of its surface illumination should be considered. Whether the pattern of light sources is regular or varied, a lighting design should be balanced in its composition, provide an appropriate sense of rhythm, and give emphasis to what is important.

There are three methods for illuminating a space: general, local, and accent lighting. General or ambient lighting illuminates a room in a fairly uniform, generally diffuse manner. The dispersed quality of the illumination can effectively reduce the contrast between task lighting and the surrounding surfaces of a room. General lighting can also be used to soften shadows, smooth out and expand the corners of a room, and provide a comfortable level of illumination for safe movement and general maintenance.

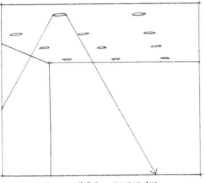

POINT SOURCES - DIRECT

Recessed downlights must have a wide beam spread to provide general lighting effectively.

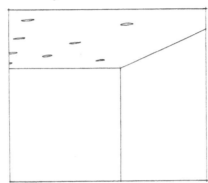

POINT SOURCES - DIRECT

Not being visually active, recessed downlights can be spaced evenly or unevenly.

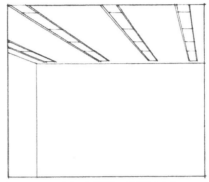

LINEAR SOURCES - DIRECT

Fluorescent luminaires parallel to our line of sight can accentuate depth.

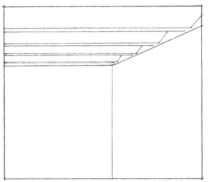

LINEAR SOURCES - DIRECT

The same fixtures perpendicular to our line of sight can increase apparent width.

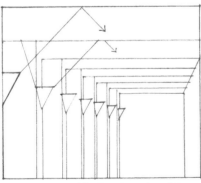

POINT SOURCES - INDIRECT

With wide-spread beams, indirect lighting fixtures can provide general lighting.

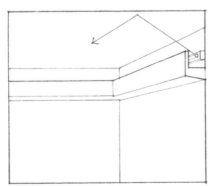

LINEAR SOURCE - INDIRECT

Cove lighting borders a room and uses the ceiling as a reflector to provide general lighting.

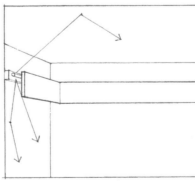

LINEAR - DIRECT/INDIRECT

Similar to cove lighting, valence lighting also illuminates the wall planes below.

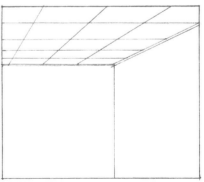

PLANAR SOURCE - DIRECT

Luminous ceilings combine high illumination and diffusion with low brightness.

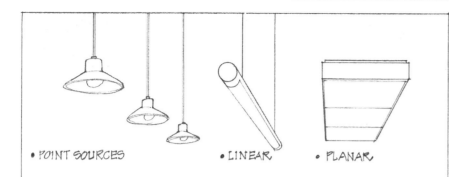

• POINT SOURCES   • LINEAR   • PLANAR

TASK LIGHTING MAY CONSIST OF LUMINAIRES SUSPENDED
DIRECTLY OVER THE VISUAL TASK SURFACE. FOR FLEXIBILITY,
SOME LUMINAIRES MAY BE TRACK MOUNTED.

# TASK LIGHTING

Local or task lighting illuminates specific areas of a space for
the performance of visual tasks or activities. The light sources
are usually placed close to – either above or beside – the task
surface, enabling the available wattage to be used more
efficiently than with general lighting. The luminaires are
normally of the direct type, and adjustability in terms of
brightness (with dimmers or rheostats) and direction is always
desirable.

To minimize the risk of an unacceptable brightness ratio
between task and surroundings, task lighting is often
combined with general lighting. Depending on the types of
luminaires used, local lighting can also contribute to the
general illumination of a space.

In addition to making a visual task easier to see, local lighting
can also create variety and interest, partition a space into a
number of areas, encompass a furniture grouping, or reinforce
the social character of a room.

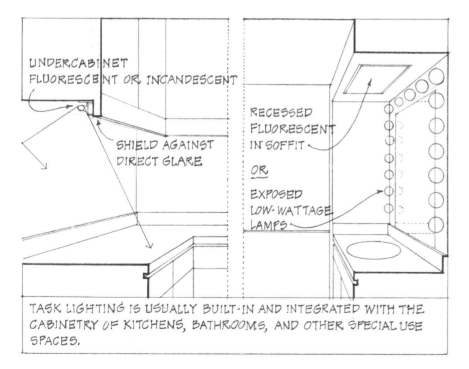

UNDERCABINET
FLUORESCENT OR INCANDESCENT

SHIELD AGAINST
DIRECT GLARE

RECESSED
FLUORESCENT
IN SOFFIT
OR
EXPOSED
LOW-WATTAGE
LAMPS

TASK LIGHTING IS USUALLY BUILT-IN AND INTEGRATED WITH THE
CABINETRY OF KITCHENS, BATHROOMS, AND OTHER SPECIAL USE
SPACES.

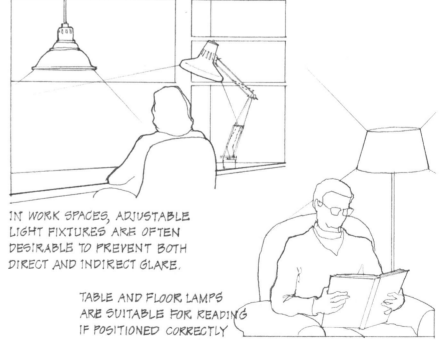

IN WORK SPACES, ADJUSTABLE
LIGHT FIXTURES ARE OFTEN
DESIRABLE TO PREVENT BOTH
DIRECT AND INDIRECT GLARE.

TABLE AND FLOOR LAMPS
ARE SUITABLE FOR READING
IF POSITIONED CORRECTLY

Accent lighting is a form of local lighting which creates focal points or rhythmic patterns of light and dark within a space. Instead of serving simply to illuminate a task or activity, accent lighting can be used to relieve the monotony of general lighting, emphasize a room's features, or highlight art objects or prized possessions.

**ACCENT LIGHTING**

RECESSED DOWNLIGHTS CAN PROVIDE DIFFERENT TYPES OF LIGHT DEPENDING ON THE TYPE OF LAMP AND INTERNAL REFLECTOR USED.

CAST SHADOWS          FRAME ARTWORK          EMPHASIZE TEXTURE

DOWNLIGHTS WITH RELATIVELY WIDE-SPREAD BEAMS ARE USED TO WASH WALLS WITH LIGHT. THE UNIFORMITY OF THE ILLUMINATION DEPENDS ON HOW WIDELY THE LUMINAIRES ARE SPACED AND HOW FAR THEY ARE SET FROM THE WALL.

# DESIGN PRINCIPLES

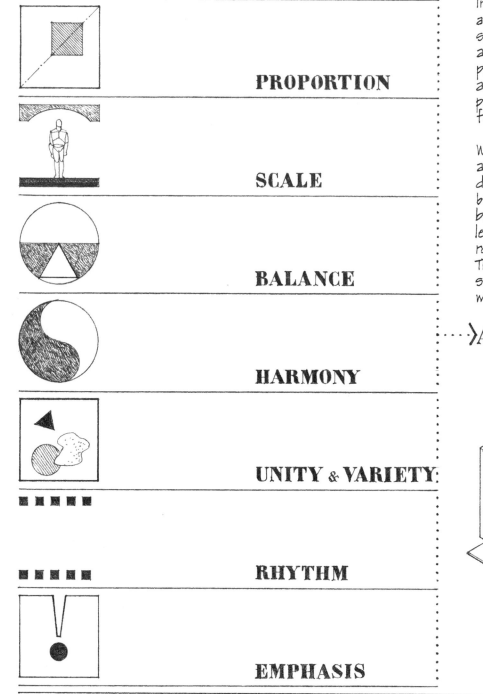

PROPORTION

SCALE

BALANCE

HARMONY

UNITY & VARIETY

RHYTHM

EMPHASIS

Interior design involves the selection of interior design elements and the arrangement of them within a spatial enclosure to satisfy certain functional and aesthetic needs and wishes. This arrangement of elements in a space includes the act of making patterns. No one single part or element in a space stands alone. In a design pattern, all of the parts, elements, or pieces depend on one another for their visual impact, function, and meaning.

We are concerned here with the visual relationships established among the interior design elements in a space. The following design principles are not intended to be hard and fast rules, but rather guidelines to the possible ways design elements can be arranged into recognizable patterns. Ultimately, we must learn to judge the appropriateness of a pattern, its visual role in a space, and its meaning to the users of the space. These principles, however, can help develop and maintain a sense of visual order among the design elements of a space while accommodating their intended use and function.

## ⟩ARRANGING DESIGN PATTERNS

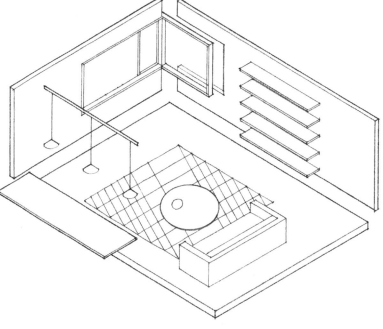

Proportion refers to the relationship of one part to another or to the whole, or between one object and another. This relationship may be one of magnitude, quantity, or degree.

MAGNITUDE

QUANTITY

DEGREE

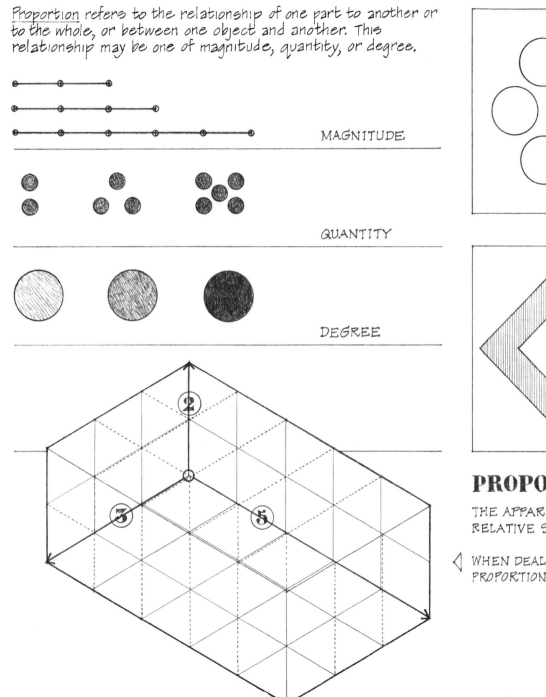

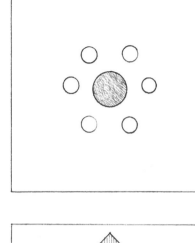

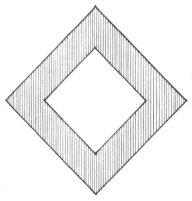

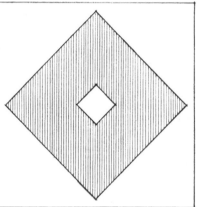

# PROPORTION

THE APPARENT SIZE OF AN OBJECT IS INFLUENCED BY THE RELATIVE SIZES OF OTHER OBJECTS IN ITS ENVIRONMENT.

◁ WHEN DEALING WITH FORMS IN SPACE, ONE MUST CONSIDER PROPORTION IN THREE DIMENSIONS.

**RATIO** ............ $A : B$ $\quad \dfrac{A}{B}$

**PROPORTION** ... $A : B : C$ $\quad \dfrac{A}{B} = \dfrac{B}{C}$

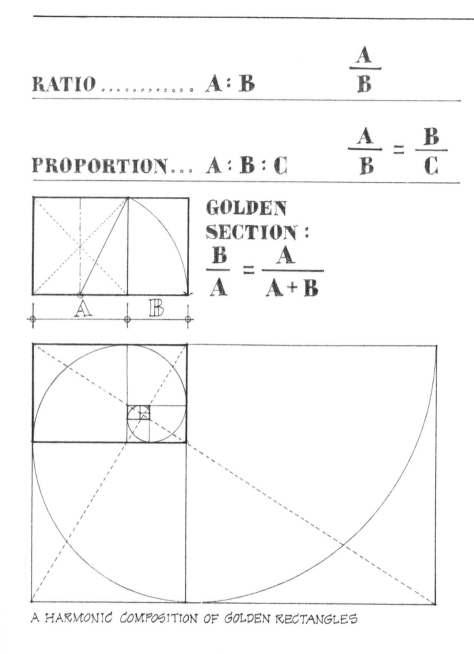

**GOLDEN SECTION :**

$$\dfrac{B}{A} = \dfrac{A}{A + B}$$

A HARMONIC COMPOSITION OF GOLDEN RECTANGLES

# 1, 1, 2, 3, 5, 8, 13, 21, 34, 55 ............

In the course of history, several mathematical or geometric methods have been developed to determine the ideal proportion of things. These proportioning systems go beyond functional and technical determinants in an attempt to establish a measure of beauty – an aesthetic rationale for the dimensional relationships among the parts and elements of a visual construction.

According to Euclid, the ancient Greek mathematician, a ratio refers to the quantitative comparison of two similar things, while proportion refers to the equality of ratios. Underlying any proportioning system, therefore, is a characteristic ratio, a permanent quality that is transmitted from one ratio to another.

Perhaps the most familiar proportioning system is the golden section established by the ancient Greeks. It defines the unique relationship between two unequal parts of a whole in which the ratio between the smaller and greater parts is equal to the ratio between the greater part and the whole.

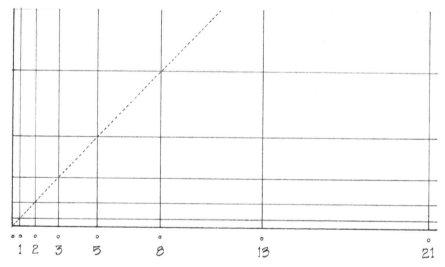

1 2 3   5   8   13   21

THE FIBONACCI SERIES IS A PROGRESSION OF WHOLE NUMBERS WHERE EACH TERM IS THE SUM OF THE PRECEDING TWO. THE RATIO BETWEEN TWO CONSECUTIVE TERMS APPROXIMATES THE GOLDEN SECTION.

Although often defined in mathematical terms, a proportioning system establishes a consistent set of visual relationships among the parts of a composition. It can be a useful design tool in promoting unity and harmony. Our perception of the physical dimensions of things is, however, often imprecise. The foreshortening of perspective, viewing distance, even cultural bias, can distort our perception.

The matter of proportion is still primarily one of critical visual judgment. In this respect, significant differences in the relative dimensions of things are important. Ultimately, a proportion will appear to be correct for a given situation when we sense that neither too little nor too much of an element or characteristic is present.

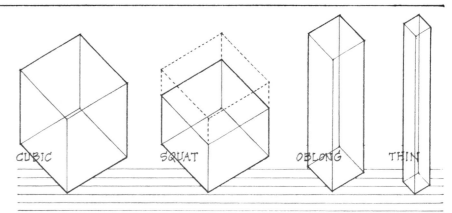

SIGNIFICANT DIFFERENCES IN PROPORTION

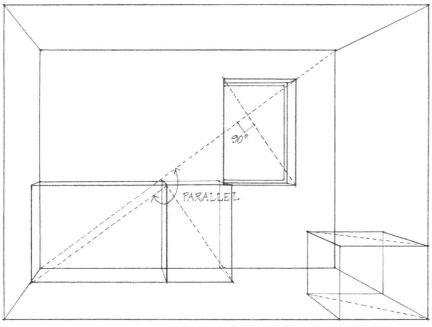

DIAGONALS WHICH ARE PARALLEL OR PERPENDICULAR TO EACH OTHER INDICATE THAT THE RECTANGLES THEY BISECT HAVE SIMILAR PROPORTIONS.

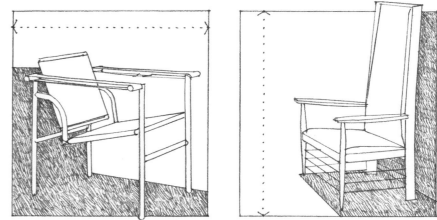

FURNITURE THAT DIFFERS SIGNIFICANTLY IN ITS PROPORTIONS

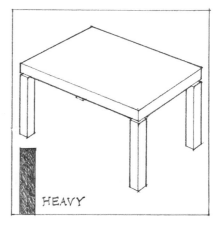

# PROPORTIONAL RELATIONSHIPS

In interior design, we are concerned with the proportional relationships between the parts of a design element, between several design elements, and between the elements and the spatial form and enclosure.

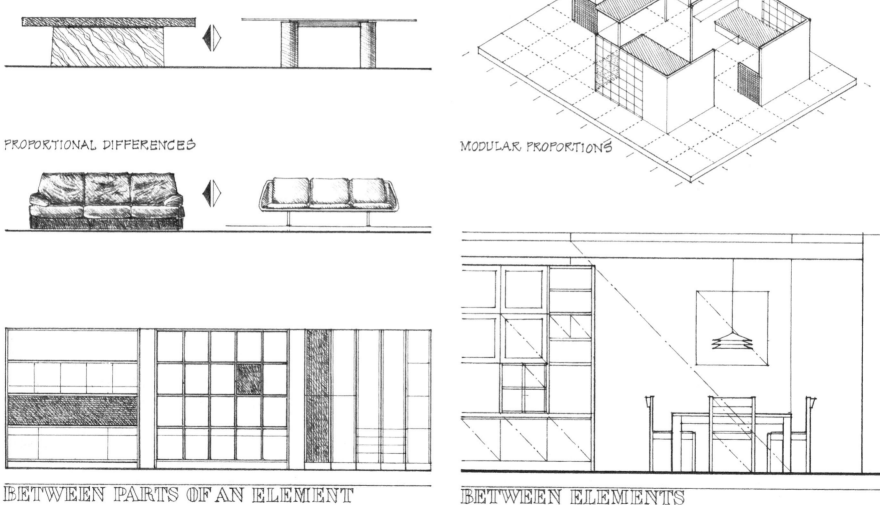

PROPORTIONAL DIFFERENCES

MODULAR PROPORTIONS

BETWEEN PARTS OF AN ELEMENT

BETWEEN ELEMENTS

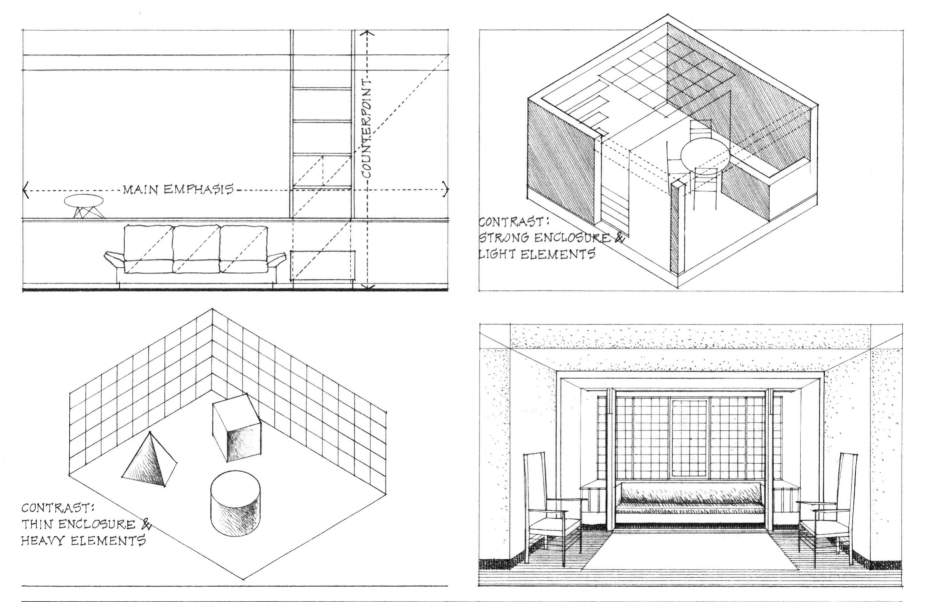

MAIN EMPHASIS

COUNTERPOINT

CONTRAST:
STRONG ENCLOSURE &
LIGHT ELEMENTS

CONTRAST:
THIN ENCLOSURE &
HEAVY ELEMENTS

BETWEEN ELEMENTS & SPATIAL ENCLOSURE

# SCALE

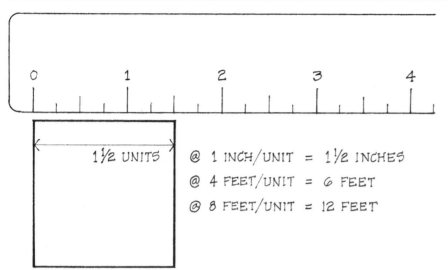

1½ UNITS

@ 1 INCH/UNIT = 1½ INCHES
@ 4 FEET/UNIT = 6 FEET
@ 8 FEET/UNIT = 12 FEET

The design principle of scale is related to proportion. Both proportion and scale deal with the relative sizes of things. If there is a difference, proportion pertains to the relationships between the parts of a composition, while scale refers specifically to the size of something, relative to some known standard or recognized constant.

Mechanical scale is the calculation of something's physical size according to a standard system of measurement. For example, we can say that a table is, according to the U.S. Customary System, 3 feet wide, 6 feet long, and 29 inches high. If we are familiar with this system and with objects of similar size, we can visualize how big the table is. Using the International Metric System, the same table would measure 914 mm wide, 1829 mm long, and 737 mm high.

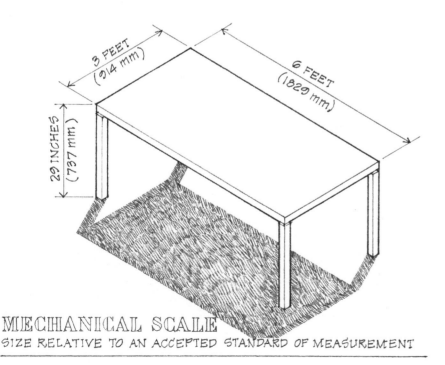

3 FEET
(914 mm)

6 FEET
(1829 mm)

29 INCHES
(737 mm)

## MECHANICAL SCALE
SIZE RELATIVE TO AN ACCEPTED STANDARD OF MEASUREMENT

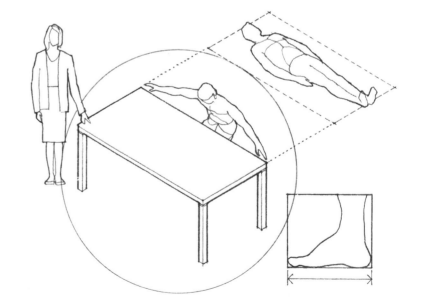

OUR BODIES CAN ALSO SERVE AS A SYSTEM OF MEASUREMENT

Visual scale refers to the bigness something appears to have when measured against other things around it. Thus, an object's scale is often a judgment we make based on the relative or known sizes of other nearby or surrounding elements. For example, the aforementioned table can appear to be in scale or out of scale with a room, depending on the relative size and proportions of the space.

We can refer to something as being small-scale if we are measuring it against other things which are generally much larger in size. Similarly, an object can be considered to be large-scale if it is grouped with relatively small items, or if it appears to be larger than what is considered normal or average in size.

SMALL-SCALE SPACE OR LARGE-SCALE FURNITURE

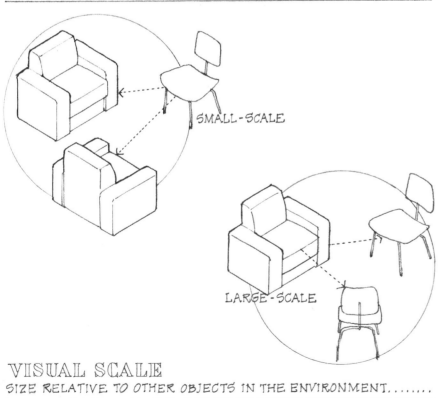

SMALL-SCALE

LARGE-SCALE

# VISUAL SCALE
SIZE RELATIVE TO OTHER OBJECTS IN THE ENVIRONMENT........

OR TO THE SURROUNDING SPACE

137

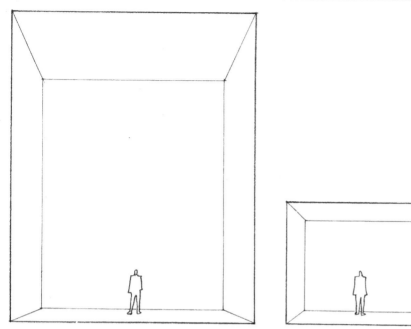

Human scale refers to the feeling of bigness something gives us. If the dimensions of an interior space or the sizes of elements within it make us feel small, we can say they lack human scale. If, on the other hand, the space does not dwarf us or if the elements offer a comfortable fit with our dimensional requirements of reach, clearance, or movement, we can say they are human in scale.

Most of the elements we use to ascertain human scale are those whose dimensions we have become accustomed to through contact and use. These include doorways, stairs, tables and counters, and various types of seating. These elements can be used to humanize a space that would otherwise lack human scale.

# HUMAN SCALE

THE FEELING OF SMALLNESS OR BIGNESS A SPACE OR AN INTERIOR ELEMENT GIVES US.

COMMON ELEMENTS WHOSE DIMENSIONS WE HAVE BECOME ACCUSTOMED TO

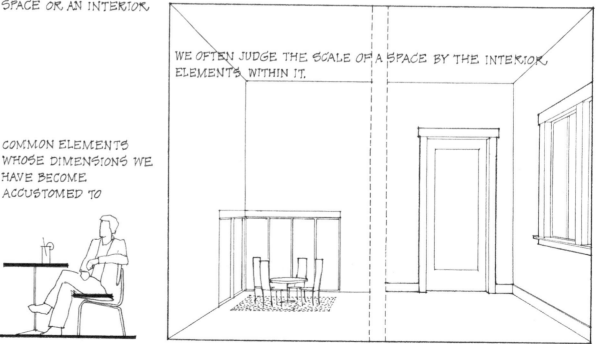

WE OFTEN JUDGE THE SCALE OF A SPACE BY THE INTERIOR ELEMENTS WITHIN IT.

The issue of scale in an interior space is not limited to one set of relationships. Interior elements can be related simultaneously to the whole space, to each other, and to those people who use the space. It is not unusual for some elements to have a normal, orderly scale relationship but have an exceptional scale when compared to other elements. Unusually scaled elements can be used to attract attention or create and emphasize a focal point.

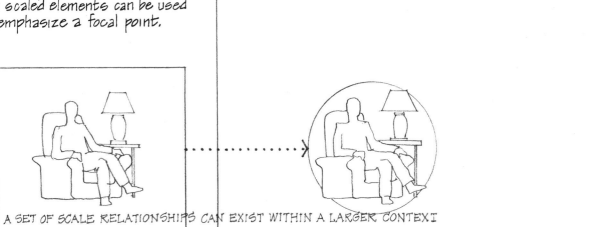

A SET OF SCALE RELATIONSHIPS CAN EXIST WITHIN A LARGER CONTEXT

FIREPLACE MASS SCALED TO SPACE WHILE RAISED HEARTH IS AT SEAT HEIGHT.

DOORWAY AND WINDOWS ARE SCALED TO SPACE WHILE SILL HEIGHTS AND WAINSCOT RETAIN A MORE HUMAN SCALE.

# BALANCE

INTERIORS: A MIX OF SHAPES, COLORS, AND TEXTURES

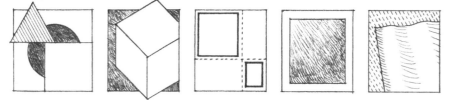

Interior spaces - and their elements of enclosure, furnishings, lighting, and accessories - often include a mix of shapes, sizes, colors, and textures. How these elements are organized is a response to functional needs and aesthetic desires. At the same time, these elements should be arranged to achieve visual balance - a state of equilibrium among the visual forces projected by the elements.

Each element in the ensemble of interior space has specific characteristics of shape, form, size, color, and texture. These characteristics, along with the factors of location and orientation, determine the visual weight of each element and how much attention each will attract in the overall pattern of space.

Characteristics that will enhance or increase the visual weight of an element - and attract our attention - are:

- Irregular or contrasting shapes
- Bright colors and contrasting textures
- Large dimensions and unusual proportions
- Elaborate details

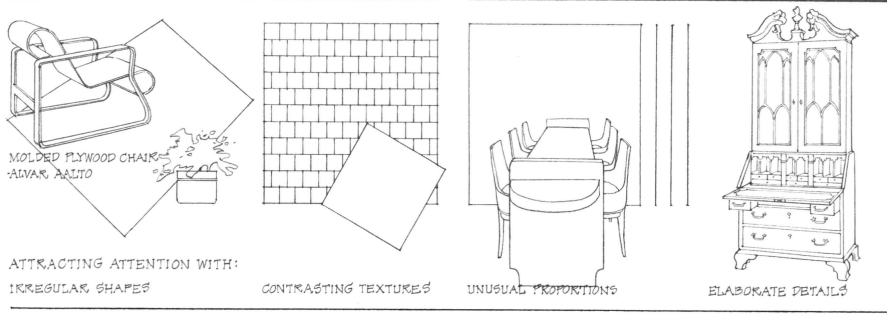

MOLDED PLYWOOD CHAIR -ALVAR AALTO

ATTRACTING ATTENTION WITH:

IRREGULAR SHAPES          CONTRASTING TEXTURES          UNUSUAL PROPORTIONS          ELABORATE DETAILS

Our perception of a room and the composition of its elements is altered as we use it and move through its space. Our perspective varies as our point of view shifts from here to there. A room also undergoes changes over time as it is illuminated by the light of day and lamps at night, occupied by people and paraphernalia, and modified by time itself. The visual balance among the elements in a space should therefore be considered in three dimensions and be strong enough to withstand the changes brought about through time and use.

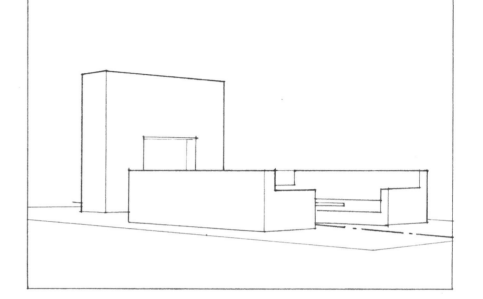

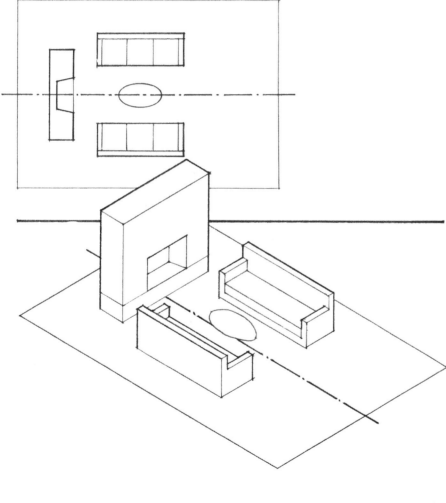

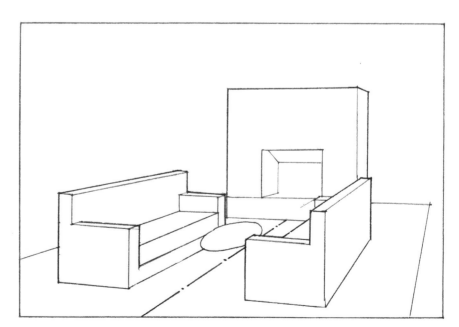

VISUAL BALANCE MUST BE CONSIDERED IN THREE DIMENSIONS.

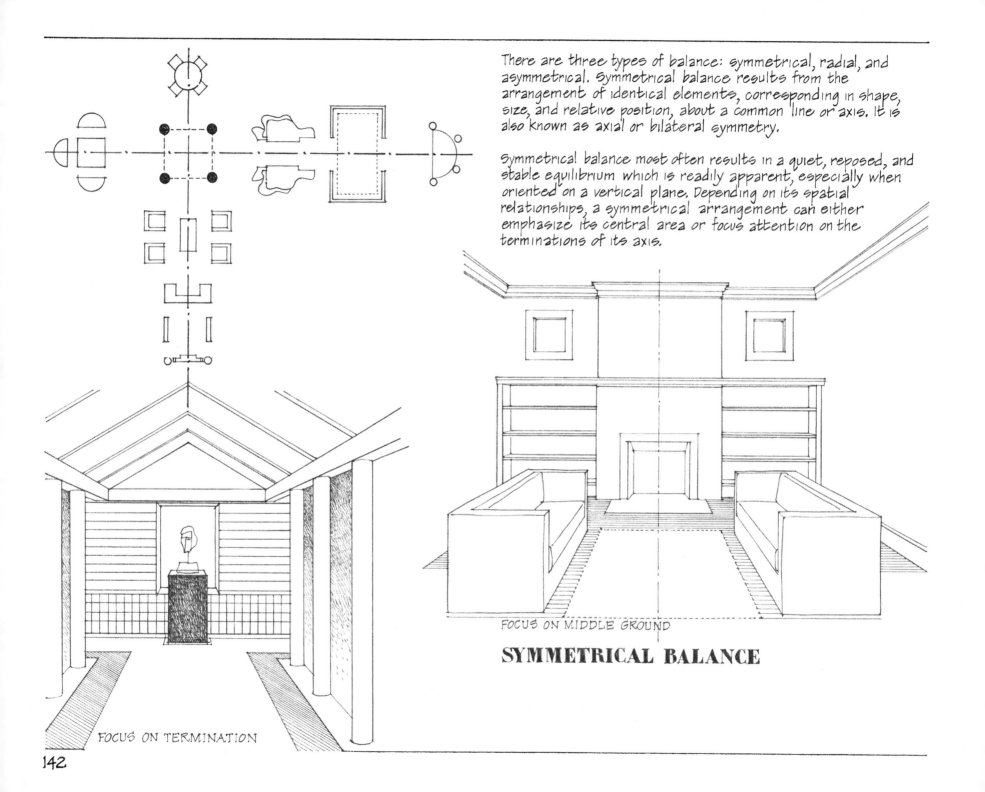

There are three types of balance: symmetrical, radial, and asymmetrical. Symmetrical balance results from the arrangement of identical elements, corresponding in shape, size, and relative position, about a common line or axis. It is also known as axial or bilateral symmetry.

Symmetrical balance most often results in a quiet, reposed, and stable equilibrium which is readily apparent, especially when oriented on a vertical plane. Depending on its spatial relationships, a symmetrical arrangement can either emphasize its central area or focus attention on the terminations of its axis.

FOCUS ON TERMINATION

FOCUS ON MIDDLE GROUND

## SYMMETRICAL BALANCE

Symmetry is a simple yet powerful device to establish visual order. If carried far enough, it can impose a strict formality on an interior space. Total symmetry, however, is often undesirable or difficult to achieve, because of function or circumstance.

It is often possible or desirable to arrange one or more parts of a space in a symmetrical manner and produce local symmetry. Symmetrical groupings within a space are easily recognized and have a quality of wholeness that can serve to simplify or organize the room's composition.

The second type of balance, radial balance, results from the arrangement of elements about a center point. It produces a centralized composition which stresses the middle ground as a focal point. The elements can focus inward toward the center, face outward from the center, or simply be placed about a central element.

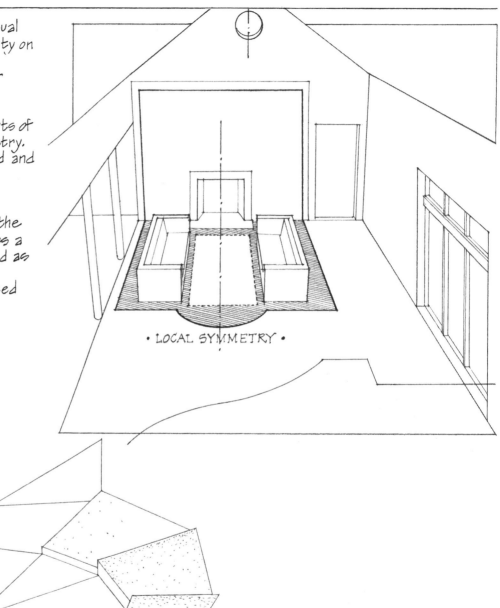

· LOCAL SYMMETRY ·

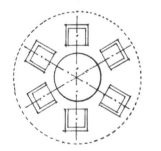

# RADIAL BALANCE

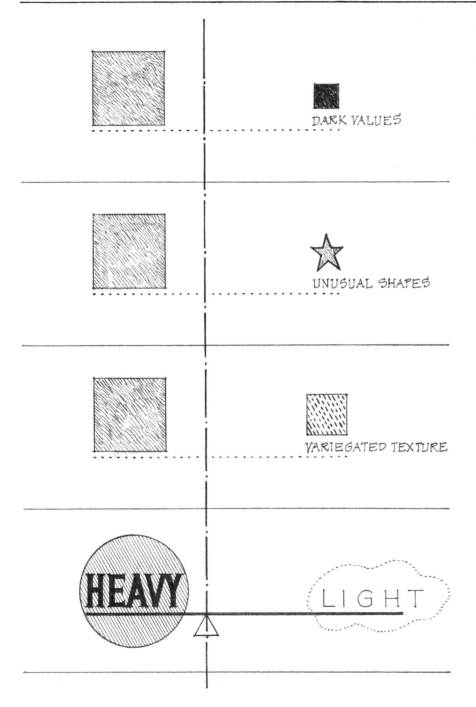

DARK VALUES

UNUSUAL SHAPES

VARIEGATED TEXTURE

HEAVY    LIGHT

Asymmetry is recognized as the lack of correspondence in size, shape, color, or relative position among the elements of a composition. While a symmetrical composition requires the use of pairs of identical elements, an asymmetrical composition incorporates dissimilar elements.

To achieve an occult or optical balance, an asymmetrical composition must take into account the visual weight or force of each of its elements and employ the principle of leverage in their arrangement. Elements which are visually forceful and attract our attention - unusual shapes, bright colors, dark values, variegated textures - must be counterbalanced by less forceful elements which are larger or placed farther away from the center of the composition.

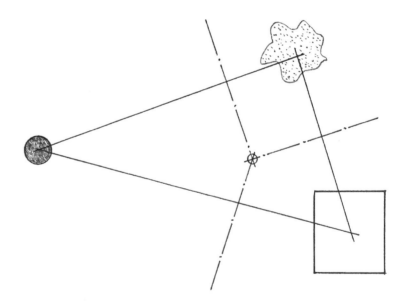

## ASYMMETRICAL BALANCE

Asymmetrical balance is not as obvious as symmetry and is often more visually active and dynamic. It is capable of expressing movement, change, even exuberance. It is also more flexible than symmetry and can adapt more readily to varying conditions of function, space, and circumstance.

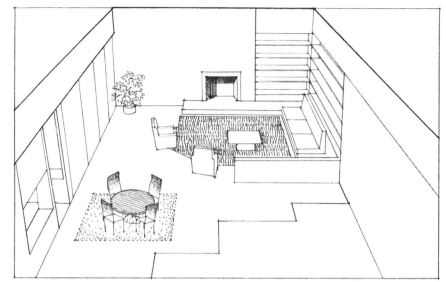

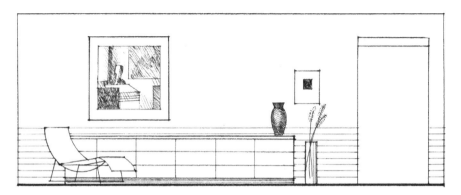

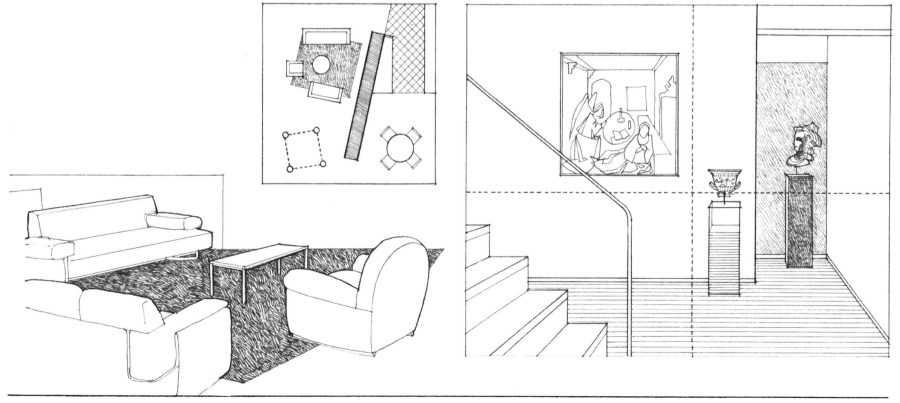

# HARMONY

Harmony can be defined as consonance or the pleasing agreement of parts or combination of parts in a composition. While balance achieves unity through the careful arrangement of both similar and dissimilar elements, the principle of harmony involves the careful selection of elements that share a common trait or characteristic, such as shape, color, texture, or material. It is the repetition of a common trait that produces unity and visual harmony among the elements in an interior setting.

SHARING A COMMON TRAIT:

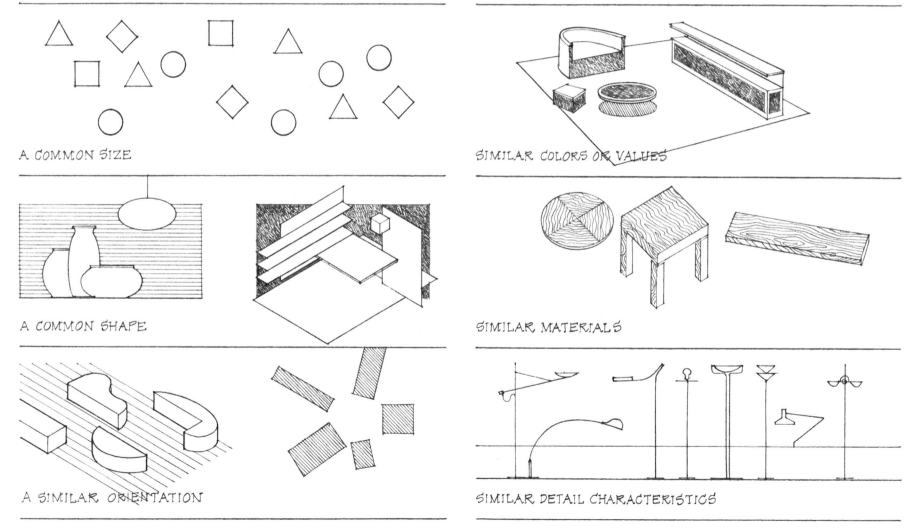

A COMMON SIZE

SIMILAR COLORS OR VALUES

A COMMON SHAPE

SIMILAR MATERIALS

A SIMILAR ORIENTATION

SIMILAR DETAIL CHARACTERISTICS

Harmony, when carried too far in the use of elements with similar traits, can result in a unified but uninteresting composition. Variety, on the other hand, when carried to an extreme for the sake of interest, can result in visual chaos. It is the careful and artistic tension between order and disorder - between unity and variety - that enlivens harmony and creates interest in an interior setting.

## INTRODUCING VARIETY:

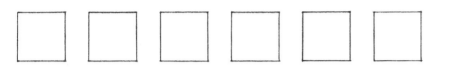

GIVEN A SET OF IDENTICAL SHAPES, VARIETY CAN BE INTRODUCED BY:

VARYING ORIENTATION

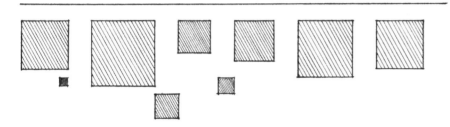

## VARYING SIZE

VARYING DETAIL CHARACTERISTICS

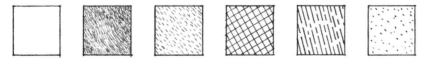

## VARYING TEXTURE

## VARYING COLOR

# UNITY & VARIETY

It is important to note that the principles of balance and harmony, in promoting unity, do not exclude the pursuit of variety and interest. Rather, the means for achieving balance and harmony are intended to include in their patterns the presence of dissimilar elements and characteristics.

For example, asymmetrical balance produces equilibrium among elements that differ in size, shape, color, or texture. The harmony produced by elements that share a common characteristic permits the same elements to also have a variety of unique, individual traits.

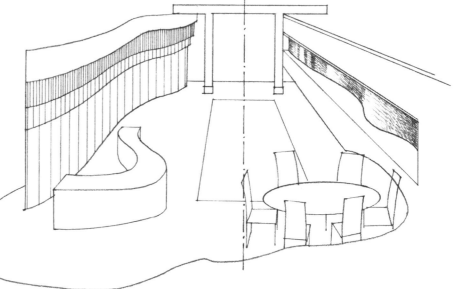

ASYMMETRICAL SCHEMES CAN ORGANIZE A VARIETY OF SHAPES, COLORS, AND TEXTURES INTO THEIR LAYOUTS.

OFFICE CHAIRS WITH SIMILAR DIMENSIONS, BUT VARIED IN CONTOUR AND OTHER DETAILS.

Another method for organizing a number of dissimilar elements is simply to arrange them in close proximity to one another. We tend to read such a grouping as an entity to the exclusion of other elements farther away. To further reinforce the visual unity of the composition, continuity of line or contour can be established among the elements' shapes.

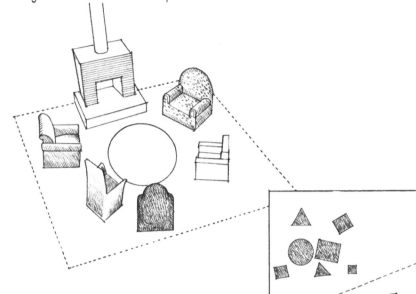

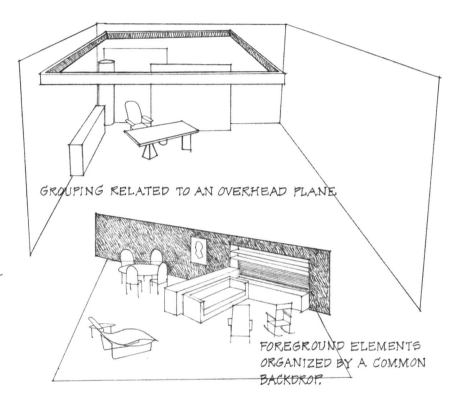

GROUPING RELATED TO AN OVERHEAD PLANE.

DISSIMILAR ELEMENTS CAN BE ORGANIZED BY GROUPING THEM IN CLOSE PROXIMITY, OR BY RELATING THEM TO A COMMON LINE OR PLANE.

FOREGROUND ELEMENTS ORGANIZED BY A COMMON BACKDROP.

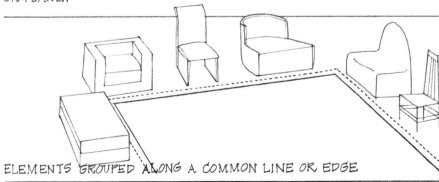

ELEMENTS GROUPED ALONG A COMMON LINE OR EDGE

# RHYTHM

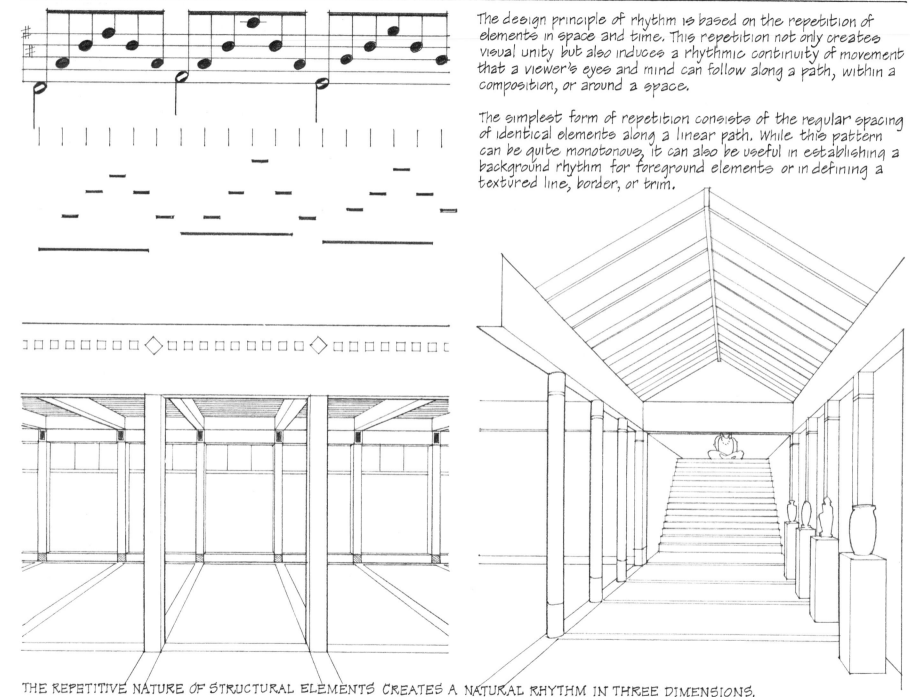

The design principle of rhythm is based on the repetition of elements in space and time. This repetition not only creates visual unity but also induces a rhythmic continuity of movement that a viewer's eyes and mind can follow along a path, within a composition, or around a space.

The simplest form of repetition consists of the regular spacing of identical elements along a linear path. While this pattern can be quite monotonous, it can also be useful in establishing a background rhythm for foreground elements or in defining a textured line, border, or trim.

THE REPETITIVE NATURE OF STRUCTURAL ELEMENTS CREATES A NATURAL RHYTHM IN THREE DIMENSIONS.

More intricate patterns of rhythm can be produced by taking into account the tendency for elements to be visually related by their proximity to one another or their sharing of a common trait.

The spacing of the recurring elements, and thus the pace of the visual rhythm, can be varied to create sets and subsets and to emphasize certain points in the pattern. The resulting rhythm may be graceful and flowing, or crisp and sharp. The contour of the rhythmic pattern and the shape of the individual elements can further reinforce the nature of the sequence.

While the recurring elements must, for continuity, share a common trait, they can also vary in shape, detail, color, or texture. These differences, whether subtle or distinct, create visual interest and can introduce other levels of complexity. An alternating rhythm can be superimposed over a more regular one, or the variations can be progressively graded in size or color value to give direction to the sequence.

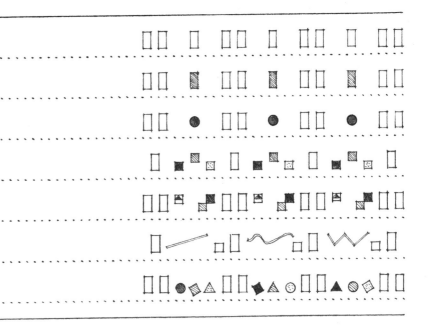

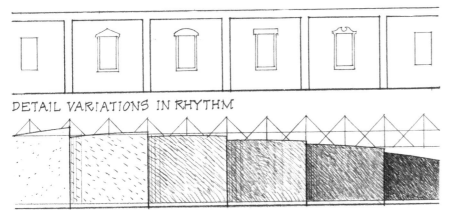

DETAIL VARIATIONS IN RHYTHM

GRADATION IN VALUE OR COLOR

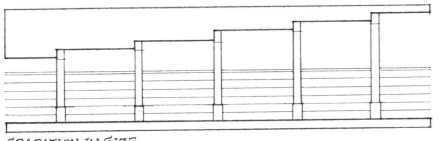

GRADATION IN SIZE

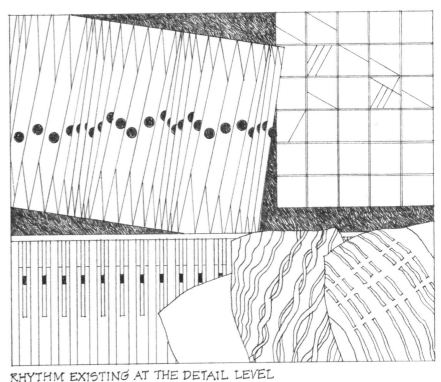

RHYTHM EXISTING AT THE DETAIL LEVEL

Visual rhythm is most easily recognized when the repetition forms a linear pattern. Within an interior space, however, nonlinear sequences of shape, color, and texture can provide more subtle rhythms which may not be immediately obvious to the eye.

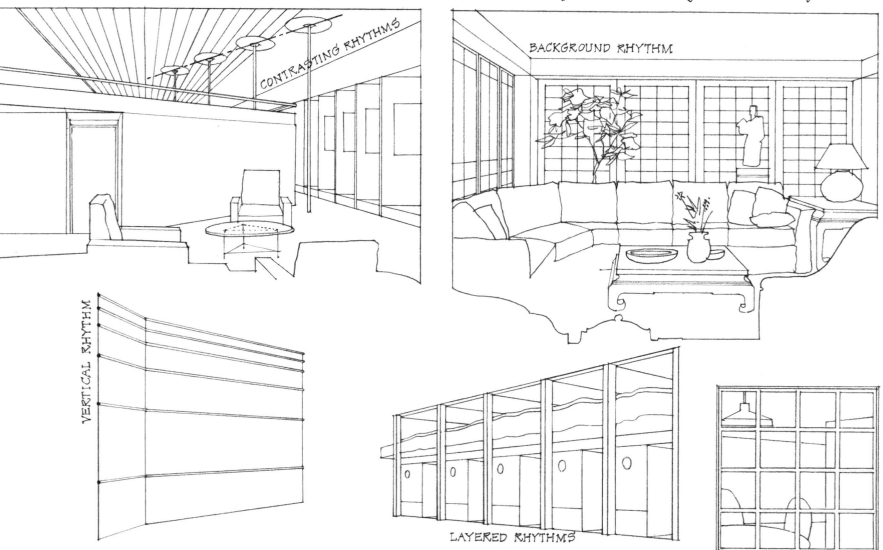

CONTRASTING RHYTHMS

BACKGROUND RHYTHM

VERTICAL RHYTHM

LAYERED RHYTHMS

FOREGROUND RHYTHM

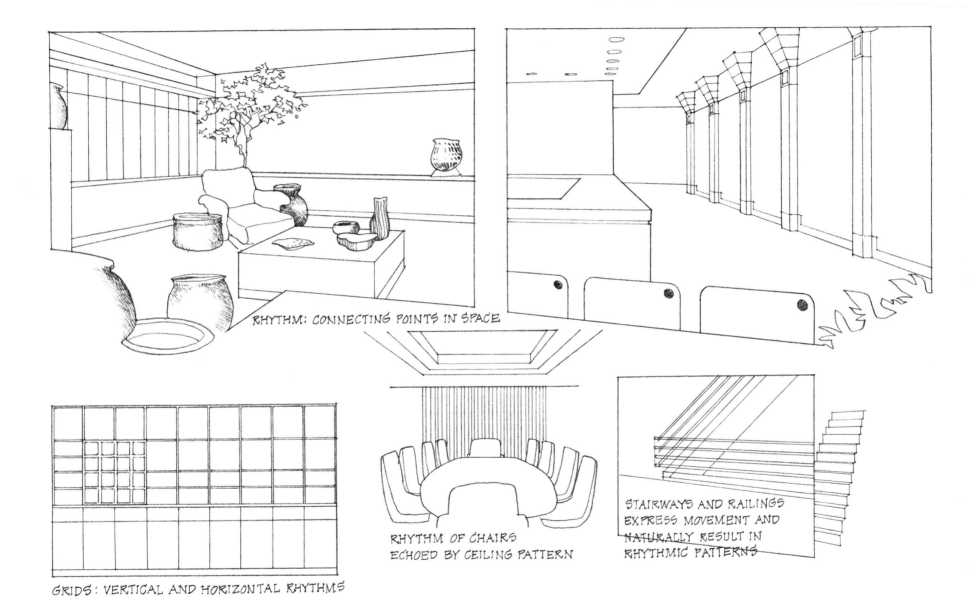

RHYTHM: CONNECTING POINTS IN SPACE

GRIDS: VERTICAL AND HORIZONTAL RHYTHMS

RHYTHM OF CHAIRS
ECHOED BY CEILING PATTERN

STAIRWAYS AND RAILINGS
EXPRESS MOVEMENT AND
NATURALLY RESULT IN
RHYTHMIC PATTERNS

# EMPHASIS

NO DOMINANT ELEMENTS -
NO EMPHASIS

TOO MANY DOMINANT
ELEMENTS - NO EMPHASIS

POINTS OF EMPHASIS CAN BE
CREATED BY A PERCEPTIBLE
CONTRAST IN SIZE, SHAPE,
COLOR, OR VALUE.

The principle of emphasis assumes the coexistence of dominant and subordinate elements in the composition of an interior setting. A design without any dominant elements would be bland and monotonous. If there are too many assertive elements, the design would be cluttered and chaotic, detracting from what may truly be important. Each part of a design should be given proper significance according to its degree of importance in the overall scheme.

An important element or feature can be given visual emphasis by endowing it with significant size, a unique shape, or a contrasting color, value, or texture. In each case, a discernible contrast must be established between the dominant element or feature and the subordinate aspects of the space. Such contrast would attract our attention by interrupting the normal pattern of the composition.

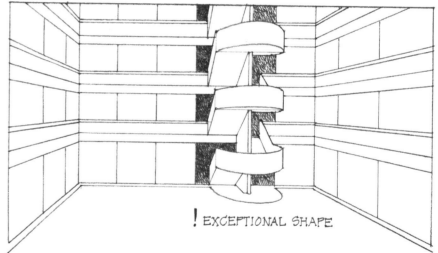

! EXCEPTIONAL SHAPE

! EXCEPTIONAL SIZE

An element or feature can also be visually emphasized by its strategic position and orientation in a space. It can be centered within the space or serve as the centerpiece of a symmetrical organization. In an asymmetric composition, it can be offset or isolated from the rest of the elements. It can be the termination of a linear sequence or a path of movement.

To further enhance its visual importance, an element can be oriented to contrast with the normal geometry of the space and the other elements within it. It can be lit in a special manner. The lines of secondary and subordinate elements can be arranged to focus our attention on the significant element or feature.

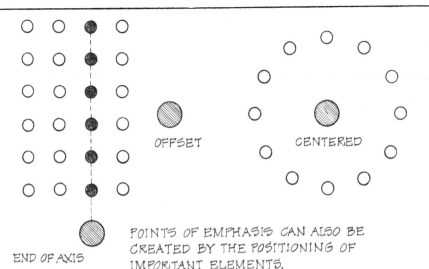

OFFSET          CENTERED

END OF AXIS

POINTS OF EMPHASIS CAN ALSO BE CREATED BY THE POSITIONING OF IMPORTANT ELEMENTS.

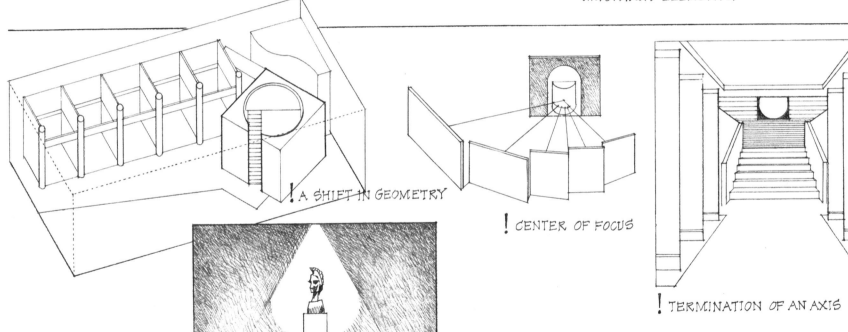

! A SHIFT IN GEOMETRY

! CENTER OF FOCUS

! TERMINATION OF AN AXIS

! SPOTLIGHTED

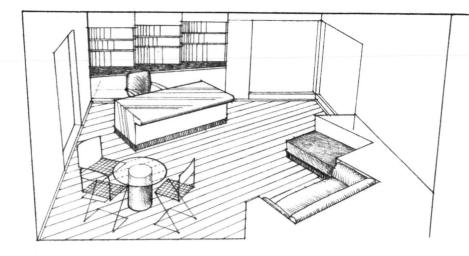

Just as there may be varying degrees of importance among the elements in an interior setting, there can also be varying degrees of emphasis given to them. Once the significant elements or features are established, then a strategy for orchestrating the subordinate elements must be devised to enhance the dominant ones.

A room's focal points should be created with some subtlety and restraint. They should not be so visually dominant that they cease to be integral parts of the overall design. Secondary points of emphasis - visual accents - can often help knit together dominant and subordinate elements. Following the principle of harmony, related shapes, colors, and values can also help retain unity of design.

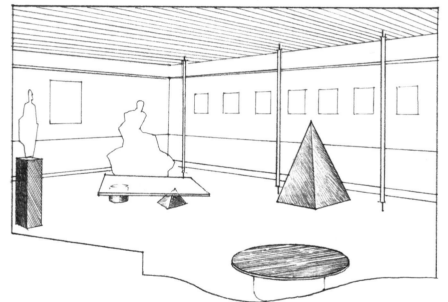

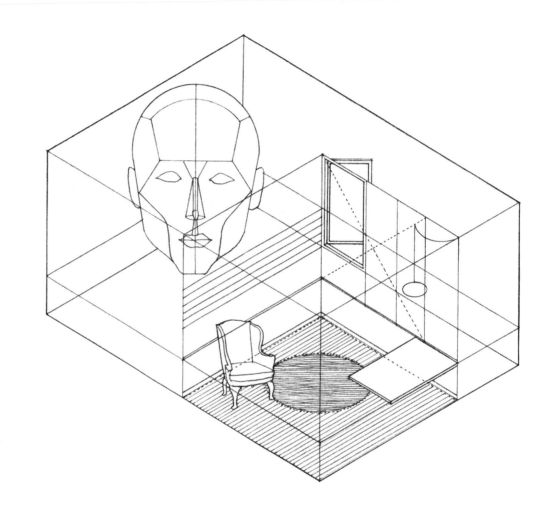

# 4
# INTERIOR DESIGN
# ELEMENTS

# INTERIOR DESIGN ELEMENTS

Interior spaces within buildings are defined by the architectural elements of structure and enclosure - columns, walls, floors, and roofs. These elements give a building its form, demarcate a portion of infinite space, and set up a pattern of interior spaces. This chapter outlines the major elements of interior design with which we develop, modify, and enhance these interior spaces and make them habitable - functionally fit, aesthetically pleasing, and psychologically satisfying - for our activities.

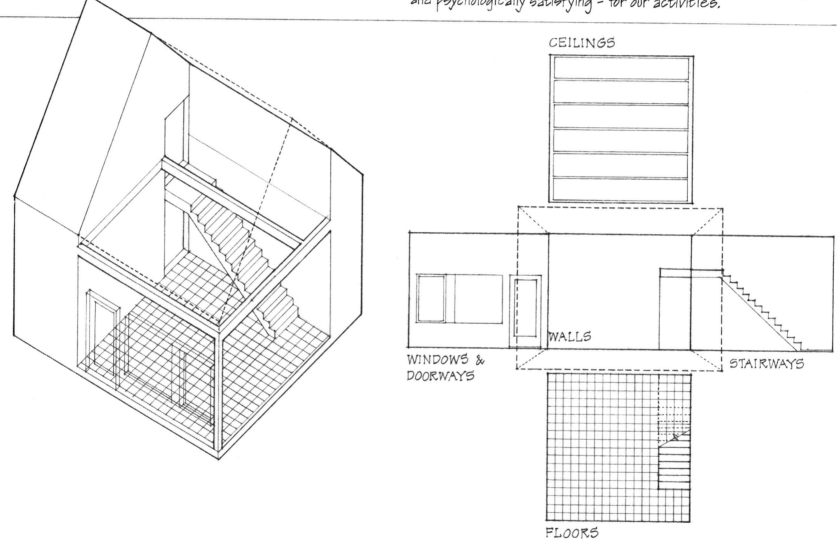

CEILINGS

WALLS

WINDOWS & DOORWAYS

STAIRWAYS

FLOORS

These design elements, and the choices they represent, are the interior designer's palette. The manner in which we select and manipulate these elements into a spatial, visual, sensory pattern will affect not only the function and use of a space but also its expressive qualities of form and style.

SEATING

TABLES

BEDS

WORK SURFACES

STORAGE

LIGHTING

ACCESSORIES

# FLOORS

Floors are the flat, level base planes of interior space. As the platforms that support our interior activities and furnishings, they must be structured to carry these loads safely, and their surfaces must be durable enough to withstand continual use and wear.

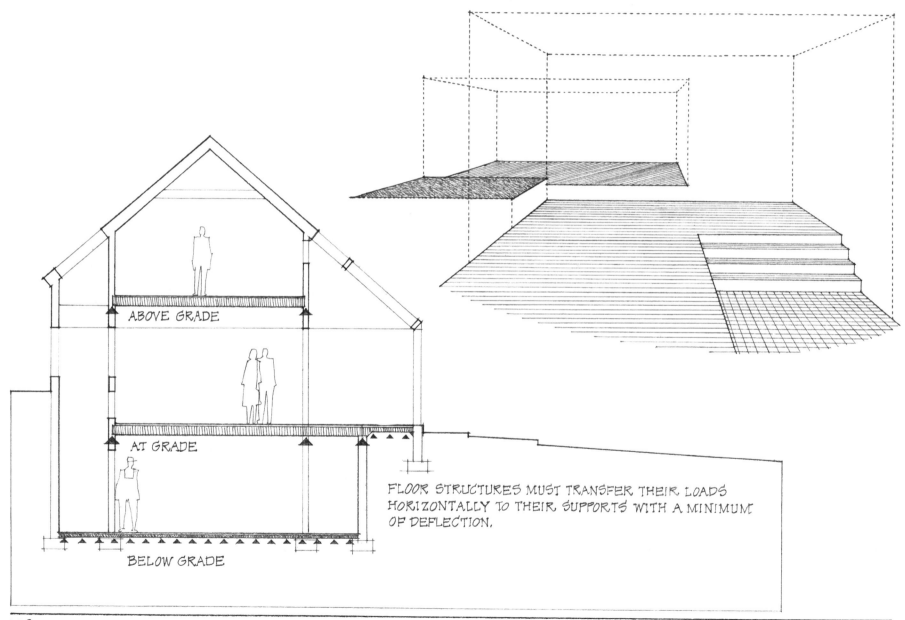

ABOVE GRADE

AT GRADE

BELOW GRADE

FLOOR STRUCTURES MUST TRANSFER THEIR LOADS HORIZONTALLY TO THEIR SUPPORTS WITH A MINIMUM OF DEFLECTION.

A typical floor consists of a series of joists spanning beams or load-bearing walls. This horizontal frame is then layered with a subfloor - a structural material such as plywood or steel decking capable of extending across the joists. The subfloor and joists are secured so that they act together as a structural unit in resisting stresses and transferring loads.

A floor may also consist of a concrete slab, reinforced with steel and capable of extending in one or two directions. The form of a slab's underside often reflects the manner in which it extends across space and transfers its loads. Instead of being cast monolithically in place, a slab can also be precast as planks.

Whether a floor is a concrete slab or framed with joists, its surface must be smooth, level, and dense enough to receive the finish flooring material. To compensate for any roughness or unevenness, a layer of underlayment or a cement topping is required for some flooring materials.

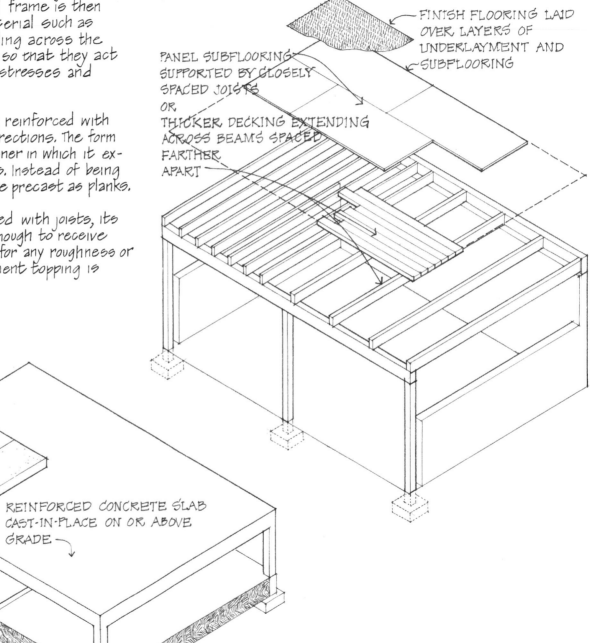

FINISH FLOORING LAID OVER LAYERS OF UNDERLAYMENT AND SUBFLOORING

PANEL SUBFLOORING SUPPORTED BY CLOSELY SPACED JOISTS OR THICKER DECKING EXTENDING ACROSS BEAMS SPACED FARTHER APART

FINISH FLOORING LAID OVER UNDERLAYMENT OR A CEMENT LEVELING COURSE

PRECAST CONCRETE SLABS OR PLANKS

REINFORCED CONCRETE SLAB CAST-IN-PLACE ON OR ABOVE GRADE

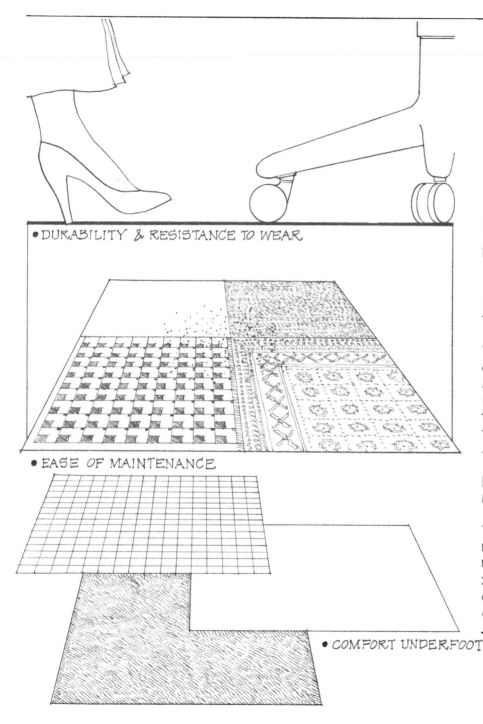

The finish flooring is the final layer of the floor structure. Since the flooring is subject to direct wear and represents a major portion of a room's surface area, it should be selected with both functional and aesthetic criteria in mind.

Durability is of utmost importance because of the wear and use a flooring material must withstand from our feet as well as the occasional moving of furniture and equipment. The flooring material should be resistant to physical abrasion, denting, and scuffing.

• DURABILITY & RESISTANCE TO WEAR

Directly related to a flooring's durability is the ease with which it can be maintained in good condition. For durability as well as ease of maintenance, a flooring material should be resistant to dirt, moisture, grease, and staining, especially in work and high-traffic areas.

There are several strategies for disguising the dirt that normally collects on a floor. One is to use neutral colors of middle value. Another is to use a pattern that camouflages any dirt and surface marks. Still another is to use a material whose natural color and texture is attractive and more noticeable than any dirt on the floor.

• EASE OF MAINTENANCE

Foot comfort is related to the degree of resilience a flooring material has and, to a lesser degree, its warmth.

The warmth of a floor may be real or apparent. A flooring material may be warmed by radiant heat and kept warm by insulating the floor. The flooring may also appear warm if it has a soft texture, a middle to dark value, or a warm hue. Of course, in warm climates, a cool floor surface would be more comfortable than a warm one.

• COMFORT UNDERFOOT

# FINISH FLOORING: FUNCTIONAL CRITERIA

In areas susceptible to wetting, it is advisable to avoid using hard, slick flooring materials.

Hard floor surfaces reflect airborne sound originating from within a room, and amplify impact noise caused by our footwear or the moving of equipment. Resilient flooring can cushion some of this impact noise. Soft, plush, or porous flooring materials reduce impact noise as well as help muffle airborne sound reaching their surfaces.

Light-colored flooring will reflect more of the light falling on its surface and help make a room seem brighter than will dark, textured flooring.

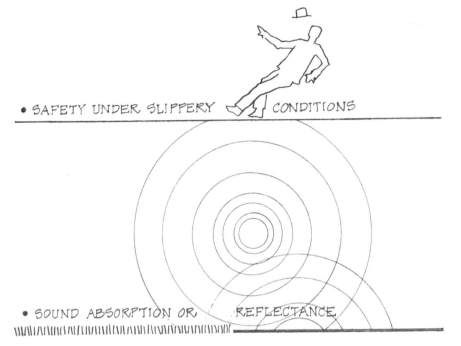

- SAFETY UNDER SLIPPERY CONDITIONS

- SOUND ABSORPTION OR REFLECTANCE

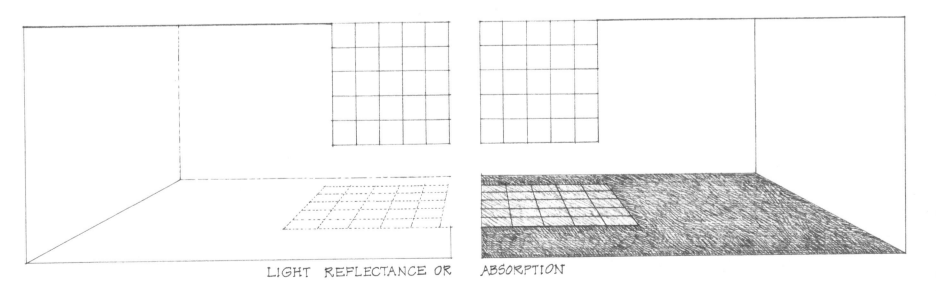

LIGHT REFLECTANCE OR ABSORPTION

Although generally considered to be a utilitarian surface and a visual background for an interior space, the floor can, through its color, pattern, and texture, play an active role in determining the character of a space.

A light-colored floor will enhance the light level within a room, while a dark floor will absorb much of the light falling on its surface. A warm, light color has an elevating effect on a floor, while a warm, dark floor conveys a sense of security. A cool, light color suggests spaciousness and emphasizes the smoothness of polished floors. A cool, dark color gives a floor plane depth and weight.

• COLOR

Unlike the wall and ceiling surfaces of a room, a floor transmits its tactile qualities - its texture and density - directly to us as we walk across its surface.

The physical texture of a flooring material and how the material is laid are directly related to the visual pattern created. It is this visual texture that communicates to us the nature of the flooring material and the character of a space.

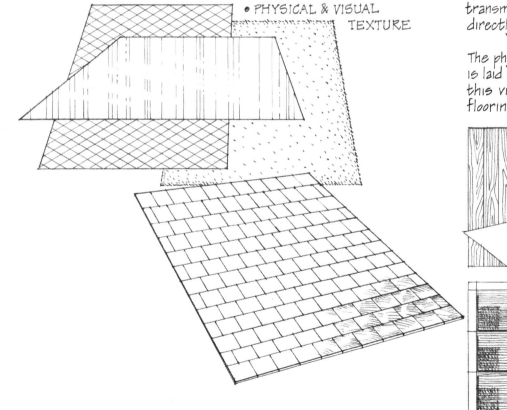

• PHYSICAL & VISUAL TEXTURE

# FINISH FLOORING: AESTHETIC CRITERIA

While a neutral, patternless floor can serve as a simple background for a room's occupants and furnishings, a floor can also become, through the use of pattern, a dominant element in an interior space. The pattern can be used to define areas, suggest paths of movement, or simply provide textural interest.

Our perception of a flooring pattern is affected by the laws of perspective. Thus a small-scale pattern may often be seen as a fine texture or a blended tone rather than as a composition of individual design elements.

In addition, any continuous linear elements in a flooring pattern will dominate. Directional patterns can often affect the apparent proportion of a floor, either exaggerating or foreshortening one of its dimensions.

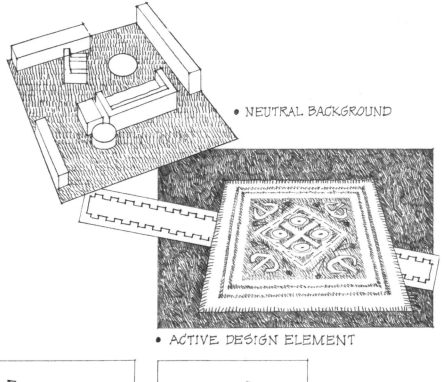

• NEUTRAL BACKGROUND

• ACTIVE DESIGN ELEMENT

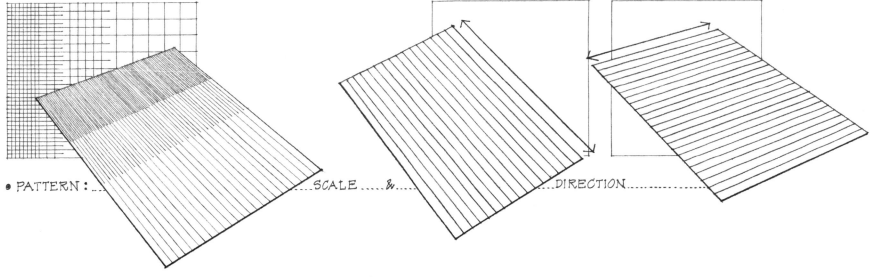

• PATTERN: ........................ SCALE .... & .................... DIRECTION ...............

# WOOD FLOORING

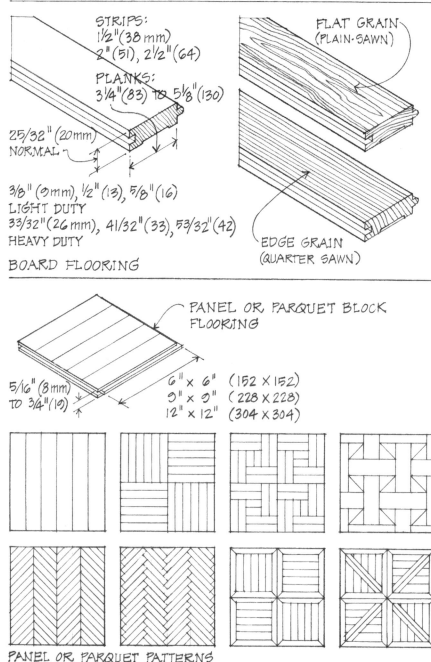

STRIPS:
1½" (38 mm)
2" (51), 2½" (64)

PLANKS:
3¼" (83) TO 5⅛" (130)

25/32" (20mm)
NORMAL

3/8" (9mm), ½" (13), 5/8" (16)
LIGHT DUTY
33/32" (26mm), 41/32" (33), 53/32" (42)
HEAVY DUTY

BOARD FLOORING

FLAT GRAIN
(PLAIN-SAWN)

EDGE GRAIN
(QUARTER SAWN)

PANEL OR PARQUET BLOCK
FLOORING

5/16" (8mm)
TO 3/4" (19)

6" x 6"  (152 x 152)
9" x 9"  (228 x 228)
12" x 12" (304 x 304)

PANEL OR PARQUET PATTERNS

Wood flooring is admired for its warm, natural appearance and its attractive blend of comfort, resilience, and durability. It is also fairly easy to maintain and, if damaged, can be refinished or replaced.

Durable, close-grained species of hardwoods (white and red oak, maple, birch, beech, and pecan) and softwoods (Southern pine, Douglas fir, Western larch, hemlock, and others) are used for wood flooring. Of these, oak, Southern pine, and Douglas fir are the most common. The best grades are Clear or Select and will minimize or exclude defects, such as knots, streaks, checks, and torn grain.

Wood flooring is available in boards or manufactured blocks and panels. Board flooring is usually in the form of narrow strips, although planks up to 6" (152 mm) wide are also available in the softwoods. Parquet blocks consist of strip flooring factory-assembled into squares with various geometric patterns. Prefinished panels which have the appearance of traditional strip flooring are another type of factory-made flooring.

Wood flooring is most often finished with clear polyurethane, varnish, or a penetrating sealer; the finishes can range from high gloss to satin or a dull sheen. Ideally, the finish should enhance the durability of the wood and its resistance to water, dirt, and staining without concealing the wood's natural beauty. Stains are used to add some color to the natural color of the wood without obscuring the wood grain. Wood flooring can also be painted or even stenciled, but painted surfaces require more maintenance.

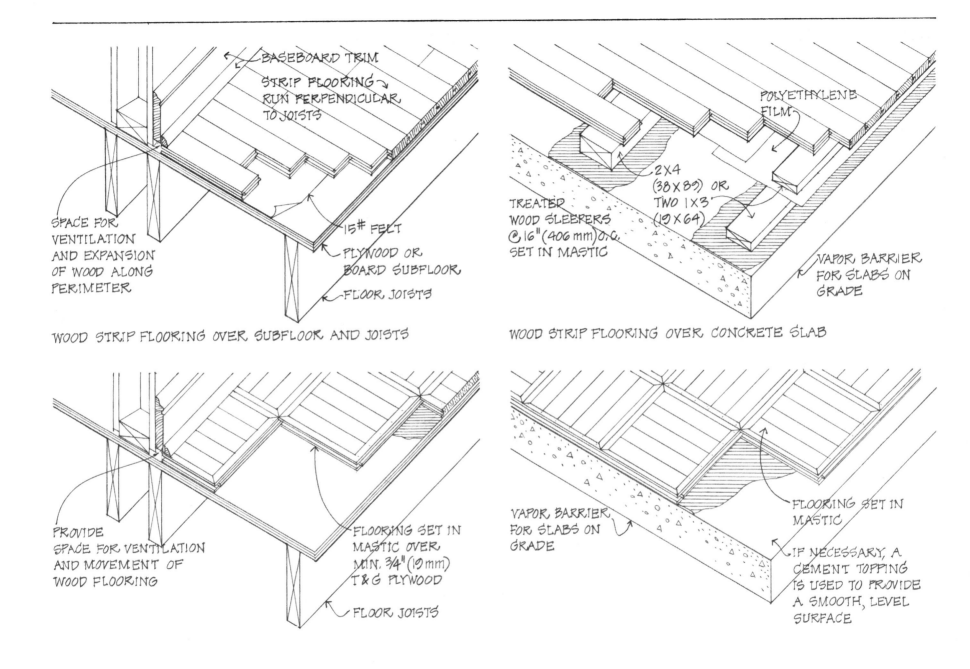

BASEBOARD TRIM

STRIP FLOORING
RUN PERPENDICULAR
TO JOISTS

SPACE FOR
VENTILATION
AND EXPANSION
OF WOOD ALONG
PERIMETER

15# FELT

PLYWOOD OR
BOARD SUBFLOOR

FLOOR JOISTS

WOOD STRIP FLOORING OVER SUBFLOOR AND JOISTS

POLYETHYLENE
FILM

2X4
(38 X 89) OR
TWO 1X3"
(19 X 64)

TREATED
WOOD SLEEPERS
@ 16" (406 mm) O.C.
SET IN MASTIC

VAPOR BARRIER
FOR SLABS ON
GRADE

WOOD STRIP FLOORING OVER CONCRETE SLAB

PROVIDE
SPACE FOR VENTILATION
AND MOVEMENT OF
WOOD FLOORING

FLOORING SET IN
MASTIC OVER
MIN. 3/4" (19 mm)
T & G PLYWOOD

FLOOR JOISTS

PANEL OR PARQUET BLOCK FLOORING OVER SUBFLOOR

VAPOR BARRIER
FOR SLABS ON
GRADE

FLOORING SET IN
MASTIC

IF NECESSARY, A
CEMENT TOPPING
IS USED TO PROVIDE
A SMOOTH, LEVEL
SURFACE

PANEL OR BLOCK FLOORING OVER CONCRETE SLAB

# TILE & STONE FLOORING

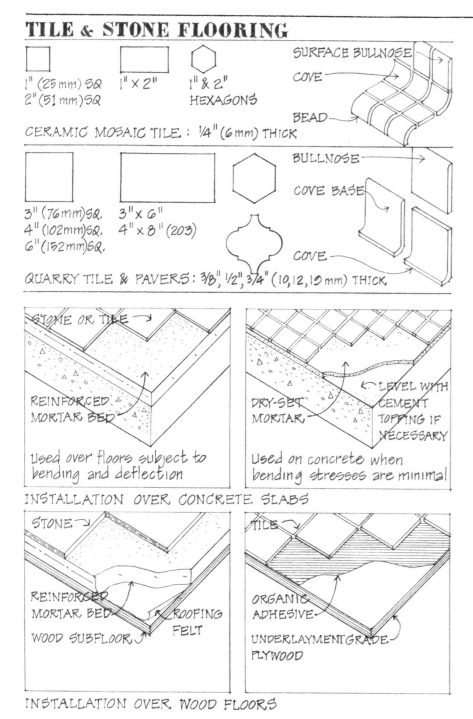

1" (25 mm) SQ.
2" (51 mm) SQ.

1" x 2"

1" & 2"
HEXAGONS

SURFACE BULLNOSE
COVE
BEAD

CERAMIC MOSAIC TILE : 1/4" (6mm) THICK

3" (76mm) SQ.
4" (102mm) SQ.
6" (152mm) SQ.

3" x 6"
4" x 8" (203)

BULLNOSE
COVE BASE
COVE

QUARRY TILE & PAVERS : 3/8", 1/2", 3/4" (10, 12, 19 mm) THICK

STONE OR TILE

REINFORCED
MORTAR BED

Used over floors subject to
bending and deflection

DRY-SET
MORTAR

LEVEL WITH
CEMENT
TOPPING IF
NECESSARY

Used on concrete when
bending stresses are minimal

INSTALLATION OVER CONCRETE SLABS

STONE

REINFORCED
MORTAR BED
WOOD SUBFLOOR

ROOFING
FELT

TILE

ORGANIC
ADHESIVE

UNDERLAYMENT GRADE
PLYWOOD

INSTALLATION OVER WOOD FLOORS

Tile and stone flooring materials are solid and durable.
Depending on the shape of the individual pieces and the
pattern in which they are laid, these flooring materials can
have a cool, formal appearance or convey an informal feeling
to a room.

Ceramic tile used for flooring are the mosaics - relatively
small, modular units of natural clay or porcelain composition.
The natural clay type is unglazed, with muted earth colors; the
porcelains can have bright colors and are vitreous (made
dense and impervious).

Quarry tiles and pavers are larger modular flooring
materials. Quarry tiles are unglazed units of heat-hardened
clay; pavers are similar to ceramic mosaic tile. Both are
practically impervious to moisture, dirt, and stains.

Stone flooring materials provide a solid, permanent, highly
durable floor surface. Colors range from the tans, beiges,
and reddish browns of flagstone to the grays and blacks
of slate. A random pattern of flagstone conveys an informal
feeling. Slate, available in square or irregular shapes, can be
formal or informal. Marble lends itself to formal elegance.

Concrete can also be used as a finish flooring surface if
smooth and level enough. It should be sealed against stains
and grease. It can be painted, stained, or integrally colored
when cast. An exposed aggregate finish can provide
textural interest. Terrazzo is a special type of exposed
aggregate finish with mosaic-like patterns created by
the marble chips used.

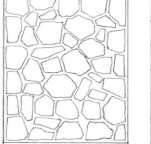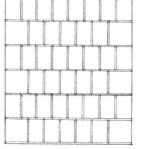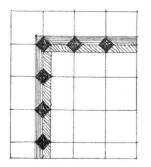

STONE FLOORING PATTERNS

Resilient flooring materials provide an economical, dense, non-absorbent flooring surface with relatively good durability and ease of maintenance. Their degree of resilience enables them to resist permanent indentation while contributing to their quietness and comfort underfoot. The degree of comfort provided will depend not only on the material's resilience, but also on the type of backing used and the hardness of the supporting substrate.

Linoleum and vinyl sheets come in rolls 6 feet (1829 mm) to 15 feet (4572 mm) wide. The other resilient flooring materials are available as tiles, typically 9 inches (228 mm) and 12 inches (304 mm) square. While sheet goods provide a seamless floor, tiles are easier to install if the floor outline is irregular. Individual tiles can also be replaced if damaged.

None of the resilient flooring types is superior in all respects. Listed below are the types which perform well in specific areas.

| | |
|---|---|
| RESILIENCE & QUIETNESS | Cork tile, rubber tile, cork tile with vinyl coating, vinyl sheet |
| RESISTANCE TO: INDENTATION | Vinyl tiles and sheets, cork tile with vinyl coating, cork and rubber tiles |
| STAINING | Vinyl tiles and sheets, vinyl asbestos tile, linoleum |
| GREASE | Vinyl tiles and sheets, cork tile with vinyl coating, linoleum, vinyl asbestos tile |
| CIGARETTE BURNS | Cork tile, Rubber tile, cork tile with vinyl coating, vinyl tile |
| EASE OF MAINTENANCE | Vinyl tiles and sheets, vinyl asbestos tile, cork tile with vinyl coating. |

The wood or concrete substrate for resilient flooring should be clean, dry, flat, and smooth since any irregularities in the base material would show through.

# RESILIENT FLOORING

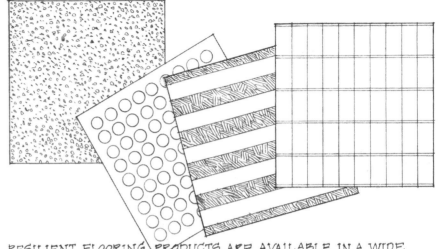

RESILIENT FLOORING PRODUCTS ARE AVAILABLE IN A WIDE RANGE OF COLORS AND PATTERNS.

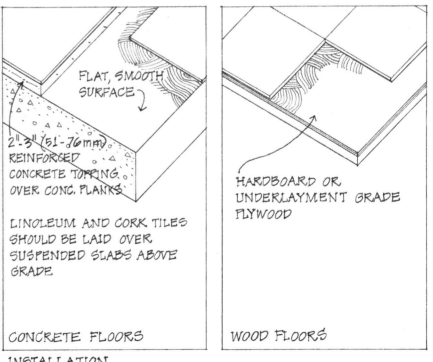

FLAT, SMOOTH SURFACE

2"-3" (51-76 mm) REINFORCED CONCRETE TOPPING OVER CONC. PLANKS

LINOLEUM AND CORK TILES SHOULD BE LAID OVER SUSPENDED SLABS ABOVE GRADE

HARDBOARD OR UNDERLAYMENT GRADE PLYWOOD

CONCRETE FLOORS

WOOD FLOORS

INSTALLATION

# FLOOR COVERINGS

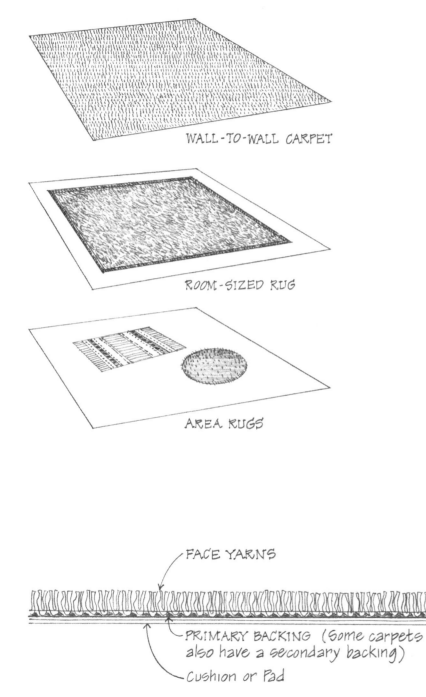

WALL-TO-WALL CARPET

ROOM-SIZED RUG

AREA RUGS

FACE YARNS

PRIMARY BACKING (Some carpets also have a secondary backing)

Cushion or Pad

Floor coverings - as opposed to flooring materials - refer to carpeting and rugs. These soft coverings provide floors with both visual and textural softness, resilience, and warmth in a wide range of colors and patterns. These qualities, in turn, enable carpeting to absorb sound, reduce impact noise, and provide a comfortable and safe surface to walk on. As a group, carpeting is also fairly easy to maintain.

There are two major categories of soft floor coverings -- carpeting and rugs. Carpeting is manufactured in strips 15 inches to 27 feet wide. It is sold by the square yard, cut to fit, and normally fastened to a floor with tackless strips or adhesive.

Carpeting normally is installed wall-to-wall, covering the entire floor of a room. It can be laid directly over a subfloor and underlayment pad, obviating the need for a finish floor. It can also be laid over an existing floor.

Because carpeting is usually fastened to a floor, it must be cleaned in place and cannot be turned to equalize wear. It is also difficult to move and, if moved, only a portion can be reused.

## CARPET FIBERS

| | |
|---|---|
| WOOL | Excellent resilience and warmth: good soil, flame and solvent resistance; cleanable |
| ACRYLIC | Approximates wool in appearance; good crush resistance; mildew and moisture resistant |
| NYLON | Predominant face fiber; excellent wearability; soil and mildew resistant; anti-static properties achieved through the use of conductive filaments |
| POLYESTER | Combines look of wool with durability of nylon; Good soil- and abrasion-resistance; low cost |
| OLEFIN | (Polypropylene) Good resistance to abrasion, soil, and mildew; used extensively in outdoor carpeting |
| COTTON | Not as durable as other face fibers, but softness and colorability used to advantage in flat-woven rugs |

Each carpet manufacturer offers blends of the generic face fibers which improve on specific characteristics such as durability, soil-resistance, cleanability, color, and luster.

Carpet tiles are modular pieces of carpet which can be laid to resemble a seamless wall-to-wall installation, or can be arranged in subtle or bold patterns. They offer the following advantages:

- They can be easily cut to fit odd-shaped contours with a minimum of waste.
- Individual tiles can be replaced if worn or damaged.
- Carpet tiles can be moved easily and reused.
- In commercial installations, the tiles can be removed for access to underfloor utilities.

Residential carpet tiles are 9 or 12 inches square with a rubber backing and self-stick adhesive. Commercial-grade carpet tiles are 18 inches square with a backing strong enough to prevent shrinkage or expansion of the tile and to protect the carpet edges from unraveling. Some commercial-grade carpet tiles are intended to be glued down, while others are laid loosely with only enough adhesive to prevent the tiles from shifting along the edges of the installation and in high-traffic areas.

## CARPET CONSTRUCTION

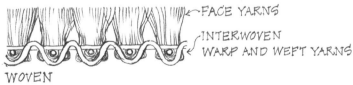

TUFTED
— FACE YARNS
— PRIMARY BACKING
— LATEX
— SECONDARY BACKING

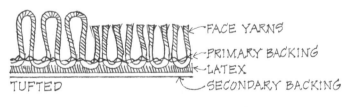

WOVEN
— FACE YARNS
— INTERWOVEN WARP AND WEFT YARNS

FUSION BONDED
— FACE YARNS
— VINYL
— SECONDARY BACKING

TUFTED CARPET:
The majority of carpet produced today is tufted. Tufting involves stitching face yarns into a backing material with multi-needled machines. The fibers are secured to the pre-woven backing with a heavy latex coating. A secondary backing may be added for greater dimensional stability.

WOVEN CARPET:
Woven carpet is longer wearing and more stable than tufted carpet, but it is slower and more expensive to produce. There is no separate backing since the backing yarns are interwoven with the face yarns. There are three basic weaving techniques: Velvet, Wilton, and Axminster.

FUSION BONDED:
Fusion bonding is a method wherein face yarns are heat-fused to a vinyl backing that is supported by other materials.

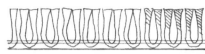

**PLUSH**
Smooth cut pile; cut yarn ends blend; when dense pile is cut close, called velvet plush.

**SAXONY PLUSH**
Texture between plush and shag; thicker yarn.

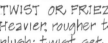

**TWIST OR FRIEZE**
Heavier, rougher texture than plush; twist set into yarn.

**SHAG**
Very textured surface created by long, twisted yarns.

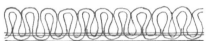

**LEVEL LOOP**
Looped tufts are at the same height; very sturdy; little textural variation.

**RIBBED LOOP**
Creates directional, ribbed or corrugated texture.

**HI-LO LOOP**
Adds another dimension to the loop texture.

**MULTI LEVEL LOOP**
Capable of producing sculptured patterns.

**CUT AND LOOP**
Cut and uncut loops alternate in a uniform fashion; adds a degree of softness and warmth to loop texture.

**CUT AND LOOP**
Texture is mostly loop pile with symmetrical geometric figures created by cut rows.

After color, texture is a carpet's prime visual characteristic. The various carpet textures available are a result of the pile construction, pile height, and the manner in which the carpet is cut. There are three major groups of carpet textures:

- CUT PILE, where every yarn loop is cut, can produce a range of textures from informal shags to short, dense velvets. Cut pile can be produced in tufted, woven, or bonded constructions.

- LOOP PILE is tougher and more easily maintained than cut pile, but is less versatile in color and pattern. Loop pile also lacks the softness of cut pile since light tends to be reflected off the carpet surface. Loop pile can be produced through tufted, woven, and knitted techniques.

- COMBINATION LOOP AND PILE adds a degree of warmth to all-loop pile. It can be produced in tufted and woven constructions.

SOME USEFUL TERMS

**PILE HEIGHT**

PITCH refers to the number of ends of yarn in 27" (685 mm) of width of woven carpet

GAUGE refers to the needle spacing across the width of a tufting machine; expressed in fractions of an inch.

FACE WEIGHT is the total weight of face yarns measured in OZ./SQ.YD.

DENSITY is a measure of the amount of pile fiber by weight in a given area of carpet. Increased density generally results in better performance.

$$\text{DENSITY} = \frac{\text{AVG. PILE WEIGHT (oz/yd}^2)}{\text{AVG. PILE HEIGHT (inches)}}$$

Rugs are single pieces of floor coverings manufactured or cut to standard sizes, often with a finished border. They are not intended to cover the entire floor of a room and are therefore simply laid over another finish flooring material.

Room-sized rugs cover most of a room's floor, leaving a strip of finish flooring exposed along the room's edges. They approximate the appearance of wall-to-wall carpeting but can be moved if desired, removed for cleaning when necessary, and turned for more even distribution of wear.

Area rugs cover a smaller portion of a room's floor, and can be used to define an area, unify a furniture grouping, or delineate a path. Decorative rugs, especially handmade ones, can also serve as a dominant design element and provide a focal point for a room's arrangement.

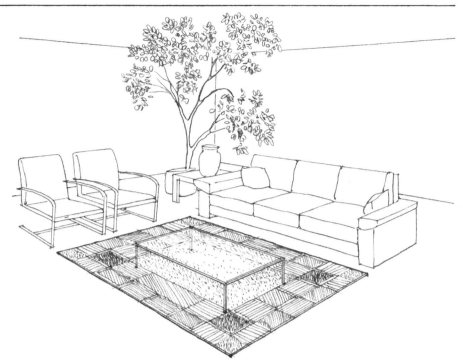

AFGHANISTAN BOKHARA

CHINESE BENGALI

INDIAN NUMDAH

NAVAJO RUG

# WALLS

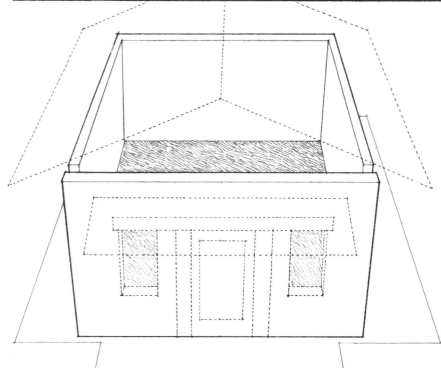

Walls are essential architectural elements of any building. They have traditionally served as structural supports for floors above grade, ceilings, and roofs. They form the facades of buildings. They provide protection and privacy for the interior spaces they create.

As structural elements, walls must be laid out in a pattern that is coordinated with the spans of the floor and roof structures they support. At the same time, this structural pattern will begin to dictate the possible sizes, shapes, and layouts of interior spaces.

When the size and shape requirements of interior spaces and the activities they house do not or would not correspond well with a firm pattern of structural walls, a post-and-beam system can be used. Nonstructural walls and partitions could then be free to define and enclose interior spaces as required. This is often done in commercial, multistory, and other buildings where flexibility in the layout of spaces is desirable.

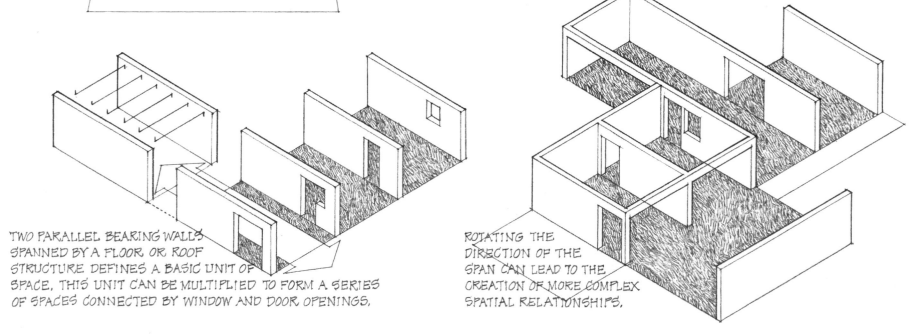

TWO PARALLEL BEARING WALLS SPANNED BY A FLOOR OR ROOF STRUCTURE DEFINES A BASIC UNIT OF SPACE. THIS UNIT CAN BE MULTIPLIED TO FORM A SERIES OF SPACES CONNECTED BY WINDOW AND DOOR OPENINGS.

ROTATING THE DIRECTION OF THE SPAN CAN LEAD TO THE CREATION OF MORE COMPLEX SPATIAL RELATIONSHIPS.

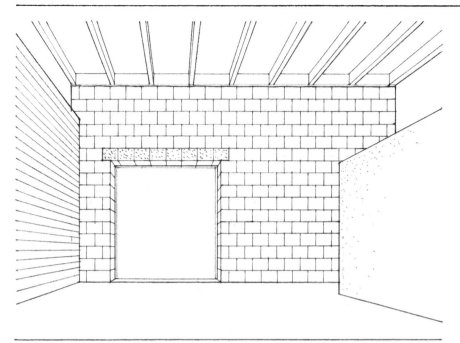

BEARING WALLS DEFINE THE BOUNDARIES OF SPACE.

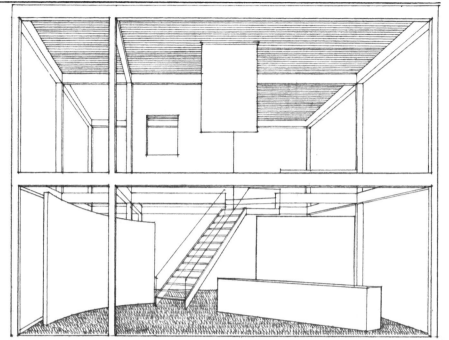

COLUMNS AND BEAMS IMPLY THE EDGES OF INTERIOR SPACE.

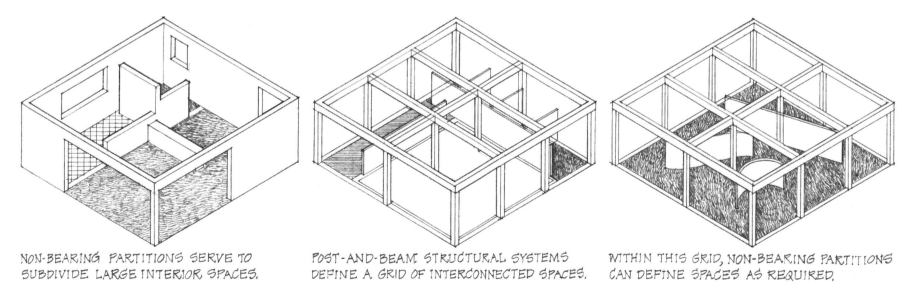

NON-BEARING PARTITIONS SERVE TO SUBDIVIDE LARGE INTERIOR SPACES.

POST-AND-BEAM STRUCTURAL SYSTEMS DEFINE A GRID OF INTERCONNECTED SPACES.

WITHIN THIS GRID, NON-BEARING PARTITIONS CAN DEFINE SPACES AS REQUIRED.

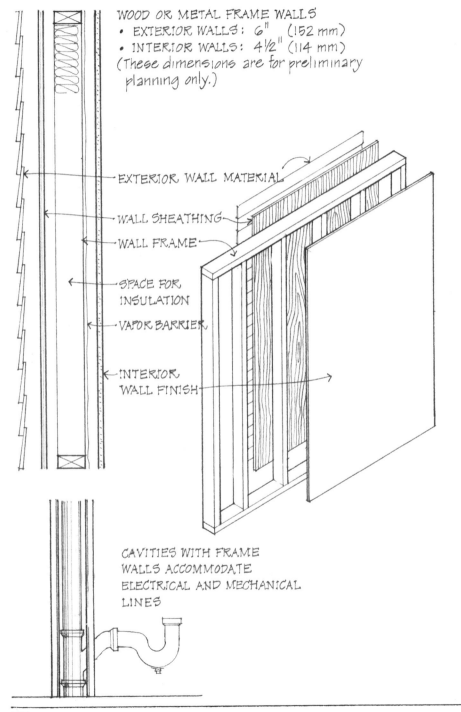

WOOD OR METAL FRAME WALLS
- EXTERIOR WALLS:  6"  (152 mm)
- INTERIOR WALLS:  4½"  (114 mm)
(These dimensions are for preliminary planning only.)

EXTERIOR WALL MATERIAL

WALL SHEATHING

WALL FRAME

SPACE FOR INSULATION

VAPOR BARRIER

INTERIOR WALL FINISH

CAVITIES WITH FRAME WALLS ACCOMMODATE ELECTRICAL AND MECHANICAL LINES

Most walls are made up of several layers of materials. The wall frame itself usually consists of wood or metal studs tied together by sole and top plates. Onto this frame are laid one or more layers of sheet material, such as plywood or gypsum board, which help to make the wall rigid.

The sheet material may serve as the finish surface on the exterior faces of walls, but more often, it serves as a support for a separate layer of siding, shingles, stucco, or masonry veneer. In either case, the exterior wall surface must be weather-resistant.

Interior wall surfaces do not have to withstand climatic elements and can therefore be selected from a wider range of materials.

To control the passage of heat, moisture, and sound through a wall's thickness, a wall construction can be layered or filled with an insulating material and lined with a vapor barrier.

EXTERIOR WALLS MUST CONTROL PASSAGE OF HEAT, MOISTURE, AND SOUND, AND WITHSTAND:

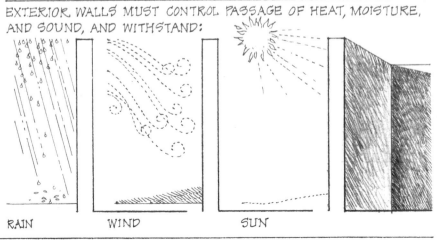

RAIN          WIND          SUN

Walls of concrete, masonry, or stone are usually employed as load-bearing walls in situations that require fire-resistant construction, or where the natural color, texture, and permanence of brick or stone are desired.

Concrete and masonry walls are usually thicker than stud frame walls since they depend on their mass for their strength and stability. While strong in compression, they require cross walls and steel reinforcement to resist bending from lateral forces.

The attractive color and texture of stone and brick are, of course, almost always left exposed as the finish wall surface. Even concrete and concrete masonry walls can now be constructed with attractive colors and textures. If desired, however, a separate finish can be applied over furring.

Concrete and masonry walls are fire-resistant but comparatively poor thermal insulators. Space for insulation and cavities for mechanical, plumbing, or electrical lines must be planned for prior to construction.

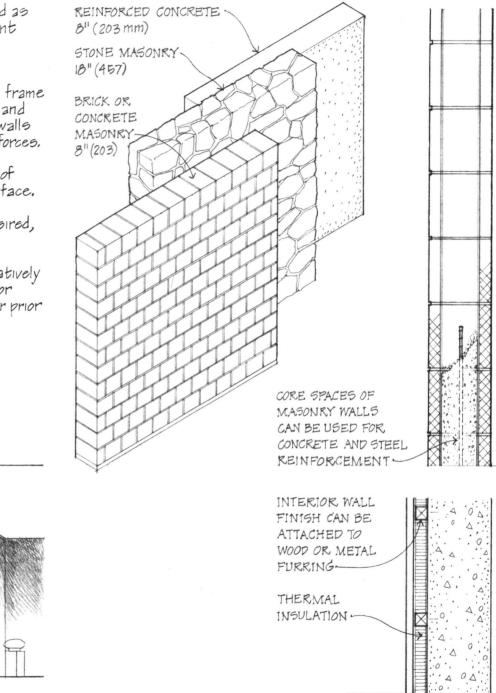

REINFORCED CONCRETE 8" (203 mm)

STONE MASONRY 18" (457)

BRICK OR CONCRETE MASONRY 8" (203)

CORE SPACES OF MASONRY WALLS CAN BE USED FOR CONCRETE AND STEEL REINFORCEMENT

INTERIOR WALL FINISH CAN BE ATTACHED TO WOOD OR METAL FURRING

THERMAL INSULATION

INTERIOR WALLS CONTROL:

OUR VIEW.......THE PASSAGE OF SOUND...HEAT...AND LIGHT.

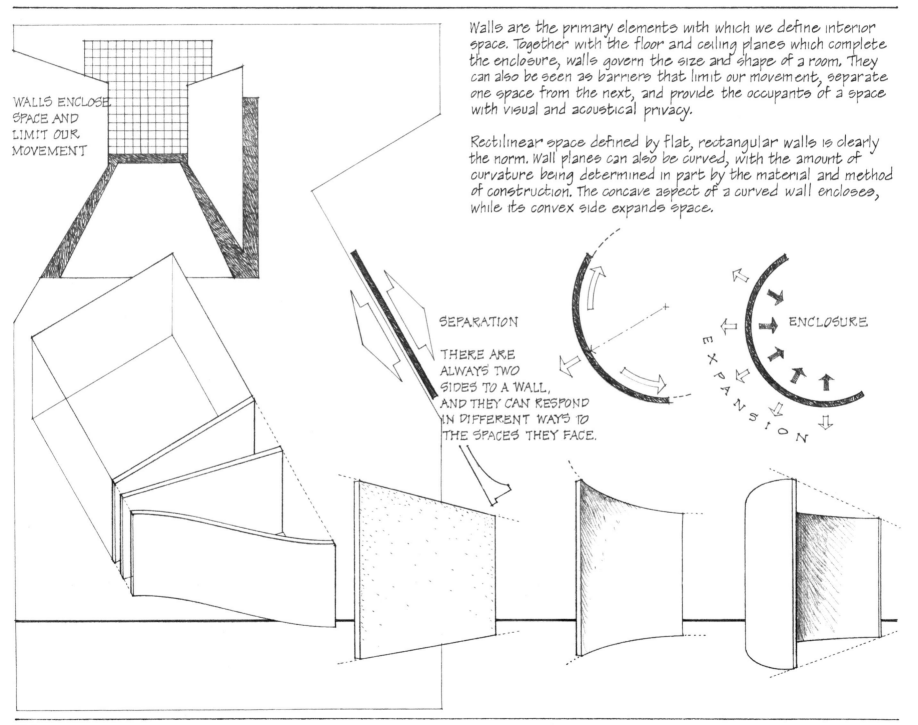

Walls are the primary elements with which we define interior space. Together with the floor and ceiling planes which complete the enclosure, walls govern the size and shape of a room. They can also be seen as barriers that limit our movement, separate one space from the next, and provide the occupants of a space with visual and acoustical privacy.

Rectilinear space defined by flat, rectangular walls is clearly the norm. Wall planes can also be curved, with the amount of curvature being determined in part by the material and method of construction. The concave aspect of a curved wall encloses, while its convex side expands space.

WALLS ENCLOSE SPACE AND LIMIT OUR MOVEMENT

SEPARATION

THERE ARE ALWAYS TWO SIDES TO A WALL, AND THEY CAN RESPOND IN DIFFERENT WAYS TO THE SPACES THEY FACE.

EXPANSION

ENCLOSURE

Openings within or between wall planes allow for continuity and our physical movement between spaces, as well as the passage of light, heat, and sound. As they increase in size, the openings also begin to erode the sense of enclosure the walls provide and visually expand the space to include adjacent spaces. Views seen through the openings become part of the enclosed space. Enlarging the openings further would result ultimately in an implied separation of space defined by a framework of columns and beams.

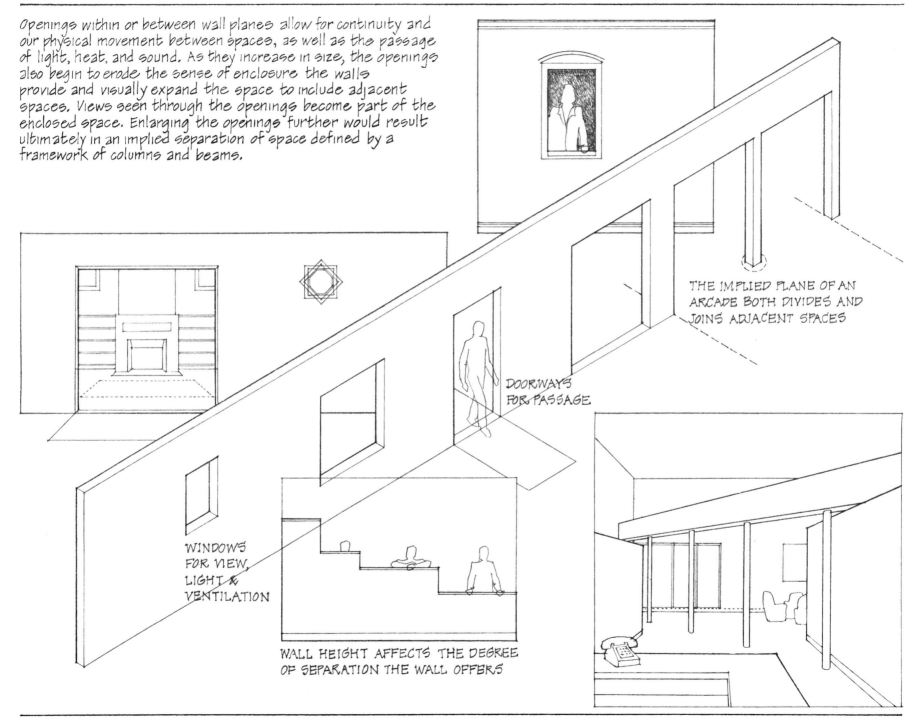

THE IMPLIED PLANE OF AN ARCADE BOTH DIVIDES AND JOINS ADJACENT SPACES

DOORWAYS FOR PASSAGE

WINDOWS FOR VIEW, LIGHT & VENTILATION

WALL HEIGHT AFFECTS THE DEGREE OF SEPARATION THE WALL OFFERS

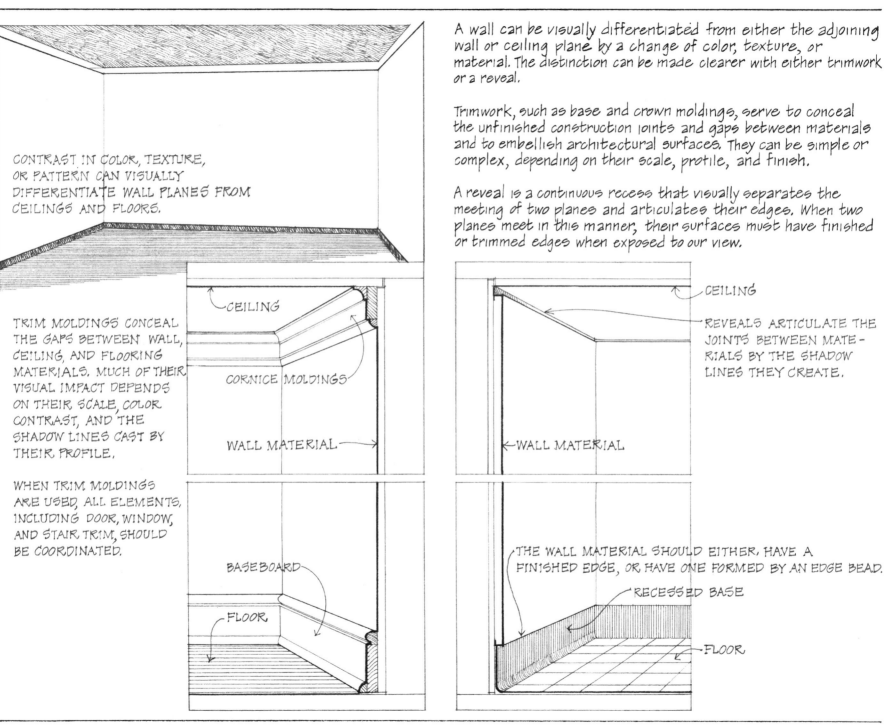

CONTRAST IN COLOR, TEXTURE, OR PATTERN CAN VISUALLY DIFFERENTIATE WALL PLANES FROM CEILINGS AND FLOORS.

A wall can be visually differentiated from either the adjoining wall or ceiling plane by a change of color, texture, or material. The distinction can be made clearer with either trimwork or a reveal.

Trimwork, such as base and crown moldings, serve to conceal the unfinished construction joints and gaps between materials and to embellish architectural surfaces. They can be simple or complex, depending on their scale, profile, and finish.

A reveal is a continuous recess that visually separates the meeting of two planes and articulates their edges. When two planes meet in this manner, their surfaces must have finished or trimmed edges when exposed to our view.

TRIM MOLDINGS CONCEAL THE GAPS BETWEEN WALL, CEILING, AND FLOORING MATERIALS. MUCH OF THEIR VISUAL IMPACT DEPENDS ON THEIR SCALE, COLOR CONTRAST, AND THE SHADOW LINES CAST BY THEIR PROFILE.

WHEN TRIM MOLDINGS ARE USED, ALL ELEMENTS, INCLUDING DOOR, WINDOW, AND STAIR TRIM, SHOULD BE COORDINATED.

CEILING

CORNICE MOLDINGS

WALL MATERIAL

BASEBOARD

FLOOR

CEILING

REVEALS ARTICULATE THE JOINTS BETWEEN MATERIALS BY THE SHADOW LINES THEY CREATE.

WALL MATERIAL

THE WALL MATERIAL SHOULD EITHER HAVE A FINISHED EDGE, OR HAVE ONE FORMED BY AN EDGE BEAD.

RECESSED BASE

FLOOR

A wall surface material can be a continuation of the floor or ceiling treatment. Continuing the floor treatment up the lower portion of a wall can visually enlarge the floor area while reducing the apparent wall height. Continuing the ceiling treatment down a portion of a wall can similarly reduce the vertical scale of the wall.

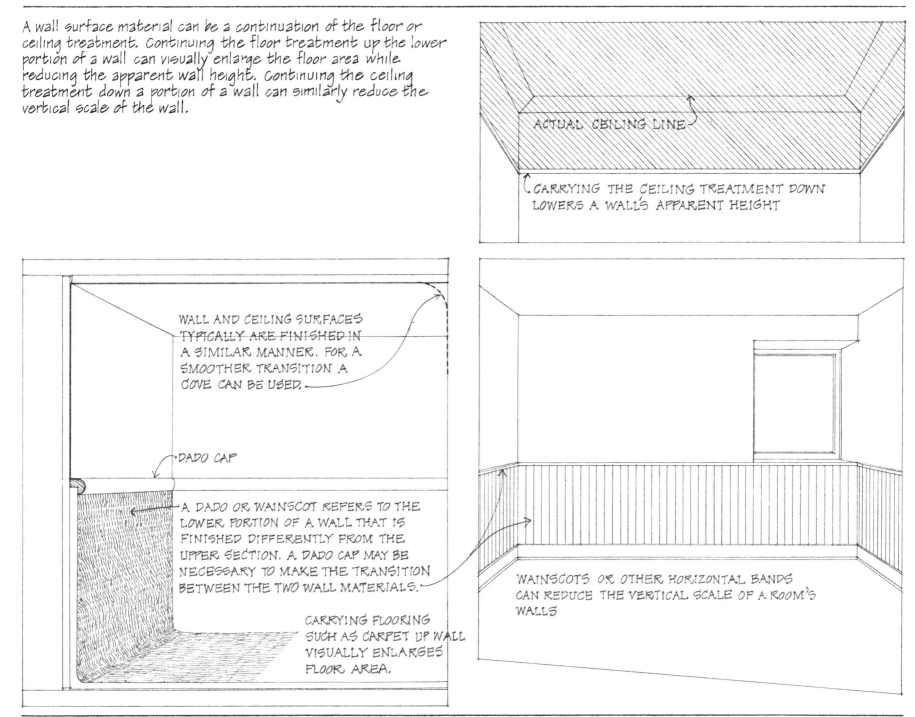

ACTUAL CEILING LINE

CARRYING THE CEILING TREATMENT DOWN LOWERS A WALL'S APPARENT HEIGHT

WALL AND CEILING SURFACES TYPICALLY ARE FINISHED IN A SIMILAR MANNER. FOR A SMOOTHER TRANSITION A COVE CAN BE USED.

DADO CAP

A DADO OR WAINSCOT REFERS TO THE LOWER PORTION OF A WALL THAT IS FINISHED DIFFERENTLY FROM THE UPPER SECTION. A DADO CAP MAY BE NECESSARY TO MAKE THE TRANSITION BETWEEN THE TWO WALL MATERIALS.

CARRYING FLOORING SUCH AS CARPET UP WALL VISUALLY ENLARGES FLOOR AREA.

WAINSCOTS OR OTHER HORIZONTAL BANDS CAN REDUCE THE VERTICAL SCALE OF A ROOM'S WALLS

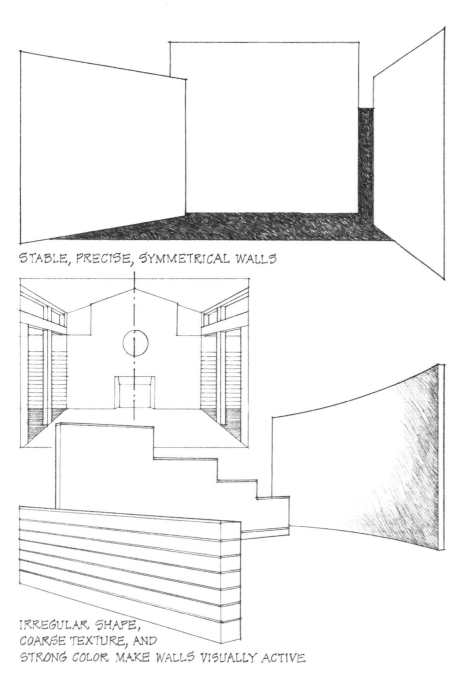

The vertical orientation of walls makes them visually active in our field of vision. In defining the boundaries of a room, they give form and shape to the space and play a major role in determining its character.

Stable, precise, symmetrical walls convey a feeling of formality, one which can be considerably enhanced with the use of smooth textures. Irregularly shaped walls, on the other hand, are more dynamic. When combined with a rough texture, they can impart an informal character to a space.

Walls provide a background for a room's furnishings and occupants. If smooth and neutral in color, they serve as passive backdrops for foreground elements. When irregular in shape, or given texture, pattern, or a vigorous color, the walls become more active and compete for our attention.

STABLE, PRECISE, SYMMETRICAL WALLS

IRREGULAR SHAPE,
COARSE TEXTURE, AND
STRONG COLOR MAKE WALLS VISUALLY ACTIVE

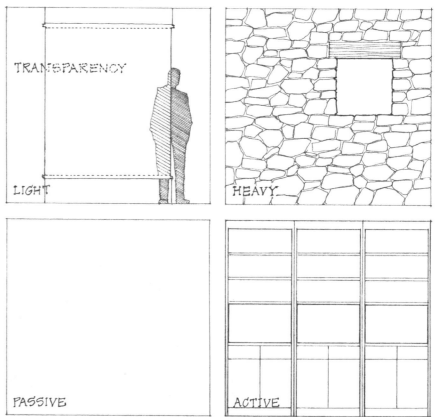

TRANSPARENCY

LIGHT

HEAVY

PASSIVE

ACTIVE

Light-colored walls reflect light effectively and serve as efficient backdrops for elements placed in front of them. Light, warm colors on a wall exude warmth, while light, cool colors increase a room's spaciousness.

Dark-colored walls absorb light, make a room more difficult to illuminate, and convey an enclosed, intimate feeling.

A wall's texture also affects how much light it will reflect or absorb. Smooth walls reflect more light than textured ones, which tend to diffuse the light striking their surfaces. In a similar manner, smooth, hard wall surfaces will reflect more sound back into a space than porous or soft-textured walls.

COLOR, PATTERN, AND TEXTURE CAN BE USED TO DIFFERENTIATE ONE WALL PLANE FROM THE NEXT AND TO ARTICULATE THE FORM OF THE SPACE.

AS WITH COLOR, THE JUXTAPOSITION OF CONTRASTING TEXTURES ENHANCES BOTH THE COARSE AND THE SMOOTH.

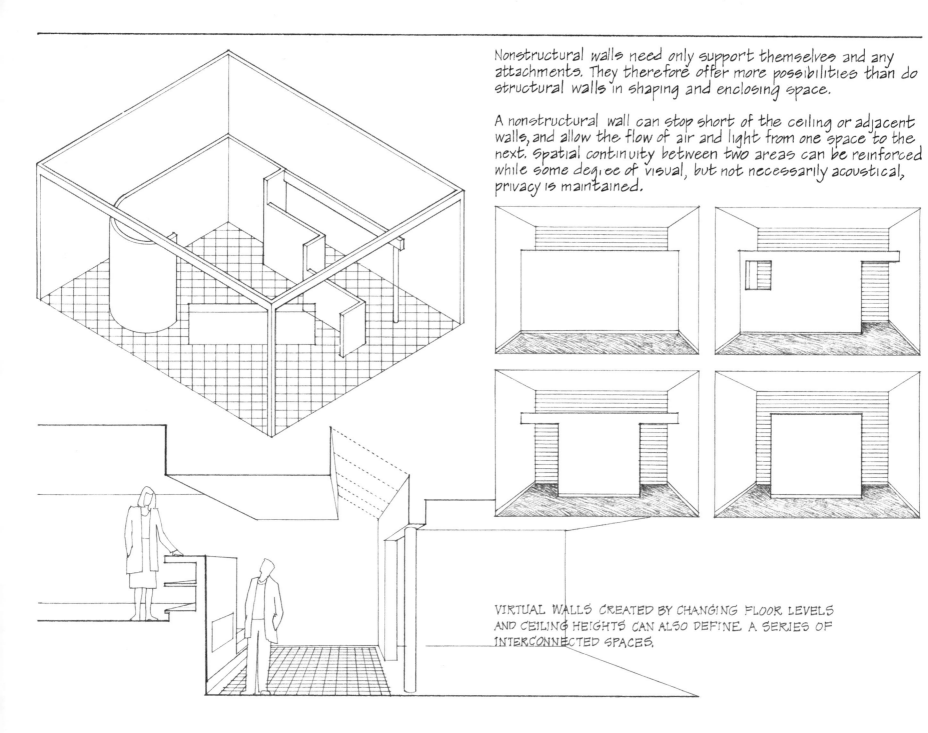

Nonstructural walls need only support themselves and any attachments. They therefore offer more possibilities than do structural walls in shaping and enclosing space.

A nonstructural wall can stop short of the ceiling or adjacent walls, and allow the flow of air and light from one space to the next. Spatial continuity between two areas can be reinforced while some degree of visual, but not necessarily acoustical, privacy is maintained.

VIRTUAL WALLS CREATED BY CHANGING FLOOR LEVELS AND CEILING HEIGHTS CAN ALSO DEFINE A SERIES OF INTERCONNECTED SPACES.

Instead of being strictly a background element in interior space, a wall can also be structured to support furnishing elements, such as seating, shelving, tabletops, and lighting. A wall can also incorporate these elements into its thickness and become itself a piece of furniture.

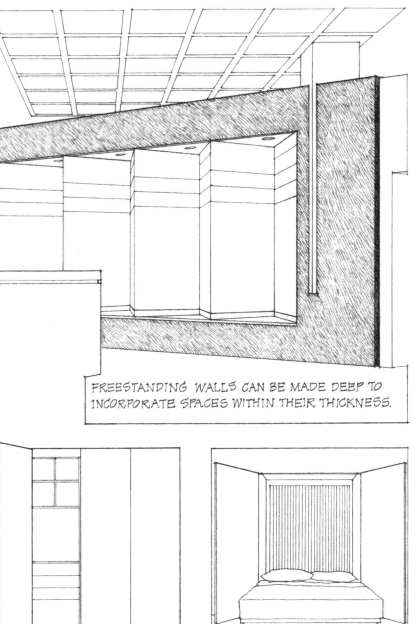

FREESTANDING WALLS CAN BE MADE DEEP TO INCORPORATE SPACES WITHIN THEIR THICKNESS.

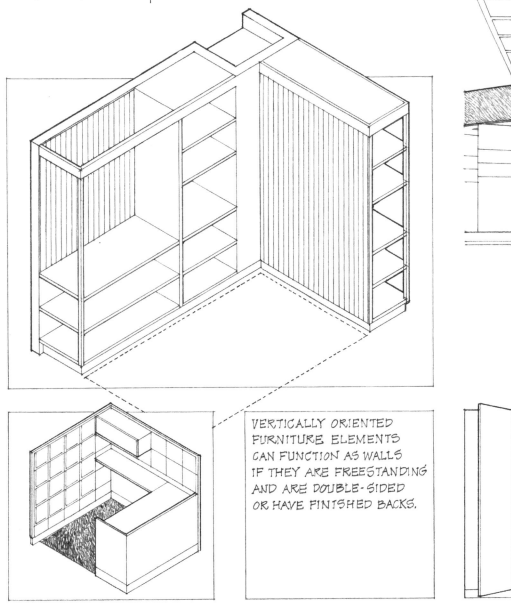

VERTICALLY ORIENTED FURNITURE ELEMENTS CAN FUNCTION AS WALLS IF THEY ARE FREESTANDING AND ARE DOUBLE-SIDED OR HAVE FINISHED BACKS.

# WALL FINISHES

Some wall finishes are an integral part of a wall's material structure, while others are separate layers attached to a wall frame. Still others are thin coatings or coverings which are applied over a wall surface. In addition to aesthetic factors such as color, texture, and pattern, functional considerations in selecting a wall material and finish include the following.

- If it is an applied material, what type of support or base is required?
- If the wall exists, what type of finish, coating, or covering can it accept?
- How durable must the material or finish be, and how easy is it to maintain?
- What degree of sound absorption, light reflectance, and fire resistance is required?
- How much does it cost to purchase and to install or apply?

The following is an outline of major types of wall materials and finishes, and their general characteristics.

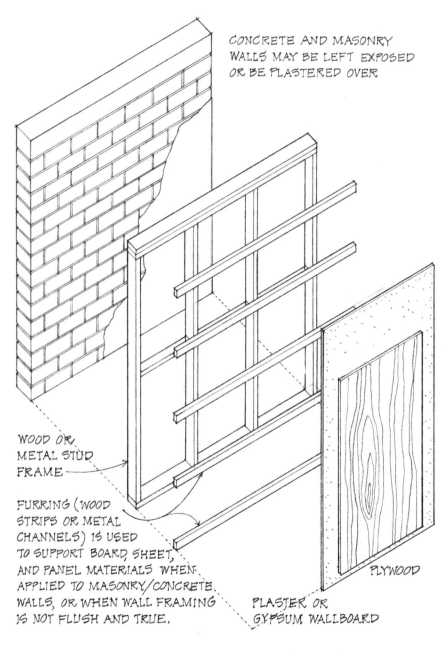

CONCRETE AND MASONRY WALLS MAY BE LEFT EXPOSED OR BE PLASTERED OVER

WOOD OR METAL STUD FRAME

FURRING (WOOD STRIPS OR METAL CHANNELS) IS USED TO SUPPORT BOARD, SHEET, AND PANEL MATERIALS WHEN APPLIED TO MASONRY/CONCRETE WALLS, OR WHEN WALL FRAMING IS NOT FLUSH AND TRUE.

PLASTER OR GYPSUM WALLBOARD

PLYWOOD

BASIC TYPES OF WALL MATERIALS

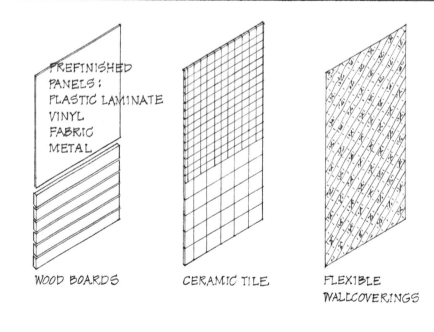

PREFINISHED PANELS:
PLASTIC LAMINATE
VINYL
FABRIC
METAL

WOOD BOARDS

CERAMIC TILE

FLEXIBLE WALLCOVERINGS

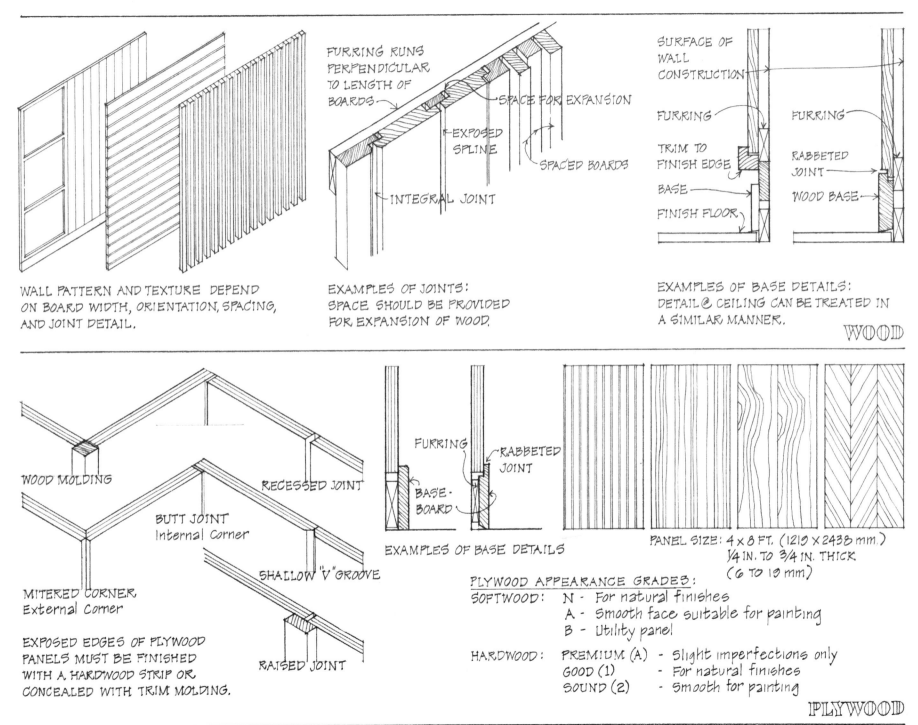

WALL PATTERN AND TEXTURE DEPEND
ON BOARD WIDTH, ORIENTATION, SPACING,
AND JOINT DETAIL.

FURRING RUNS PERPENDICULAR TO LENGTH OF BOARDS

SPACE FOR EXPANSION

EXPOSED SPLINE

SPACED BOARDS

INTEGRAL JOINT

EXAMPLES OF JOINTS:
SPACE SHOULD BE PROVIDED
FOR EXPANSION OF WOOD.

SURFACE OF WALL CONSTRUCTION

FURRING

TRIM TO FINISH EDGE

BASE

FINISH FLOOR

FURRING

RABBETED JOINT

WOOD BASE

EXAMPLES OF BASE DETAILS:
DETAIL @ CEILING CAN BE TREATED IN
A SIMILAR MANNER.

**WOOD**

WOOD MOLDING

RECESSED JOINT

BUTT JOINT
Internal Corner

MITERED CORNER
External Corner

SHALLOW "V" GROOVE

EXPOSED EDGES OF PLYWOOD
PANELS MUST BE FINISHED
WITH A HARDWOOD STRIP OR
CONCEALED WITH TRIM MOLDING.

RAISED JOINT

FURRING

RABBETED JOINT

BASE-BOARD

EXAMPLES OF BASE DETAILS

PANEL SIZE: 4 x 8 FT. (1219 x 2438 mm.)
1/4 IN. TO 3/4 IN. THICK
(6 TO 19 mm)

PLYWOOD APPEARANCE GRADES:
SOFTWOOD:  N - For natural finishes
           A - Smooth face suitable for painting
           B - Utility panel

HARDWOOD:  PREMIUM (A) - Slight imperfections only
           GOOD (1)    - For natural finishes
           SOUND (2)   - Smooth for painting

**PLYWOOD**

189

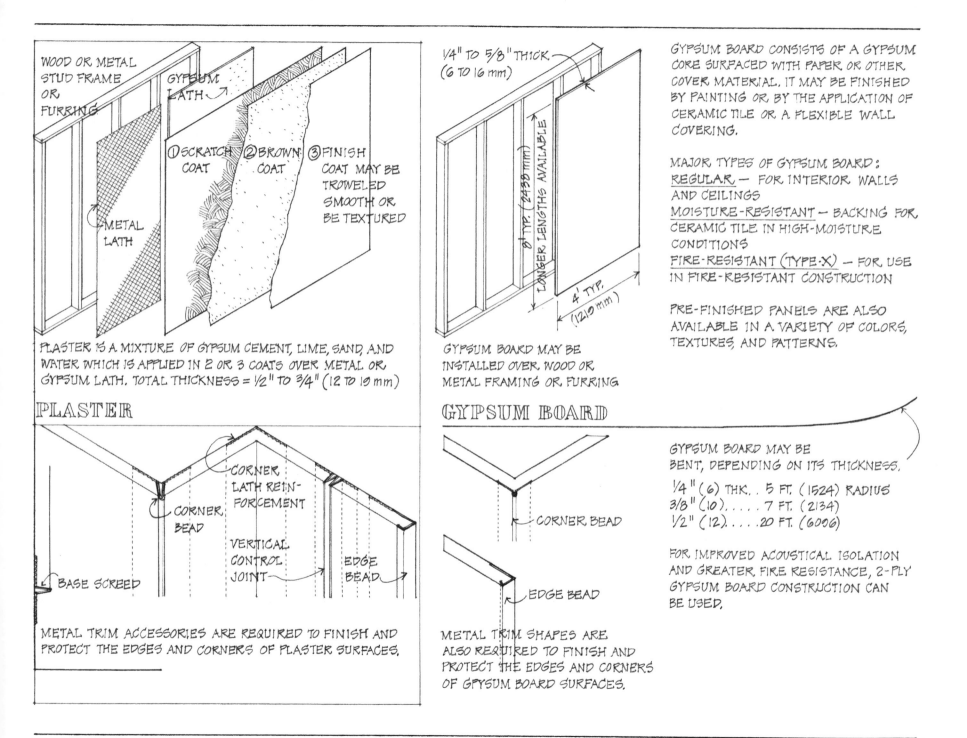

WOOD OR METAL STUD FRAME OR FURRING

GYPSUM LATH

METAL LATH

① SCRATCH COAT ② BROWN COAT ③ FINISH COAT MAY BE TROWELED SMOOTH OR BE TEXTURED

PLASTER IS A MIXTURE OF GYPSUM CEMENT, LIME, SAND, AND WATER WHICH IS APPLIED IN 2 OR 3 COATS OVER METAL OR GYPSUM LATH. TOTAL THICKNESS = ½" TO ¾" (12 TO 19 mm)

## PLASTER

CORNER LATH REINFORCEMENT

CORNER BEAD

VERTICAL CONTROL JOINT

EDGE BEAD

BASE SCREED

METAL TRIM ACCESSORIES ARE REQUIRED TO FINISH AND PROTECT THE EDGES AND CORNERS OF PLASTER SURFACES.

¼" TO ⅝" THICK (6 TO 16 mm)

8' TYP. (2438 mm) LONGER LENGTHS AVAILABLE

4' TYP. (1219 mm)

GYPSUM BOARD MAY BE INSTALLED OVER WOOD OR METAL FRAMING OR FURRING

## GYPSUM BOARD

CORNER BEAD

EDGE BEAD

METAL TRIM SHAPES ARE ALSO REQUIRED TO FINISH AND PROTECT THE EDGES AND CORNERS OF GYPSUM BOARD SURFACES.

GYPSUM BOARD CONSISTS OF A GYPSUM CORE SURFACED WITH PAPER OR OTHER COVER MATERIAL. IT MAY BE FINISHED BY PAINTING OR BY THE APPLICATION OF CERAMIC TILE OR A FLEXIBLE WALL COVERING.

MAJOR TYPES OF GYPSUM BOARD:
REGULAR — FOR INTERIOR WALLS AND CEILINGS
MOISTURE-RESISTANT — BACKING FOR CERAMIC TILE IN HIGH-MOISTURE CONDITIONS
FIRE-RESISTANT (TYPE-X) — FOR USE IN FIRE-RESISTANT CONSTRUCTION

PRE-FINISHED PANELS ARE ALSO AVAILABLE IN A VARIETY OF COLORS, TEXTURES, AND PATTERNS.

GYPSUM BOARD MAY BE BENT, DEPENDING ON ITS THICKNESS.

¼" (6) THK.. 5 FT. (1524) RADIUS
⅜" (10).... 7 FT. (2134)
½" (12)....20 FT. (6006)

FOR IMPROVED ACOUSTICAL ISOLATION AND GREATER FIRE RESISTANCE, 2-PLY GYPSUM BOARD CONSTRUCTION CAN BE USED.

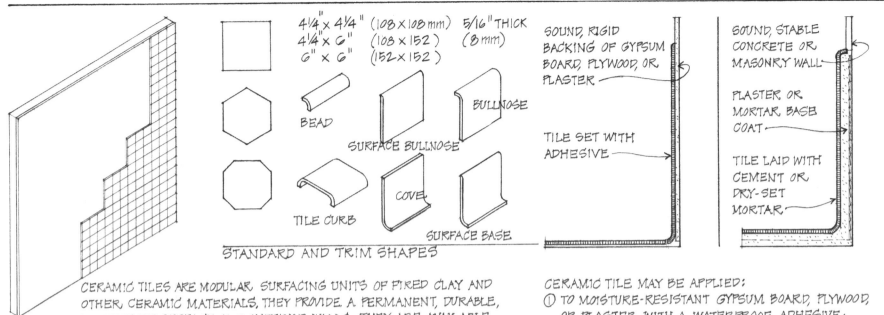

4¼" x 4¼" (108 x 108 mm)
4¼" x 6" (108 x 152)
6" x 6" (152 x 152)

5/16" THICK (8 mm)

BEAD

BULLNOSE

SURFACE BULLNOSE

TILE CURB

COVE

SURFACE BASE

SOUND, RIGID BACKING OF GYPSUM BOARD, PLYWOOD, OR PLASTER

TILE SET WITH ADHESIVE

SOUND, STABLE CONCRETE OR MASONRY WALL

PLASTER OR MORTAR BASE COAT

TILE LAID WITH CEMENT OR DRY-SET MORTAR

## STANDARD AND TRIM SHAPES

CERAMIC TILES ARE MODULAR SURFACING UNITS OF FIRED CLAY AND OTHER CERAMIC MATERIALS. THEY PROVIDE A PERMANENT, DURABLE, WATERPROOF SURFACE FOR INTERIOR WALLS. THEY ARE AVAILABLE IN BRIGHT OR MATTE GLAZES IN A WIDE RANGE OF COLORS AND SURFACE DESIGNS. CONSULT MANUFACTURER FOR DETAILS.

CERAMIC TILE MAY BE APPLIED:
① TO MOISTURE-RESISTANT GYPSUM BOARD, PLYWOOD, OR PLASTER, WITH A WATERPROOF ADHESIVE;
② OVER FRAME CONSTRUCTION, SET WITH CEMENT MORTAR OVER METAL OR GYPSUM LATH.

# CERAMIC TILE

IN ADDITION TO BEING PAINTED, SMOOTH PLASTER AND GYPSUM BOARD SURFACES CAN BE FINISHED WITH A VARIETY OF FLEXIBLE WALL COVERINGS
• WALLPAPER
• CLOTH OR PAPER BACKED VINYL
• FABRIC (WOOL, LINEN, COTTON)
• GRASS CLOTH
• BURLAP
• CORK

THESE WALL COVERINGS ARE AVAILABLE IN AN ALMOST INFINITE RANGE OF COLORS, PATTERNS, AND DESIGNS. CONSULT MANUFACTURER FOR SAMPLES, ROLL WIDTHS AND LENGTHS, AND TYPE OF ADHESIVE REQUIRED FOR APPLICATION.

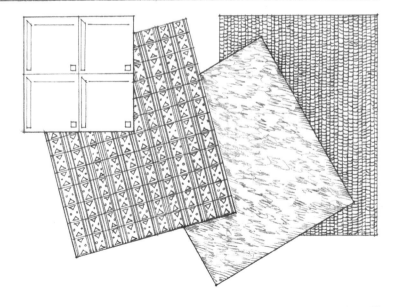

# WALL COVERINGS

# CEILINGS

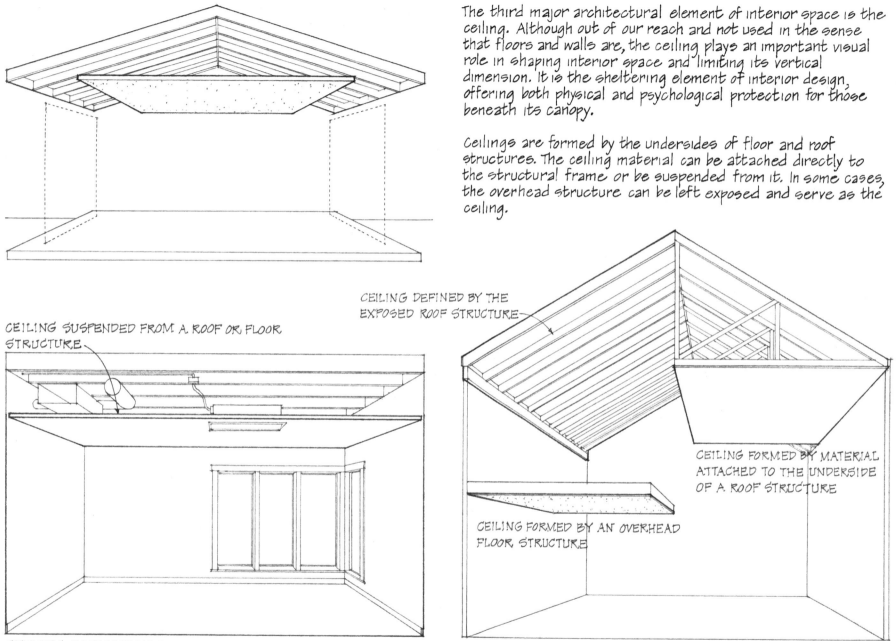

The third major architectural element of interior space is the ceiling. Although out of our reach and not used in the sense that floors and walls are, the ceiling plays an important visual role in shaping interior space and limiting its vertical dimension. It is the sheltering element of interior design, offering both physical and psychological protection for those beneath its canopy.

Ceilings are formed by the undersides of floor and roof structures. The ceiling material can be attached directly to the structural frame or be suspended from it. In some cases, the overhead structure can be left exposed and serve as the ceiling.

CEILING DEFINED BY THE EXPOSED ROOF STRUCTURE

CEILING SUSPENDED FROM A ROOF OR FLOOR STRUCTURE

CEILING FORMED BY MATERIAL ATTACHED TO THE UNDERSIDE OF A ROOF STRUCTURE

CEILING FORMED BY AN OVERHEAD FLOOR STRUCTURE

CEILING FORMATIONS

The height of a ceiling has a major impact on the scale of a space. While a ceiling's height should be considered relative to a room's other dimensions, and to its occupancy and use, some generalizations can still be made about the vertical dimension of space.

High ceilings tend to give space an open, airy, lofty feeling. They can also provide an air of dignity or formality, especially when regular in shape and form. Instead of merely hovering over a space, they can soar.

Low ceilings, on the other hand, emphasize their sheltering quality and tend to create intimate, cozy spaces.

Changing the ceiling height within a space, or from one space to the next, helps to define spatial boundaries and to differentiate between adjacent areas. Each ceiling height emphasizes, by contrast, the lowness or height of the other.

THE "NORMAL" HEIGHT OF A CEILING SHOULD BE IN PROPORTION TO A ROOM'S HORIZONTAL DIMENSIONS AND ITS USE.

HIGH CEILINGS CAN, BY COMPARISON, DIMINISH THE APPARENT WIDTH OF A SPACE.

CEILING HEIGHT AND SCALE

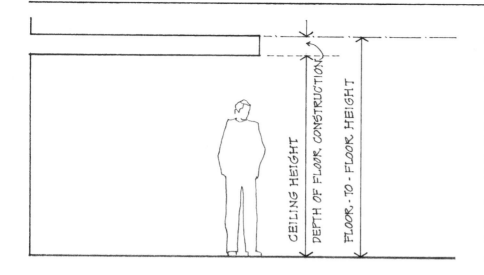

When a flat ceiling is formed by a floor above, its height is fixed by the floor-to-floor height and the depth of the floor construction. Given this dimension, the apparent height of a ceiling can be altered in several ways.

Since light values appear to recede, smooth, light-colored ceilings that reflect light convey a feeling of spaciousness. Carrying the wall material or finish onto the ceiling plane can also make a ceiling appear higher than it is, especially when a cove is used to make the transition between wall and ceiling.

The apparent height of a ceiling can be lowered by using a dark, bright color that contrasts with the wall color, or by carrying the ceiling material or finish down onto the walls.

SMOOTH, LIGHT, COOL-COLORED CEILINGS CONVEY SPACIOUSNESS; CARRYING WALL FINISH ONTO CEILING WITH A COVE ALSO RAISES APPARENT CEILING HEIGHT.

VISUAL WEIGHT OF DARK, BRIGHT COLORS LOWERS APPARENT CEILING HEIGHT; CARRY CEILING FINISH DOWN ONTO WALL PLANE ENLARGES CEILING AND LOWERS WALL HEIGHT.

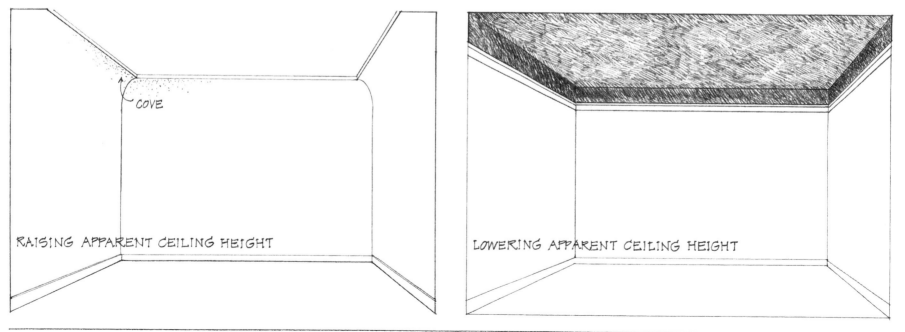

RAISING APPARENT CEILING HEIGHT

LOWERING APPARENT CEILING HEIGHT

Instead of being surfaced with a smooth, planar material, a ceiling can consist of or express the structural pattern of the floor or roof above. Linear members can create parallel, grid, or radial patterns. Any ceiling pattern will tend to attract our attention and appear to be lower than it is because of its visual weight. Since linear patterns direct the eye, they can also emphasize that dimension of space to which they are parallel.

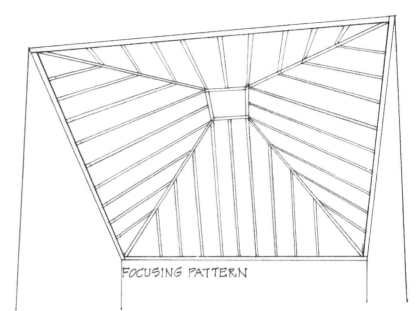

FOCUSING PATTERN

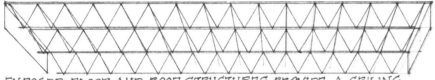

EXPOSED FLOOR AND ROOF STRUCTURES PROVIDE A CEILING WITH TEXTURE, PATTERN, DEPTH, AND DIRECTION. THESE CHARACTERISTICS ATTRACT OUR ATTENTION AND ARE BEST DISPLAYED IN CONTRAST TO SMOOTH WALL PLANES.

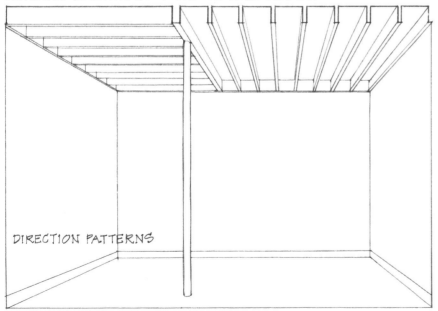

DIRECTION PATTERNS

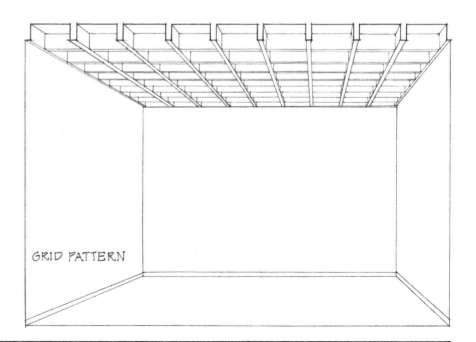

GRID PATTERN

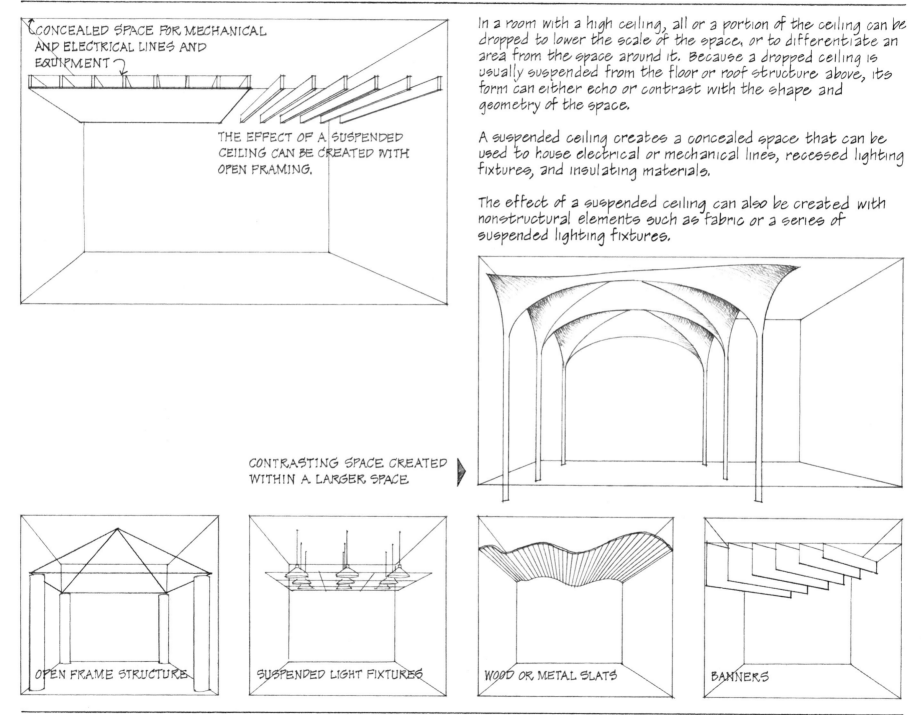

CONCEALED SPACE FOR MECHANICAL AND ELECTRICAL LINES AND EQUIPMENT

THE EFFECT OF A SUSPENDED CEILING CAN BE CREATED WITH OPEN FRAMING.

In a room with a high ceiling, all or a portion of the ceiling can be dropped to lower the scale of the space, or to differentiate an area from the space around it. Because a dropped ceiling is usually suspended from the floor or roof structure above, its form can either echo or contrast with the shape and geometry of the space.

A suspended ceiling creates a concealed space that can be used to house electrical or mechanical lines, recessed lighting fixtures, and insulating materials.

The effect of a suspended ceiling can also be created with nonstructural elements such as fabric or a series of suspended lighting fixtures.

CONTRASTING SPACE CREATED WITHIN A LARGER SPACE

OPEN FRAME STRUCTURE

SUSPENDED LIGHT FIXTURES

WOOD OR METAL SLATS

BANNERS

In commercial spaces, a modular suspended ceiling system is often used to integrate and provide flexibility in the layout of lighting fixtures and air distribution outlets. The typical system consists of modular ceiling tiles supported by a metal grid suspended from the overhead structure. The tiles are usually removable for access to the ceiling space.

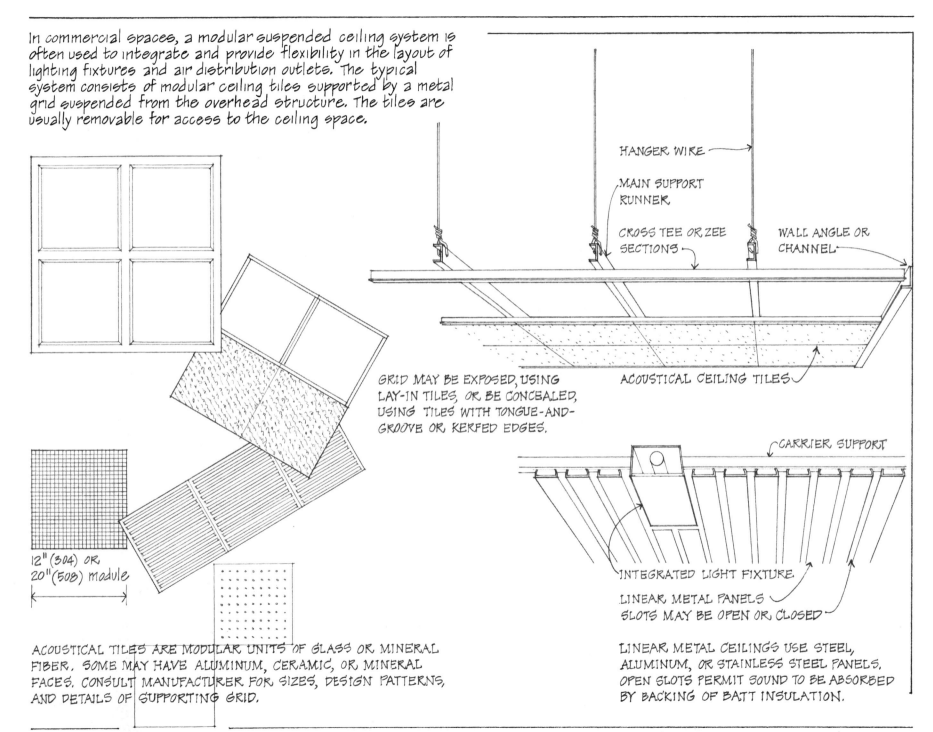

HANGER WIRE

MAIN SUPPORT RUNNER

CROSS TEE OR ZEE SECTIONS

WALL ANGLE OR CHANNEL

ACOUSTICAL CEILING TILES

GRID MAY BE EXPOSED, USING LAY-IN TILES, OR BE CONCEALED, USING TILES WITH TONGUE-AND-GROOVE OR KERFED EDGES.

12" (304) OR 20" (508) module

ACOUSTICAL TILES ARE MODULAR UNITS OF GLASS OR MINERAL FIBER. SOME MAY HAVE ALUMINUM, CERAMIC, OR MINERAL FACES. CONSULT MANUFACTURER FOR SIZES, DESIGN PATTERNS, AND DETAILS OF SUPPORTING GRID.

CARRIER SUPPORT

INTEGRATED LIGHT FIXTURE

LINEAR METAL PANELS SLOTS MAY BE OPEN OR CLOSED

LINEAR METAL CEILINGS USE STEEL, ALUMINUM, OR STAINLESS STEEL PANELS. OPEN SLOTS PERMIT SOUND TO BE ABSORBED BY BACKING OF BATT INSULATION.

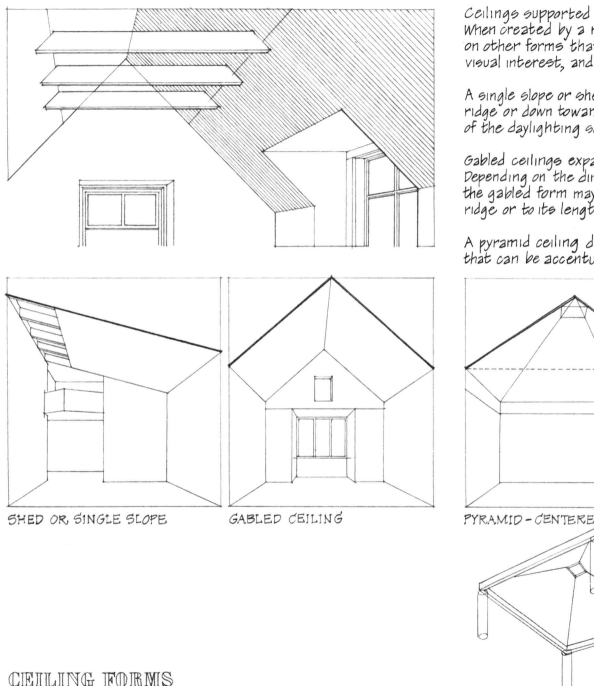

Ceilings supported by a floor structure above are normally flat. When created by a roof structure, however, a ceiling can take on other forms that reflect the shape of the structure, add visual interest, and give direction to the space.

A single slope or shed form may lead the eye upward toward the ridge or down toward the eave line, depending on the location of the daylighting sources within the room.

Gabled ceilings expand space upward toward the ridge line. Depending on the direction of any exposed structural elements, the gabled form may direct our attention to the height of the ridge or to its length.

A pyramid ceiling directs the eye upward to its peak, a focus that can be accentuated further with an illuminating skylight.

SHED OR SINGLE SLOPE     GABLED CEILING     PYRAMID — CENTERED PEAK     PYRAMID — OFF·CENTER PEAK

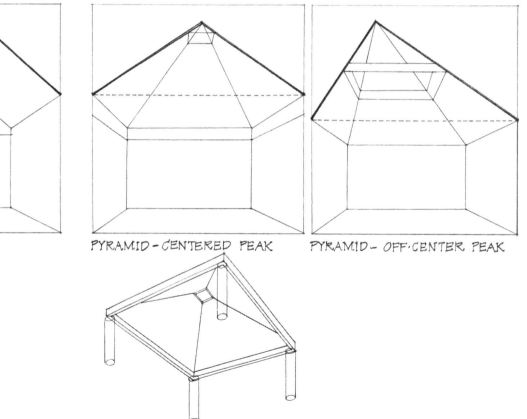

CEILING FORMS

A coved ceiling uses a curved surface to soften its meeting with the surrounding wall planes. The resulting merger of vertical and horizontal surfaces gives the enclosed space a plastic quality.

Increasing the scale of the cove further leads to vaulted and domed ceiling forms. A vaulted ceiling directs our eyes upward and along its length. A dome is a centralized form that expands space upward and focuses our attention on the space beneath its center.

Freeform ceilings contrast with the planar quality of walls and floors, and therefore attract our attention. Whether curvilinear or crystalline in nature, they are decorative and can often dominate the other elements of interior space.

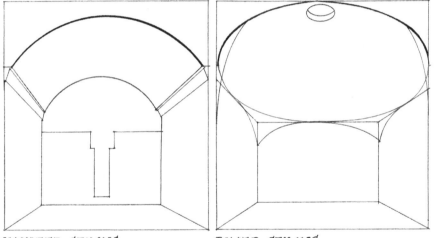

VAULTED CEILING   DOMED CEILING

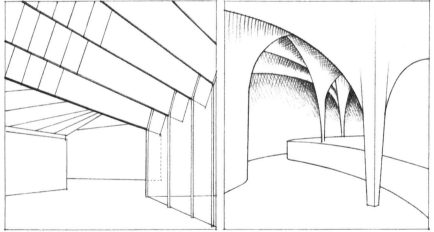

FREEFORM – RECTILINEAR   FREEFORM – CURVILINEAR

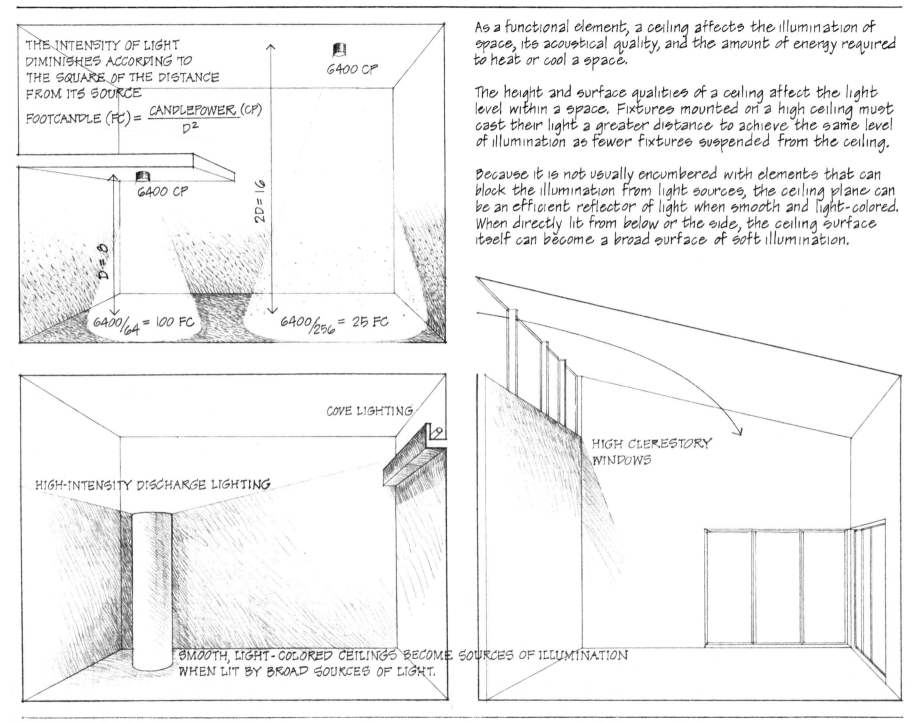

THE INTENSITY OF LIGHT DIMINISHES ACCORDING TO THE SQUARE OF THE DISTANCE FROM ITS SOURCE

$$FOOTCANDLE\ (FC) = \frac{CANDLEPOWER\ (CP)}{D^2}$$

6400 CP

6400 CP

$2D = 16$

$D = 8$

$6400/64 = 100\ FC$

$6400/256 = 25\ FC$

As a functional element, a ceiling affects the illumination of space, its acoustical quality, and the amount of energy required to heat or cool a space.

The height and surface qualities of a ceiling affect the light level within a space. Fixtures mounted on a high ceiling must cast their light a greater distance to achieve the same level of illumination as fewer fixtures suspended from the ceiling.

Because it is not usually encumbered with elements that can block the illumination from light sources, the ceiling plane can be an efficient reflector of light when smooth and light-colored. When directly lit from below or the side, the ceiling surface itself can become a broad surface of soft illumination.

COVE LIGHTING

HIGH-INTENSITY DISCHARGE LIGHTING

HIGH CLERESTORY WINDOWS

SMOOTH, LIGHT-COLORED CEILINGS BECOME SOURCES OF ILLUMINATION WHEN LIT BY BROAD SOURCES OF LIGHT.

Since the ceiling represents the largest unused surface of a room, its form and texture can have a significant impact on the room's acoustics. The smooth, hard surfaces of most ceiling materials reflect airborne sound within a space. In most situations, this is acceptable since other elements and surfaces in a space can employ sound-absorbing materials. In offices, stores, and restaurants, where additional sound-absorbing surfaces may be required to reduce the reflection of noise from numerous sources, acoustical ceilings can be employed.

Undesirable flutter within a space results when repeated echoes traverse back and forth between two non-absorbing parallel planes, such as a hard, flat ceiling opposite a hard-surface floor. Concave domes and vaults focus reflected sound and can intensify echoes and flutter. A remedy for flutter is to add absorbing surfaces. Another is to slope the ceiling plane or use one with a multifaceted surface.

Warm air rises while cooler air falls. Thus a high ceiling allows the warmer air in a room to rise and cooler air to settle at floor level. This pattern of air movement makes a high-ceilinged space more comfortable in warm weather, but also more difficult to heat in cold weather. Conversely, a low-ceilinged space traps warm air and is easier to heat in cold weather, but can be uncomfortably warm in hot weather.

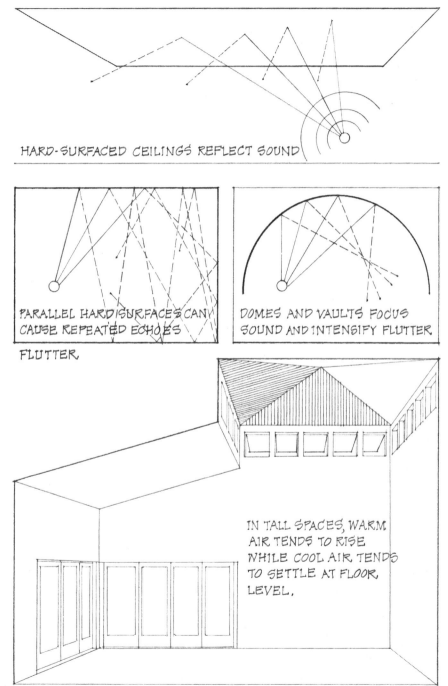

HARD-SURFACED CEILINGS REFLECT SOUND

PARALLEL HARD SURFACES CAN CAUSE REPEATED ECHOES

DOMES AND VAULTS FOCUS SOUND AND INTENSIFY FLUTTER

FLUTTER

IN TALL SPACES, WARM AIR TENDS TO RISE WHILE COOL AIR TENDS TO SETTLE AT FLOOR LEVEL.

The underside of the floor or roof structure above can be left exposed and serve as the ceiling. More often, however, a separate ceiling material is attached to or hung from a supporting structure. The range of ceiling materials is similar to that for walls except for those which are too heavy to be hung from an overhead structure.

## PLASTER & GYPSUM BOARD

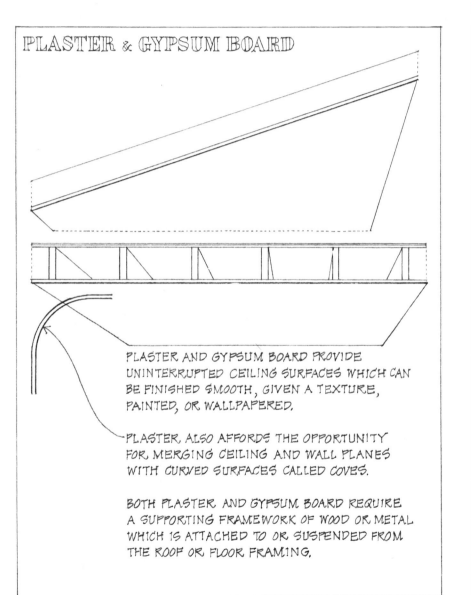

PLASTER AND GYPSUM BOARD PROVIDE UNINTERRUPTED CEILING SURFACES WHICH CAN BE FINISHED SMOOTH, GIVEN A TEXTURE, PAINTED, OR WALLPAPERED.

PLASTER ALSO AFFORDS THE OPPORTUNITY FOR MERGING CEILING AND WALL PLANES WITH CURVED SURFACES CALLED COVES.

BOTH PLASTER AND GYPSUM BOARD REQUIRE A SUPPORTING FRAMEWORK OF WOOD OR METAL WHICH IS ATTACHED TO OR SUSPENDED FROM THE ROOF OR FLOOR FRAMING.

## WOOD

WOOD DECKING OR PLANKS SPAN BETWEEN BEAMS TO FORM THE STRUCTURAL PLATFORM OF A FLOOR OR ROOF. THE UNDERSIDE OF THE PLANKS MAY BE LEFT EXPOSED AS THE FINISH CEILING.

WOOD PLANKS ARE NORMALLY 5¼ INCHES (133 mm) WIDE AND HAVE "V" GROOVE, TONGUE-AND-GROOVE JOINTS. CHANNEL GROOVE, STRIATED, AND OTHER MACHINED PATTERNS ARE AVAILABLE.

WITH THIS STRUCTURAL SYSTEM, THERE IS NO CONCEALED CEILING SPACE.

## METAL

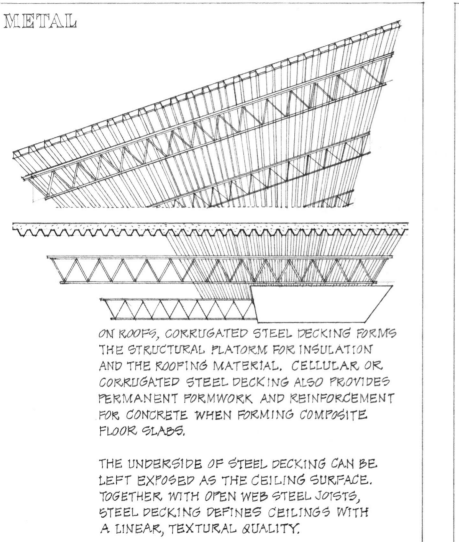

ON ROOFS, CORRUGATED STEEL DECKING FORMS
THE STRUCTURAL PLATFORM FOR INSULATION
AND THE ROOFING MATERIAL. CELLULAR OR
CORRUGATED STEEL DECKING ALSO PROVIDES
PERMANENT FORMWORK AND REINFORCEMENT
FOR CONCRETE WHEN FORMING COMPOSITE
FLOOR SLABS.

THE UNDERSIDE OF STEEL DECKING CAN BE
LEFT EXPOSED AS THE CEILING SURFACE.
TOGETHER WITH OPEN WEB STEEL JOISTS,
STEEL DECKING DEFINES CEILINGS WITH
A LINEAR, TEXTURAL QUALITY.

## MODULAR

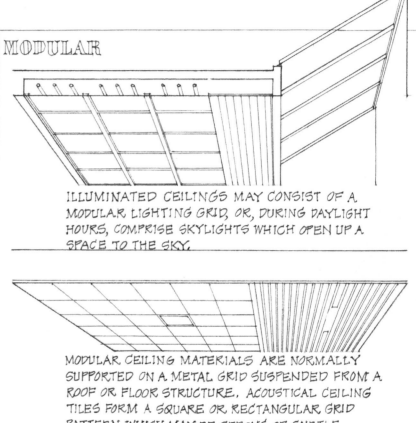

ILLUMINATED CEILINGS MAY CONSIST OF A
MODULAR LIGHTING GRID, OR, DURING DAYLIGHT
HOURS, COMPRISE SKYLIGHTS WHICH OPEN UP A
SPACE TO THE SKY.

MODULAR CEILING MATERIALS ARE NORMALLY
SUPPORTED ON A METAL GRID SUSPENDED FROM A
ROOF OR FLOOR STRUCTURE. ACOUSTICAL CEILING
TILES FORM A SQUARE OR RECTANGULAR GRID
PATTERN WHICH MAY BE STRONG OR SUBTLE,
DEPENDING ON THE TILE DESIGN. IN CONTRAST
TO THIS, LONG, NARROW METAL PANELS FORM A
LINEAR PATTERN ON CEILINGS. IN BOTH CASES,
LIGHT FIXTURES, AIR DIFFUSERS, AND OTHER
EQUIPMENT CAN BE INTEGRATED INTO THE
MODULAR SYSTEM.

# WINDOWS

Windows and doorways interrupt the wall planes that give a building its form and interior spaces their definition. They are the transitional elements of architectural and interior design that link, both visually and physically, one space to another, and inside to outside.

The size, shape, and placement of windows affect the visual integrity of a wall surface and the sense of enclosure it provides. A window can be seen as a bright area within a wall, an opening framed by a wall, or a void separating two wall planes. It can also be enlarged to the point where it becomes the physical wall plane - a transparent window wall that visually unites an interior space with the outdoors or an adjacent interior space.

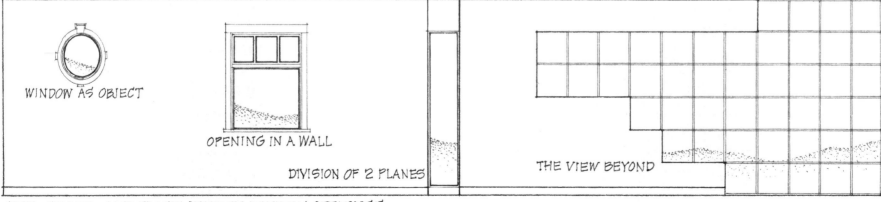

WINDOW AS OBJECT

OPENING IN A WALL

DIVISION OF 2 PLANES

THE VIEW BEYOND

SIZE, SHAPE, AND PLACEMENT OF WINDOW OPENINGS

The scale of a window is related not only to the surrounding wall plane but also to our own dimensions. We are accustomed to a window head height slightly above our height and to a sill height that corresponds to our waistline. When a large window is used to visually expand a space, broaden its outlook, or complement its scale, the window can be subdivided into smaller units to maintain a human scale.

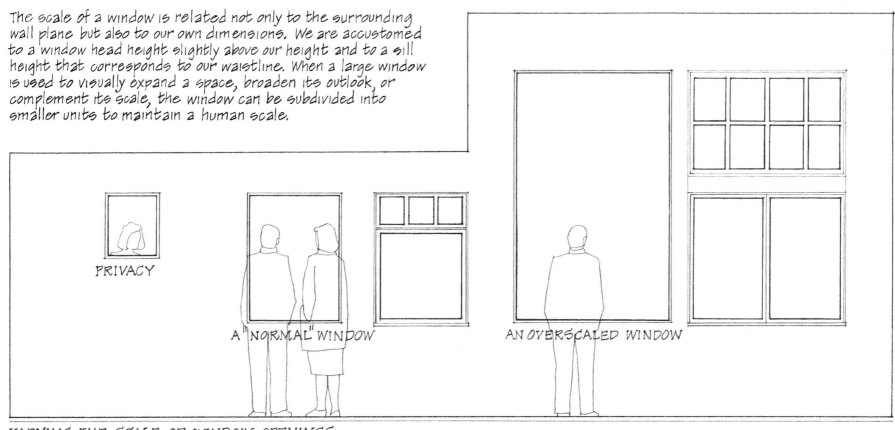

PRIVACY

A "NORMAL" WINDOW

AN OVERSCALED WINDOW

VARYING THE SCALE OF WINDOW OPENINGS

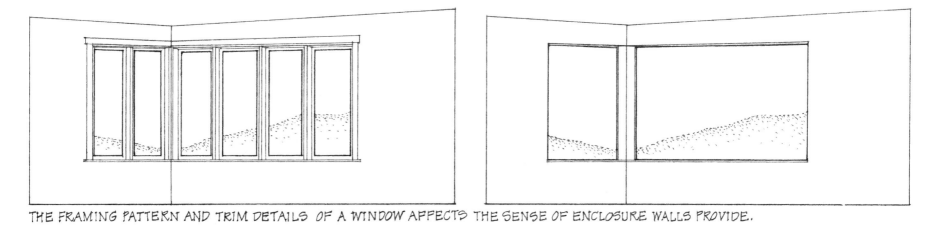

THE FRAMING PATTERN AND TRIM DETAILS OF A WINDOW AFFECTS THE SENSE OF ENCLOSURE WALLS PROVIDE.

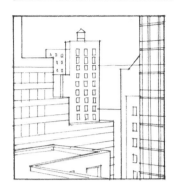

Views from windows become an integral part of the fabric of interior space. They not only provide an outward focus from within a room; they also convey visual information to us about where we are. They form a connection between inside and outside.

In determining the size, shape, and placement of windows in a room, consideration should be given to what can be seen through the window openings, how these views are framed, and how the visual scenes shift as we move about the room.

Windows do more than simply frame views. In daylighting a space and providing for its ventilation, a window may also expose a less than desirable view. In such a case, the treatment of a window can fragment, filter, or divert our view. Exterior landscaping can also aid in shielding an interior space from an undesirable view, or even create a pleasant outlook where none exists.

WAYS TO DEAL WITH AN UNSIGHTLY VIEW:

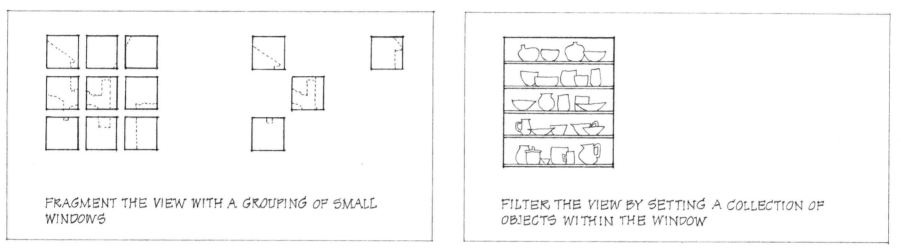

FRAGMENT THE VIEW WITH A GROUPING OF SMALL WINDOWS

FILTER THE VIEW BY SETTING A COLLECTION OF OBJECTS WITHIN THE WINDOW

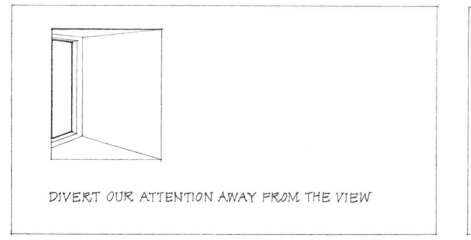

DIVERT OUR ATTENTION AWAY FROM THE VIEW

WHERE NO VIEW EXISTS, CREATE A GARDEN OR COURTYARD VIEW.

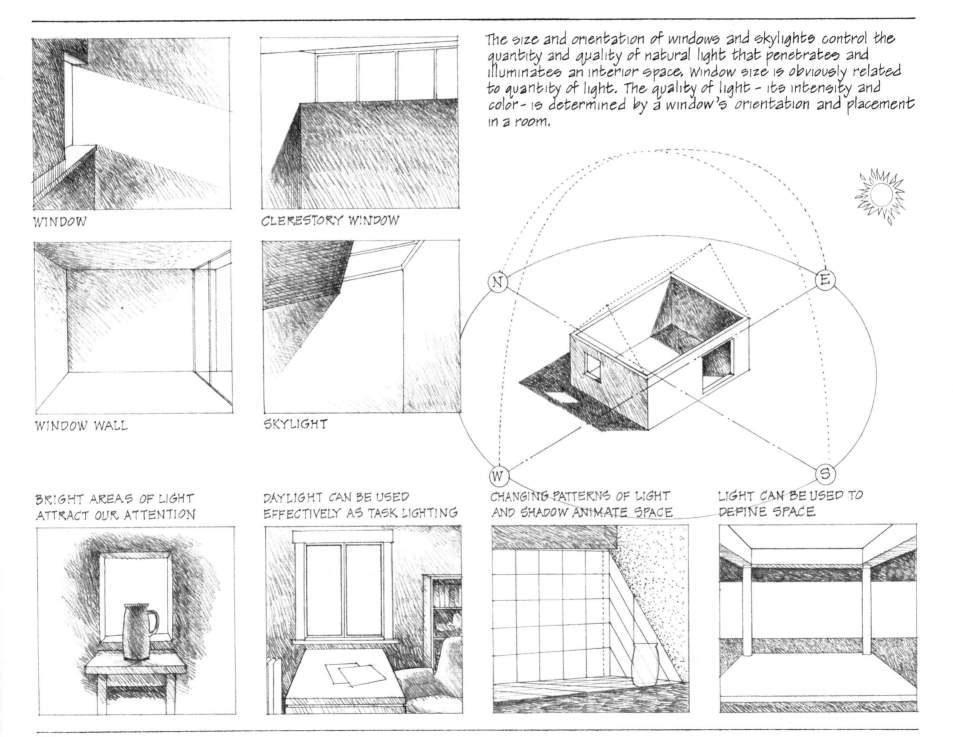

WINDOW

CLERESTORY WINDOW

The size and orientation of windows and skylights control the quantity and quality of natural light that penetrates and illuminates an interior space. Window size is obviously related to quantity of light. The quality of light – its intensity and color – is determined by a window's orientation and placement in a room.

WINDOW WALL

SKYLIGHT

BRIGHT AREAS OF LIGHT ATTRACT OUR ATTENTION

DAYLIGHT CAN BE USED EFFECTIVELY AS TASK LIGHTING

CHANGING PATTERNS OF LIGHT AND SHADOW ANIMATE SPACE

LIGHT CAN BE USED TO DEFINE SPACE

A problem associated with daylighting is glare, which is caused by excessive contrast between the brightness of a window opening and the darker wall surfaces adjacent to it. When one deals with glare, the placement of windows is as important as their size. The optimum condition is balanced lighting from at least two directions — from two walls or a wall and the ceiling. Skylights, in particular, can help soften the harshness of direct sunlight.

In rooms with windows close to the floor, glare can be caused by the light reflected off of the exterior ground surface. This ground glare can be reduced through the use of shade trees or a vertical screen of horizontal louvers.

Locating a window adjacent to a perpendicular wall or ceiling surface maximizes the light entering the window. The perpendicular surface is illuminated by the entering light and becomes itself a broad source of reflected light.

GLARE RESULTS WHEN OUR EYES CANNOT ADJUST SIMULTANEOUSLY TO WIDELY CONTRASTING AREAS OF BRIGHTNESS.

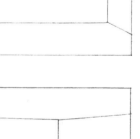

OUR EYES ADJUST TO THE BRIGHTEST LIGHT, REDUCING OUR ABILITY TO SEE LESS BRIGHTLY LIT AREAS.

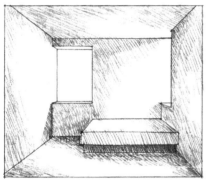

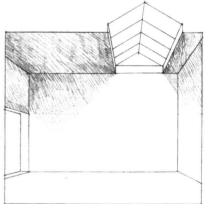

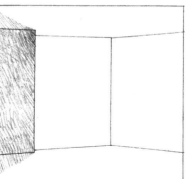

BIDIRECTIONAL DAYLIGHTING RAISES THE LEVEL OF DIFFUSED LIGHT IN A SPACE AND REDUCES THE POSSIBILITY OF GLARE.

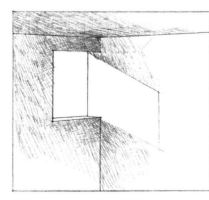

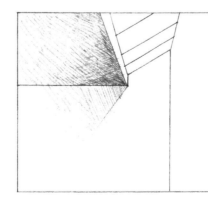

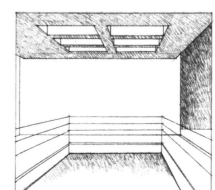

NATURAL VENTILATION REQUIRES THE USE OF OPERABLE WINDOWS.

Wind velocity, temperature, and direction are important site considerations in locating windows in all climatic regions. During hot periods, wind-induced ventilation is desirable for cooling by evaporation or conduction. In cold weather, wind should be avoided or screened from windows to minimize the infiltration of cold air into a building. At all times, some degree of ventilation is desirable for good health and the removal of stale air and odors from interior spaces.

Natural ventilation in the interior spaces of buildings is generated by differences in air pressure as well as temperature. Air flow patterns induced by these forces are affected more by building geometry than air speed.

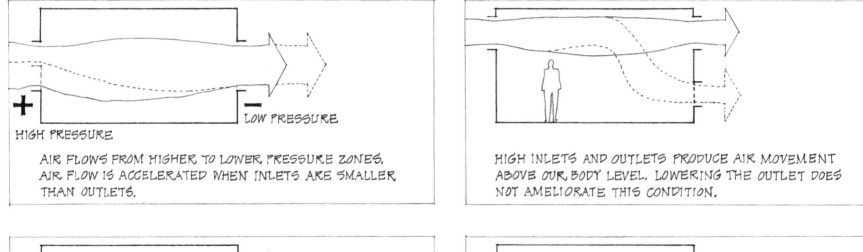

HIGH PRESSURE    LOW PRESSURE

AIR FLOWS FROM HIGHER TO LOWER PRESSURE ZONES. AIR FLOW IS ACCELERATED WHEN INLETS ARE SMALLER THAN OUTLETS.

HIGH INLETS AND OUTLETS PRODUCE AIR MOVEMENT ABOVE OUR BODY LEVEL. LOWERING THE OUTLET DOES NOT AMELIORATE THIS CONDITION.

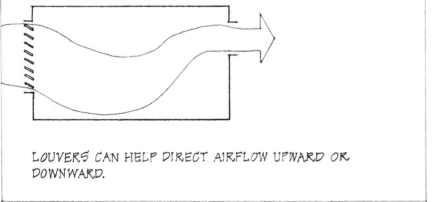

LOUVERS CAN HELP DIRECT AIRFLOW UPWARD OR DOWNWARD.

INTERIOR PARTITIONS AND TALL FURNISHINGS CAN ADVERSELY ALTER THE PATTERN OF AIR FLOW.

Ventilation is provided by window openings. Even when closed, windows are sources of heat gain and loss. Heat gain, desirable in cold winter months and undesirable in hot summer months, is due to solar radiation through a window's glazing. Heat loss through a window, undesirable in cold weather, is due to the temperature differential between a heated interior space and the colder outside air.

Glass is a poor thermal insulator. To increase its resistance to heat flow, a window can be double- or triple-glazed, so that the trapped air space between the glass panes can be used as insulation.

A window's orientation is a more cost-effective factor in controlling solar radiation than is its construction.

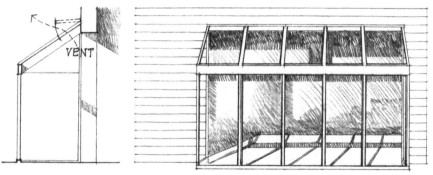

SOUTHERLY ORIENTATION OF WINDOWS ADMITS SOLAR RADIATION

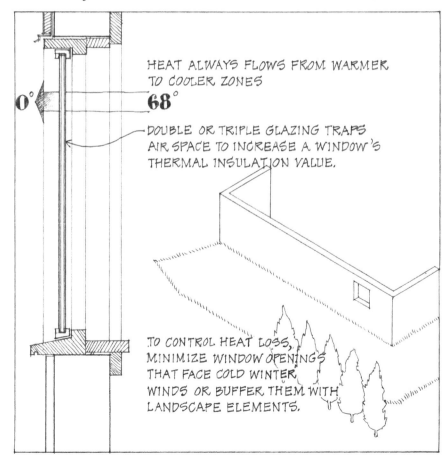

HEAT ALWAYS FLOWS FROM WARMER TO COOLER ZONES

0°    68°

DOUBLE OR TRIPLE GLAZING TRAPS AIR SPACE TO INCREASE A WINDOW'S THERMAL INSULATION VALUE.

TO CONTROL HEAT LOSS, MINIMIZE WINDOW OPENINGS THAT FACE COLD WINTER WINDS OR BUFFER THEM WITH LANDSCAPE ELEMENTS.

ONE OF THE METHODS FOR PASSIVE SOLAR HEATING UTILIZES A SUN SPACE FOR SOLAR COLLECTION AND THERMAL STORAGE ELEMENTS, SUCH AS MASONRY FLOORS AND WALLS. PROVISION FOR SOME OPERABLE GLAZING IS NECESSARY SO THAT THE SPACE CAN BE VENTILATED IN WARM WEATHER.

In addition to their aesthetic impact on the interior environment, windows also influence the physical arrangement of furnishings within a room. Their brightness during daylight hours and the views they offer attract our attention and often persuade us to gather about or orient a furniture grouping toward them.

Windows occupy wall space. When locating windows, one planning consideration is how much wall area remains between window openings and whether the size and proportion of these wall segments can accommodate the furnishings placed in front of them. If wall space is at a premium, clerestory windows and skylights can be considered as alternatives.

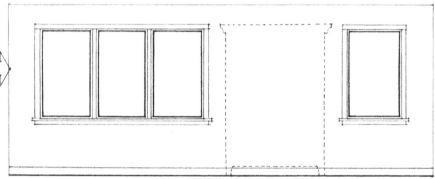

WINDOW LOCATIONS FRAGMENT WALL SPACE.

WITH WINDOWS REPOSITIONED, WALL SPACE IS CONSOLIDATED.

LOCATING WINDOW AWAY FROM CORNER CAN ALLOW FOR DEPTH OF FURNITURE PLACED ON PERPENDICULAR WALL.

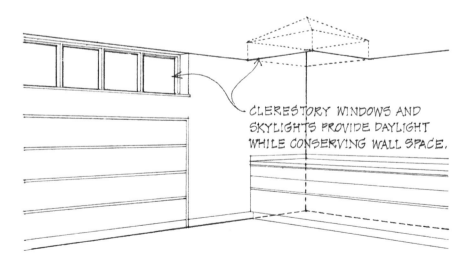

CLERESTORY WINDOWS AND SKYLIGHTS PROVIDE DAYLIGHT WHILE CONSERVING WALL SPACE.

The sill height of a window also affects what can be placed below it. A low sill height may dictate that the floor area in front of the window be left open, thereby reducing the amount of usable floor space in a room. This is especially pertinent when window walls extend down to the floor to promote visual continuity between interior and exterior space.

Another consideration in the placement of windows is the adverse effect direct sunlight can have on a room's occupants (heat and glare) and on the finishes of its carpet and furnishings (fading and deterioration).

WINDOWS EXPOSE THE BACKS OF FURNITURE PLACED AGAINST THEM.

WINDOWSILL

COUNTERTOP

WHEN POSSIBLE, COORDINATE WINDOWS WITH BUILT-IN ELEMENTS.

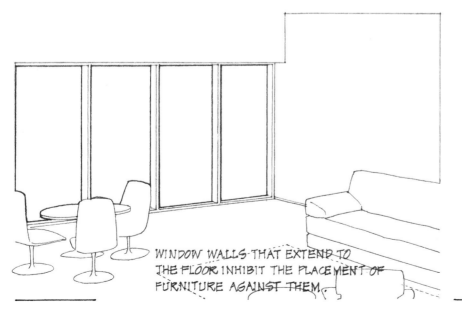

WINDOW WALLS THAT EXTEND TO THE FLOOR INHIBIT THE PLACEMENT OF FURNITURE AGAINST THEM.

WHEN EXPOSED TO DIRECT SUNLIGHT, SOME MATERIALS ARE SUBJECT TO FADING AND DETERIORATION.

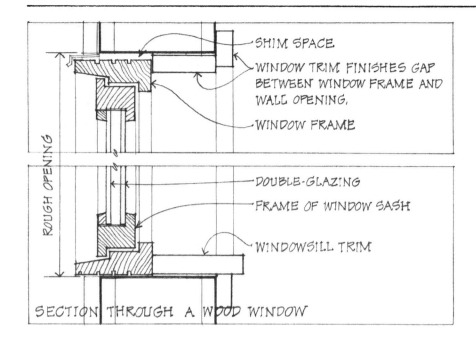

- SHIM SPACE
- WINDOW TRIM FINISHES GAP BETWEEN WINDOW FRAME AND WALL OPENING.
- WINDOW FRAME

ROUGH OPENING

- DOUBLE-GLAZING
- FRAME OF WINDOW SASH
- WINDOWSILL TRIM

SECTION THROUGH A WOOD WINDOW

Most windows used today are prefabricated units with frames of wood or metal. Wood frames are generally constructed of kiln-dried, clear, straight-grain material. They are usually treated in the factory with preservatives or water-repellants. The exterior of the frame may be ordered unfinished, primed for painting, or clad with aluminum or vinyl for reduced maintenance. The interior of the frame is usually left unfinished.

Metal frames are stronger and therefore usually thinner in profile than wood frames. Aluminum and steel are the most common types, although stainless steel and bronze windows are also available. Aluminum frames may have a natural, mill finish, or be anodized for additional protection and color. Steel window frames must be galvanized and/or primed and painted for corrosion-resistance. Since metal is an efficient conductor of heat, moisture can condense on the inner face of metal sashes in cold weather unless a thermal break is built into their construction.

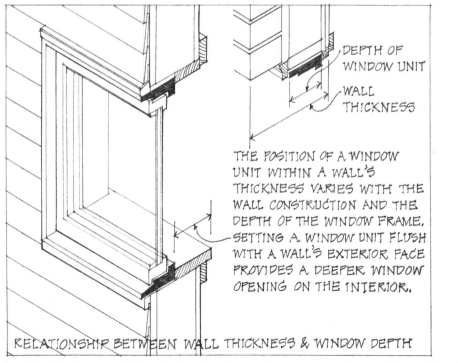

- DEPTH OF WINDOW UNIT
- WALL THICKNESS

THE POSITION OF A WINDOW UNIT WITHIN A WALL'S THICKNESS VARIES WITH THE WALL CONSTRUCTION AND THE DEPTH OF THE WINDOW FRAME. SETTING A WINDOW UNIT FLUSH WITH A WALL'S EXTERIOR FACE PROVIDES A DEEPER WINDOW OPENING ON THE INTERIOR.

RELATIONSHIP BETWEEN WALL THICKNESS & WINDOW DEPTH

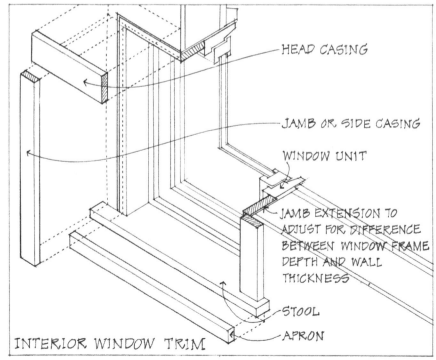

- HEAD CASING
- JAMB OR SIDE CASING
- WINDOW UNIT
- JAMB EXTENSION TO ADJUST FOR DIFFERENCE BETWEEN WINDOW FRAME DEPTH AND WALL THICKNESS
- STOOL
- APRON

INTERIOR WINDOW TRIM

Factory-manufactured windows come in stock sizes, but these vary with each manufacturer. Custom sizes and shapes are available, but often at additional cost.

Rough openings in wall construction usually allow ½ to ¾ inch on each side and along the top for leveling and plumbing up of the window units. Flashing and caulking on the exterior side of the frames help to make the joints weathertight and minimize the infiltration of air.

Casing and trimwork are used to conceal and finish the gaps between a window unit and its rough opening. The type of interior trim used contributes significantly to the character of a space.

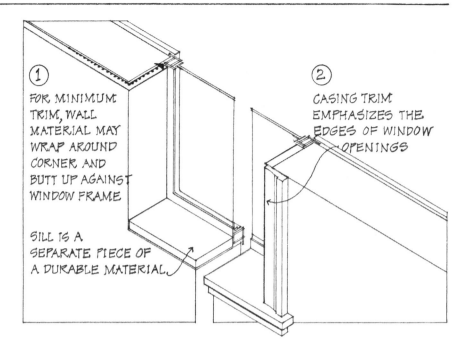

① FOR MINIMUM TRIM, WALL MATERIAL MAY WRAP AROUND CORNER AND BUTT UP AGAINST WINDOW FRAME

SILL IS A SEPARATE PIECE OF A DURABLE MATERIAL.

② CASING TRIM EMPHASIZES THE EDGES OF WINDOW OPENINGS

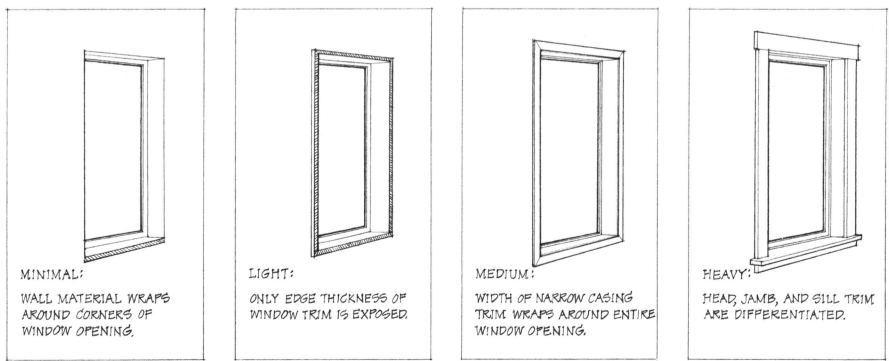

MINIMAL:
WALL MATERIAL WRAPS AROUND CORNERS OF WINDOW OPENING.

LIGHT:
ONLY EDGE THICKNESS OF WINDOW TRIM IS EXPOSED.

MEDIUM:
WIDTH OF NARROW CASING TRIM WRAPS AROUND ENTIRE WINDOW OPENING.

HEAVY:
HEAD, JAMB, AND SILL TRIM ARE DIFFERENTIATED.

Windows can be categorized into two major groups: fixed and ventilating. While both groups provide interior spaces with light and views, fixed windows do not allow for the passage of air as do ventilating windows. Fixed windows can never be opened; ventilating windows can always be closed. It would seem then that the decision to use fixed windows should be a carefully considered one.

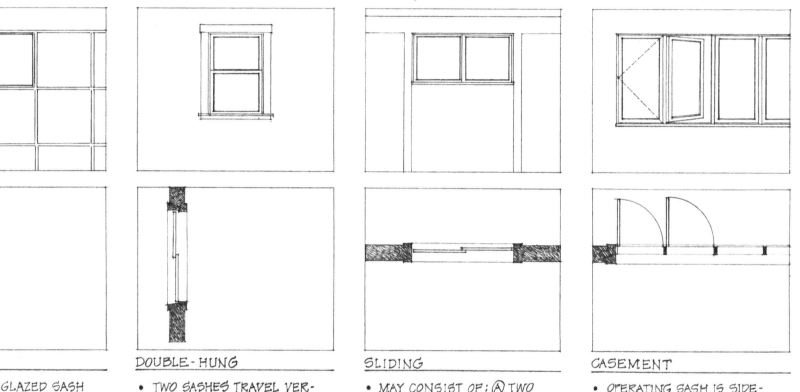

## FIXED

- FRAME AND GLAZED SASH ARE STATIONARY
- NO VENTILATION POSSIBLE
- FLEXIBLE SIZE & SHAPE DEPENDING ON GLAZING SIZE AVAILABLE
- CAN TAKE ON A THREE-DIMENSIONAL FORM, I.E., A BAY WINDOW
- NO HARDWARE OR SCREENS REQUIRED

## DOUBLE-HUNG

- TWO SASHES TRAVEL VERTICALLY AND ARE HELD IN DESIRED POSITION BY FRICTION OR A BALANCING DEVICE
- NO RAIN PROTECTION
- CAN BE WEATHERPROOFED EFFECTIVELY
- SCREENED ON OUTSIDE
- 50% VENTILATION
- DIFFICULT TO PAINT & CLEAN WITHOUT PIVOTING SASH

## SLIDING

- MAY CONSIST OF: Ⓐ TWO SASHES OF WHICH ONE SLIDES HORIZONTALLY (50% VENTILATION), OR Ⓑ THREE SASHES OF WHICH THE MIDDLE IS FIXED WHILE THE OTHER TWO SLIDE (66% VENTILATION)
- NO RAIN PROTECTION
- SCREENED ON OUTSIDE
- SLIDING PATIO DOORS ARE LIKE LARGE SLIDING WINDOWS.

## CASEMENT

- OPERATING SASH IS SIDE-HINGED, USUALLY SWINGING OUTWARD; INSIDE SCREEN
- 100% VENTILATION; CAN DIRECT OR DEFLECT BREEZES
- NO RAIN PROTECTION
- PROJECTING SASH CAN BE AN OBSTRUCTION
- ROTO-HARDWARE OR FRICTION HARDWARE USED FOR STABILITY OF SASH WHEN OPEN

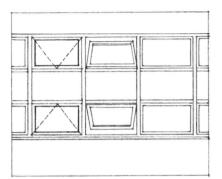

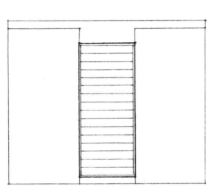

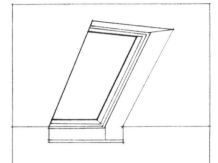

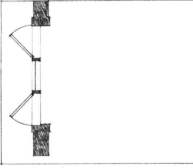

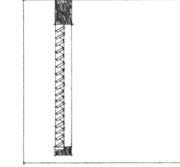

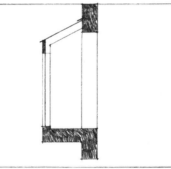

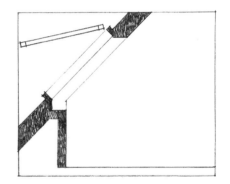

## AWNING/HOPPER

- SIMILAR TO CASEMENTS BUT HINGED AT TOP (AWNING) OR BOTTOM (HOPPER)
- 100% VENTILATION
- BOTH TYPES PROVIDE DRAFT-FREE VENTILATION; AWNINGS ALSO PROVIDE SOME RAIN PROTECTION
- MAY BE DIFFICULT TO WEATHERPROOF
- REQUIRES SPACE FOR SWING OF SASH

## JALOUSIE

- SIMILAR IN PRINCIPLE TO AWNING WINDOWS EXCEPT THAT A SERIES OF NARROW OPAQUE OR TRANSLUCENT STRIPS ARE USED
- ABLE TO DIRECT FLOW OF INCOMING AIR
- DIFFICULT TO CLEAN & WEATHERPROOF; USED IN WARM CLIMATES WHERE VENTILATION IS REQUIRED ALONG WITH PRIVACY.

## BAY WINDOWS & SKYLIGHTS

- SKYLIGHTS MAY BE FIXED OR VENTILATING UNITS
- SAFETY GLASS (TEMPERED OR WIRE GLASS) OR ACRYLIC REQUIRED
- SKYLIGHTS PROVIDE DAYLIGHTING WITHOUT INTERFERING WITH FURNITURE ARRANGEMENT AND WHILE MAINTAINING PRIVACY FROM UNWANTED VIEW
- VENTILATING SKYLIGHTS CAN BE EFFECTIVE COOLING MECHANISMS, ALLOWING HOT AIR TO ESCAPE IN WARM WEATHER
- BAY WINDOWS MAY USE A COMBINATION OF FIXED AND OPERABLE WINDOWS AND SKYLIGHTS TO PROJECT A PORTION OF INTERIOR SPACE OUTWARD INTO THE SURROUNDING LANDSCAPE

# WINDOW TREATMENTS

In the broad category of window treatments are included devices that provide additional control of light, available views, and the passage of air, heat, and cold. Exterior treatments are normally designed as integral elements of a building's architecture. If added to an existing building, such alterations should respect the existing architectural style.

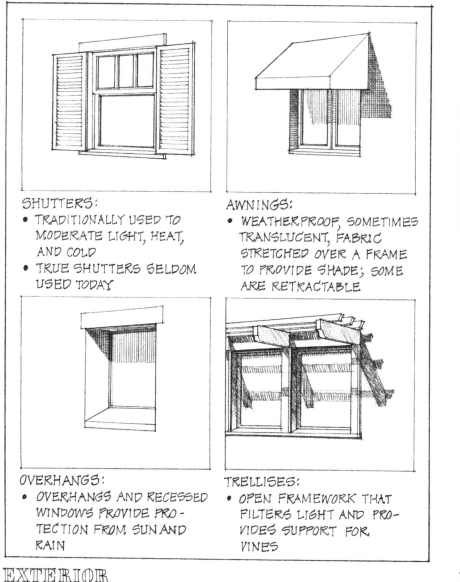

SHUTTERS:
- TRADITIONALLY USED TO MODERATE LIGHT, HEAT, AND COLD
- TRUE SHUTTERS SELDOM USED TODAY

AWNINGS:
- WEATHERPROOF, SOMETIMES TRANSLUCENT, FABRIC STRETCHED OVER A FRAME TO PROVIDE SHADE; SOME ARE RETRACTABLE

OVERHANGS:
- OVERHANGS AND RECESSED WINDOWS PROVIDE PROTECTION FROM SUN AND RAIN

TRELLISES:
- OPEN FRAMEWORK THAT FILTERS LIGHT AND PROVIDES SUPPORT FOR VINES

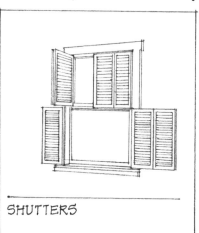

SHUTTERS

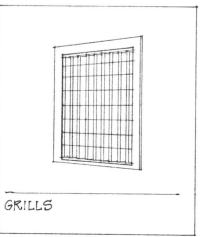

GRILLS

- RIGID PANELS, USUALLY OF WOOD, ARE HINGED TO OPEN AND CLOSE LIKE MINIATURE DOORS
- PANELS USUALLY HAVE ADJUSTABLE LOUVERS SO THAT FILTERING OF LIGHT AND VIEW CAN BE CONTROLLED
- SHUTTERS PROVIDE A CLEAN, PRECISE, UNCLUTTERED APPEARANCE
- WHEN CLOSED, SHUTTERS ENHANCE SENSE OF ENCLOSURE

- GRILLS ARE DECORATIVE SCREENS OF WOOD OR METAL THAT CAN BE USED TO MASK VIEWS, FILTER LIGHT, OR DIFFUSE VENTILATION.
- DEGREE OF MASKING, FILTRATION, OR DIFFUSION DEPENDS ON SPACING AND ORIENTATION OF MEMBERS
- MAY BE FIXED OR ADJUSTABLE
- DESIGN OF GRILL PATTERN CAN BE IMPORTANT VISUAL ELEMENT

EXTERIOR

INTERIOR

Interior window treatments vary according to how they temper the light, ventilation, and view a window provides, and how they alter a window's form and appearance. They also differ in how they open and close; a window treatment should not interfere with a window's operation or restrict access to its hardware.

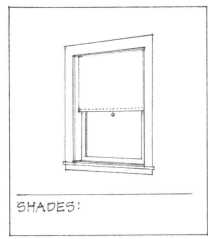

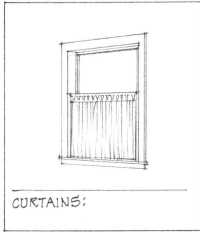

## SHADES:

- SHADES ARE ECONOMICAL WINDOW TREATMENTS OF FABRIC, VINYL, OR BAMBOO
- SHADES OPERATE FROM THE TOP DOWN TO COVER PART OR ALL OF A WINDOW OPENING
- SHADE MATERIAL MAY BE TRANSLUCENT OR OPAQUE
- SHADES REDUCE LIGHT WHILE PROVIDING PRIVACY
- BAMBOO PRESENTS A PLEASING TEXTURE WHILE FILTERING LIGHT AND VIEW
- SHADES MAY BE ROLLED OR GATHERED WHEN OPENED

## BLINDS:

- HORIZONTAL BLINDS CONSIST OF THIN OR WIDE SLATS
- SLATS MAY BE OF WOOD OR METAL
- SPACING AND ADJUSTABILITY OF SLATS PROVIDE GOOD CONTROL OF LIGHT AND AIR FLOW; THIN SLATS OBSTRUCT VIEW LESS THAN WIDE SLATS
- DIFFICULT TO CLEAN

- VERTICAL BLINDS HAVE SLATS, GENERALLY OF OPAQUE OR TRANSLUCENT FABRIC, THAT PIVOT AT THE TOP AND BOTTOM
- VERTICAL BLINDS ENHANCE THE HEIGHT OF A ROOM, GATHER LESS DUST, AND CAN BE MADE TO FIT ODD-SHAPED OPENINGS

## DRAPERIES:

- DRAPERIES REFER TO ANY FABRIC THAT HANGS STRAIGHT IN LOOSE FOLDS
- DRAPERIES ARE USUALLY OF HEAVY FABRIC; THEY MAY BE TIED BACK OR HUNG LIKE A TAPESTRY; THEY OFTEN HAVE A VALENCE OR WIDE CORNICE AT THE TOP

- DRAW CURTAINS OF OPAQUE OR TRANSLUCENT FABRIC ARE MOUNTED ON TRAVERSE RODS
- THEY SHOULD BE FULL AND HANG STRAIGHT, STARTING AT THE CEILING OR SLIGHTLY ABOVE THE TOP OF THE FRAME AND ENDING SLIGHTLY BELOW THE BOTTOM OF THE FRAME OR NEAR THE FLOOR

## CURTAINS:

- GLASS CURTAINS ARE OF SHEER, LIGHTWEIGHT MATERIAL HUNG CLOSE TO THE GLASS OF A WINDOW OR FRENCH DOOR
- SHEERNESS SOFTENS AND DIFFUSES LIGHT, FILTERS THE VIEW, AND PROVIDES DAYTIME PRIVACY
- CAN BE HUNG WITHIN WINDOW FRAME, OR OUTSIDE TO UNIFY A GROUP OF WINDOWS

- SASH CURTAINS ARE LIKE GLASS CURTAINS, BUT THEY ARE HUNG OR STRETCHED ACROSS THE SASH OF A WINDOW

# DOORS

Doors and doorways allow physical access for ourselves, furnishings, and goods in and out of a building and from room to room within it. Through their design, construction, and location, they can control the use of a room, the views from one space to the next, and the passage of light, sound, warmth, and cool breezes.

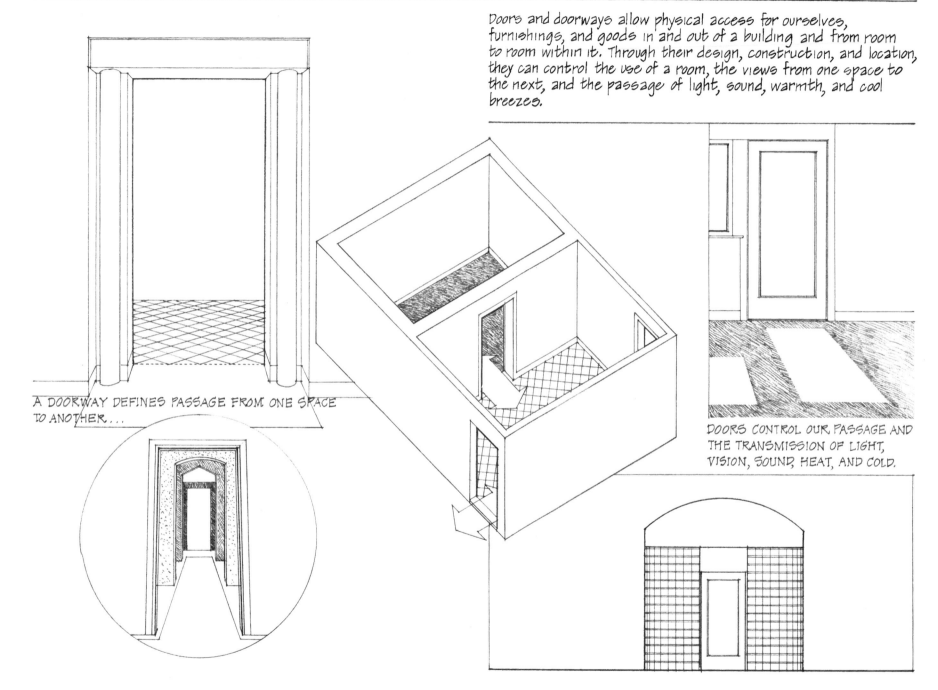

A DOORWAY DEFINES PASSAGE FROM ONE SPACE TO ANOTHER...

DOORS CONTROL OUR PASSAGE AND THE TRANSMISSION OF LIGHT, VISION, SOUND, HEAT, AND COLD.

Doors may have wood or metal frames surfaced with wood, metal, or a specialty material such as plastic laminate. They may be factory-primed for painting, pre-painted, or clad in various materials. They may be glazed for transparency, or contain louvers for ventilation.

Special doors include those constructed to have a fire-resistance rating, an acoustical rating, or entrance doors with a thermal insulation value.

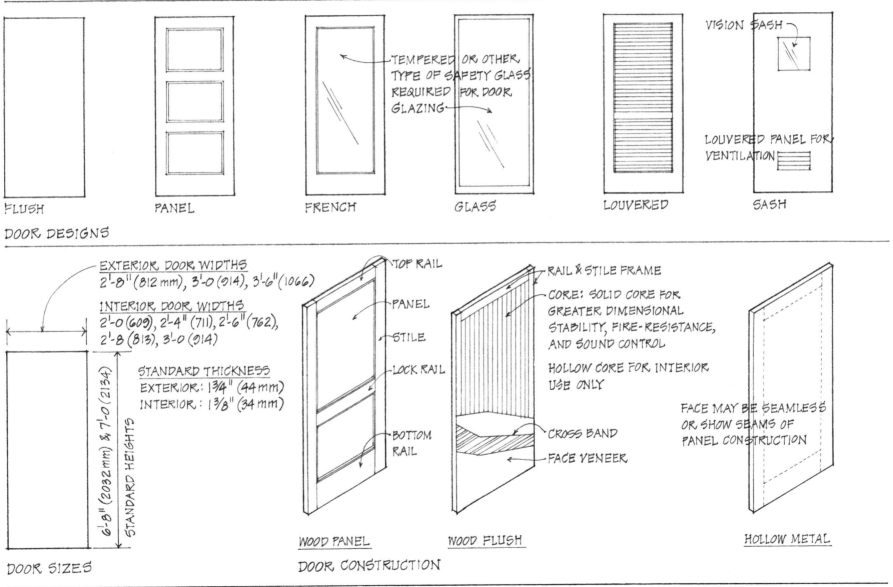

FLUSH  PANEL  FRENCH  GLASS  LOUVERED  SASH

TEMPERED OR OTHER TYPE OF SAFETY GLASS REQUIRED FOR DOOR GLAZING

VISION SASH

LOUVERED PANEL FOR VENTILATION

DOOR DESIGNS

EXTERIOR DOOR WIDTHS
2'-8" (812 mm), 3'-0 (914), 3'-6" (1066)

INTERIOR DOOR WIDTHS
2'-0 (609), 2'-4" (711), 2'-6" (762),
2'-8 (813), 3'-0 (914)

STANDARD THICKNESS
EXTERIOR: 1¾" (44 mm)
INTERIOR: 1⅜" (34 mm)

6'-8" (2032mm) & 7'-0 (2134) STANDARD HEIGHTS

DOOR SIZES

TOP RAIL
PANEL
STILE
LOCK RAIL
BOTTOM RAIL

WOOD PANEL

RAIL & STILE FRAME
CORE: SOLID CORE FOR GREATER DIMENSIONAL STABILITY, FIRE-RESISTANCE, AND SOUND CONTROL

HOLLOW CORE FOR INTERIOR USE ONLY

CROSS BAND
FACE VENEER

WOOD FLUSH

FACE MAY BE SEAMLESS OR SHOW SEAMS OF PANEL CONSTRUCTION

HOLLOW METAL

DOOR CONSTRUCTION

# DOOR TYPES

In addition to how they are designed and constructed, doors may be categorized according to how they operate.

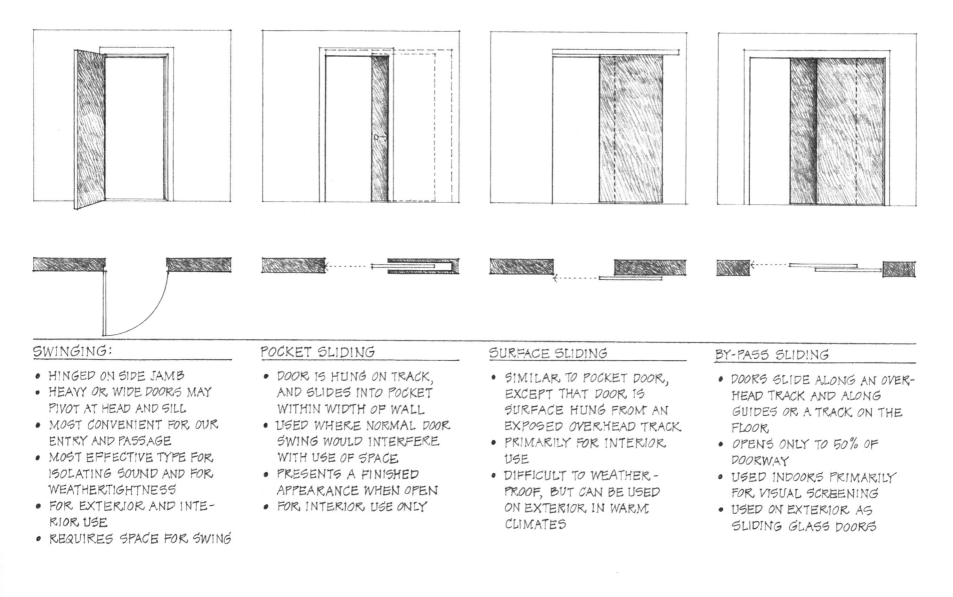

## SWINGING:

- HINGED ON SIDE JAMB
- HEAVY OR WIDE DOORS MAY PIVOT AT HEAD AND SILL
- MOST CONVENIENT FOR OUR ENTRY AND PASSAGE
- MOST EFFECTIVE TYPE FOR ISOLATING SOUND AND FOR WEATHERTIGHTNESS
- FOR EXTERIOR AND INTERIOR USE
- REQUIRES SPACE FOR SWING

## POCKET SLIDING

- DOOR IS HUNG ON TRACK, AND SLIDES INTO POCKET WITHIN WIDTH OF WALL
- USED WHERE NORMAL DOOR SWING WOULD INTERFERE WITH USE OF SPACE
- PRESENTS A FINISHED APPEARANCE WHEN OPEN
- FOR INTERIOR USE ONLY

## SURFACE SLIDING

- SIMILAR TO POCKET DOOR, EXCEPT THAT DOOR IS SURFACE HUNG FROM AN EXPOSED OVERHEAD TRACK
- PRIMARILY FOR INTERIOR USE
- DIFFICULT TO WEATHER-PROOF, BUT CAN BE USED ON EXTERIOR IN WARM CLIMATES

## BY-PASS SLIDING

- DOORS SLIDE ALONG AN OVERHEAD TRACK AND ALONG GUIDES OR A TRACK ON THE FLOOR
- OPENS ONLY TO 50% OF DOORWAY
- USED INDOORS PRIMARILY FOR VISUAL SCREENING
- USED ON EXTERIOR AS SLIDING GLASS DOORS

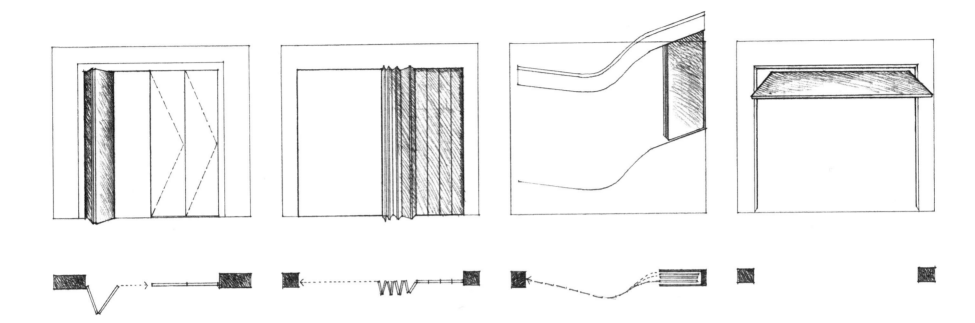

## BI-FOLD

- CONSISTS OF HINGED DOOR PANELS THAT SLIDE ON AN OVERHEAD TRACK
- FOR INTERIOR USE ONLY
- COMMONLY USED AS A VISUAL SCREEN TO CLOSE OFF STORAGE AND CLOSET SPACES

## ACCORDION FOLDING

- SIMILAR TO BI-FOLD DOORS EXCEPT THAT PANELS ARE SMALLER
- FOR INTERIOR USE ONLY
- USED TO SUBDIVIDE LARGE SPACES INTO SMALLER ROOMS

## SPECIAL FOLDING

- DOOR PANELS SLIDE ON OVERHEAD TRACKS
- TRACKS CAN BE CONFIGURED TO FOLLOW A CURVILINEAR PATH
- PANELS CAN BE STORED IN POCKET OR RECESS
- FOR INTERIOR USE

## OVERHEAD DOORS

- CONSISTS OF HINGED DOOR SECTIONS THAT ROLL UPWARD ON AN OVERHEAD TRACK
- CAPABLE OF CLOSING OFF UNUSUALLY TALL OR WIDE OPENINGS
- FOR EXTERIOR OR INTERIOR USE
- NOT FOR FREQUENT USE

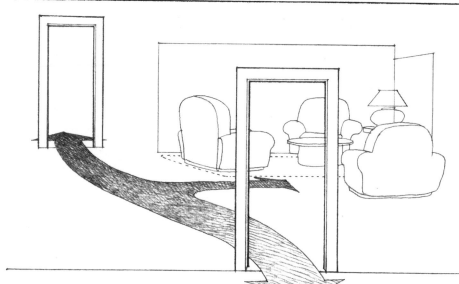

In linking the interior spaces of a building, doorways connect pathways. Their locations influence our patterns of movement from space to space as well as within a space. The nature of these patterns should be appropriate to the uses and activities housed within the interior spaces.

Space must be provided for our comfortable movement and the operation of doors. At the same time, there must also be sufficient and appropriately proportioned space remaining for the arrangement of furnishings.

Generally speaking, a room should have as few doorways as is feasible, and the paths that connect them should be as short and direct as possible without interfering with activity areas within the space.

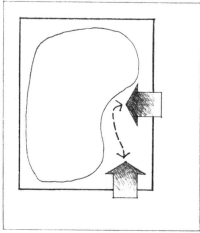

TWO DOORWAYS CLOSE TO EACH OTHER DEFINE A SHORT PATH THAT LEAVES A MAXIMUM AMOUNT OF USABLE FLOOR SPACE.

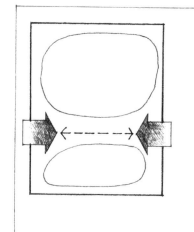

DOORWAYS SITUATED AT OR CLOSE TO CORNERS CAN DEFINE PATHS THAT RUN ALONG A ROOM'S WALLS. LOCATING THE DOORWAYS A COUPLE OF FEET AWAY FROM THE CORNERS ALLOWS FURNISHINGS SUCH AS STORAGE UNITS TO BE PLACED ALONG THE WALLS.

OPPOSING DOORWAYS DEFINE A STRAIGHT PATH THAT SUBDIVIDES A ROOM INTO TWO ZONES.

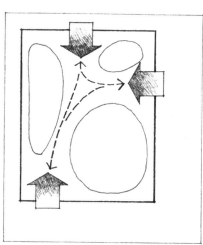

THREE DOORWAYS ON THREE WALLS CAN PRESENT A PROBLEM IF THE POSSIBLE PATHWAYS TAKE UP MUCH OF THE FLOOR AREA AND LEAVE A FRAGMENTED SERIES OF USABLE SPACES.

Another consideration in determining the location of a doorway is the view seen through its opening both from the adjacent space and upon entering. When visual privacy for a room is desired, a doorway, even when open, should not permit a direct view into the private zone of the space.

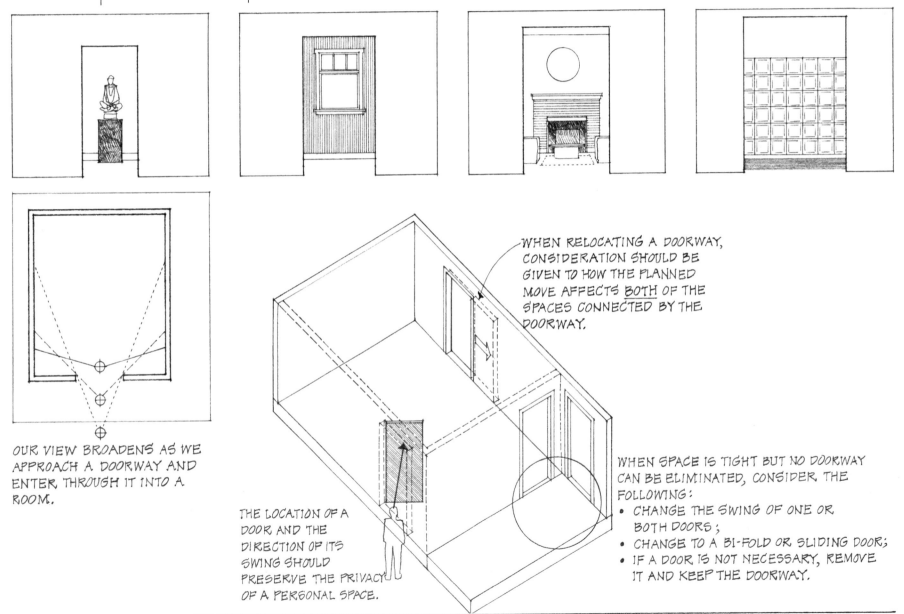

OUR VIEW BROADENS AS WE APPROACH A DOORWAY AND ENTER THROUGH IT INTO A ROOM.

WHEN RELOCATING A DOORWAY, CONSIDERATION SHOULD BE GIVEN TO HOW THE PLANNED MOVE AFFECTS BOTH OF THE SPACES CONNECTED BY THE DOORWAY.

THE LOCATION OF A DOOR AND THE DIRECTION OF ITS SWING SHOULD PRESERVE THE PRIVACY OF A PERSONAL SPACE.

WHEN SPACE IS TIGHT BUT NO DOORWAY CAN BE ELIMINATED, CONSIDER THE FOLLOWING:
• CHANGE THE SWING OF ONE OR BOTH DOORS;
• CHANGE TO A BI-FOLD OR SLIDING DOOR;
• IF A DOOR IS NOT NECESSARY, REMOVE IT AND KEEP THE DOORWAY.

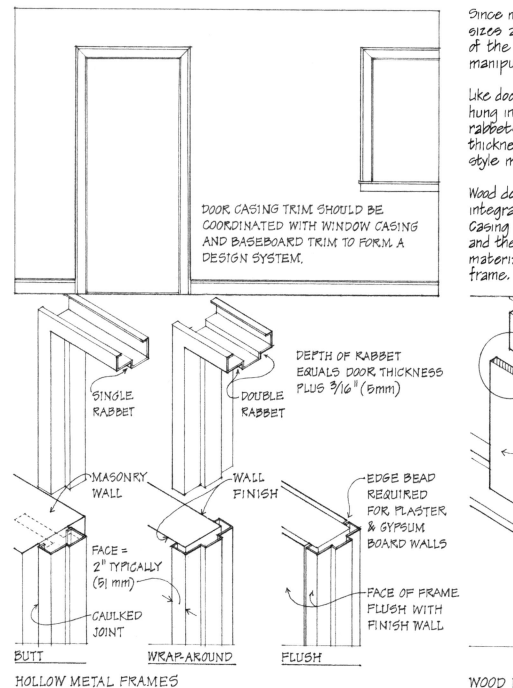

DOOR CASING TRIM SHOULD BE COORDINATED WITH WINDOW CASING AND BASEBOARD TRIM TO FORM A DESIGN SYSTEM.

Since most doors are manufactured in a number of standard sizes and styles, the treatment of the opening and the design of the casing trim are the areas where the designer can manipulate the scale and character of a doorway.

Like doors, door frames are standard items. Hollow metal doors are hung in hollow metal frames. These may have single or double rabbets, and may either butt up against or wrap around the wall thickness. In addition to the standard flat face, various trim style moldings are available.

Wood doors use wood frames. Exterior door frames usually have integral stops, while interior frames may have applied stops. Casing trim is used to conceal the gap between the door frame and the wall surface. Casing trim can be omitted if the wall material can be finished neatly and butt up against the door frame.

SINGLE RABBET

DOUBLE RABBET

DEPTH OF RABBET EQUALS DOOR THICKNESS PLUS 3/16" (5mm)

MASONRY WALL

WALL FINISH

EDGE BEAD REQUIRED FOR PLASTER & GYPSUM BOARD WALLS

FACE = 2" TYPICALLY (51 mm)

CAULKED JOINT

FACE OF FRAME FLUSH WITH FINISH WALL

BUTT          WRAP-AROUND          FLUSH

HOLLOW METAL FRAMES

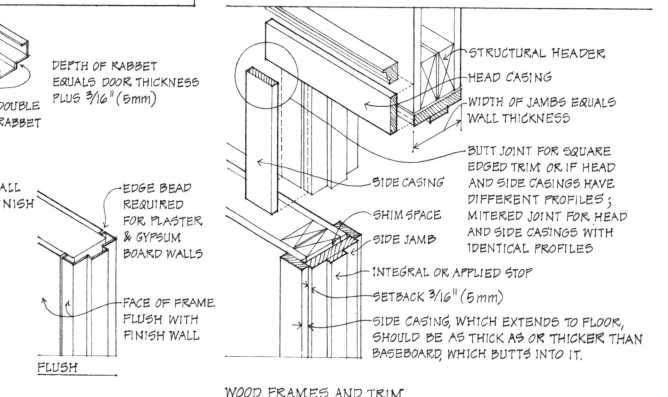

STRUCTURAL HEADER

HEAD CASING

WIDTH OF JAMBS EQUALS WALL THICKNESS

BUTT JOINT FOR SQUARE EDGED TRIM OR IF HEAD AND SIDE CASINGS HAVE DIFFERENT PROFILES; MITERED JOINT FOR HEAD AND SIDE CASINGS WITH IDENTICAL PROFILES

SIDE CASING

SHIM SPACE

SIDE JAMB

INTEGRAL OR APPLIED STOP

SETBACK 3/16" (5mm)

SIDE CASING, WHICH EXTENDS TO FLOOR, SHOULD BE AS THICK AS OR THICKER THAN BASEBOARD, WHICH BUTTS INTO IT.

WOOD FRAMES AND TRIM

Door casing trim, through its form and color, can accentuate a doorway and articulate the door as a distinct visual element in a space. The doorway opening itself can also be enlarged physically with sidelights and transoms, or visually with color and trimwork.

Conversely, a door frame and trim can, if desired, be minimized visually to reduce the scale of a doorway or to have it appear as a simple void in a wall.

If flush with the surrounding wall, a door can be finished to merge with and become part of the wall surface.

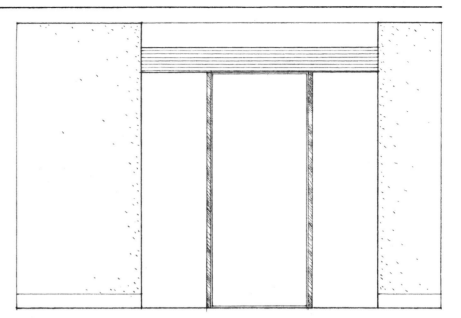

DOORWAY OPENING IS ENLARGED WITH ADDITIONAL GLAZING ABOVE DOOR AND SIDE LIGHTS TO ENHANCE ITS SCALE.

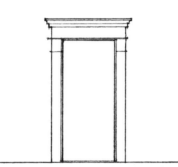

DOORWAY IS ELABORATED WITH TRIM WORK TO VISUALLY PRONOUNCE THE ENTRANCE INTO A ROOM. THE STYLE OF THE ELABORATION CAN GIVE A HINT AS TO WHAT LIES BEYOND.

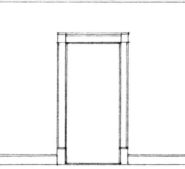

EVEN SIMPLE TRIMWORK CAN EMPHASIZE THE OPENING OF A DOORWAY IN A WALL PLANE.

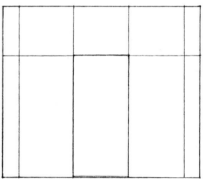

A DOOR CAN MERGE WITH THE SURROUNDING WALL SURFACE AND BECOME AN OBSCURE ELEMENT IN A SPACE.

IN EACH OF THE ABOVE CASES, HOW COLOR AND VALUE IS USED CAN MODIFY OUR PERCEPTION OF THE RELATIONSHIP BETWEEN A DOOR, ITS FRAME AND TRIM, AND THE SURROUNDING WALL SURFACE.

# STAIRS

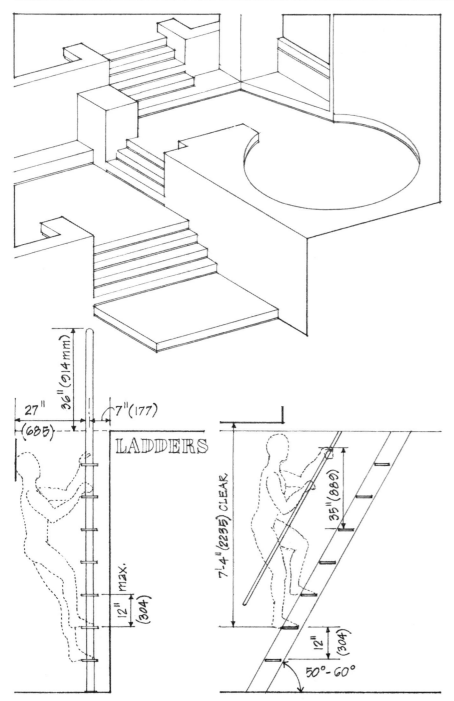

Stairs and stairways provide for our vertical movement between the various floor levels of a building. The two most important functional criteria in the design of stairs are safety and ease of ascent and descent. The dimensions of a stair's risers and treads should be proportioned to fit our body movement. Their pitch, if steep, can make ascent physically tiring as well as psychologically forbidding, and can make descent precarious. If shallow, a stair must have treads deep enough to fit our stride.

Building codes regulate the maximum and minimum dimensions of risers and treads. In addition, there are three rules of thumb that can be used to determine the proper proportion between the riser and tread dimensions of a stairway.

- Riser × Tread  = 70 to 75     (Measurement in inches)
- Riser + Tread  = 17 to 17½
- (2) Riser + Tread = 24 to 25

To determine the actual riser dimension of a stair, divide the total rise (the floor-to-floor height) by a whole number that gives a riser dimension closest to the one desired. The actual tread dimension can then be determined by using one of the rule-of-thumb formulas. Since in any flight of stairs there is one less tread than the number of risers, the total run can be easily determined.

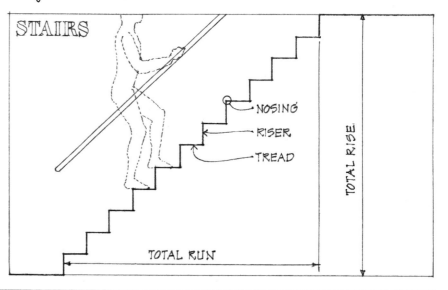

A stairway should be wide enough to comfortably accommodate our passage as well as any furnishings and equipment that must be moved up or down the steps. Building codes specify minimum widths based on occupant loads. Beyond these minimums, however, the width of a stairway also provides a visual clue to the public or private quality of the stairway.

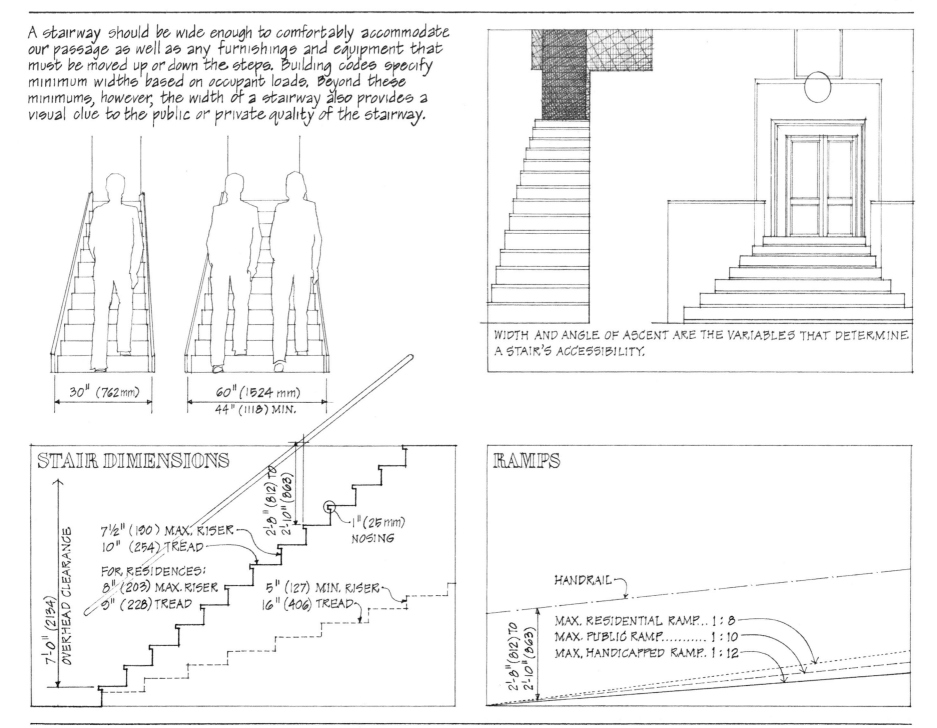

30" (762 mm)

60" (1524 mm)
44" (1118) MIN.

WIDTH AND ANGLE OF ASCENT ARE THE VARIABLES THAT DETERMINE A STAIR'S ACCESSIBILITY.

## STAIR DIMENSIONS

7½" (190) MAX. RISER
10" (254) TREAD

FOR RESIDENCES:
8" (203) MAX. RISER
9" (228) TREAD

5" (127) MIN. RISER
16" (406) TREAD

1" (25 mm) NOSING

2'-8" (812) TO 2'-10" (863)

7'-0" (2134) OVERHEAD CLEARANCE

## RAMPS

HANDRAIL

2'-8" (812) TO 2'-10" (863)

MAX. RESIDENTIAL RAMP... 1 : 8
MAX. PUBLIC RAMP............ 1 : 10
MAX. HANDICAPPED RAMP.. 1 : 12

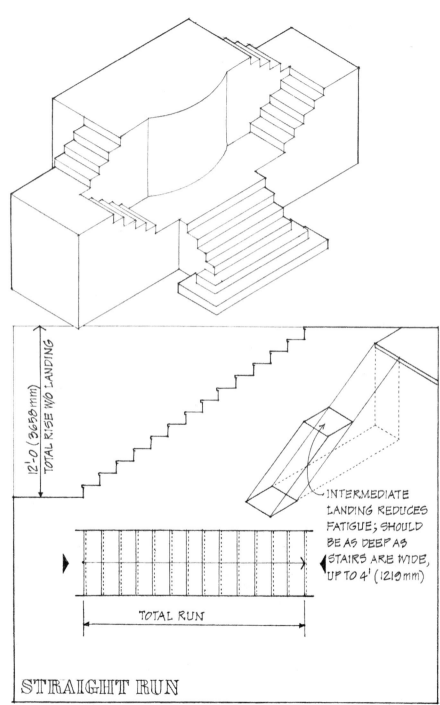

The configuration of a stairway determines the direction of our path as we ascend or descend its steps. There are several basic ways in which to configure the runs of a stairway. These variations result from the use of landings, which interrupt a stair run and enable it to change direction. Landings also provide opportunities for rest and possibilities for access and outlook from the stairway. Together with the pitch of a stair, the locations of landings determine the rhythm of our movement up or down a stair.

An important consideration in the planning of any stairway is how it links the paths of movement at each floor level. Another is the amount of space the stair requires. Each basic stair type has inherent proportions that will affect its possible location relative to other spaces around it. These proportions can be altered to some degree by adjusting the location of landings in the pattern. In each case, space should be provided at both the top and bottom of a stairway for safe and comfortable access and egress.

12'-0 (3658mm) TOTAL RISE W/O LANDING

INTERMEDIATE LANDING REDUCES FATIGUE; SHOULD BE AS DEEP AS STAIRS ARE WIDE, UP TO 4' (1219mm)

TOTAL RUN

## STRAIGHT RUN

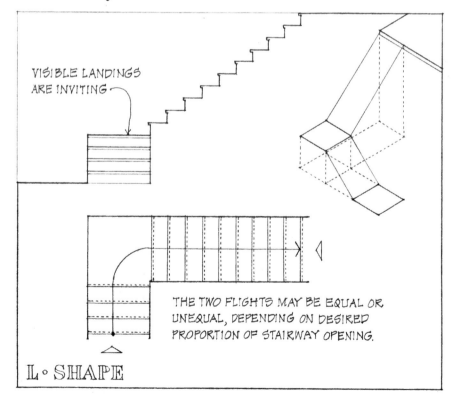

VISIBLE LANDINGS ARE INVITING

THE TWO FLIGHTS MAY BE EQUAL OR UNEQUAL, DEPENDING ON DESIRED PROPORTION OF STAIRWAY OPENING.

## L·SHAPE

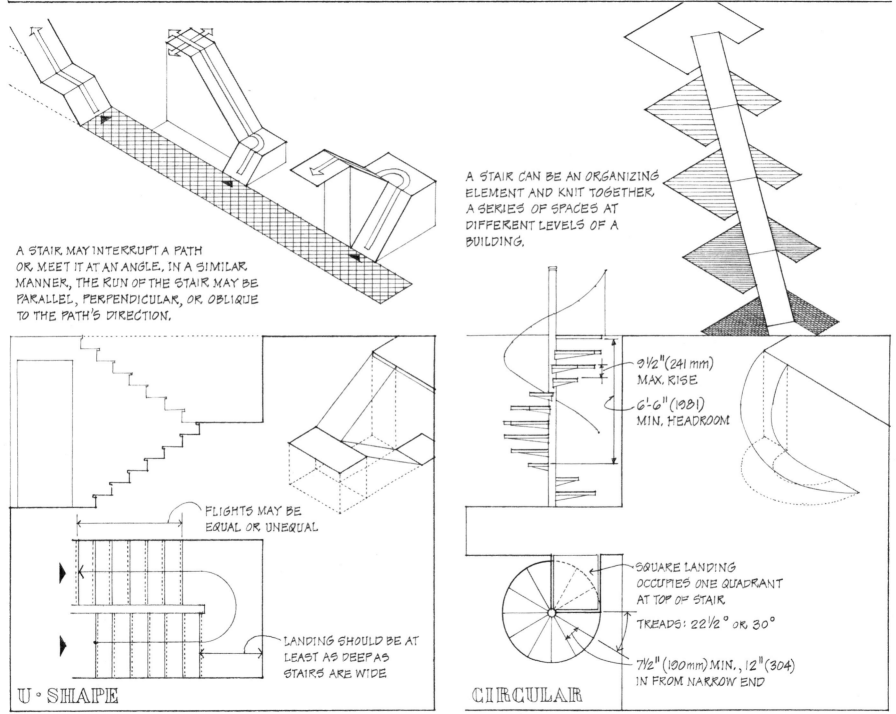

A STAIR MAY INTERRUPT A PATH
OR MEET IT AT AN ANGLE. IN A SIMILAR
MANNER, THE RUN OF THE STAIR MAY BE
PARALLEL, PERPENDICULAR, OR OBLIQUE
TO THE PATH'S DIRECTION.

A STAIR CAN BE AN ORGANIZING
ELEMENT AND KNIT TOGETHER
A SERIES OF SPACES AT
DIFFERENT LEVELS OF A
BUILDING.

9½" (241 mm)
MAX. RISE

6'-6" (1981)
MIN. HEADROOM

FLIGHTS MAY BE
EQUAL OR UNEQUAL

LANDING SHOULD BE AT
LEAST AS DEEP AS
STAIRS ARE WIDE

SQUARE LANDING
OCCUPIES ONE QUADRANT
AT TOP OF STAIR

TREADS: 22½° OR 30°

7½" (190mm) MIN., 12" (304)
IN FROM NARROW END

## U·SHAPE

## CIRCULAR

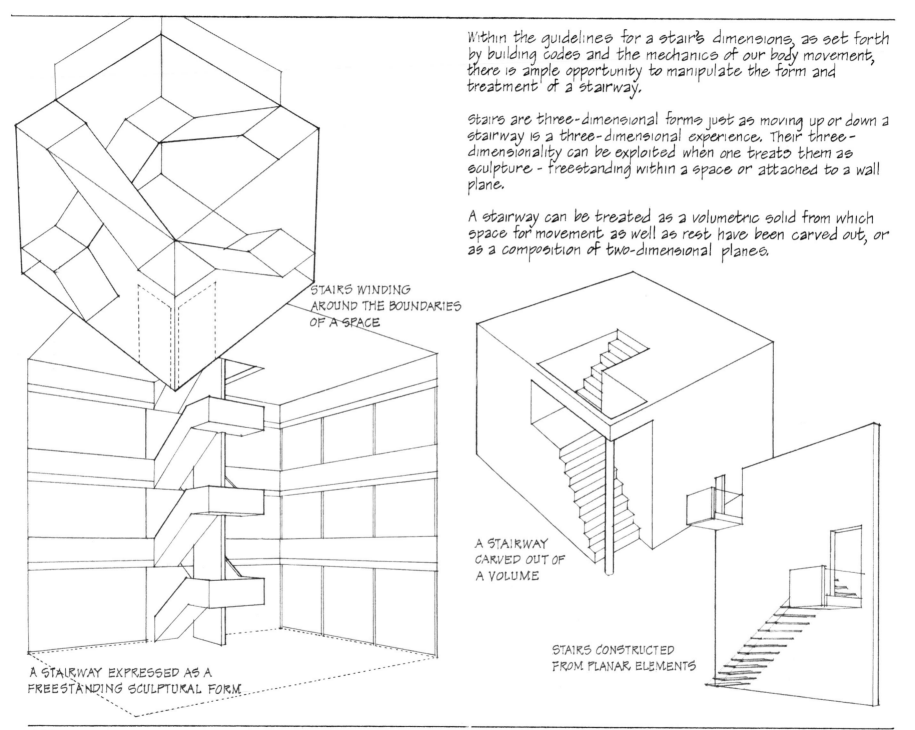

Within the guidelines for a stair's dimensions, as set forth by building codes and the mechanics of our body movement, there is ample opportunity to manipulate the form and treatment of a stairway.

Stairs are three-dimensional forms just as moving up or down a stairway is a three-dimensional experience. Their three-dimensionality can be exploited when one treats them as sculpture - freestanding within a space or attached to a wall plane.

A stairway can be treated as a volumetric solid from which space for movement as well as rest have been carved out, or as a composition of two-dimensional planes.

STAIRS WINDING AROUND THE BOUNDARIES OF A SPACE

A STAIRWAY EXPRESSED AS A FREESTANDING SCULPTURAL FORM

A STAIRWAY CARVED OUT OF A VOLUME

STAIRS CONSTRUCTED FROM PLANAR ELEMENTS

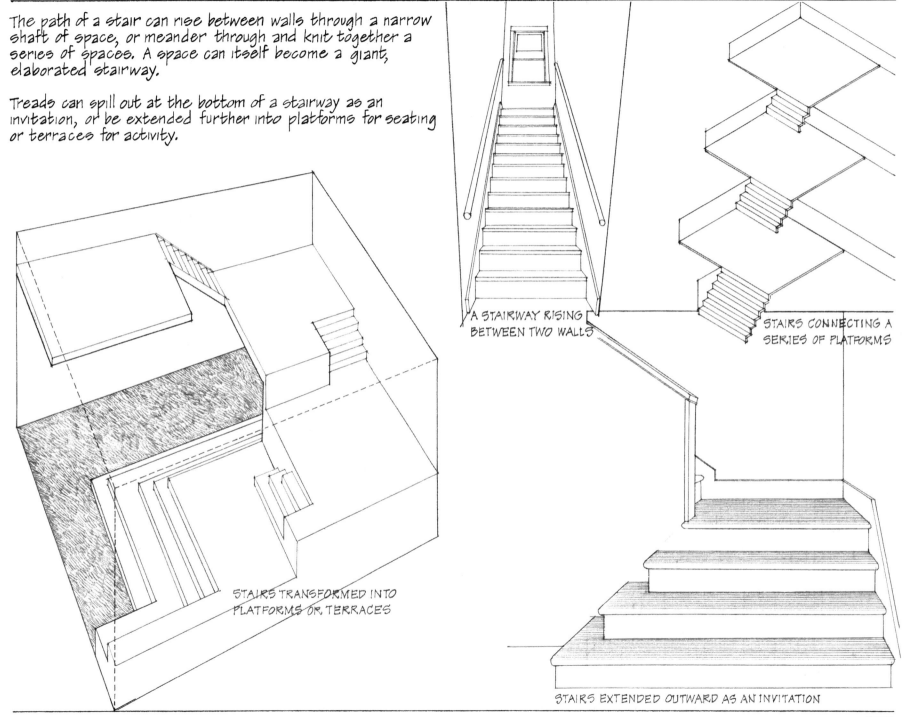

The path of a stair can rise between walls through a narrow shaft of space, or meander through and knit together a series of spaces. A space can itself become a giant, elaborated stairway.

Treads can spill out at the bottom of a stairway as an invitation, or be extended further into platforms for seating or terraces for activity.

A STAIRWAY RISING BETWEEN TWO WALLS

STAIRS CONNECTING A SERIES OF PLATFORMS

STAIRS TRANSFORMED INTO PLATFORMS OR TERRACES

STAIRS EXTENDED OUTWARD AS AN INVITATION

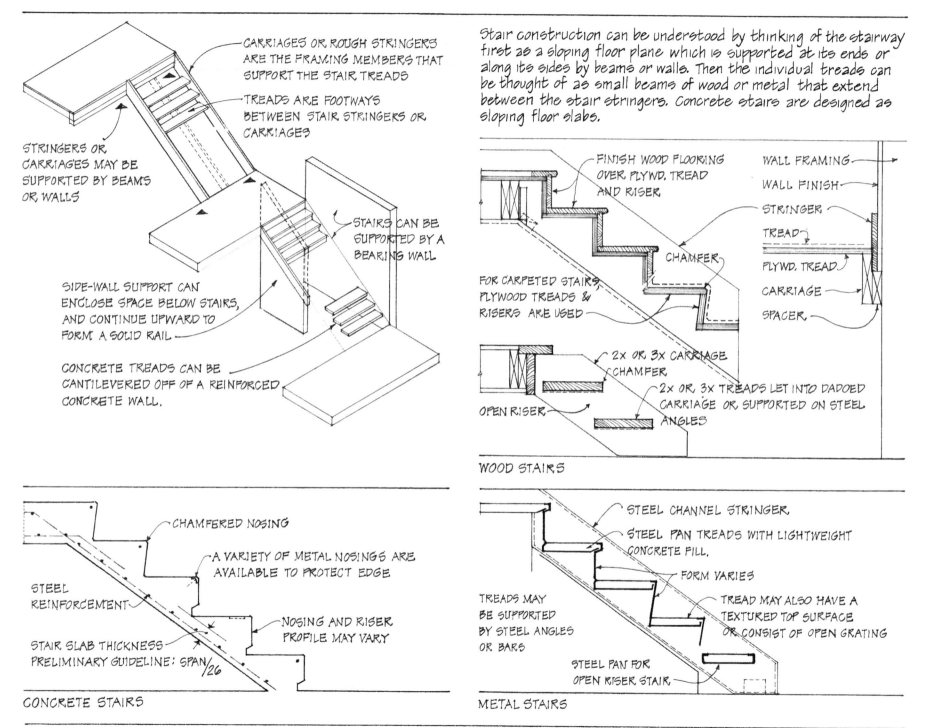

CARRIAGES OR ROUGH STRINGERS ARE THE FRAMING MEMBERS THAT SUPPORT THE STAIR TREADS

TREADS ARE FOOTWAYS BETWEEN STAIR STRINGERS OR CARRIAGES

STRINGERS OR CARRIAGES MAY BE SUPPORTED BY BEAMS OR WALLS

STAIRS CAN BE SUPPORTED BY A BEARING WALL

SIDE-WALL SUPPORT CAN ENCLOSE SPACE BELOW STAIRS, AND CONTINUE UPWARD TO FORM A SOLID RAIL

CONCRETE TREADS CAN BE CANTILEVERED OFF OF A REINFORCED CONCRETE WALL.

Stair construction can be understood by thinking of the stairway first as a sloping floor plane which is supported at its ends or along its sides by beams or walls. Then the individual treads can be thought of as small beams of wood or metal that extend between the stair stringers. Concrete stairs are designed as sloping floor slabs.

FINISH WOOD FLOORING OVER PLYWD. TREAD AND RISER.

WALL FRAMING

WALL FINISH

STRINGER

TREAD

CHAMFER

PLYWD. TREAD.

CARRIAGE

SPACER

FOR CARPETED STAIRS, PLYWOOD TREADS & RISERS ARE USED

2x OR 3x CARRIAGE

CHAMFER

2x OR 3x TREADS LET INTO DADOED CARRIAGE OR SUPPORTED ON STEEL ANGLES

OPEN RISER

**WOOD STAIRS**

CHAMFERED NOSING

A VARIETY OF METAL NOSINGS ARE AVAILABLE TO PROTECT EDGE

STEEL REINFORCEMENT

NOSING AND RISER PROFILE MAY VARY

STAIR SLAB THICKNESS PRELIMINARY GUIDELINE: SPAN/26

**CONCRETE STAIRS**

STEEL CHANNEL STRINGER

STEEL PAN TREADS WITH LIGHTWEIGHT CONCRETE FILL.

FORM VARIES

TREADS MAY BE SUPPORTED BY STEEL ANGLES OR BARS

TREAD MAY ALSO HAVE A TEXTURED TOP SURFACE OR CONSIST OF OPEN GRATING

STEEL PAN FOR OPEN RISER STAIR.

**METAL STAIRS**

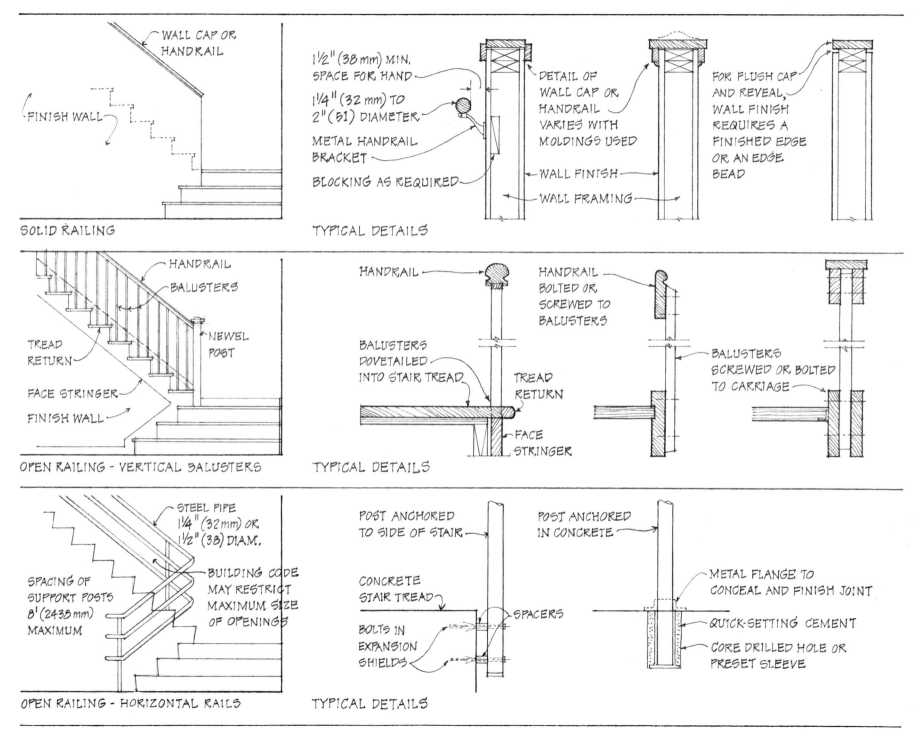

WALL CAP OR HANDRAIL

FINISH WALL

SOLID RAILING

1½" (38 mm) MIN. SPACE FOR HAND

1¼" (32 mm) TO 2" (51) DIAMETER

METAL HANDRAIL BRACKET

BLOCKING AS REQUIRED

DETAIL OF WALL CAP OR HANDRAIL VARIES WITH MOLDINGS USED

WALL FINISH

WALL FRAMING

FOR FLUSH CAP AND REVEAL, WALL FINISH REQUIRES A FINISHED EDGE OR AN EDGE BEAD

TYPICAL DETAILS

HANDRAIL

BALUSTERS

NEWEL POST

TREAD RETURN

FACE STRINGER

FINISH WALL

OPEN RAILING - VERTICAL BALUSTERS

HANDRAIL

BALUSTERS DOVETAILED INTO STAIR TREAD

TREAD RETURN

FACE STRINGER

HANDRAIL BOLTED OR SCREWED TO BALUSTERS

BALUSTERS SCREWED OR BOLTED TO CARRIAGE

TYPICAL DETAILS

STEEL PIPE 1¼" (32 mm) OR 1½" (38) DIAM.

BUILDING CODE MAY RESTRICT MAXIMUM SIZE OF OPENINGS

SPACING OF SUPPORT POSTS 8' (2438 mm) MAXIMUM

OPEN RAILING - HORIZONTAL RAILS

POST ANCHORED TO SIDE OF STAIR

CONCRETE STAIR TREAD

BOLTS IN EXPANSION SHIELDS

SPACERS

POST ANCHORED IN CONCRETE

METAL FLANGE TO CONCEAL AND FINISH JOINT

QUICK-SETTING CEMENT

CORE DRILLED HOLE OR PRESET SLEEVE

TYPICAL DETAILS

# FIREPLACES

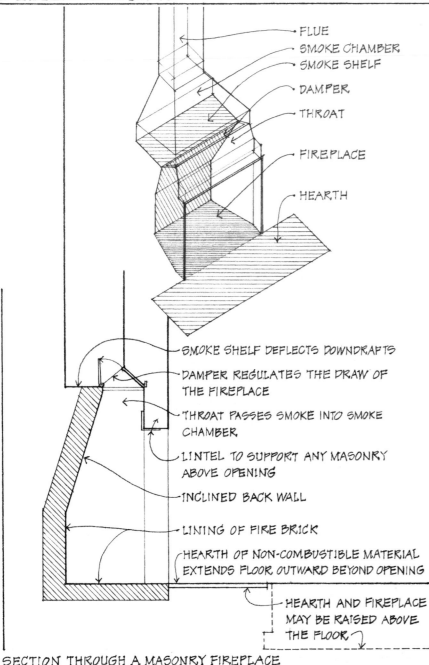

Labels (top diagram):
- FLUE
- SMOKE CHAMBER
- SMOKE SHELF
- DAMPER
- THROAT
- FIREPLACE
- HEARTH

Labels (section diagram):
- SMOKE SHELF DEFLECTS DOWNDRAFTS
- DAMPER REGULATES THE DRAW OF THE FIREPLACE
- THROAT PASSES SMOKE INTO SMOKE CHAMBER
- LINTEL TO SUPPORT ANY MASONRY ABOVE OPENING
- INCLINED BACK WALL
- LINING OF FIRE BRICK
- HEARTH OF NON-COMBUSTIBLE MATERIAL EXTENDS FLOOR OUTWARD BEYOND OPENING
- HEARTH AND FIREPLACE MAY BE RAISED ABOVE THE FLOOR

SECTION THROUGH A MASONRY FIREPLACE

While a traditional fireplace is not as efficient for heating an interior space as a good stove, few would dispute the special attraction it holds for people. The warmth and flames of an open fire are like a magnet, enticing people to gather around a fireplace. Even without a fire, a fireplace can be a unique center of interest, and serve as the focal point about which a room can be arranged.

A fireplace must be designed to draw properly, to sustain combustion safely, and to carry smoke away efficiently. Thus the proportions of a fireplace and the arrangement of its components are subject to both the laws of nature and the local building code. It is important for the interior designer to note the amount of space a fireplace requires, and how the face - the opening, surround, and hearth - can be treated.

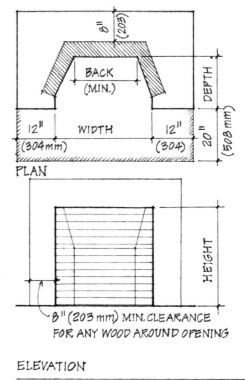

PLAN

8" (203 mm) MIN. CLEARANCE FOR ANY WOOD AROUND OPENING

ELEVATION

GUIDELINES FOR FIREPLACE DIMENSIONS:

| WIDTH | HEIGHT | DEPTH | BACK |
|-------|--------|-------|------|
| 24" | 24" | 16"-18" | 14" |
| 28" | 24" | 16"-18" | 14" |
| 30" | 28"-30" | 16"-18" | 16" |
| 36" | 28"-30" | 16"-18" | 22" |
| 42" | 28"-30" | 16"-18" | 28" |
| 48" | 32" | 18"-20" | 32" |

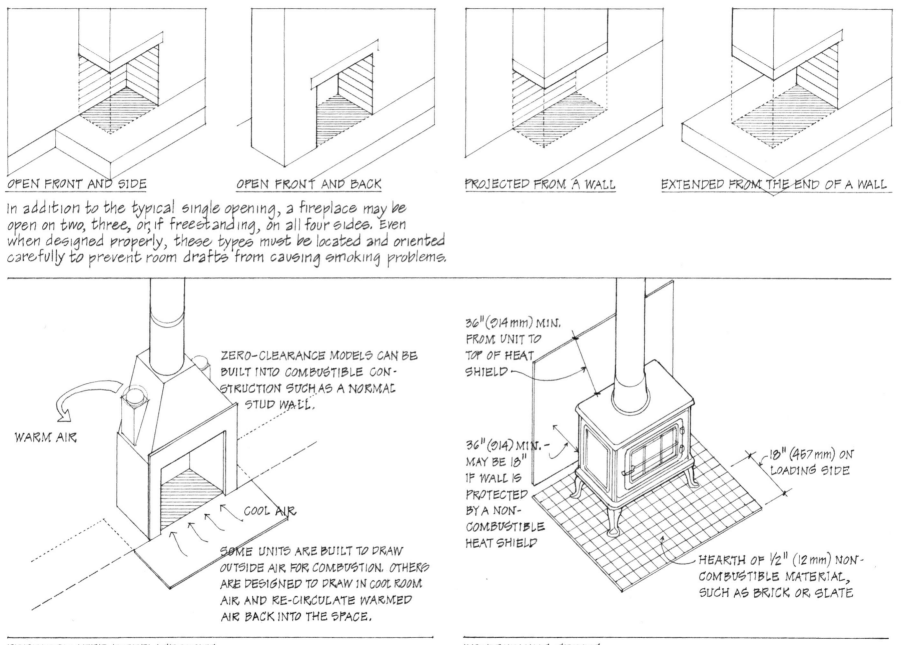

OPEN FRONT AND SIDE

OPEN FRONT AND BACK

PROJECTED FROM A WALL

EXTENDED FROM THE END OF A WALL

In addition to the typical single opening, a fireplace may be open on two, three, or, if freestanding, on all four sides. Even when designed properly, these types must be located and oriented carefully to prevent room drafts from causing smoking problems.

ZERO-CLEARANCE MODELS CAN BE BUILT INTO COMBUSTIBLE CONSTRUCTION SUCH AS A NORMAL STUD WALL.

WARM AIR

COOL AIR

SOME UNITS ARE BUILT TO DRAW OUTSIDE AIR FOR COMBUSTION. OTHERS ARE DESIGNED TO DRAW IN COOL ROOM AIR AND RE-CIRCULATE WARMED AIR BACK INTO THE SPACE.

PREFABRICATED FIREPLACE UNITS

36" (914mm) MIN. FROM UNIT TO TOP OF HEAT SHIELD

36" (914) MIN. — MAY BE 18" IF WALL IS PROTECTED BY A NON-COMBUSTIBLE HEAT SHIELD

18" (457mm) ON LOADING SIDE

HEARTH OF 1/2" (12mm) NON-COMBUSTIBLE MATERIAL, SUCH AS BRICK OR SLATE

WOODBURNING STOVES

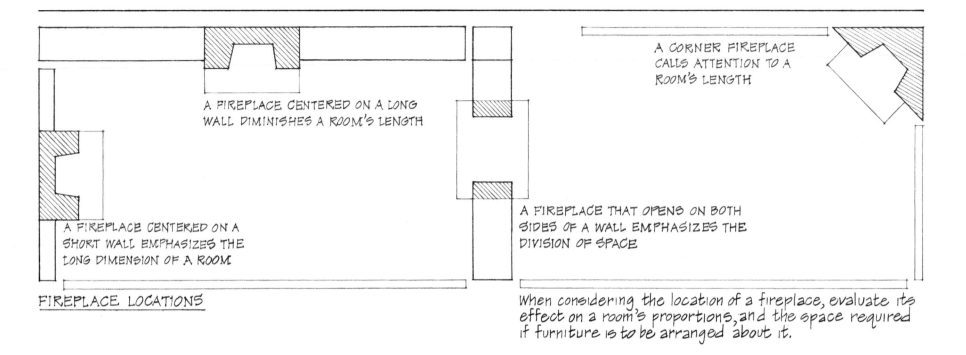

A FIREPLACE CENTERED ON A LONG WALL DIMINISHES A ROOM'S LENGTH

A CORNER FIREPLACE CALLS ATTENTION TO A ROOM'S LENGTH

A FIREPLACE CENTERED ON A SHORT WALL EMPHASIZES THE LONG DIMENSION OF A ROOM

A FIREPLACE THAT OPENS ON BOTH SIDES OF A WALL EMPHASIZES THE DIVISION OF SPACE

FIREPLACE LOCATIONS

When considering the location of a fireplace, evaluate its effect on a room's proportions, and the space required if furniture is to be arranged about it.

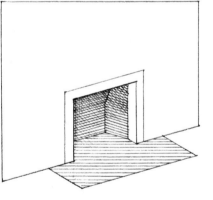

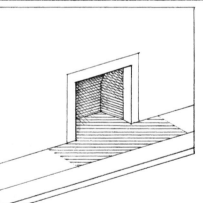

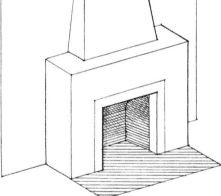

OPENING FLUSH WITH WALL SURFACE

Fireplace can be unobtrusive or be visually active depending on treatment of surround.

OPENING AND HEARTH RAISED OFF FLOOR

Fireplace and hearth together become more of an integral part of a room.

OPENING AND FIREPLACE PROJECTED FROM WALL

Fireplace becomes a three-dimensional form and a forceful element in space.

RELATIONSHIP BETWEEN FIREPLACE AND THE WALL PLANE

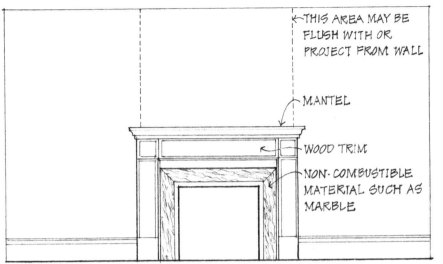

THIS AREA MAY BE FLUSH WITH OR PROJECT FROM WALL

MANTEL

WOOD TRIM

NON-COMBUSTIBLE MATERIAL SUCH AS MARBLE

THE TREATMENT OF THE SURROUND VISUALLY ENLARGES THE FIREPLACE OPENING, ENHANCES IT AS A FOCAL POINT, AND INTEGRATES IT WITH THE REST OF A ROOM'S TRIMWORK.

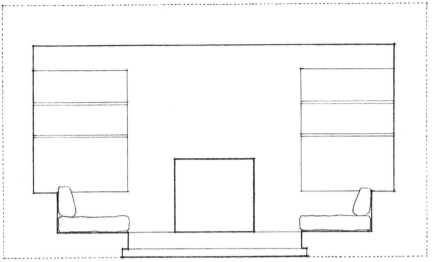

THE RAISED HEARTH OF A FIREPLACE CAN BE EXTENDED TO FORM A PLATFORM FOR SEATING. THIS PLATFORM ALONG WITH THE FIREPLACE CAN BEGIN TO DEFINE AN ALCOVE SPACE.

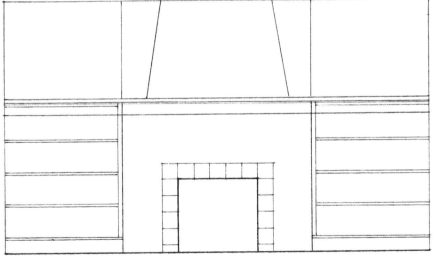

WHEN PROJECTING INTO A ROOM, A FIREPLACE ALSO FORMS RECESSES TO EITHER SIDE THAT CAN BE USED FOR STORAGE.

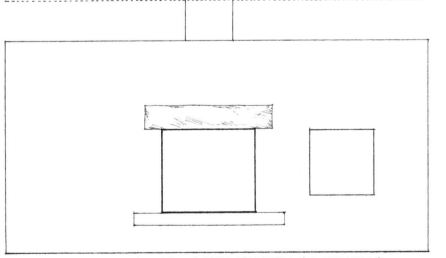

A LINTEL OR BEAM THAT SPANS THE FIREPLACE OPENING IN A MASONRY WALL CAN BE EXPOSED AND EMBELLISHED AS A VISUAL DESIGN ELEMENT.

FIREPLACE TREATMENTS

# FURNITURE

Furniture is the one category of design elements that lies almost wholly within the realm of interior design. While walls, floors, ceilings, windows, and doors are established in the architectural design of a building, the selection and arrangement of furniture within the building's spaces are major tasks of interior design.

Furniture mediates between architecture and people. It offers a transition in form and scale between an interior space and the individual. It makes interiors habitable by providing comfort and utility in the tasks and activities we undertake.

In addition to fulfilling specific functions, furniture contributes to the visual character of interior settings. The form, lines, color, texture, and scale of individual pieces, as well as their spatial organization, play a major role in establishing the expressive qualities of a room.

The pieces can be linear, planar, or volumetric in form; their lines may be rectilinear or curvilinear, angular or freeflowing. They can have horizontal or vertical proportions; they can be light and airy, or sturdy and solid. Their texture can be slick and shiny, smooth and satiny, warm and plush, or rough and heavy; their color can be natural or transparent in quality, warm or cool in temperature, light or dark in value.

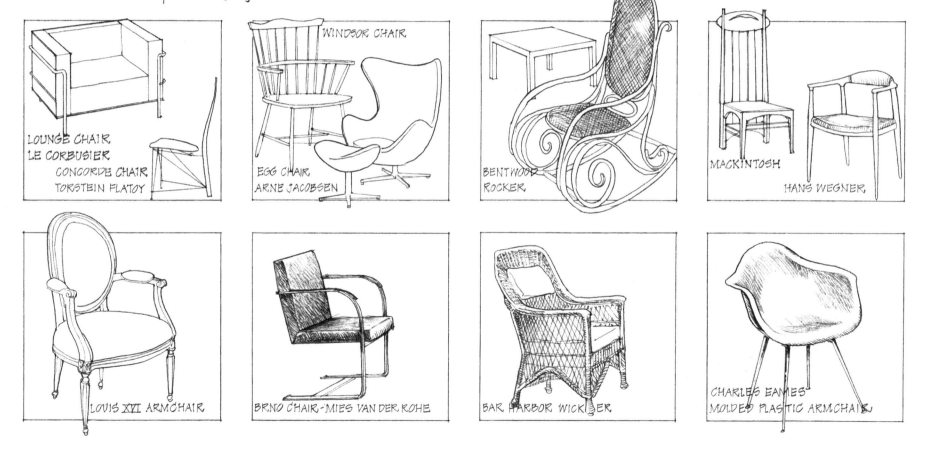

LOUNGE CHAIR
LE CORBUSIER

CONCORDE CHAIR
TORSTEIN FLATOY

WINDSOR CHAIR

EGG CHAIR
ARNE JACOBSEN

BENTWOOD
ROCKER

MACKINTOSH

HANS WEGNER

LOUIS XVI ARMCHAIR

BRNO CHAIR - MIES VAN DER ROHE

BAR HARBOR WICKER

CHARLES EAMES
MOLDED PLASTIC ARMCHAIR

Furniture can, depending on the quality of its design, either offer or limit physical comfort in a real and tangible way. Our bodies will tell us if a chair is uncomfortable, or if a table is too high or too low for our use. There is definite feedback which tells us whether a piece of furniture is appropriate for its intended use.

Human factors, therefore, are a major influence on the form, proportion, and scale of furniture. To provide utility and comfort in the execution of our tasks, furniture should be designed first to respond or correspond to our dimensions, the clearances required by our patterns of movement, and the nature of the activity we are engaged in.

Our perception of comfort is, of course, conditioned by the nature of the task or activity being performed, its duration, and other circumstantial factors such as the quality of lighting and even our state of mind. At times, the effectiveness of a furniture element may depend on its correct use – on our learning how to use it.

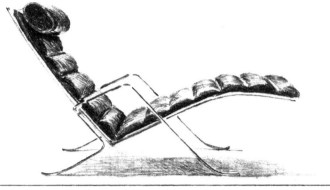

KNOLL INTERNATIONAL INC.

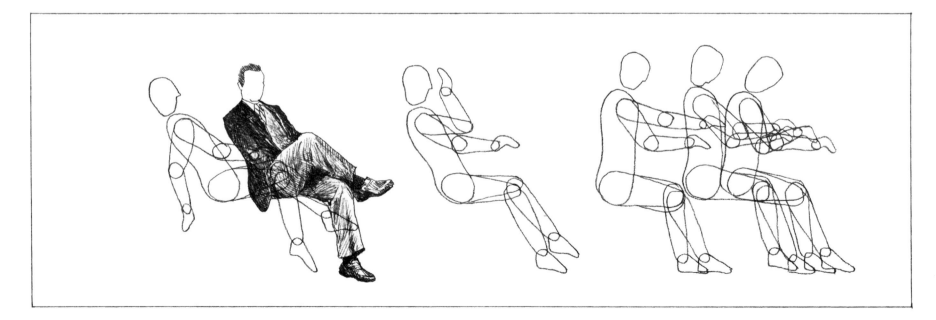

The way furniture is arranged in a room will affect how the space is used and perceived. Furniture can simply be placed as sculptural objects in space. More often, however, furniture is organized into functional groupings. These groupings, in turn, can be arranged to organize and structure space.

Most furniture consists of individual or unit pieces which allow for flexibility in their arrangement. The pieces are movable and may consist of various specialized elements as well as a mix of forms and styles.

Built-in arrangements of furniture, on the other hand, allow for the flexible use of more space. There is generally more continuity of form among the furniture elements with fewer gaps between them.

Modular units combine the unified appearance of built-in furniture with the flexibility and movability of individual unit pieces.

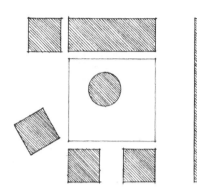

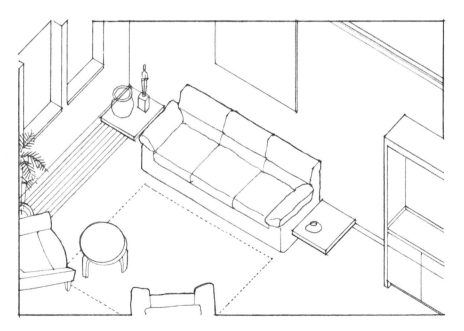

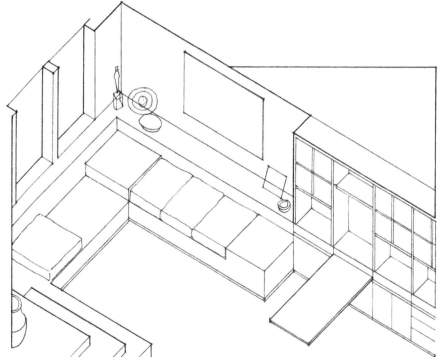

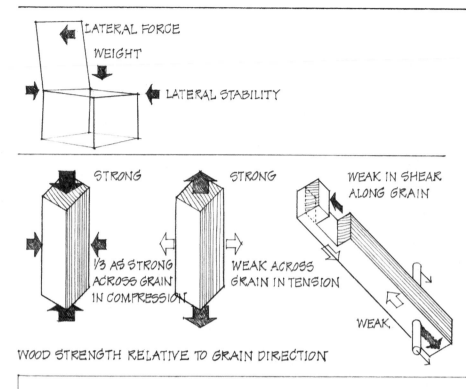

LATERAL FORCE

WEIGHT

LATERAL STABILITY

STRONG

STRONG

WEAK IN SHEAR ALONG GRAIN

⅓ AS STRONG ACROSS GRAIN IN COMPRESSION

WEAK ACROSS GRAIN IN TENSION

WEAK

WOOD STRENGTH RELATIVE TO GRAIN DIRECTION

Furniture may be constructed of wood, metal, or plastic. Each material has strengths and weaknesses which should be recognized in furniture design and construction if a piece is to be strong, stable, and durable in use.

Wood is the standard furniture material. A primary consideration in how it is used and joined is its grain direction. Wood is strong in compression with the grain but can be dented under loading perpendicular to the grain. In tension, wood can be pulled in the direction of its grain, but will split when pulled at a right angle to the grain. Wood is weakest in shear along its grain. Another important consideration is the expansion and contraction of wood across its grain with changes in moisture content. All these factors bear on the way wood members are configured and joined in furniture construction.

Plywood is a sheet material which consists of an odd number of plies layed at right angles in grain direction to each other. Thus, a plywood panel has strength in two directions. In addition, the quality of the face veneer can be controlled in appearance.

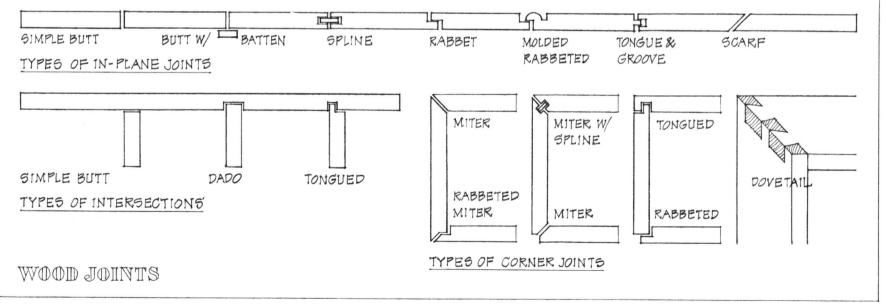

SIMPLE BUTT     BUTT W/ BATTEN     SPLINE     RABBET     MOLDED RABBETED     TONGUE & GROOVE     SCARF

TYPES OF IN-PLANE JOINTS

SIMPLE BUTT     DADO     TONGUED

TYPES OF INTERSECTIONS

MITER     MITER W/ SPLINE     TONGUED

RABBETED MITER     MITER     RABBETED

DOVETAIL

WOOD JOINTS

TYPES OF CORNER JOINTS

Like wood, metal is strong both in compression and tension, but it does not have a strong grain direction and it is ductile. These factors, along with a high strength-to-weight ratio, enable metal to have relatively thin cross sections and to be curved or bent in furniture construction. Methods for joining metal are analogous to those for wood. Instead of being nailed, metal can be screwed, bolted, or riveted; instead of being glued, metal can be welded.

Plastic is a unique material in the way it can be shaped, formed, textured, colored, and used. This is due to the numerous types and variations of plastic materials available and under development today. While not as strong as wood or metal, plastic can be strengthened with glass fiber. More significantly, it can be easily shaped into structurally stable and rigid forms. For this reason, plastic furniture almost always consists of a single piece without joints or connections.

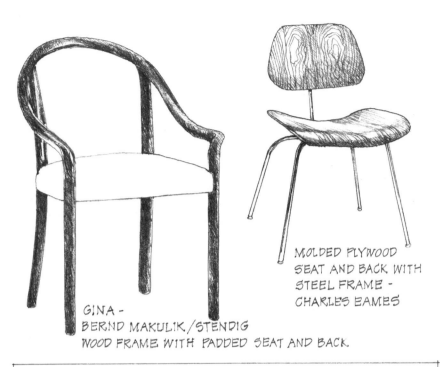

GINA -
BERND MAKULIK/STENDIG
WOOD FRAME WITH PADDED SEAT AND BACK.

MOLDED PLYWOOD
SEAT AND BACK WITH
STEEL FRAME -
CHARLES EAMES

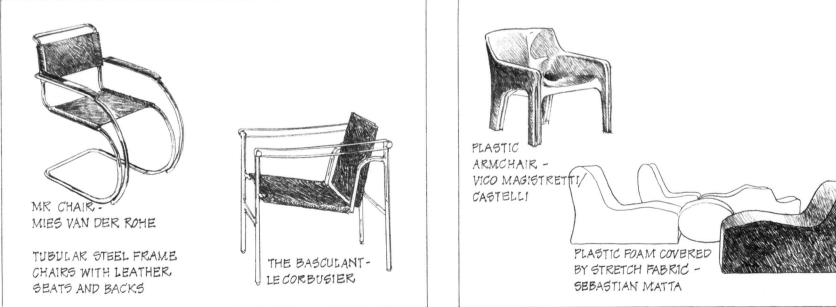

MR CHAIR -
MIES VAN DER ROHE

TUBULAR STEEL FRAME
CHAIRS WITH LEATHER
SEATS AND BACKS

THE BASCULANT -
LE CORBUSIER

PLASTIC
ARMCHAIR -
VICO MAGISTRETTI/
CASTELLI

PLASTIC FOAM COVERED
BY STRETCH FABRIC -
SEBASTIAN MATTA

# SEATING

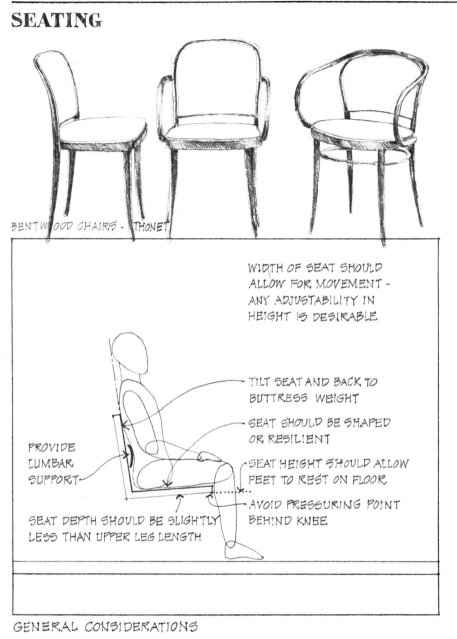

BENTWOOD CHAIRS - THONET

Seating should be designed to comfortably support the weight and shape of the user/occupants. Because of the great variation in body size, however, and the danger of designing too precisely what conditions would result in a comfortable seating device, what is illustrated on these two pages are the factors which affect our personal judgment of comfort and a range of dimensions which should serve only as guidelines.

The comfort factor is also affected by the nature of the activity the user might be engaged in at the time. There are different types of chairs and seating for different uses. On the following pages are illustrations intended to show the range of seating available to the interior designer.

WIDTH OF SEAT SHOULD ALLOW FOR MOVEMENT - ANY ADJUSTABILITY IN HEIGHT IS DESIRABLE

TILT SEAT AND BACK TO BUTTRESS WEIGHT

SEAT SHOULD BE SHAPED OR RESILIENT

SEAT HEIGHT SHOULD ALLOW FEET TO REST ON FLOOR

AVOID PRESSURING POINT BEHIND KNEE

PROVIDE LUMBAR SUPPORT

SEAT DEPTH SHOULD BE SLIGHTLY LESS THAN UPPER LEG LENGTH

GENERAL CONSIDERATIONS

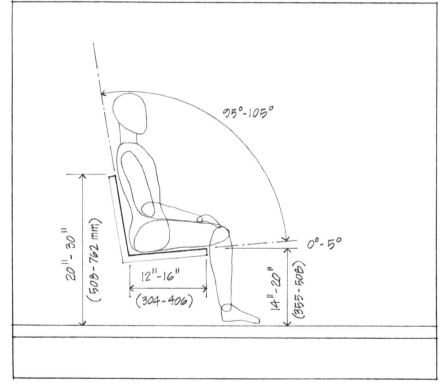

95°-105°

0°-5°

20"- 30" (508 - 762 mm)

12"-16" (304-406)

14"- 20" (355-508)

GENERAL PURPOSE CHAIR

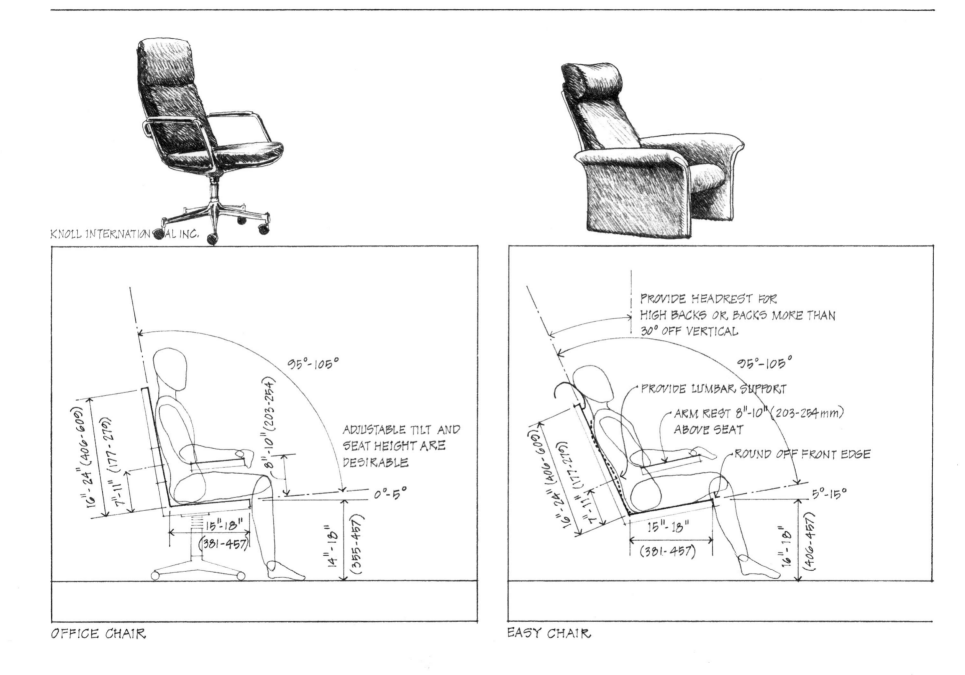

KNOLL INTERNATIONAL INC.

95°-105°

8"-10" (203-254)

ADJUSTABLE TILT AND
SEAT HEIGHT ARE
DESIRABLE

0°-5°

16"-24" (406-609)

7"-11" (177-279)

15"-18"
(381-457)

14"-18"
(355-457)

OFFICE CHAIR

PROVIDE HEADREST FOR
HIGH BACKS OR BACKS MORE THAN
30° OFF VERTICAL

95°-105°

PROVIDE LUMBAR SUPPORT

ARM REST 8"-10" (203-254mm)
ABOVE SEAT

ROUND OFF FRONT EDGE

5°-15°

16"-24" (406-609)

7"-11" (177-279)

15"-18"
(381-457)

16"-18"
(406-457)

EASY CHAIR

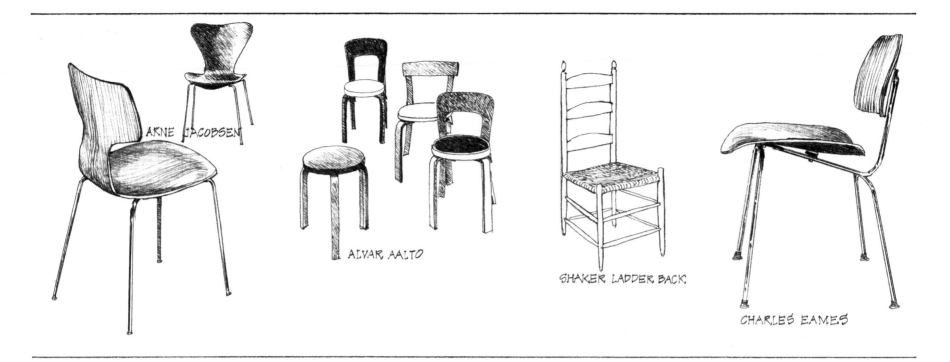

ARNE JACOBSEN

ALVAR AALTO

SHAKER LADDER BACK

CHARLES EAMES

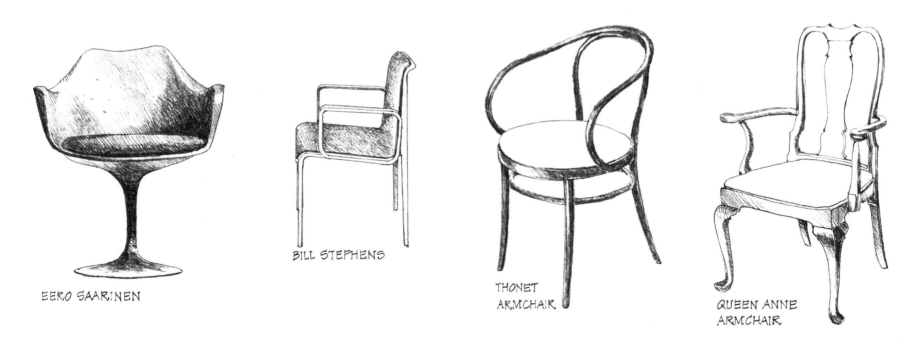

EERO SAARINEN

BILL STEPHENS

THONET
ARMCHAIR

QUEEN ANNE
ARMCHAIR

ANGELO MANGIAROTTI

AFRA & TOBIA SCARPA.

VICO MAGISTRETTI

BJÖRN ALGE

HANS WEGNER

HARRY BERTOIA

HANS WEGNER

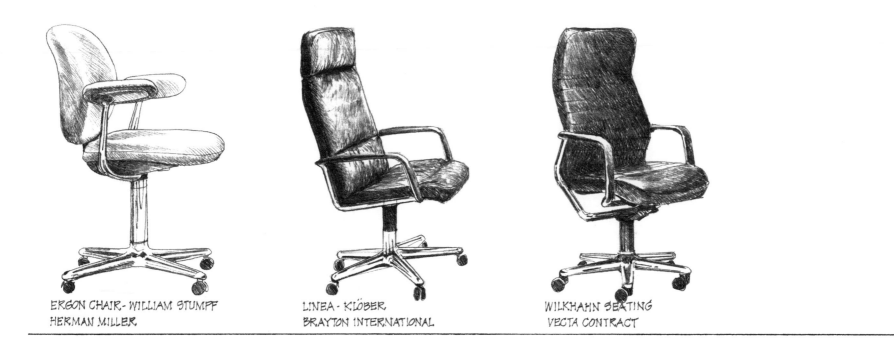

ERGON CHAIR - WILLIAM STUMPF
HERMAN MILLER

LINEA - KLÖBER
BRAYTON INTERNATIONAL

WILKHAHN SEATING
VECTA CONTRACT

CHAISE LONGUE - MARTIN SZEKELY

LOUNGE CHAIR - CHARLES EAMES
HERMAN MILLER

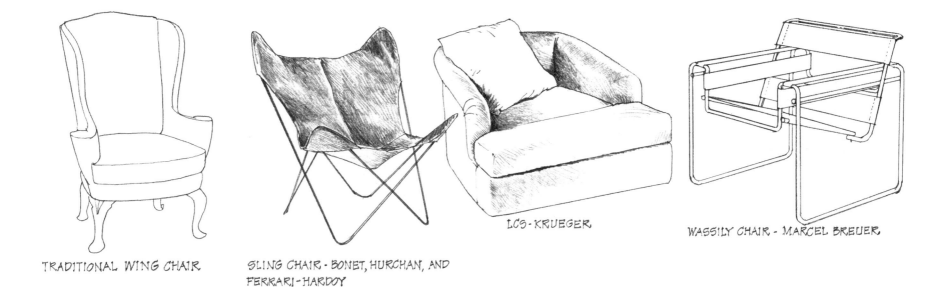

TRADITIONAL WING CHAIR

SLING CHAIR - BONET, HURCHAN, AND
FERRARI-HARDOY

LCS - KRUEGER

WASSILY CHAIR - MARCEL BREUER

PIERLUIGI MOLINARI

ALESSANDRO MENDINI

4 SOFAS - WARD BENNETT DESIGNS - BRICKEL ASSOCIATES

MAURO LIPPARINI · ROBERTO TAPINASSI

BURKHARDT VOGTHERR

# TABLES

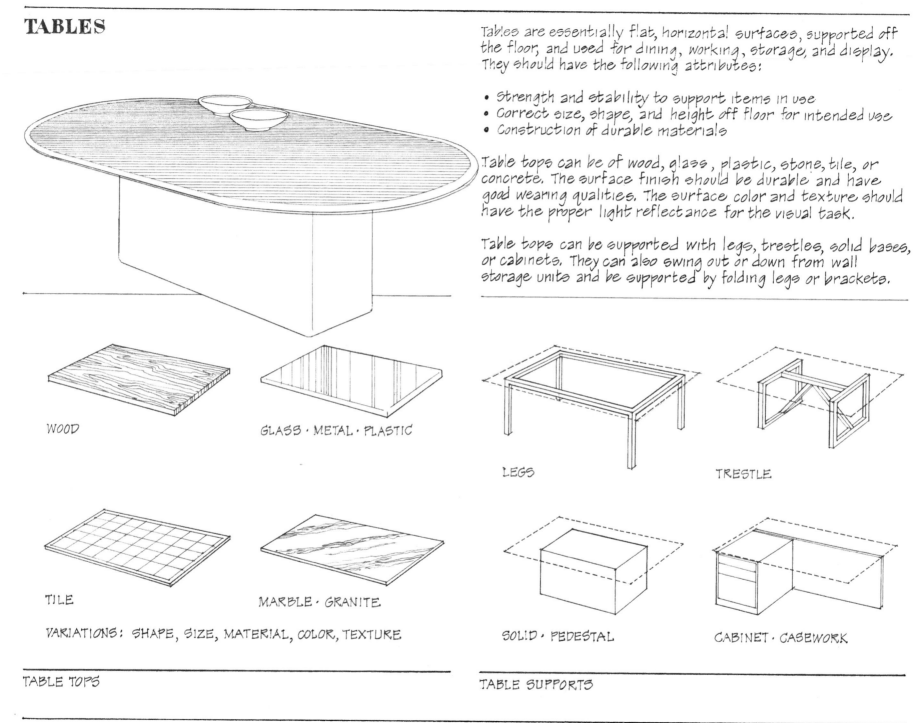

Tables are essentially flat, horizontal surfaces, supported off the floor, and used for dining, working, storage, and display. They should have the following attributes:

- Strength and stability to support items in use
- Correct size, shape, and height off floor for intended use
- Construction of durable materials

Table tops can be of wood, glass, plastic, stone, tile, or concrete. The surface finish should be durable and have good wearing qualities. The surface color and texture should have the proper light reflectance for the visual task.

Table tops can be supported with legs, trestles, solid bases, or cabinets. They can also swing out or down from wall storage units and be supported by folding legs or brackets.

WOOD

GLASS · METAL · PLASTIC

LEGS

TRESTLE

TILE

MARBLE · GRANITE

SOLID · PEDESTAL

CABINET · CASEWORK

VARIATIONS: SHAPE, SIZE, MATERIAL, COLOR, TEXTURE

TABLE TOPS

TABLE SUPPORTS

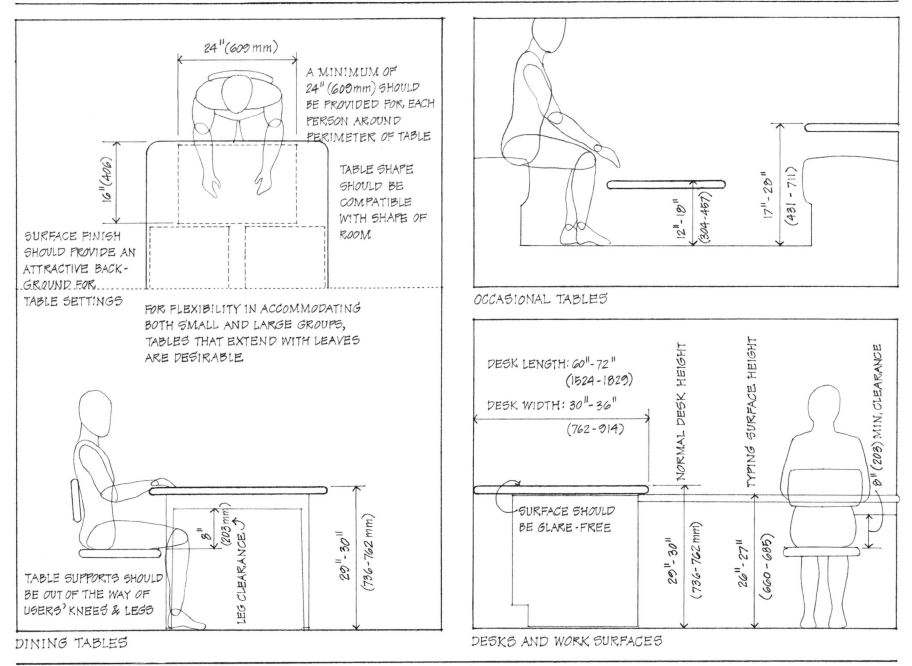

24" (600mm)

A MINIMUM OF 24" (609mm) SHOULD BE PROVIDED FOR EACH PERSON AROUND PERIMETER OF TABLE

16" (406)

TABLE SHAPE SHOULD BE COMPATIBLE WITH SHAPE OF ROOM

SURFACE FINISH SHOULD PROVIDE AN ATTRACTIVE BACK-GROUND FOR TABLE SETTINGS

FOR FLEXIBILITY IN ACCOMMODATING BOTH SMALL AND LARGE GROUPS, TABLES THAT EXTEND WITH LEAVES ARE DESIRABLE

8" (203mm)

LEG CLEARANCE

29" - 30" (736-762 mm)

TABLE SUPPORTS SHOULD BE OUT OF THE WAY OF USERS' KNEES & LEGS

DINING TABLES

OCCASIONAL TABLES

12" - 18" (304-457)

17" - 28" (431 - 711)

DESK LENGTH: 60" - 72" (1524 - 1829)

DESK WIDTH: 30" - 36" (762 - 914)

NORMAL DESK HEIGHT

TYPING SURFACE HEIGHT

8" (203) MIN. CLEARANCE

SURFACE SHOULD BE GLARE-FREE

29" - 30" (736-762 mm)

26" - 27" (660 - 685)

DESKS AND WORK SURFACES

TABLE DIMENSIONS

QUEEN ANNE TEA TABLE

DROP-LEAF TABLE

SMALL ACCESSORY TABLE

TILT-TOP TABLE

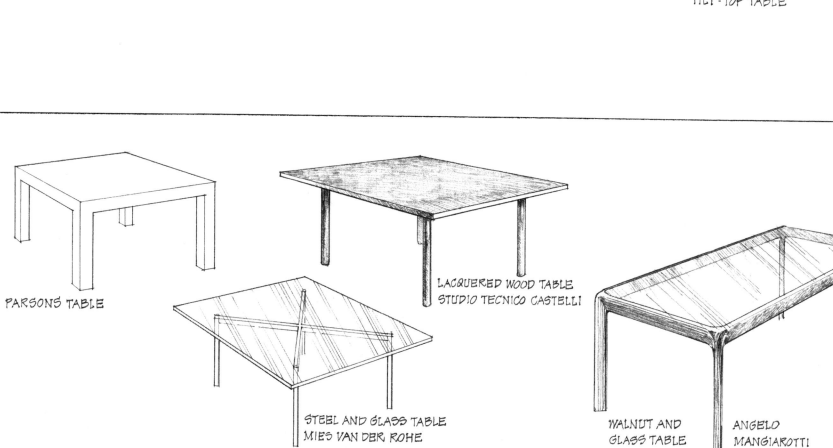

PARSONS TABLE

LACQUERED WOOD TABLE
STUDIO TECNICO CASTELLI

STEEL AND GLASS TABLE
MIES VAN DER ROHE

WALNUT AND
GLASS TABLE

ANGELO
MANGIAROTTI

GLASS TOP AND ENCAUSTIC PAINTED
METAL BASE - LELLA E MASSIMO
VIGNELLI / DAVID LAW

GLASS TOP AND PAINTED METAL BASE
MICHELLE DE LUCHI

MARBLE TOP AND LACQUERED WOOD
BASE - IGNAZIO GARDELLA

MARBLE AND WOOD TOP WITH METAL
LEGS - DANIELA PUPPA

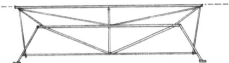

GLASS TOP AND METAL BASE -
KURT ZIEHMER

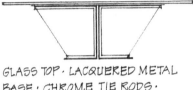

GLASS TOP · LACQUERED METAL
BASE · CHROME TIE RODS ·
R, CARTA MANTIGLIA

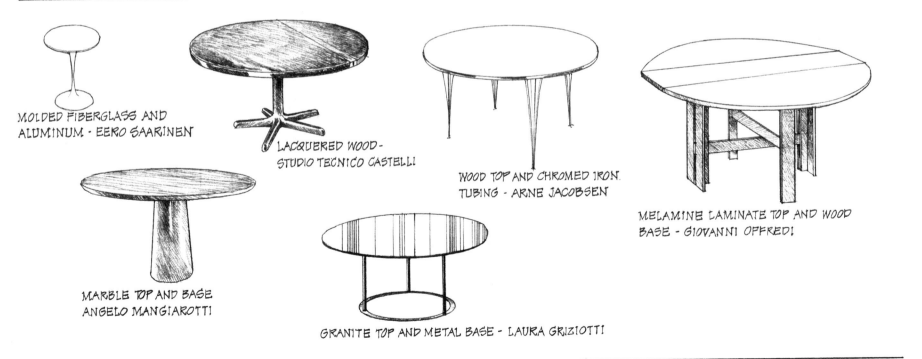

MOLDED FIBERGLASS AND
ALUMINUM · EERO SAARINEN

LACQUERED WOOD -
STUDIO TECNICO CASTELLI

WOOD TOP AND CHROMED IRON.
TUBING - ARNE JACOBSEN

MELAMINE LAMINATE TOP AND WOOD
BASE - GIOVANNI OFFREDI

MARBLE TOP AND BASE
ANGELO MANGIAROTTI

GRANITE TOP AND METAL BASE - LAURA GRIZIOTTI

# WORK STATIONS

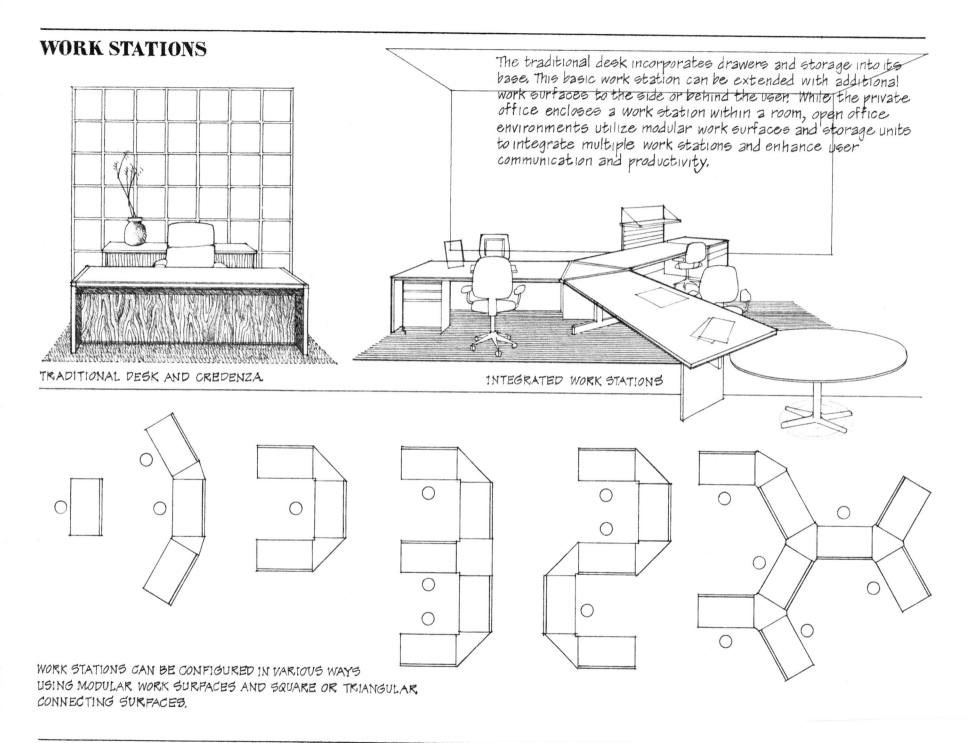

The traditional desk incorporates drawers and storage into its base. This basic work station can be extended with additional work surfaces to the side or behind the user. While the private office encloses a work station within a room, open office environments utilize modular work surfaces and storage units to integrate multiple work stations and enhance user communication and productivity.

TRADITIONAL DESK AND CREDENZA

INTEGRATED WORK STATIONS

WORK STATIONS CAN BE CONFIGURED IN VARIOUS WAYS USING MODULAR WORK SURFACES AND SQUARE OR TRIANGULAR CONNECTING SURFACES.

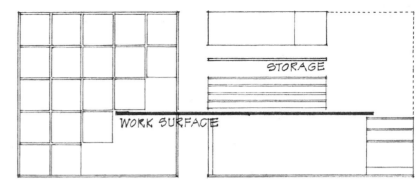

STORAGE

WORK SURFACE

PANEL

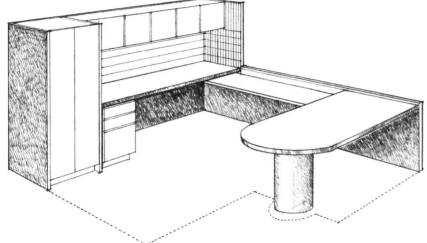

## OPEN OFFICE SYSTEM

Open office systems offer flexibility in plan arrangements, efficiency in space utilization, and the ability to tailor a work station to suit individual needs and specific tasks. While the details of office systems vary with each manufacturer, the basic components remain the same. Modular panels are configured for stability and support the required work surfaces, storage units, lighting, and accessories. The panels are available in a variety of heights, widths, and finishes; some include glazing. Wiring for power, lighting, and telecommunications is often incorporated into the panel frames.

THE LAYOUT OF OPEN OFFICE SYSTEMS REQUIRES CAREFUL ANALYSIS OF USER NEEDS FOR ACOUSTIC AND VISUAL PRIVACY, COMMUNICATIONS, ACTIVITY REQUIREMENTS, AND EFFICIENT UTILIZATION OF SPACE.

# BEDS

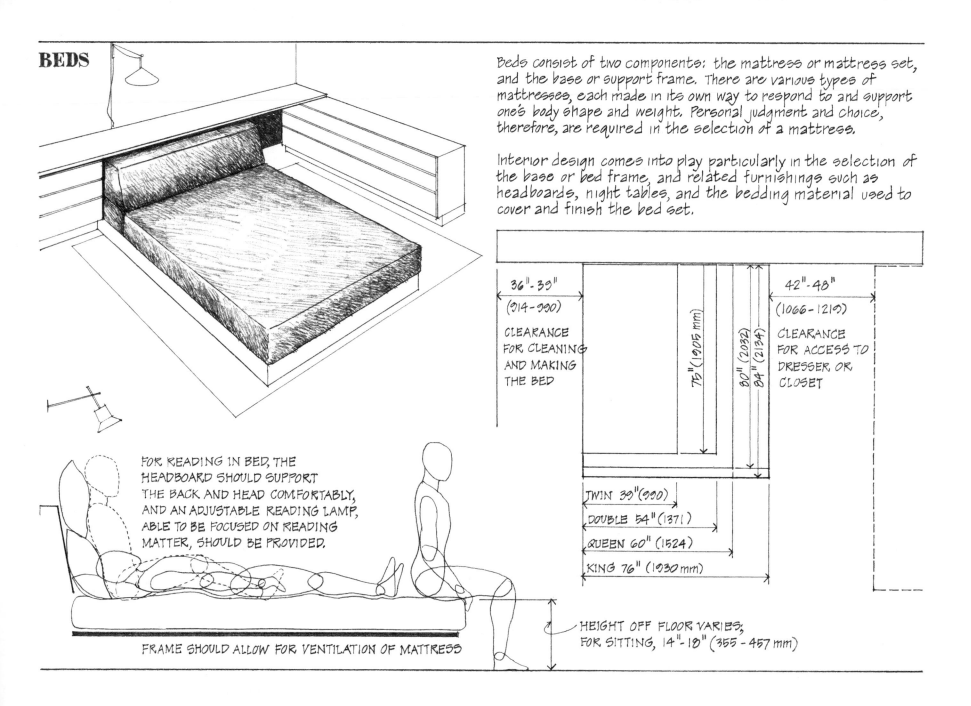

Beds consist of two components: the mattress or mattress set, and the base or support frame. There are various types of mattresses, each made in its own way to respond to and support one's body shape and weight. Personal judgment and choice, therefore, are required in the selection of a mattress.

Interior design comes into play particularly in the selection of the base or bed frame, and related furnishings such as headboards, night tables, and the bedding material used to cover and finish the bed set.

36"-39"
(914-990)
CLEARANCE FOR CLEANING AND MAKING THE BED

42"-48"
(1066-1219)
CLEARANCE FOR ACCESS TO DRESSER, OR CLOSET

76" (1905 mm)

80" (2032)
84" (2134)

TWIN 39" (990)
DOUBLE 54" (1371)
QUEEN 60" (1524)
KING 76" (1930 mm)

FOR READING IN BED, THE HEADBOARD SHOULD SUPPORT THE BACK AND HEAD COMFORTABLY, AND AN ADJUSTABLE READING LAMP, ABLE TO BE FOCUSED ON READING MATTER, SHOULD BE PROVIDED.

HEIGHT OFF FLOOR VARIES; FOR SITTING, 14"-18" (355-457 mm)

FRAME SHOULD ALLOW FOR VENTILATION OF MATTRESS

258

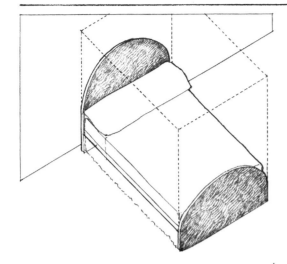

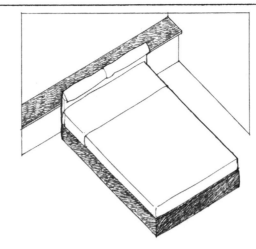

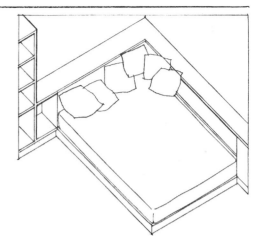

HEADBOARDS, FOOTBOARDS, AND CANOPIES DEFINE THE VOLUME OF SPACE OCCUPIED BY A BED.

A BED CAN SIMPLY REST ON A PLATFORM BASE, EMPHASIZING THE HORIZONTALITY OF THE SETTING

A BED CAN BE NESTLED INTO A CORNER OR ALCOVE. THIS BUILT-IN SETTING TAKES UP LESS FLOOR SPACE BUT BED MAY BE DIFFICULT TO MAKE.

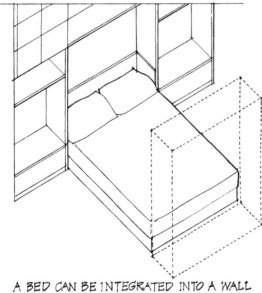

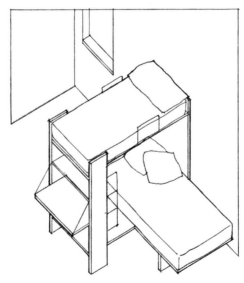

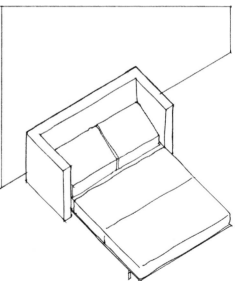

A BED CAN BE INTEGRATED INTO A WALL STORAGE SYSTEM AT THE HEAD AND/OR THE FOOT OF THE BED.

BUNK BEDS UTILIZE VERTICAL SPACE TO STACK SLEEPING LEVELS. STORAGE AND DESK SURFACES CAN ALSO BE INTEGRATED INTO THE SYSTEM.

SOFAS AND ARMCHAIRS THAT CONVERT INTO BEDS OFFER CONVENIENT SHORT-TERM SLEEPING ARRANGE-MENTS.

# STORAGE

Providing adequate and properly designed storage is an important concern in the planning of interior spaces, particularly where space is tight or where an uncluttered appearance is desired. To determine storage requirements, analyze the following:

- Accessibility: Where is storage needed?
- Convenience: What type of storage should be provided? What sizes and shapes of items are to be stored? What is the frequency of use?
- Visibility: Are items to be on display, or concealed?

Storage should be distributed where needed. How far we can reach while seated, standing, or kneeling should govern the means of access to the storage area. Active storage of often-used items should be readily accessible while dead storage of little-used or seasonal items can be hidden away.

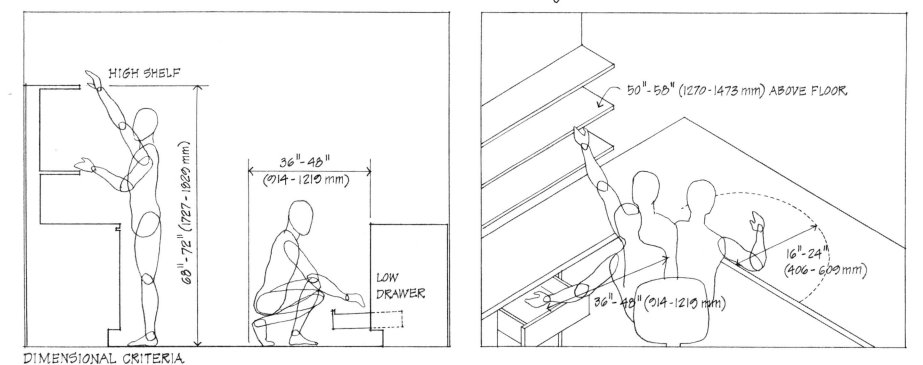

HIGH SHELF

68" - 72" (1727 - 1829 mm)

36" - 48" (914 - 1219 mm)

LOW DRAWER

DIMENSIONAL CRITERIA

50" - 58" (1270 - 1473 mm) ABOVE FLOOR

16" - 24" (406 - 609 mm)

36" - 48" (914 - 1219 mm)

The size, proportion, and type of storage units used depend on the type and amount of items to be stored, the frequency of use, and the degree of visibility desired. Basic types of storage units are shelves, drawers, and cabinets. These may be suspended from the ceiling, mounted on a wall, or simply be placed on the floor as a piece of furniture. Storage units can also be built into the thickness of a wall, occupy a niche, or utilize otherwise unusable space such as under a stairway.

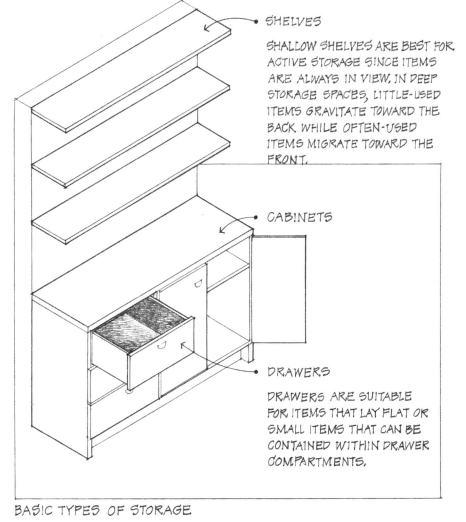

SHELVES

SHALLOW SHELVES ARE BEST FOR ACTIVE STORAGE SINCE ITEMS ARE ALWAYS IN VIEW. IN DEEP STORAGE SPACES, LITTLE-USED ITEMS GRAVITATE TOWARD THE BACK WHILE OFTEN-USED ITEMS MIGRATE TOWARD THE FRONT.

CABINETS

DRAWERS

DRAWERS ARE SUITABLE FOR ITEMS THAT LAY FLAT OR SMALL ITEMS THAT CAN BE CONTAINED WITHIN DRAWER COMPARTMENTS.

BASIC TYPES OF STORAGE

• UNIT FURNITURE

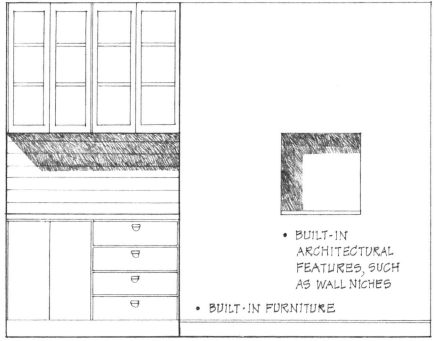

• BUILT-IN ARCHITECTURAL FEATURES, SUCH AS WALL NICHES

• BUILT-IN FURNITURE

FORMS OF STORAGE

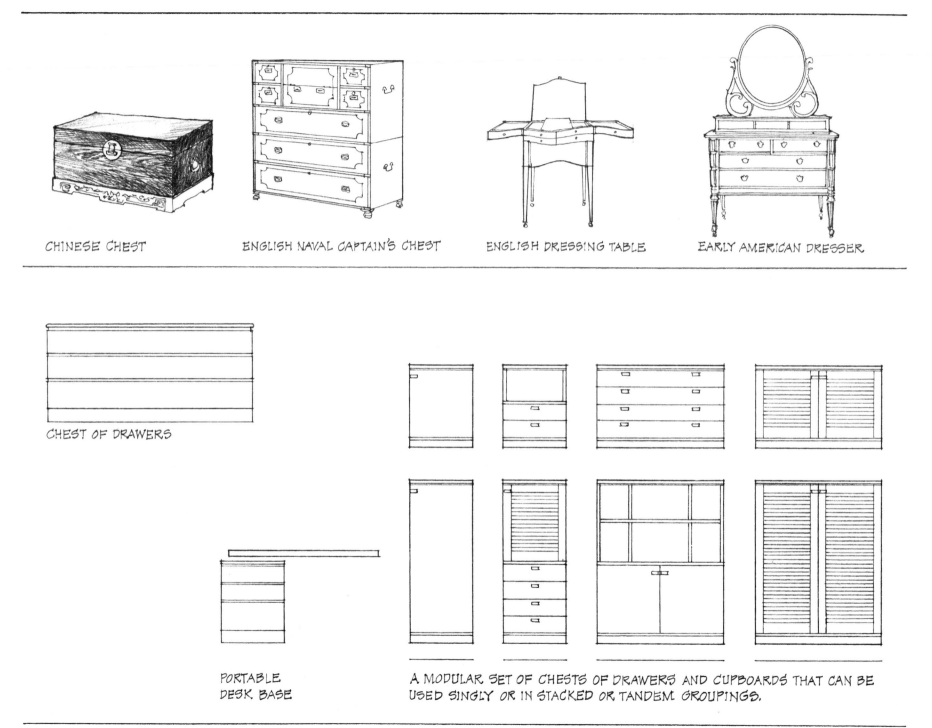

CHINESE CHEST

ENGLISH NAVAL CAPTAIN'S CHEST

ENGLISH DRESSING TABLE

EARLY AMERICAN DRESSER

CHEST OF DRAWERS

PORTABLE
DESK BASE

A MODULAR SET OF CHESTS OF DRAWERS AND CUPBOARDS THAT CAN BE
USED SINGLY OR IN STACKED OR TANDEM GROUPINGS.

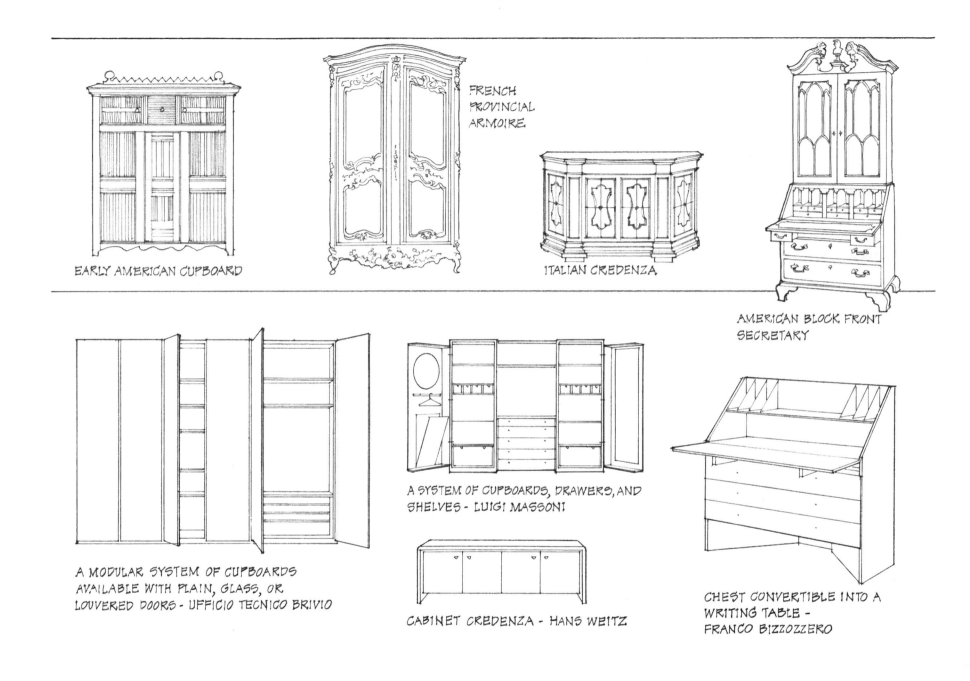

EARLY AMERICAN CUPBOARD

FRENCH PROVINCIAL ARMOIRE

ITALIAN CREDENZA

AMERICAN BLOCK FRONT SECRETARY

A MODULAR SYSTEM OF CUPBOARDS AVAILABLE WITH PLAIN, GLASS, OR LOUVERED DOORS - UFFICIO TECNICO BRIVIO

A SYSTEM OF CUPBOARDS, DRAWERS, AND SHELVES - LUIGI MASSONI

CABINET CREDENZA - HANS WEITZ

CHEST CONVERTIBLE INTO A WRITING TABLE - FRANCO BIZZOZZERO

A WALL STORAGE SYSTEM FORMING A SHALLOW ALCOVE SPACE

A WALL SYSTEM SERVING AS A FREESTANDING ROOM DIVIDER

WALL STORAGE SYSTEMS CONSIST OF MODULAR SHELVING, DRAWER, AND CABINET UNITS WHICH CAN BE COMBINED IN VARIOUS WAYS TO FORM SELF-SUPPORTING ASSEMBLIES. THE UNITS MAY HAVE OPEN FRONTS OR BE FITTED WITH SOLID, GLASS, OR LOUVERED DOORS. SOME SYSTEMS INTEGRATE DISPLAY LIGHTING INTO THEIR CONSTRUCTION.

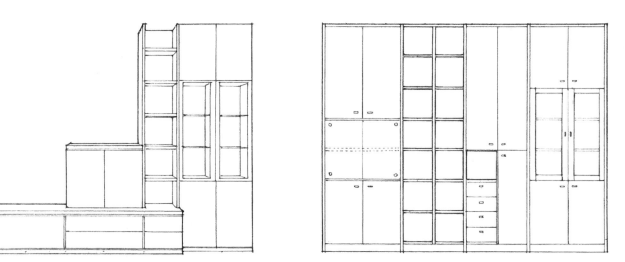

A WALL STORAGE SYSTEM MAY BE A FREESTANDING ASSEMBLY OR BE PLACED INTO A WALL RECESS.

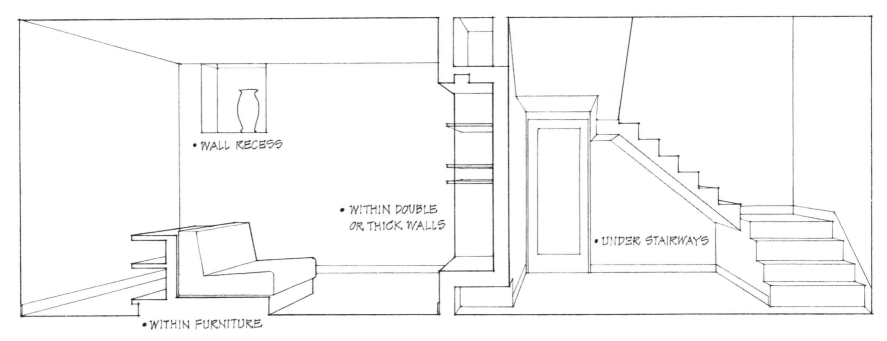

• WALL RECESS

• WITHIN DOUBLE
OR THICK WALLS

• UNDER STAIRWAYS

• WITHIN FURNITURE

□ FINDING SPACE FOR STORAGE

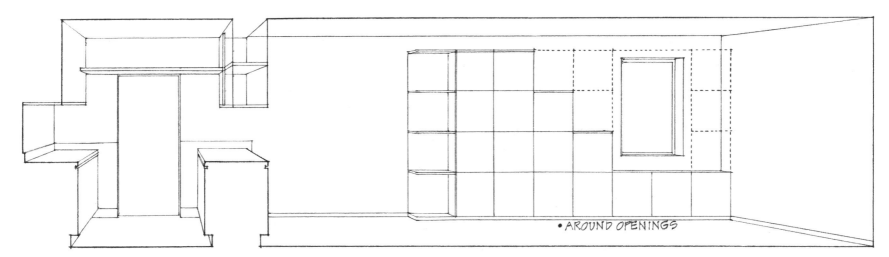

• AROUND OPENINGS

BUILT-IN STORAGE AND CABINETRY ARE MOST COMMON IN KITCHENS,
PANTRIES, AND BATHROOM SPACES, BUT CAN EFFECTIVELY BE
EXTENDED INTO OTHER SPACES AS WELL.

# LIGHTING FIXTURES

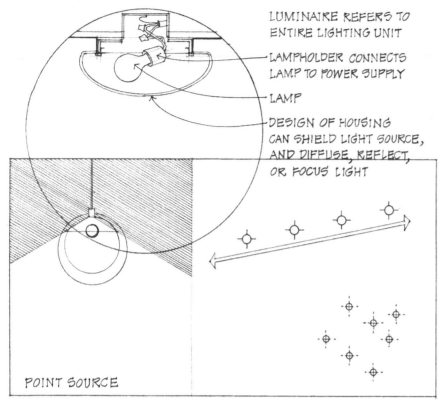

LUMINAIRE REFERS TO ENTIRE LIGHTING UNIT

LAMPHOLDER CONNECTS LAMP TO POWER SUPPLY

LAMP

DESIGN OF HOUSING CAN SHIELD LIGHT SOURCE, AND DIFFUSE, REFLECT, OR FOCUS LIGHT

POINT SOURCE

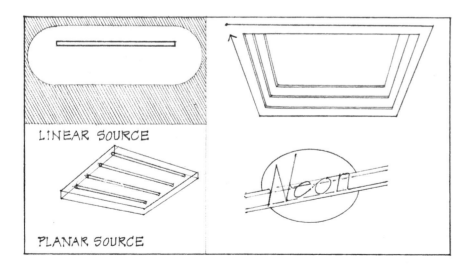

LINEAR SOURCE

PLANAR SOURCE

Neon

Light fixtures are integral parts of a building's electrical system, transforming energy into usable illumination. Light fixtures require an electrical connection or power supply, a housing assembly, and a lamp. See Chapter 5 for further discussion of lamps, light distribution, and illumination levels. This section will focus on the light fixtures themselves as design elements.

We are concerned not only with the shape and form of the fixture but also with the form of the illumination it provides. Point sources give focus to a space since the area of greatest brightness in a space tends to attract our attention. They can be used to highlight an area or an object of interest. A number of point sources can be arranged to describe rhythm and sequence. Small point sources, when grouped, can provide glitter and sparkle.

Linear sources can be used to give direction, emphasize the edges of planes, or outline an area. A parallel series of linear sources can form a plane of illumination which is effective for the general, diffused illumination of an area.

Volumetric sources are point sources expanded by the use of translucent materials into spheres, globes, or other three-dimensional forms.

VOLUMETRIC SOURCE

Light fixtures can provide direct and/or indirect illumination. The form of distribution depends on the design of the fixture as well as its placement and orientation in a space.

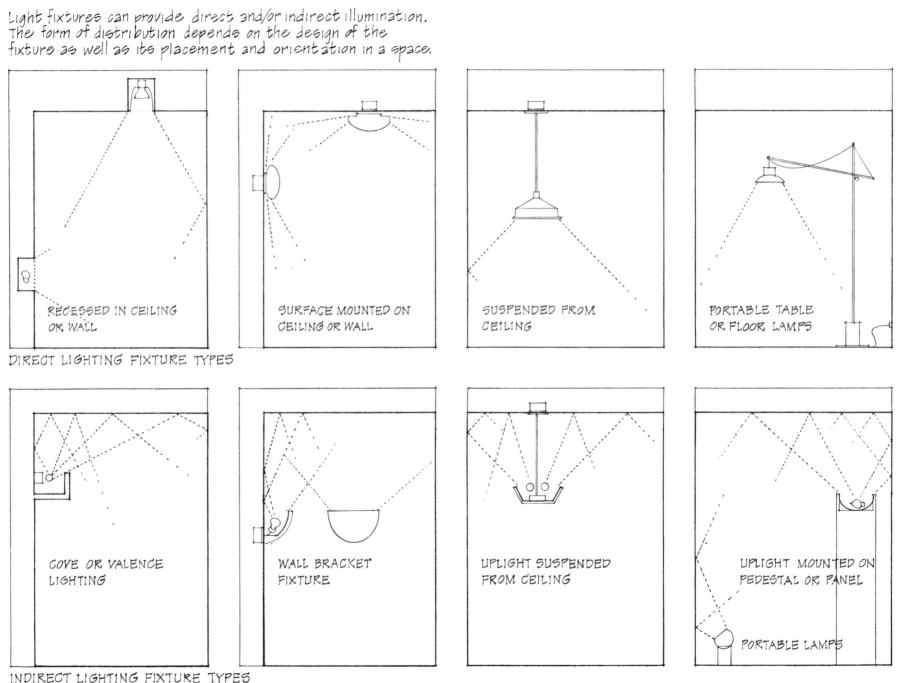

RECESSED IN CEILING OR WALL

SURFACE MOUNTED ON CEILING OR WALL

SUSPENDED FROM CEILING

PORTABLE TABLE OR FLOOR LAMPS

DIRECT LIGHTING FIXTURE TYPES

COVE OR VALENCE LIGHTING

WALL BRACKET FIXTURE

UPLIGHT SUSPENDED FROM CEILING

UPLIGHT MOUNTED ON PEDESTAL OR PANEL

PORTABLE LAMPS

INDIRECT LIGHTING FIXTURE TYPES

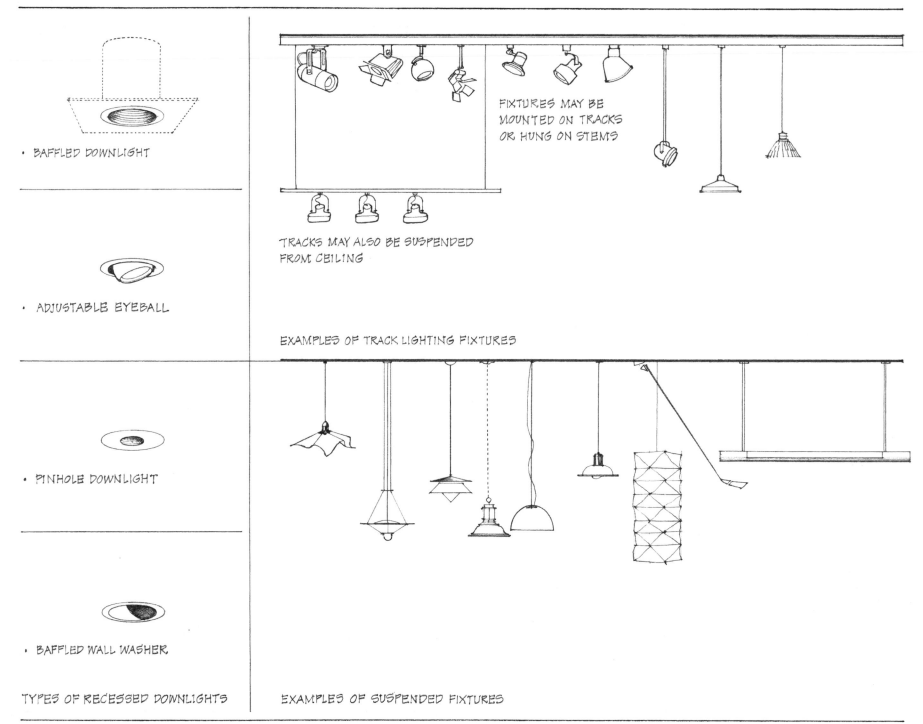

• BAFFLED DOWNLIGHT

• ADJUSTABLE EYEBALL

• PINHOLE DOWNLIGHT

• BAFFLED WALL WASHER

TYPES OF RECESSED DOWNLIGHTS

FIXTURES MAY BE
MOUNTED ON TRACKS
OR HUNG ON STEMS

TRACKS MAY ALSO BE SUSPENDED
FROM CEILING

EXAMPLES OF TRACK LIGHTING FIXTURES

EXAMPLES OF SUSPENDED FIXTURES

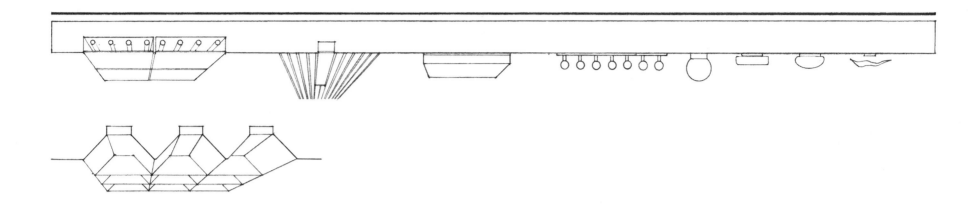

EXAMPLES OF RECESSED AND SURFACE-MOUNTED CEILING FIXTURES

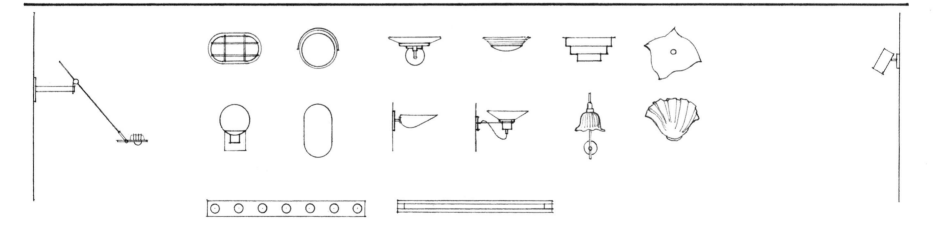

EXAMPLES OF WALL-MOUNTED FIXTURES

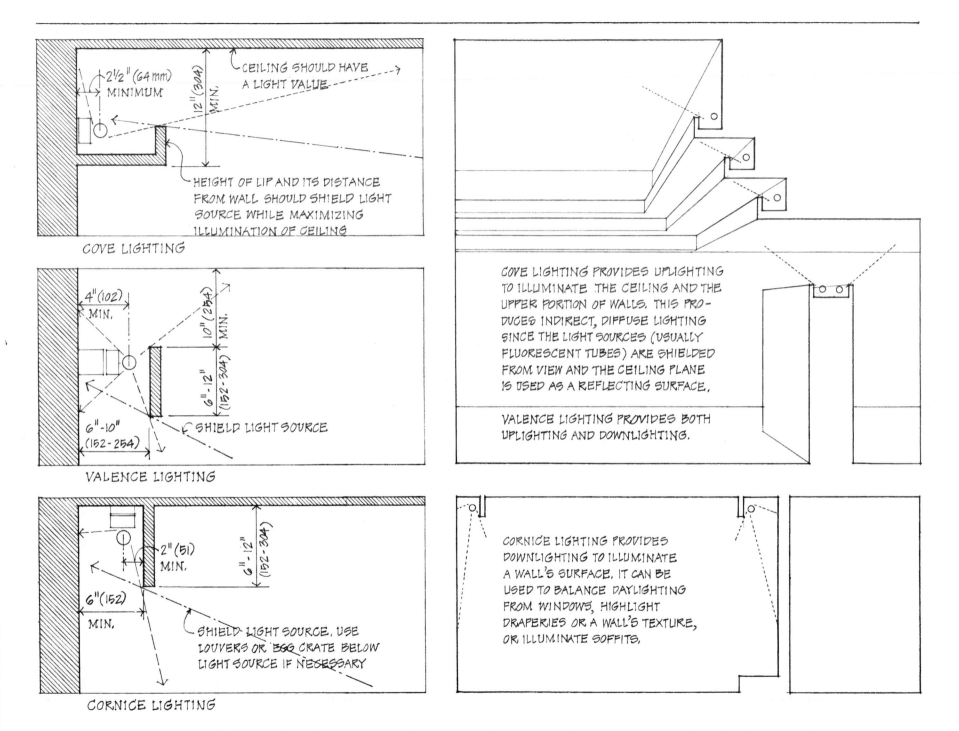

**COVE LIGHTING**

2½" (64 mm) MINIMUM

12" (304) MIN.

CEILING SHOULD HAVE A LIGHT VALUE

HEIGHT OF LIP AND ITS DISTANCE FROM WALL SHOULD SHIELD LIGHT SOURCE WHILE MAXIMIZING ILLUMINATION OF CEILING

**VALENCE LIGHTING**

4" (102) MIN.

10" (254) MIN.

6"-12" (152-304)

6"-10" (152-254)

SHIELD LIGHT SOURCE

**CORNICE LIGHTING**

2" (51) MIN.

6"-12" (152-304)

6" (152) MIN.

SHIELD LIGHT SOURCE, USE LOUVERS OR EGG CRATE BELOW LIGHT SOURCE IF NECESSARY

COVE LIGHTING PROVIDES UPLIGHTING TO ILLUMINATE THE CEILING AND THE UPPER PORTION OF WALLS. THIS PRODUCES INDIRECT, DIFFUSE LIGHTING SINCE THE LIGHT SOURCES (USUALLY FLUORESCENT TUBES) ARE SHIELDED FROM VIEW AND THE CEILING PLANE IS USED AS A REFLECTING SURFACE.

VALENCE LIGHTING PROVIDES BOTH UPLIGHTING AND DOWNLIGHTING.

CORNICE LIGHTING PROVIDES DOWNLIGHTING TO ILLUMINATE A WALL'S SURFACE. IT CAN BE USED TO BALANCE DAYLIGHTING FROM WINDOWS, HIGHLIGHT DRAPERIES OR A WALL'S TEXTURE, OR ILLUMINATE SOFFITS.

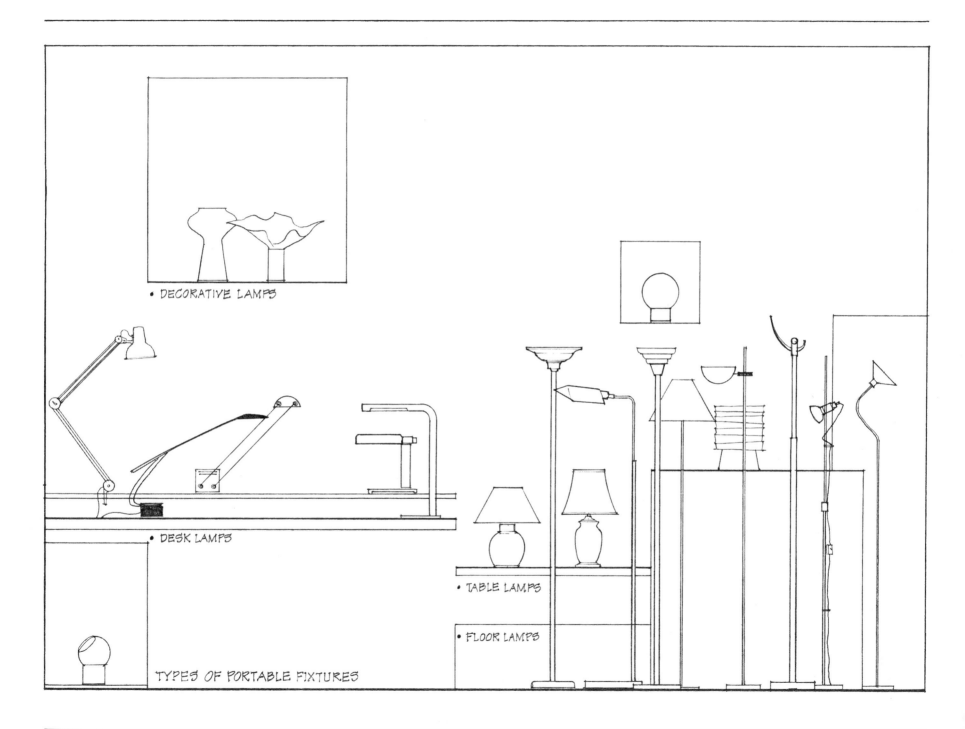

• DECORATIVE LAMPS

• DESK LAMPS

• TABLE LAMPS

• FLOOR LAMPS

TYPES OF PORTABLE FIXTURES

# ACCESSORIES

Accessories in interior design refer to those items which provide a space with aesthetic enrichment and embellishment. These items may provide visual delight for the eye, textural interest for the hand, or stimulation for the mind. Ultimately, accessories, individually or collectively, are the inevitable evidence of habitation.

Accessories which can add visual and tactile richness to an interior setting may be:

- Utilitarian - useful tools and objects
- Incidental - architectural elements and furnishings
- Decorative - artwork and plants.

Utilitarian accessories come in a range of designs and their selection over time is often a reflection of the personality of those who inhabit a place.

## UTILITARIAN

Incidental accessories enrich a space while simultaneously serving other functions. One example is architectural elements and the details which express the way materials are joined. Another would be the forms, colors, and textures of interior furnishings.

## INCIDENTAL

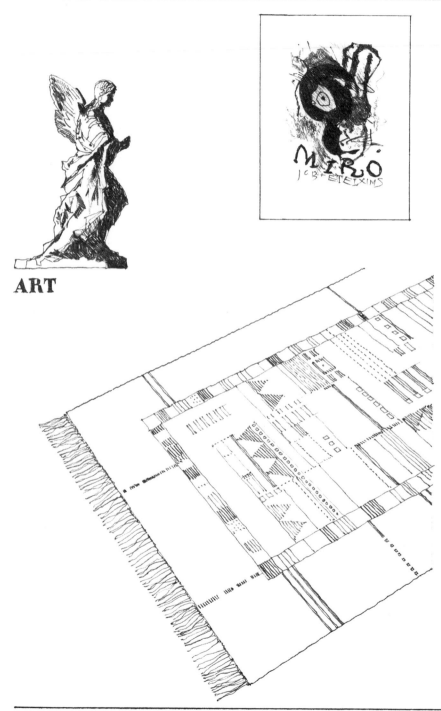

**ART**

Decorative accessories delight the eye, the hand, or the intellect without necessarily being utilitarian in purpose. These may include:

- Artwork — Enriching a space with art follows an age-old tradition of decorating objects and surfaces. Many utilitarian and incidental items can be considered as art.

- Collections — Collections of objects may be serious or not so serious but they almost always have personal meaning.

- Plants — Plants and flowers, as visible signs of nature, bring their expression of life and growth to interior spaces.

## COLLECTIONS

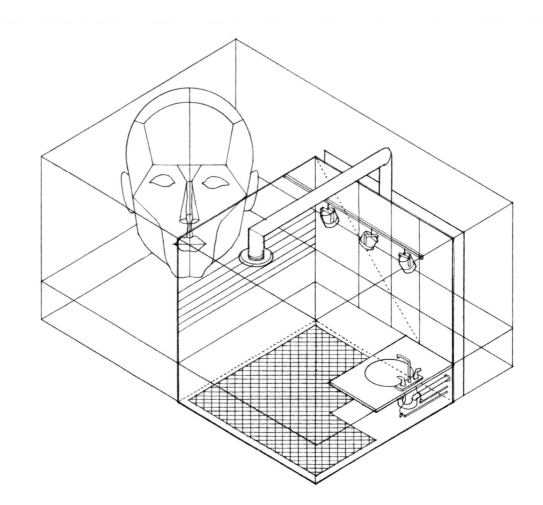

# INTERIOR ENVIRONMENTAL SYSTEMS

# INTERIOR ENVIRONMENTAL SYSTEMS

HEATING
VENTILATING
AIR CONDITIONING

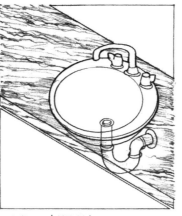

WATER SUPPLY
SANITARY DRAINAGE

Interior environmental systems are essential components of any building since they provide for occupants the thermal, visual, auditory, and sanitary conditions necessary for their comfort and convenience. These systems must be designed and laid out not only to function properly. They must also be coordinated with a building's structural system. This requires the knowledge and expertise of professional engineers and architects. The interior designer, nevertheless, should be aware that these systems exist and know how they affect the quality of the interior environment.

This chapter provides a brief description of the elements of the following systems:

- HEATING AND AIR CONDITIONING SYSTEMS
- WATER SUPPLY AND SANITARY DRAINAGE SYSTEMS
- ELECTRICAL AND LIGHTING SYSTEMS
- ACOUSTICS

ELECTRIC POWER &
LIGHTING

ROOM ACOUSTICS
NOISE CONTROL

SYSTEMS

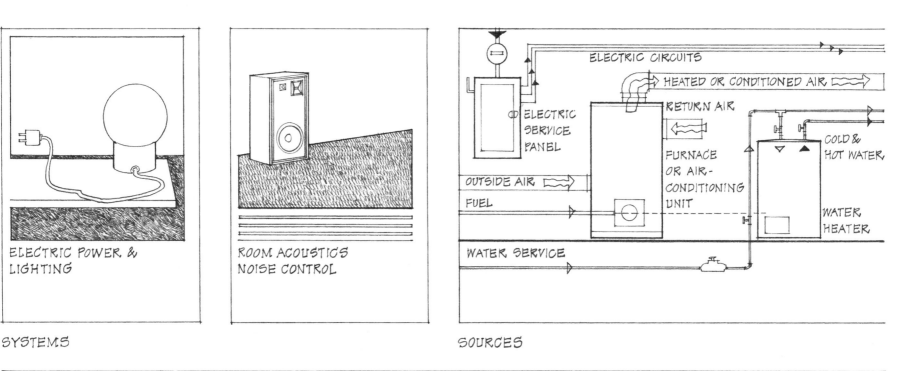

SOURCES

These environmental control systems are similar in the following respects. They all have a source or point of entry, a means of travel, and, ultimately, they deliver a result in an interior space - conditioned air, hot and cold water, electrical power and light.

The means of travel - wiring, pipes, and ducts - run vertically and horizontally through a building. Vertical travel of wiring and small pipes and ducts can be accommodated within the thickness of walls, but large lines require mechanical shaft spaces. Horizontal travel can occur within a floor structure, or if more space is required, between the floor and a hung ceiling.

Where these lines interface with an interior space affect not only their systems' performance but also how the space is used. Just as important for the interior designer is the appearance of those elements that have an impact on the visual quality of a space. Some are low-key, such as an air diffuser or a switch plate; others are more critical, such as a plumbing or light fixture.

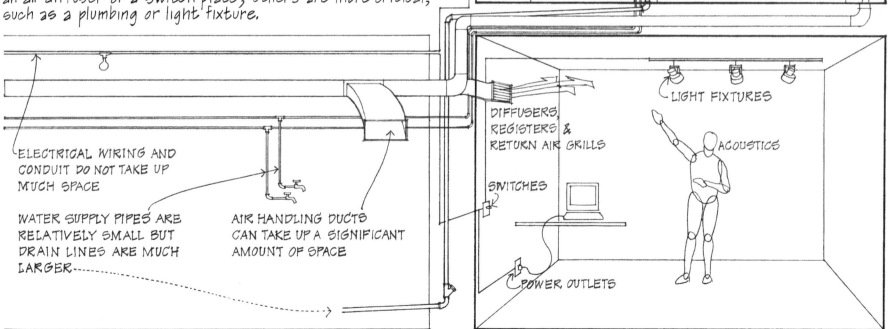

PLUMBING FIXTURES

DIFFUSERS, REGISTERS & RETURN AIR GRILLS

LIGHT FIXTURES

ACOUSTICS

SWITCHES

POWER OUTLETS

ELECTRICAL WIRING AND CONDUIT DO NOT TAKE UP MUCH SPACE

WATER SUPPLY PIPES ARE RELATIVELY SMALL BUT DRAIN LINES ARE MUCH LARGER

AIR HANDLING DUCTS CAN TAKE UP A SIGNIFICANT AMOUNT OF SPACE

TRANSMISSION

CONTROL AND OUTPUT DEVICES

# HEATING & AIR CONDITIONING

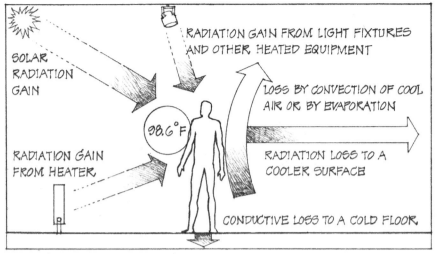

SOLAR RADIATION GAIN

RADIATION GAIN FROM LIGHT FIXTURES AND OTHER HEATED EQUIPMENT

LOSS BY CONVECTION OF COOL AIR OR BY EVAPORATION

98.6°F

RADIATION GAIN FROM HEATER

RADIATION LOSS TO A COOLER SURFACE

CONDUCTIVE LOSS TO A COLD FLOOR

MODES OF HEAT TRANSFER

The primary objective of a heating system is to replace the heat lost within an interior space. The basic heating system consists of a heat-producing medium, equipment to convert the medium to heat, a means to deliver the heat to a space, and, finally, a method for discharging the heat within the space.

While a heating system supplies heat, an air conditioner is usually considered to be a means for supplying cool air. A true air-conditioning system, however, provides all-year climate control by bringing in outside air, cleaning, heating, or cooling it, adding or removing humidity, and delivering the conditioned air to the interior spaces of a building.

RADIATION: Heat transfer from a warm surface to a cooler surface; not affected by air motion or temp.

CONVECTION: Transfer due to motion of warm or cool air across a body's surface.

CONDUCTION: Direct transfer from a warm surface in contact with a cooler surface.

EVAPORATION: Heat loss due to the process of moisture turning into vapor.

To achieve and maintain thermal comfort, a reasonable balance must be reached among the types of heat transfer that can occur in a room.

- The higher the mean radiant temperature of a room's surfaces, the cooler the air temperature should be.

- The higher the relative humidity of a space, the lower the air temperature should be.

- The cooler the moving air stream, the less velocity it should have.

THERMAL COMFORT CONSIDERATIONS

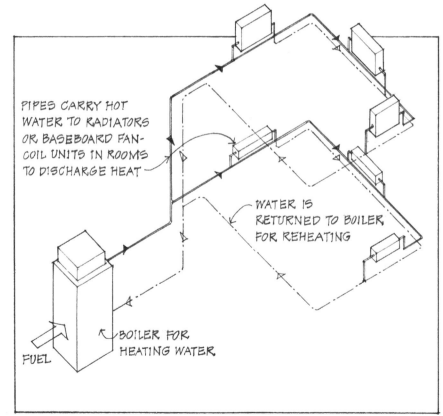

PIPES CARRY HOT WATER TO RADIATORS OR BASEBOARD FAN-COIL UNITS IN ROOMS TO DISCHARGE HEAT

WATER IS RETURNED TO BOILER FOR REHEATING

FUEL

BOILER FOR HEATING WATER

HOT WATER HEATING SYSTEM

An air-conditioning system treats air in several ways since thermal comfort is dependent not only on air temperature, but also on relative air humidity, the radiant temperature of surrounding surfaces, and air motion. Air purity and odor removal are additional comfort factors that can be controlled by an air-conditioning system.

While the architect and engineers plan a heating or air-conditioning system during the design of a building, the interior designer can influence the final result through the selection of wall, window, and floor coverings and by the adjustment of air-flow patterns.

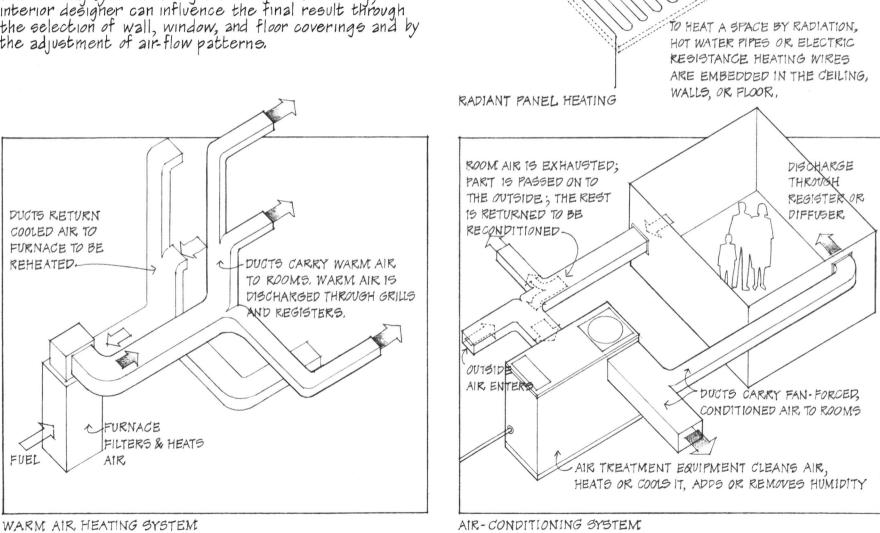

TO HEAT A SPACE BY RADIATION, HOT WATER PIPES OR ELECTRIC RESISTANCE HEATING WIRES ARE EMBEDDED IN THE CEILING, WALLS, OR FLOOR.

RADIANT PANEL HEATING

DUCTS RETURN COOLED AIR TO FURNACE TO BE REHEATED.

DUCTS CARRY WARM AIR TO ROOMS. WARM AIR IS DISCHARGED THROUGH GRILLS AND REGISTERS.

FURNACE FILTERS & HEATS AIR.

FUEL

WARM AIR HEATING SYSTEM

ROOM AIR IS EXHAUSTED; PART IS PASSED ON TO THE OUTSIDE; THE REST IS RETURNED TO BE RECONDITIONED

DISCHARGE THROUGH REGISTER OR DIFFUSER

OUTSIDE AIR ENTERS

DUCTS CARRY FAN-FORCED, CONDITIONED AIR TO ROOMS

AIR TREATMENT EQUIPMENT CLEANS AIR, HEATS OR COOLS IT, ADDS OR REMOVES HUMIDITY

AIR-CONDITIONING SYSTEM

# WATER SYSTEMS

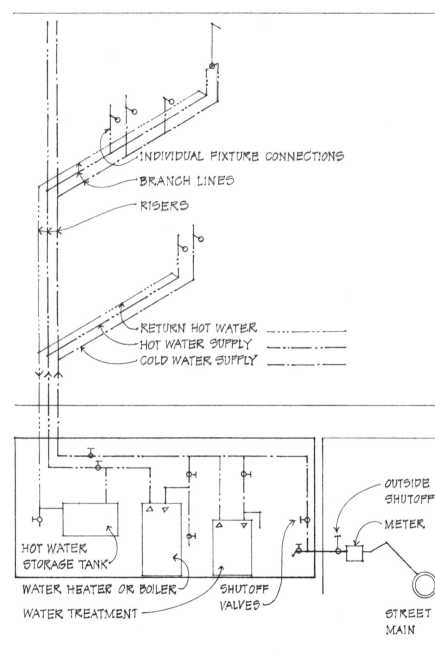

INDIVIDUAL FIXTURE CONNECTIONS

BRANCH LINES

RISERS

RETURN HOT WATER ——— ———

HOT WATER SUPPLY ——— ———

COLD WATER SUPPLY ——— ———

HOT WATER
STORAGE TANK

WATER HEATER OR BOILER

WATER TREATMENT

SHUTOFF
VALVES

OUTSIDE
SHUTOFF

METER

STREET
MAIN

SCHEMATIC OF A WATER SUPPLY SYSTEM

There are two separate but parallel networks in a water system. One supplies water for human use, and use by mechanical and fire protection systems. The other disposes of waterborne waste material once the water has been used. Water is supplied under pressure from a water main; once used, the water along with any waste material is discharged from the building and carried to a sewer line by gravity.

A water supply system must overcome the forces of gravity and friction to deliver water up to its points of use. The pressure required to upfeed water may come from the water main or from pumps within the building. When this pressure is insufficient, water can be pumped to an elevated storage tank for gravity downfeed.

A separate supply subsystem common to all buildings is the hot water supply system, leading from the heater or boiler to each required fixture. To conserve energy, the hot water supply can be a closed and constantly circulating system.

To control the flow of water at each fixture as well as be able to isolate one or more fixtures from the water supply system for repair and maintenance, a series of valves is required.

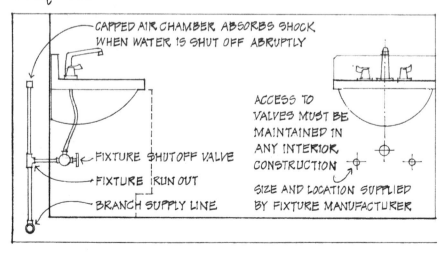

CAPPED AIR CHAMBER ABSORBS SHOCK WHEN WATER IS SHUT OFF ABRUPTLY

FIXTURE SHUTOFF VALVE

FIXTURE RUN OUT

BRANCH SUPPLY LINE

ACCESS TO VALVES MUST BE MAINTAINED IN ANY INTERIOR CONSTRUCTION

SIZE AND LOCATION SUPPLIED BY FIXTURE MANUFACTURER

The water supply system terminates at each plumbing fixture. After the water has been drawn and used, it enters the sanitary drainage system. The primary objective of this drainage system is to dispose of fluid waste and organic matter as quickly as possible.

Since a sanitary drainage system relies on gravity for its discharge, its pipes are much larger than water supply lines, which are under pressure. In addition, there are restrictions on the length and slope of horizontal runs and on the types and number of turns.

Gases are formed in drainage pipes by the decomposition of waste matter. To prevent these gases from entering the interior spaces of a building, traps or water seals are required at each fixture. In addition, the entire sanitary drainage system must be vented to the outside air. Venting prevents water seals in traps from being siphoned out and allows air to circulate within the system.

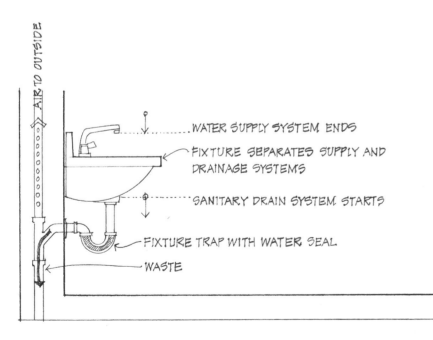

WATER SUPPLY SYSTEM ENDS

FIXTURE SEPARATES SUPPLY AND DRAINAGE SYSTEMS

SANITARY DRAIN SYSTEM STARTS

FIXTURE TRAP WITH WATER SEAL

WASTE

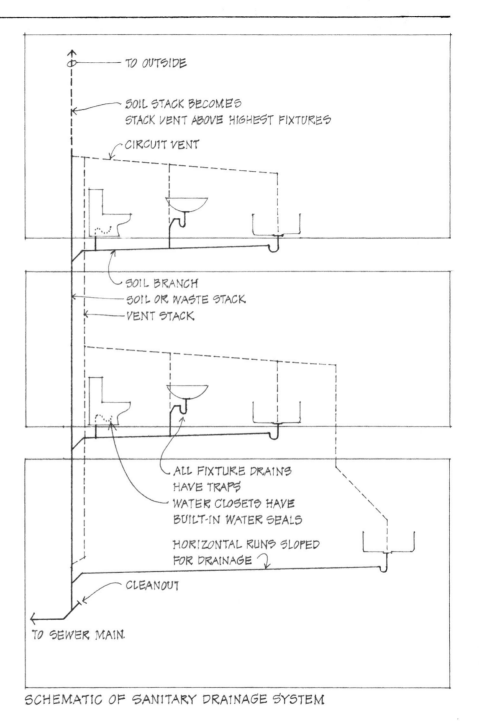

TO OUTSIDE

SOIL STACK BECOMES STACK VENT ABOVE HIGHEST FIXTURES

CIRCUIT VENT

SOIL BRANCH
SOIL OR WASTE STACK
VENT STACK

ALL FIXTURE DRAINS HAVE TRAPS
WATER CLOSETS HAVE BUILT-IN WATER SEALS

HORIZONTAL RUNS SLOPED FOR DRAINAGE

CLEANOUT

TO SEWER MAIN.

SCHEMATIC OF SANITARY DRAINAGE SYSTEM

# ELECTRICAL SYSTEMS

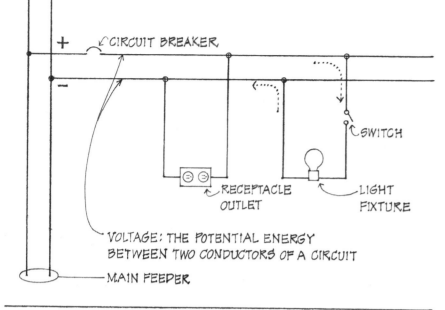

**CIRCUIT BREAKER**

**SWITCH**

**RECEPTACLE OUTLET**

**LIGHT FIXTURE**

VOLTAGE: THE POTENTIAL ENERGY BETWEEN TWO CONDUCTORS OF A CIRCUIT

MAIN FEEDER

SCHEMATIC OF A BRANCH CIRCUIT

The electrical system of a building supplies power for lighting, heating, and the operation of electrical equipment and appliances. This system should be installed to operate safely, reliably, and efficiently.

Electrical energy flows through a conductor because of a difference in electrical charge between two points in a circuit. This potential energy is measured in volts. The actual amount of energy flow or current is measured in amperes. The power required to keep an electric current flowing is measured in watts. (Power in watts = Current in amperes x Pressure in volts)

For electric current to flow, a circuit must be complete. Switches control current flow by introducing breaks in a circuit until power is required.

Power is supplied to a building by the electric utility company. The service line is first connected to a meter and a main disconnect switch, and then to a panelboard. This panelboard distributes the incoming power supply into smaller, more easily controlled circuits, and protects them from being overloaded with circuit breakers.

Most electric power is used in the form of alternating current (AC). Large pieces of machinery use direct current (DC).

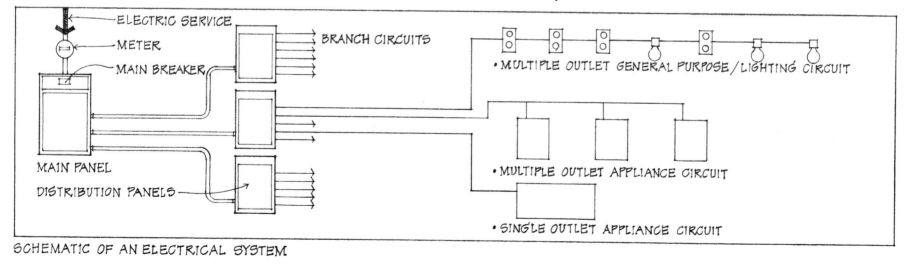

ELECTRIC SERVICE

METER

MAIN BREAKER

BRANCH CIRCUITS

MAIN PANEL

DISTRIBUTION PANELS

• MULTIPLE OUTLET GENERAL PURPOSE/LIGHTING CIRCUIT

• MULTIPLE OUTLET APPLIANCE CIRCUIT

• SINGLE OUTLET APPLIANCE CIRCUIT

SCHEMATIC OF AN ELECTRICAL SYSTEM

Branch circuits distribute electric power to the interior spaces of a building. The wiring in a circuit is sized according to the amount of current it must carry. A fuse or circuit breaker in the distribution panel disconnects a circuit when too much current is drawn for its wiring. The continuous load on a circuit should not exceed 80% of its rated capacity. For example, a 15 Amp. circuit should have a continuous load rating of 12 Amperes. On a 110 Volt line, the circuit could then be assumed to handle (12A x 110V) or 1320 Watts. Since room should be allowed for expansion, the safe capacity of a 15 Amp. circuit on a 110 Volt line is 1200 Watts.

Electrical systems are designed by electrical engineers. The interior designer can influence the location of lighting fixtures, power outlets, and switches to control their operation. The designer should also be aware of the power requirements of an electrical installation so that they can be coordinated with the existing or planned circuits.

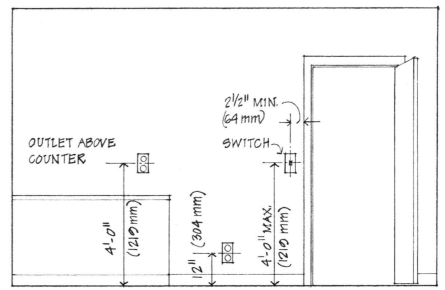

HEIGHTS OF SWITCHES AND RECEPTACLE OUTLETS

| Symbol | Description | Symbol | Description |
|---|---|---|---|
| ▬ | Lighting Panel | ▭ | Fluorescent Fixture |
| ▨ | Power Panel | ○ | Ceiling Incandescent |
| S | Singe Pole Switch | Ю | Wall Incandescent |
| S₃ | Three-Way Switch | Ⓡ | Recessed Fixture |
| ⊖ | Duplex Receptacle | Ⓧ | Exit Light Outlet |
| ⊡ | Floor Duplex Outlet | Ⓕ | Fan Outlet |
| △ | Special Purpose Outlet | Ⓔ | Electrical Outlet |
| ◄ | Telephone Outlet | Ⓜ | Motor |
| ◄ | Floor Telephone Outlet | Ⓙ | Junction Box |
| TV | Television Outlet | Ⓣ | Thermostat |

TYPICAL ELECTRICAL SYMBOLS

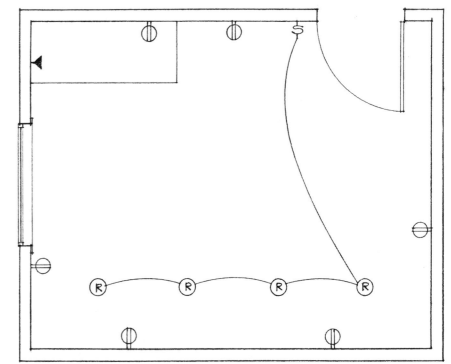

TYPICAL ELECTRICAL & LIGHTING PLAN

# LIGHTING

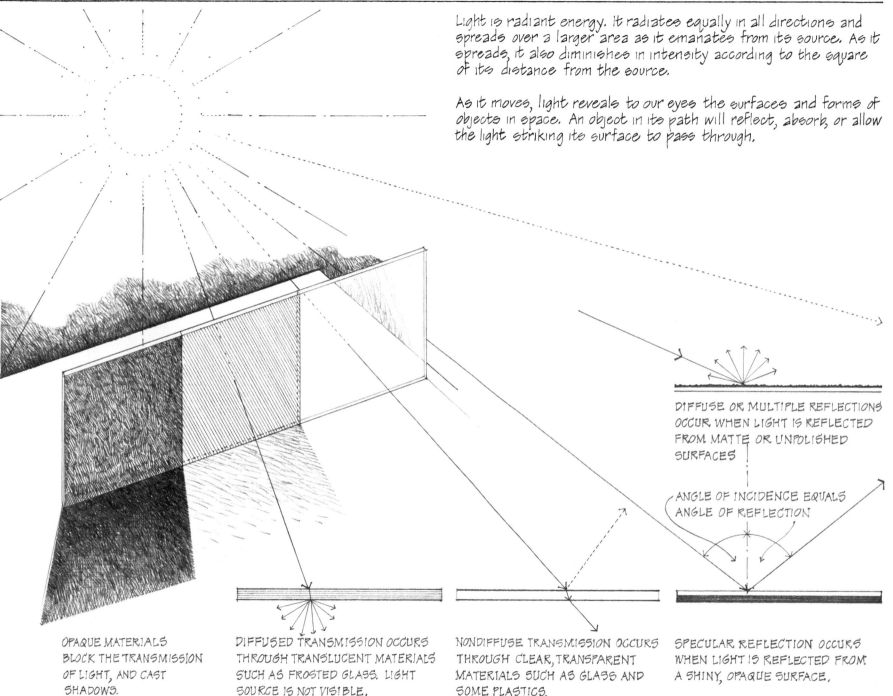

Light is radiant energy. It radiates equally in all directions and spreads over a larger area as it emanates from its source. As it spreads, it also diminishes in intensity according to the square of its distance from the source.

As it moves, light reveals to our eyes the surfaces and forms of objects in space. An object in its path will reflect, absorb, or allow the light striking its surface to pass through.

DIFFUSE OR MULTIPLE REFLECTIONS OCCUR WHEN LIGHT IS REFLECTED FROM MATTE OR UNPOLISHED SURFACES

ANGLE OF INCIDENCE EQUALS ANGLE OF REFLECTION

OPAQUE MATERIALS BLOCK THE TRANSMISSION OF LIGHT, AND CAST SHADOWS.

DIFFUSED TRANSMISSION OCCURS THROUGH TRANSLUCENT MATERIALS SUCH AS FROSTED GLASS. LIGHT SOURCE IS NOT VISIBLE.

NONDIFFUSE TRANSMISSION OCCURS THROUGH CLEAR, TRANSPARENT MATERIALS SUCH AS GLASS AND SOME PLASTICS.

SPECULAR REFLECTION OCCURS WHEN LIGHT IS REFLECTED FROM A SHINY, OPAQUE SURFACE.

The sun, stars, and electric lamps are visible to us because of the light they generate. Most of what we see, however, is visible because of the light that is reflected from the surfaces of objects. Our ability to see well – that is, to discern shape, color, and texture, and to differentiate one object from another – is affected not only by the amount of light available for illumination but also by the following factors:

- Brightness
- Contrast
- Glare
- Diffusion
- Color

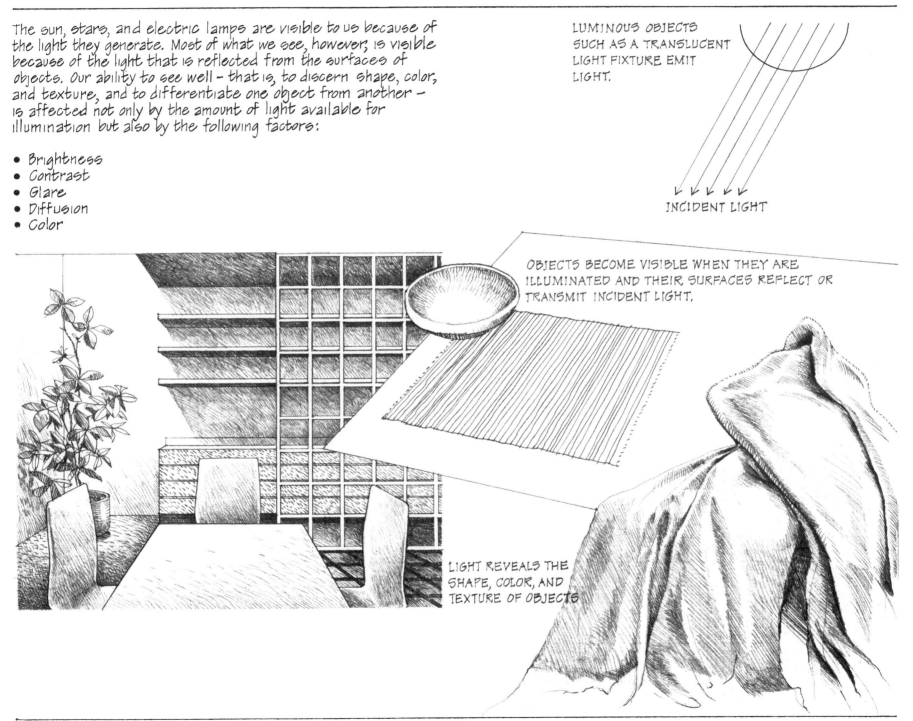

LUMINOUS OBJECTS SUCH AS A TRANSLUCENT LIGHT FIXTURE EMIT LIGHT.

INCIDENT LIGHT

OBJECTS BECOME VISIBLE WHEN THEY ARE ILLUMINATED AND THEIR SURFACES REFLECT OR TRANSMIT INCIDENT LIGHT.

LIGHT REVEALS THE SHAPE, COLOR, AND TEXTURE OF OBJECTS

Brightness refers to how much light energy is reflected by a surface. The degree of brightness of an object, in turn, depends on the color value and texture of its surface. A shiny, light-colored surface will reflect more light than a dark, matte, or rough-textured surface, even though both surfaces are lit with the same amount of illumination.

Generally speaking, visual acuity increases with object brightness. Of equal importance is the relative brightness between the object being viewed and its surroundings. To discern its shape, form, and texture, some degree of contrast or brightness ratio is required. For example, a white object on an equally bright white background would be difficult to see, as would a dark object seen against a dark background.

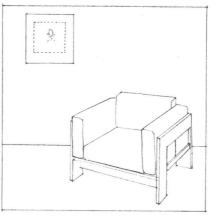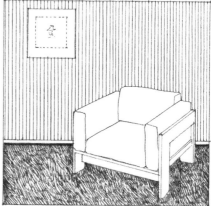

EVEN THOUGH THESE OBJECTS MAY BE UNIFORMLY ILLUMINATED, THEIR SURFACES DIFFER IN BRIGHTNESS ACCORDING TO THEIR COLOR VALUE AND TEXTURE AND CONSEQUENTLY, THEIR ABILITY TO REFLECT LIGHT.

BRIGHTNESS = ILLUMINATION × REFLECTANCE

CONTRAST IN BRIGHTNESS AIDS IN OUR PERCEPTION OF SHAPE AND FORM

# BRIGHTNESS

Contrast between an object and its background is especially critical for visual tasks that require the discrimination of shape and contour. An obvious example of this need for contrast is the printed page where dark letters can best be read when printed on light paper.

For seeing tasks requiring discrimination of surface texture and detail, less contrast between the surface and its background is desirable because our eyes adjust automatically to the average brightness of a scene. Someone seen against a brightly illuminated background would be silhouetted well but it would be difficult to discern that person's facial features.

The surface brightness of a task area should be the same as its background or be just a bit brighter. A maximum brightness ratio of 3:1 between the task surface and its background is generally recommended. Between the task area and the darkest part of the surrounding room, the brightness ratio should not exceed 5:1. Higher brightness ratios can lead to glare and associated problems of eye fatigue and loss in visual performance.

# CONTRAST

HIGH BACKGROUND BRIGHTNESS IS HELPFUL IN DELINEATING SHAPE AND OUTLINE.

TO AID IN DISCRIMINATING SURFACE DETAIL, SURFACE BRIGHTNESS MUST BE INCREASED.

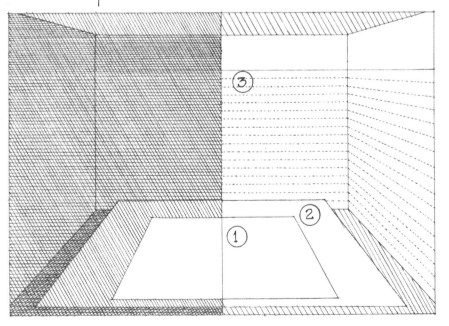

SURROUNDING AREA ③ SHOULD RANGE FROM 1/5 TO 5X THE BRIGHTNESS OF THE VISUAL TASK AREA ①

## 3:1
MAXIMUM RECOMMENDED BRIGHTNESS RATIO BETWEEN VISUAL TASK AREA ① AND ITS IMMEDIATE BACKGROUND ②

BRIGHTNESS AND CONTRAST CAN BE DESIRABLE IN CERTAIN SITUATIONS.

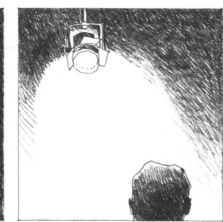

## GLARE

DIRECT GLARE IS CAUSED BY THE BRIGHTNESS OF LIGHT SOURCES IN A PERSON'S NORMAL FIELD OF VISION.

Even though our eyes prefer even lighting, particularly between a task surface and its background, our eyes are able to adapt to a wide range of brightness levels. We can respond to a minimum brightness ratio of 2:1 as well as to a maximum of 100:1 or more, but only over a period of time. Our eyes cannot respond immediately to extreme changes in lighting levels. Once our eyes have adjusted to a certain lighting level, any significant increase in brightness can lead to glare, eyestrain, and impairment of visual performance.

There are two types of glare, direct and indirect. Direct glare is caused by the brightness of light sources within our normal field of vision. The brighter the light source, the greater the glare. Possible solutions to problems of direct glare include the following:

- Locate the sources of brightness out of the direct line of vision.
- If this is not possible, use properly shielded or baffled luminaires.
- In addition, raise the background brightness of the light sources and reduce their brightness ratio.

POSSIBLE SOLUTIONS TO DIRECT GLARE:

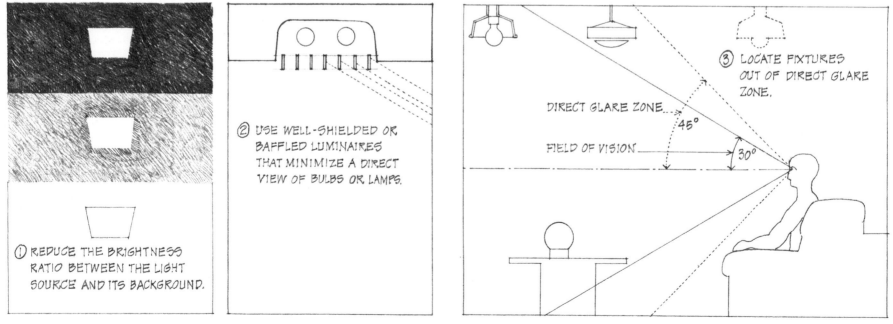

① REDUCE THE BRIGHTNESS RATIO BETWEEN THE LIGHT SOURCE AND ITS BACKGROUND.

② USE WELL-SHIELDED OR BAFFLED LUMINAIRES THAT MINIMIZE A DIRECT VIEW OF BULBS OR LAMPS.

③ LOCATE FIXTURES OUT OF DIRECT GLARE ZONE.

DIRECT GLARE ZONE

FIELD OF VISION

45°

30°

Indirect glare is caused by a task or viewing surface reflecting light from a light source into the viewer's eyes. The term _veiling reflection_ is sometimes used to describe this type of glare because the reflection of the light source creates a veiling of the image on the task surface and a resultant loss of contrast necessary for seeing the image.

Reflected glare is most severe when the task or viewing surface is shiny and has a high specular reflectance value. Using a dull, matte task surface can help alleviate, but will not eliminate, veiling reflections.

Possible solutions to problems of reflected glare include the following:

- Locate the light source so that the incident light rays will be reflected away from the viewer.
- Use luminaires with diffusers or lenses that lower their brightness levels.
- Lower the level of general overhead lighting and supplement it with localized task light closer to the work surface.

GLITTER AND SPARKLE ARE DESIRABLE TYPES OF GLARE.

INDIRECT OR REFLECTED GLARE AFFECTS OUR ABILITY TO PERFORM CRITICAL SEEING TASKS SUCH AS READING OR DRAFTING.

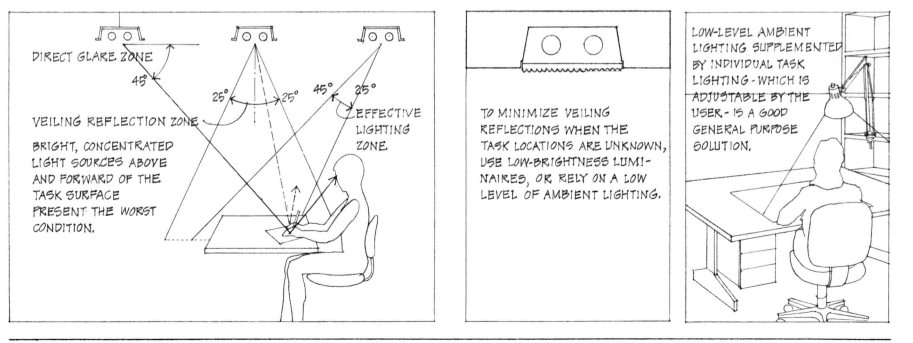

DIRECT GLARE ZONE

45°

VEILING REFLECTION ZONE

25° 25° 45° 25°

EFFECTIVE LIGHTING ZONE.

BRIGHT, CONCENTRATED LIGHT SOURCES ABOVE AND FORWARD OF THE TASK SURFACE PRESENT THE WORST CONDITION.

TO MINIMIZE VEILING REFLECTIONS WHEN THE TASK LOCATIONS ARE UNKNOWN, USE LOW-BRIGHTNESS LUMI-NAIRES, OR RELY ON A LOW LEVEL OF AMBIENT LIGHTING.

LOW-LEVEL AMBIENT LIGHTING SUPPLEMENTED BY INDIVIDUAL TASK LIGHTING - WHICH IS ADJUSTABLE BY THE USER - IS A GOOD GENERAL PURPOSE SOLUTION.

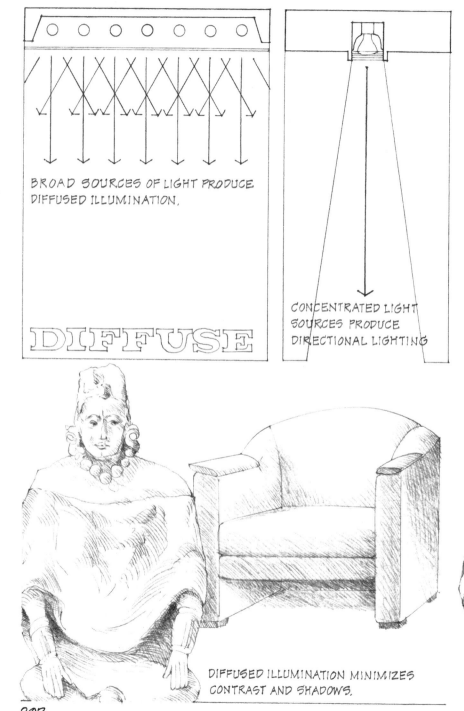

BROAD SOURCES OF LIGHT PRODUCE
DIFFUSED ILLUMINATION.

DIFFUSE

CONCENTRATED LIGHT
SOURCES PRODUCE
DIRECTIONAL LIGHTING

Diffuseness is a measure of a light's direction and dispersion as it emanates from its source. This quality of light affects both the visual atmosphere of a room and the appearance of objects within it. A broad source of light such as a luminous ceiling produces diffused illumination that is flat, fairly uniform, and generally glare-free. The soft light provided minimizes contrast and shadows, and can make the reading of surface textures difficult.

On the other hand, a point source of light such as an incandescent bulb produces a directional light with little diffusion. Directional lighting enhances our perception of shape, form, and surface texture by producing shadows and brightness variations on the objects it illuminates.

While diffused lighting is useful for general vision, it can be monotonous. Some directional lighting can help relieve this dullness by providing visual accents, introducing brightness variations, and brightening task surfaces. A mix of both diffused and directional lighting is often desirable and beneficial, especially when a variety of tasks are to be performed in a room.

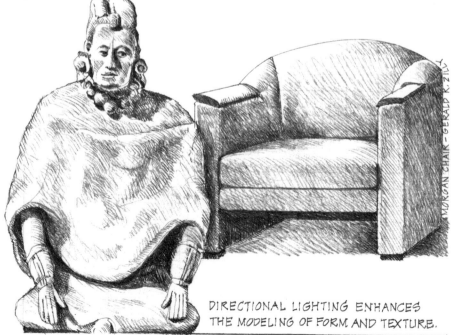

DIFFUSED ILLUMINATION MINIMIZES
CONTRAST AND SHADOWS.

DIRECTIONAL LIGHTING ENHANCES
THE MODELING OF FORM AND TEXTURE.

Another important quality of light is its color and how it affects the coloration of objects and surfaces in a room. While we assume most light to be white, the spectral distribution of light varies according to the nature of its source. The most evenly balanced white light is noon daylight. But in the early morning hours, daylight can range from purple to red. As the day progresses, it will cycle through a range of oranges and yellows to blue-white at noon, and then back again through the oranges and reds of sunset.

The spectral distribution of artificial light sources varies with the type of lamp. For example, an incandescent bulb produces a yellow-white light while a cool-white fluorescent produces a blue-white light.

The apparent color of a surface is a result of its reflection of its predominant hue and its absorption of the other colors of the light illuminating it. The spectral distribution of a light source is important because if certain wavelengths of color are missing, then those colors cannot be reflected and will appear to be missing or greyed in any surface illuminated by that light.

# THE COLOR OF LIGHT

## COLOR TEMPERATURE SCALE

| °KELVIN | LIGHT SOURCE |
|---|---|
| 10,000° | Clear blue sky (up to 25,000°K) |
| 9000° | |
| 8000° | North light |
| 7000° | |
| 6000° | Daylight fluorescent<br>Overcast sky |
| 5000° | Noon sunlight<br>Cool white fluorescent |
| 4000° | Daylight incandescent<br>Warm white fluorescent |
| 3000° | |
| 2000° | Incandescent lamp<br>Sunrise |

SPECTRALLY BALANCED WHITE LIGHT

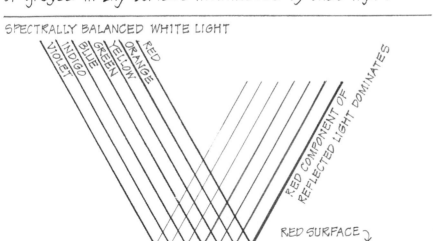

RED COMPONENT OF REFLECTED LIGHT DOMINATES

RED SURFACE

COOL WHITE FLUORESCENT

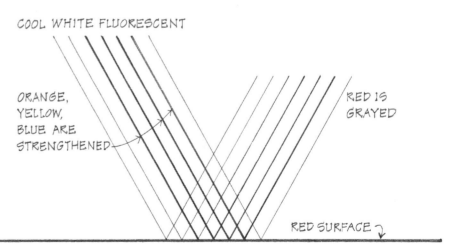

ORANGE, YELLOW, BLUE ARE STRENGTHENED

RED IS GRAYED

RED SURFACE

# LIGHT SOURCES

The source of all natural daylight is the sun. Its light is intense but will vary with the time of day, from season to season, and from place to place. It can also be diffused by cloud cover, haze, precipitation, or any pollution that may be present in the air.

In addition to direct sunlight, two other conditions must be considered when designing the daylighting of a space, reflected light from a clear sky and light from an overcast sky. While direct sunlight emphasizes hot, bright colors, skylight is more diffuse and enhances cool colors.

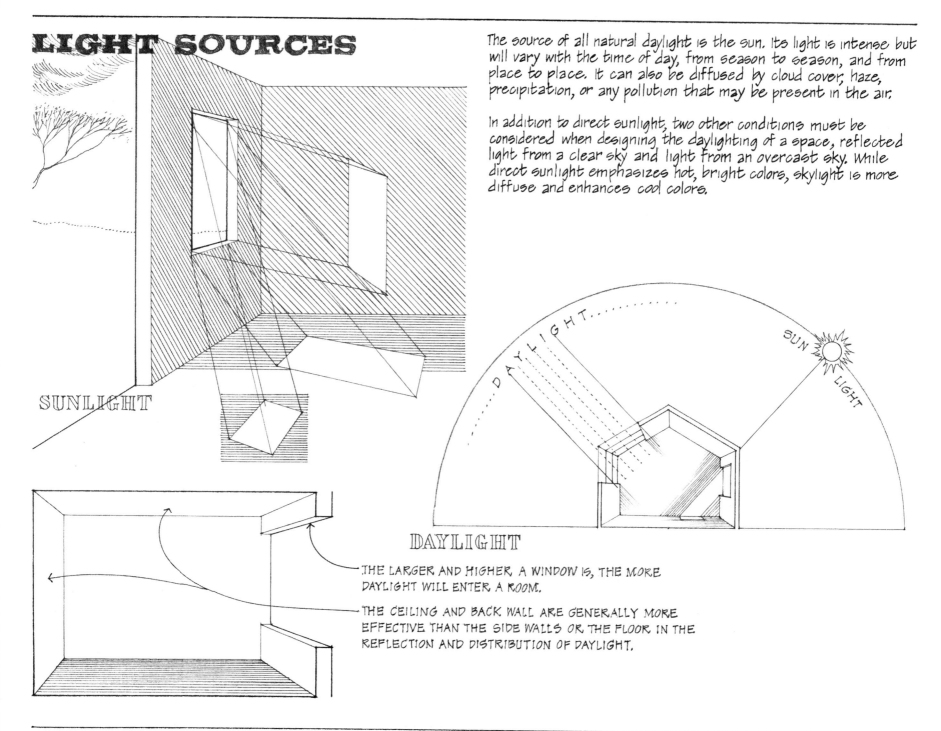

SUNLIGHT

DAYLIGHT

THE LARGER AND HIGHER A WINDOW IS, THE MORE DAYLIGHT WILL ENTER A ROOM.

THE CEILING AND BACK WALL ARE GENERALLY MORE EFFECTIVE THAN THE SIDE WALLS OR THE FLOOR IN THE REFLECTION AND DISTRIBUTION OF DAYLIGHT.

Artificial light is natural light that is produced by manufactured elements. The quantity and quality of light produced differ according to the type of lamp used. The light is further modified by the housing which holds and energizes the lamp.

There are two major types of artificial light sources in common use, incandescent and fluorescent lamps. Incandescent lamps consist of material filaments which are heated within a glass enclosure until they glow. They are generally less expensive, easier to dim with rheostats, and warmer in color than fluorescent lamps. Their relatively small size and compact shape allow them to be used as point sources of light which emphasize the form and texture of objects.

Incandescent lamps have a low efficacy rating. Only about 12% of the wattage used goes toward the production of light; the remainder is heat. They also have a comparatively short life.

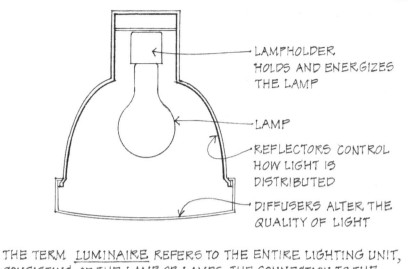

- LAMPHOLDER HOLDS AND ENERGIZES THE LAMP
- LAMP
- REFLECTORS CONTROL HOW LIGHT IS DISTRIBUTED
- DIFFUSERS ALTER THE QUALITY OF LIGHT

THE TERM LUMINAIRE REFERS TO THE ENTIRE LIGHTING UNIT, CONSISTING OF THE LAMP OR LAMPS, THE CONNECTION TO THE POWER SUPPLY, AND ELEMENTS THAT SHIELD, REFLECT, OR DIFFUSE THE LIGHT.

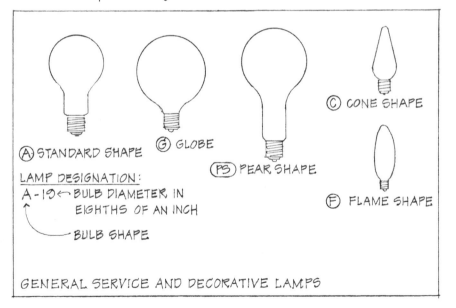

Ⓐ STANDARD SHAPE
Ⓖ GLOBE
Ⓟ Ⓢ PEAR SHAPE
Ⓒ CONE SHAPE
Ⓕ FLAME SHAPE

LAMP DESIGNATION:
A-19 ← BULB DIAMETER IN EIGHTHS OF AN INCH
↑
└ BULB SHAPE

GENERAL SERVICE AND DECORATIVE LAMPS

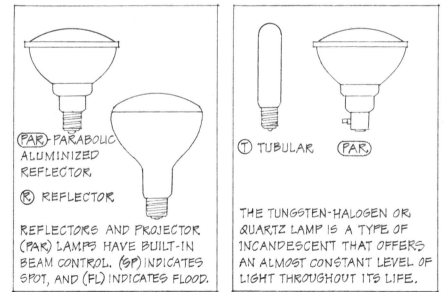

(PAR)- PARABOLIC ALUMINIZED REFLECTOR

Ⓡ REFLECTOR

REFLECTORS AND PROJECTOR (PAR) LAMPS HAVE BUILT-IN BEAM CONTROL. (SP) INDICATES SPOT, AND (FL) INDICATES FLOOD.

Ⓣ TUBULAR     (PAR)

THE TUNGSTEN-HALOGEN OR QUARTZ LAMP IS A TYPE OF INCANDESCENT THAT OFFERS AN ALMOST CONSTANT LEVEL OF LIGHT THROUGHOUT ITS LIFE.

# INCANDESCENT LAMPS

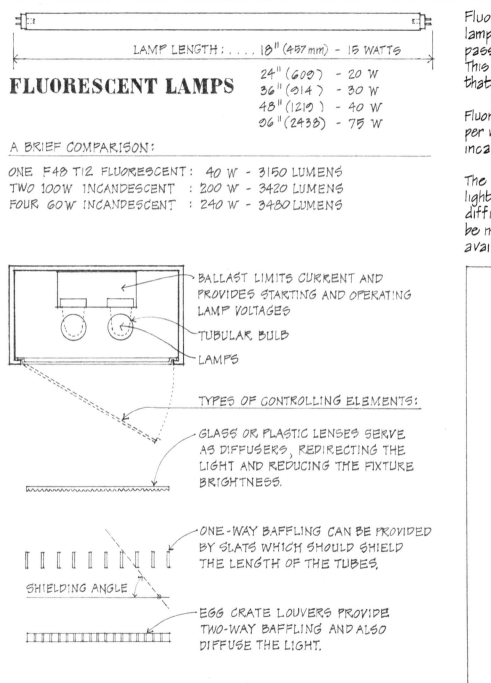

LAMP LENGTH: .... 18" (457 mm) - 15 WATTS

# FLUORESCENT LAMPS

24" (609) - 20 W
36" (914) - 30 W
48" (1219) - 40 W
96" (2438) - 75 W

A BRIEF COMPARISON:

ONE F48 T12 FLUORESCENT: 40 W - 3150 LUMENS
TWO 100 W INCANDESCENT : 200 W - 3420 LUMENS
FOUR 60 W INCANDESCENT : 240 W - 3480 LUMENS

BALLAST LIMITS CURRENT AND
PROVIDES STARTING AND OPERATING
LAMP VOLTAGES

TUBULAR BULB

LAMPS

TYPES OF CONTROLLING ELEMENTS:

GLASS OR PLASTIC LENSES SERVE
AS DIFFUSERS, REDIRECTING THE
LIGHT AND REDUCING THE FIXTURE
BRIGHTNESS.

ONE-WAY BAFFLING CAN BE PROVIDED
BY SLATS WHICH SHOULD SHIELD
THE LENGTH OF THE TUBES.

SHIELDING ANGLE

EGG CRATE LOUVERS PROVIDE
TWO-WAY BAFFLING AND ALSO
DIFFUSE THE LIGHT.

Fluorescent lamps are tubular, low-intensity, electric discharge lamps. They produce light by generating an electric arc which passes through the mercury vapor sealed within their tubes. This produces ultraviolet light which energizes the phosphors that coat the tubes' inner walls, thus emitting visible light.

Fluorescent lamps are more efficient (efficacy of 50-80 lumens per watt) and have a longer life (9,000 - 20,000 hours) than incandescent lamps. They produce little heat.

The long, tubular form of fluorescent lamps results in a linear light source which produces diffused light. This light can be difficult to control optically, and the resulting flat light can be monotonous. Circular and U-shaped lamps are also available for use in more compact fixture housings.

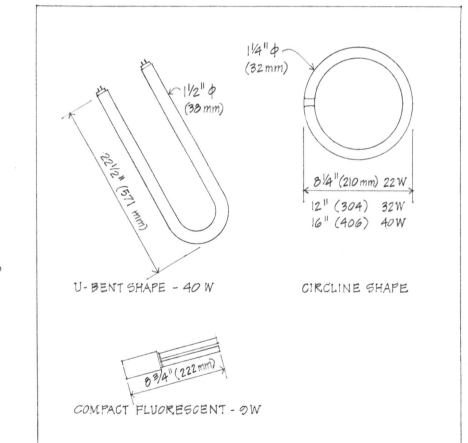

1½" φ (38 mm)

22½" (571 mm)

U-BENT SHAPE - 40 W

1¼" φ (32 mm)

8¼" (210 mm) 22 W

12" (304) 32 W
16" (406) 40 W

CIRCLINE SHAPE

8¾" (222 mm)

COMPACT FLUORESCENT - 9 W

One can control the lamp's output and color by changing the fluorescent phosphors that coat the inner wall of the tube. There are, therefore, many types of "white" light produced by the various types of fluorescent lamps.

FLUORESCENT ---------→ **F48 T12 CW · HO**

TUBE LENGTH ----------

LAMP SHAPE (TUBULAR) ----------
LAMP DIAMETER IN EIGHTHS OF AN INCH ----

---- INDICATES HIGHER OUTPUT LAMP -
REQUIRES SPECIAL CIRCUIT AND BALLAST

---- TYPE OF COLOR TINT

| COLOR PROPERTIES OF FLUORESCENT AND INCANDESCENT LAMPS | | | | SOURCE: GENERAL ELECTRIC CO. LAMP DEPARTMENT | |
|---|---|---|---|---|---|
| TYPE OF LAMP | EFFECT ON A NEUTRAL SURFACE | EFFECT ON ATMOSPHERE | COLORS STRENGTHENED | COLORS GRAYED | REMARKS |
| COOL WHITE        CW | WHITE | NEUTRAL TO MODERATELY COOL | ORANGE YELLOW BLUE | RED | BLENDS WITH NATURAL DAYLIGHT |
| DELUXE          CWX COOL WHITE | WHITE | NEUTRAL TO MODERATELY COOL | ALL NEARLY EQUALLY | NONE | BEST OVERALL COLOR RENDITION |
| WARM WHITE      WW | YELLOWISH WHITE | WARM | ORANGE YELLOW | RED GREEN BLUE | BLENDS WITH INCANDESCENT LIGHT |
| DELUXE          WWX WARM WHITE | YELLOWISH WHITE | WARM | RED, ORANGE YELLOW GREEN | BLUE | SIMULATES INCANDESCENT LIGHT |
| DAYLIGHT | BLUISH WHITE | VERY COOL | GREEN BLUE | RED ORANGE | |
| | | | | | |
| INCANDESCENT | YELLOWISH WHITE | WARM | RED ORANGE YELLOW | BLUE | GOOD COLOR RENDERING |

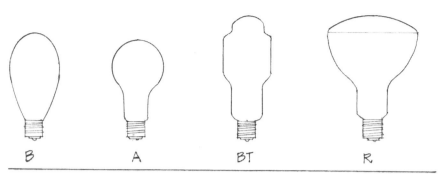

MERCURY VAPOR LAMP SHAPES

B   A   BT   R

FOR ACCURATE, CURRENT DATA ON LAMP SIZES, WATTAGES, LUMEN OUTPUT, AND AVERAGE LIFE, CONSULT MANUFACTURER'S CATALOGS.

A third major group of artificial light sources consists of high intensity discharge (HID) lamps - mercury vapor, high pressure sodium, and metal halide lamps. These lamps have a long life expectancy and consume little energy to produce a great amount of light from a relatively small source. They combine the form of an incandescent lamp with the efficiency of a fluorescent.

HID lamps were originally used primarily for street and sidewalk lighting and in large industrial spaces. Despite their efficiency, they had uneven spectral distributions and acutely distorted the color of objects they illuminated. Because of improvements in their rendition of color, however, HID lamps are increasingly being used in large commercial and public interior spaces.

Mercury lamps produce light when an arc is struck in a quartz tube containing vaporized mercury. Available in 40W to 1000W sizes, they produce twice as much light as a comparable incandescent lamp and have about the same efficacy (40-60 lumens/watt) as fluorescent lamps. Since they have a life of 16,000 - 24,000 hours, they are often used when burning hours are long and service is difficult. Clear mercury lamps cast a definite blue-green light. Phosphor-coated lamps have improved efficiency and color quality, making them usable for interior lighting.

# HIGH INTENSITY DISCHARGE LAMPS

| COLOR PROPERTIES OF MERCURY LAMPS | | | | | |
|---|---|---|---|---|---|
| | | | | SOURCE: GENERAL ELECTRIC CO. LAMP DEPARTMENT | |
| TYPE OF LAMP | EFFECT ON NEUTRAL SURFACE | EFFECT ON ATMOSPHERE | COLORS STRENGTHENED | COLORS GREYED | REMARKS |
| CLEAR MERCURY | GREENISH BLUE-WHITE | VERY COOL, GREENISH | YELLOW BLUE GREEN | RED ORANGE | POOR COLOR RENDERING |
| WHITE MERCURY | GREENISH WHITE | MODERATELY COOL, GREENISH | YELLOW GREEN BLUE | RED ORANGE | MODERATE COLOR RENDERING |
| DELUXE WHITE MERCURY | PURPLISH WHITE | WARM, PURPLISH | RED BLUE YELLOW | GREEN | COLOR ACCEPTABILITY SIMILAR TO CW FLUORESCENT |

Metal halide lamps are similar to mercury lamps except that metal halide is added to provide more light (efficacy of 80-100 lumens/watt) and better color. They are available in 400W-1500W sizes, and have a life of 1,500-15,000 hours. Because of their compact shape, their light can be optically controlled. And because they render color fairly well, they can be used both for outdoor and interior applications.

High-pressure sodium lamps are the most efficient sources of white light. Available in 75W-1000W sizes, they have an efficacy of 100-130 lumens/watt and a life of 10,000-20,000 hours. their light has a slightly yellowish cast similar to that of a warm-white fluorescent.

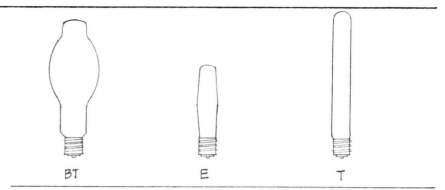

BT          E          T

METAL HALIDE AND HIGH PRESSURE SODIUM LAMP SHAPES

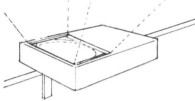

PORTABLE UNITS MAY BE PLACED ON SHELVES OR ATOP PANELS ABOVE EYE LEVEL,

FREESTANDING UNITS ARE ALSO PORTABLE

HID LIGHTS ARE AN ALTERNATIVE TO CONVENTIONAL OVERHEAD LIGHTING IN COMMERCIAL INTERIOR SPACES. THEY PROVIDE INDIRECT, AMBIENT LIGHTING BY USING THE CEILING SURFACE TO REFLECT AND DIFFUSE THEIR LIGHT.

| COLOR PROPERTIES OF METAL HALIDE AND HIGH PRESSURE SODIUM LAMPS | | | | | |
|---|---|---|---|---|---|
| | | | | SOURCE: GENERAL ELECTRIC CO. LAMP DEPARTMENT | |
| TYPE OF LAMP | EFFECT ON NEUTRAL SURFACE | EFFECT ON ATMOSPHERE | COLORS STRENGTHENED | COLORS GRAYED | REMARKS |
| METAL HALIDE | GREENISH WHITE | MODERATELY COOL, GREENISH | YELLOW GREEN BLUE | RED | COLOR ACCEPTABILITY SIMILAR TO CW FLUORESCENT |
| HIGH PRESSURE SODIUM | YELLOWISH | WARM, YELLOWISH | YELLOW GREEN ORANGE | RED BLUE | COLOR ACCEPTABILITY APPROACHES THAT OF WW FLUORESCENT |
| | | | | | |

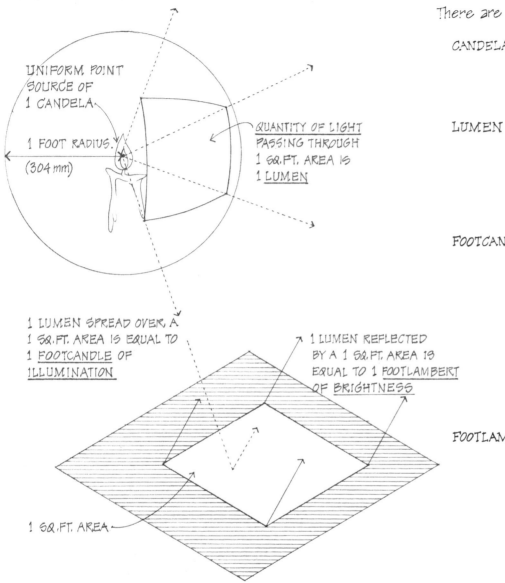

UNIFORM POINT
SOURCE OF
1 CANDELA

1 FOOT RADIUS.

(304 mm)

QUANTITY OF LIGHT
PASSING THROUGH
1 SQ.FT. AREA IS
1 <u>LUMEN</u>

1 LUMEN SPREAD OVER A
1 SQ.FT. AREA IS EQUAL TO
1 <u>FOOTCANDLE</u> OF
<u>ILLUMINATION</u>

1 LUMEN REFLECTED
BY A 1 SQ.FT. AREA IS
EQUAL TO 1 <u>FOOTLAMBERT</u>
OF <u>BRIGHTNESS</u>

1 SQ.FT. AREA

There are four basic ways to measure light.

CANDELA — The international unit of luminous intensity emitted from a source. The term <u>candlepower</u> is often used to describe the relative intensity of a light source.

LUMEN — The quantity of continuously generated light or luminous flux. One lumen is equivalent to the quantity of light, from a point source of one candela, that passes through a square foot area of a one-foot diameter sphere surrounding the point source.

FOOTCANDLE — The basic unit of illumination; a measure of the amount of light falling on a surface. One footcandle is equal to one lumen spread evenly over an area of one square foot.

ESI (Equivalent Sphere Illumination) footcandle is a measure of the usable illumination at a given location in a room. It is a better measure of lighting performance since it takes into account the ability of a fixture to control glare and reflections.

FOOTLAMBERT — The basic unit of brightness, measuring the amount of light reflected from a surface. One footlambert is equal to one lumen emitted by an area of one square foot.

Since the majority of what we see is due to the light reflected from the surfaces in a room, footlamberts reveal the nature of the space.

# LIGHTING CALCULATIONS

The basic unit of illumination, the footcandle, can be defined by the formula:

1 Footcandle = $\dfrac{1 \text{ Lumen (evenly distributed over)}}{1 \text{ Square Foot of Area}}$

This formula also provides the basis for calculating the average level of illumination in a space generated by a number of known light sources.

Illumination (Footcandles) = $\dfrac{\text{Lumens (from sources)}}{\text{Square Footage (of space)}}$

or

$\boxed{FC = \dfrac{L}{A}}$  This formula assumes all of the light generated by a room's light sources becomes usable illumination. In reality, however, there are several factors that diminish the actual lumen output of luminaires and how well this amount is utilized for task illumination in a given room.

- Fixture Efficiency:
  As soon as light is generated by a luminaire, a portion of it is lost within the fixture itself.

- Room Characteristics:
  The proportion of a room (the ratio of its vertical-to-horizontal areas) as well as the reflectances of its surfaces affect the amount of light that is lost as it strikes, and is absorbed by, the room's surfaces.

The one factor that takes these considerations into account is the Coefficient of Utilization (CU). It represents the percentage of generated light that ultimately arrives at the work plane. It is usually supplied by the fixture manufacturer for the specific luminaire being considered for use. Its use modifies the basic formula for illumination as follows:

$\boxed{FC = \dfrac{L \times CU}{A}}$

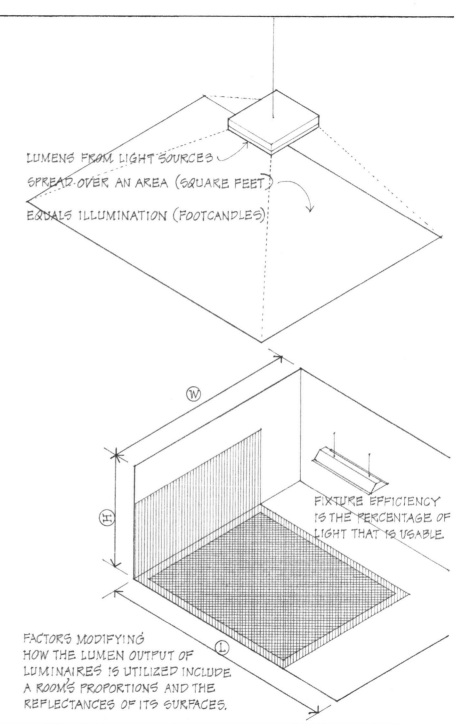

LUMENS FROM LIGHT SOURCES SPREAD OVER AN AREA (SQUARE FEET) EQUALS ILLUMINATION (FOOTCANDLES)

FIXTURE EFFICIENCY IS THE PERCENTAGE OF LIGHT THAT IS USABLE

FACTORS MODIFYING HOW THE LUMEN OUTPUT OF LUMINAIRES IS UTILIZED INCLUDE A ROOM'S PROPORTIONS AND THE REFLECTANCES OF ITS SURFACES.

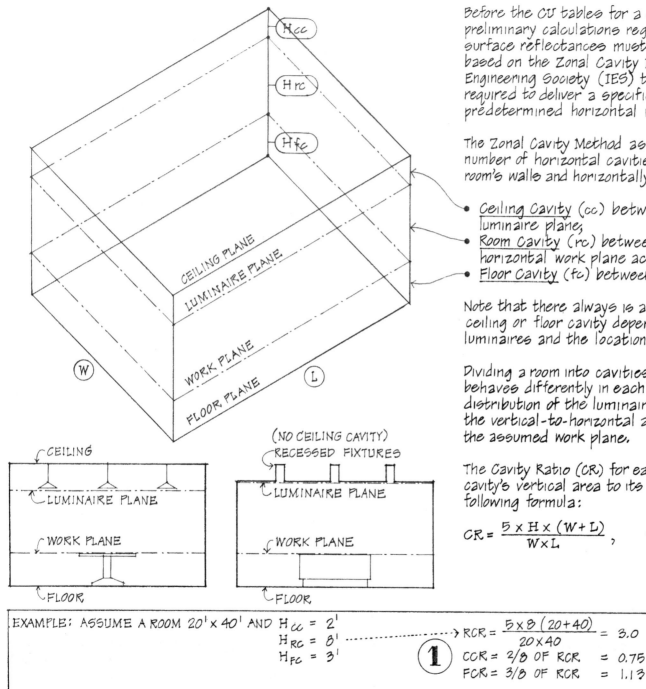

Before the CU tables for a specific luminaire can be used, some preliminary calculations regarding a room's proportions and surface reflectances must be made. These calculations are based on the Zonal Cavity Method, developed by the Illuminating Engineering Society (IES) to determine the number of luminaires required to deliver a specified amount of illumination at a predetermined horizontal work plane.

The Zonal Cavity Method assumes a room to be divided into a number of horizontal cavities, each bounded vertically by the room's walls and horizontally to form a:

- <u>Ceiling Cavity</u> (cc) between the ceiling and a horizontal luminaire plane;
- <u>Room Cavity</u> (rc) between the luminaire plane and a horizontal work plane across the task surfaces;
- <u>Floor Cavity</u> (fc) between the work plane and the floor.

Note that there always is a room cavity. The existence of a ceiling or floor cavity depends on the suspension of the luminaires and the location of the work plane.

Dividing a room into cavities permits the study of how light behaves differently in each cavity — according to the light distribution of the luminaires, the surface reflectances, and the vertical-to-horizontal areas — before the light reaches the assumed work plane.

The Cavity Ratio (CR) for each cavity is the relationship of the cavity's vertical area to its horizontal area as defined by the following formula:

$$CR = \frac{5 \times H \times (W+L)}{W \times L}, \quad \text{where} \quad \begin{aligned} H &= \text{cavity height} \\ W &= \text{cavity width} \\ L &= \text{cavity length} \end{aligned}$$

EXAMPLE: ASSUME A ROOM 20' × 40' AND $H_{cc} = 2'$
$H_{RC} = 8'$
$H_{FC} = 3'$

$RCR = \dfrac{5 \times 8 \ (20 + 40)}{20 \times 40} = 3.0$

① $CCR = 2/8 \ \text{OF} \ RCR = 0.75$
$FCR = 3/8 \ \text{OF} \ RCR = 1.13$

The "percent effective cavity reflectance," represented by the Greek letter rho (ρ), is a measure of how much light escapes the ceiling or wall cavities after a portion is absorbed within the cavity by surface reflectances. The effective reflectances for the ceiling and floor cavities, based on the Cavity Ratio and the actual ceiling, wall, and floor reflectances, can be found in tables in the IES Lighting Handbook (Illuminating Engineering Society, New York).

Given the Room Cavity Ratio (RCR), the percent effective ceiling and floor cavity reflectances, and the percent wall reflectance, the overall Coefficient of Utilization (CU) for a specific luminaire can be extracted from tables supplied by the fixture manufacturer.

EXAMPLE:
ASSUME THE ROOM DESCRIBED ON THE PREVIOUS PAGE HAS THE FOLLOWING REFLECTANCES:

CEILING REFLECTANCE: 80%
WALL REFLECTANCE : 50%
FLOOR REFLECTANCE : 20%

$$REFLECTANCE = \frac{REFLECTED\ LIGHT}{INCIDENT\ LIGHT}$$

THE HIGHER THE PERCENTAGE, THE GREATER THE REFLECTANCE.

## ③ DETERMINE THE COEFFICIENT OF UTILIZATION ASSUMING A SPECIFIC TYPE OF LUMINAIRE

| TYPE OF LUMINAIRE | DISTRIBUTION AND PER CENT LAMP LUMENS | $\rho_{CC}$ | 80 | | 70 (70) | | | 50 | | |
|---|---|---|---|---|---|---|---|---|---|---|
| | | $\rho_W$ | 30 | 10 | 50 | 30 | 10 | 50 | 30 | 10 |
| | MAINT. CAT. / MAX. S/MH GUIDE | RCR | CU TABLE FOR $\rho_{FC} = \underline{20}$ | | | | | | | |
| | IV   1.3 | 0 | .99 | .97 | .97 | .97 | .92 | . | | |
| | | 1 | .82 | .86 | .83 | .81 | .83 | . | | |
| | 0%↑ | 2 | .68 | .76 | .72 | .67 | .73 | . | | |
| | | (3) | .57 | (.67) | .61 | .57 | .65 | . | | |
| | | 4 | .49 | .60 | .53 | .48 | .58 | . | | |
| | 83½% ↓ | 5 | .41 | .53 | .46 | .41 | .51 | . | | |
| | | 6 | .35 | .47 | .40 | .35 | .46 | . | | |
| | | 7 | .30 | .42 | .35 | .30 | .41 | . | | |
| | | 8 | .26 | .38 | .31 | .26 | .37 | . | | |
| | | 9 | .23 | .34 | .27 | .23 | .33 | . | | |
| | | 10 | .20 | .31 | .24 | .20 | .30 | . | | |

(CU = .67)

If the effective floor cavity reflectance is not equal to 20, then the value for CU must be adjusted. The CU value is higher if $\rho_{FC}$ is greater than 20, and lower if $\rho_{FC}$ is less than 20.

## ② DETERMINE EFFECTIVE CEILING AND FLOOR CAVITY REFLECTANCES

| PERCENT BASE (CEILING OR FLOOR) REFLECTANCE | (80) ceiling | | | | | | (20) floor | | | | | |
|---|---|---|---|---|---|---|---|---|---|---|---|---|
| PERCENT WALL REFLECTANCE | 90 | 80 | 70 | 60 | (50) | 40 | 90 | 80 | 70 | 60 | (50) | 40 |
| CAVITY RATIO | | | | | | | | | | | | |
| 0.2 | 79 | 78 | 78 | 77 | 77 | 76 | | | | | | |
| 0.4 | 79 | 77 | 76 | 75 | 74 | 73 | | | | | | |
| 0.6 | 78 | 76 | 75 | 73 | 71 | 70 | | | | | | |
| 0.8 | 78 | 75 | 73 | 71 | 69 | 67 | | | | | | |
| 1.0 | 77 | 74 | 72 | 69 | 67 | 65 | 25 | 23 | 22 | 20 | 19 | 18 |
| 1.2 | | | | | | | 25 | 23 | 22 | 20 | 19 | 17 |
| 1.4 | | | | | | | 26 | 24 | 22 | 20 | 18 | 17 |
| 1.6 | | | | | | | 27 | 24 | 22 | 20 | 18 | 17 |
| 1.8 | | | | | | | 27 | 25 | 23 | 20 | 18 | 17 |

(CCR = 0.75)   (FCR = 1.13)

INTERPOLATING, $\rho_{CC}$ = 70 and $\rho_{FC}$ = 19

Note that, in principle, the effective reflectances for ceiling and floor cavities decrease as their cavity ratios increase and and wall reflectances decrease.

| LAMP LUMEN DEPRECIATION (LLD) FACTORS FOR SOME TYPICAL LAMPS | | | |
|---|---|---|---|
| LAMP TYPE | WATTS | MEAN | MINIMUM |
| INCANDESCENT | 75 | .90 | .86 |
| | 100 | .93 | .90 |
| | 300 | .91 | .87 |
| FLUORESCENT | 40 | .87 | .83 |
| | 60 | .93 | .89 |
| | 75 | .93 | .89 |
| HID - MERCURY | 250 | .81 | .75 |
| HID - METAL HALIDE | 250 | .83 | .76 |

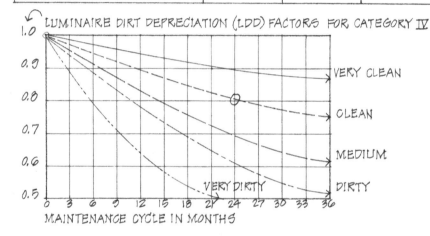

LUMINAIRE DIRT DEPRECIATION (LDD) FACTORS FOR CATEGORY IV

MAINTENANCE CYCLE IN MONTHS

There are two additional factors that contribute to the loss of light available for illumination. The Lamp Lumen Depreciation (LLD) factor takes into account the inherent loss of lumen output of lamps over time. This LLD factor varies with the type of lamp used.

The Luminaire Dirt Depreciation (LDD) factor compensates for light loss due to the accumulation of dirt on the lamp and fixture housing. The LDD factor used will depend on the type of luminaire used, the type of atmosphere in the room, and the expected maintenance practice.

Consult the IES Lighting Handbook or the manufacturer's photometric tables for LLD and LDD values. An overall Maintenance Factor (MF) combines these two values into a single quantity that modifies the working equation for illumination.

$$FC = \frac{L \times CU \times LLD \times LDD}{A}; \quad IF\ MF = LLD \times LDD, then$$

$$FC = \frac{L \times CU \times MF}{A}$$

The working formula for illumination has assumed solving for Footcandles (FC). Since the desired footcandles is normally determined by the function of a space, the formula can be transposed to solve for required Lumens (L).

$$L\ (total\ lumens\ required) = \frac{FC\ (desired) \times Area}{CU \times MF}$$

Since each luminaire has a known number of lamps and each lamp generates a known quantity of lumens, the required number of luminaires can be found by the following:

$$N^{\circ}\ of\ luminaires = \frac{FC\ (desired) \times Area}{CU \times MF \times lumens/lamp \times lamps/luminaire}$$

EXAMPLE CONTINUED FROM PREVIOUS PAGE:
ASSUME: LUMINAIRE USES A SINGLE 300 W INCANDESCENT WITH A LUMEN OUTPUT OF 6360; A CLEANING CYCLE OF 24 MONTHS UNDER CLEAN CONDITIONS.

▶ MF = LLD × LDD = .91 × 0.8 = 0.73

FROM PREVIOUS PAGES:
▶ ROOM = 20' × 40'
▶ CU = .67
DESIRED FOOTCANDLE LEVEL = 100 FC ◀

THEREFORE, REQUIRED NUMBER OF LUMINAIRES =

$$\frac{(100) \times (20 \times 40)}{0.67 \times 0.73 \times 6360 \times 1} = 25.7,.....\underline{26\ LUMINAIRES\ REQUIRED}$$

# COEFFICIENT OF UTILIZATION TABLES FOR THREE TYPES OF LUMINAIRES:
Consult the IES Lighting Handbook, or for the most current data, refer to manufacturer's catalogs.

| TYPE OF LUMINAIRE | TYPICAL DISTRIBUTION AND PERCENT LAMP LUMENS | | ρcc → | 80 | | | 70 | | | 50 | | | 30 | | | 10 | | | 0 |
|---|---|---|---|---|---|---|---|---|---|---|---|---|---|---|---|---|---|---|---|
| | | | ρw → | 50 | 30 | 10 | 50 | 30 | 10 | 50 | 30 | 10 | 50 | 30 | 10 | 50 | 30 | 10 | 0 |
| | MAINT. CAT. ↓ | MAXIMUM S M/H GUIDE ↓ | RCR ↓ | COEFFICIENTS OF UTILIZATION FOR ρFC = 20 | | | | | | | | | | | | | | | |
| DIFFUSING SPHERE WITH INCANDESCENT LAMP | V — 35%↑ 45%↓ | 1.5 | 1 | .71 | .67 | .63 | .66 | .62 | .59 | .56 | .53 | .50 | .47 | .45 | .43 | .39 | .37 | .35 | .31 |
| | | | 2 | .61 | .54 | .49 | .56 | .50 | .46 | .47 | .43 | .39 | .39 | .36 | .33 | .32 | .29 | .27 | .23 |
| | | | 3 | .52 | .45 | .39 | .48 | .42 | .37 | .41 | .36 | .31 | .34 | .30 | .26 | .27 | .24 | .22 | .18 |
| | | | 4 | .46 | .38 | .33 | .42 | .36 | .30 | .36 | .30 | .26 | .30 | .26 | .22 | .24 | .21 | .18 | .15 |
| | | | 5 | .40 | .33 | .27 | .37 | .30 | .25 | .32 | .26 | .22 | .26 | .22 | .19 | .21 | .18 | .15 | .12 |
| | | | 6 | .36 | .28 | .23 | .33 | .26 | .21 | .28 | .23 | .19 | .23 | .19 | .16 | .19 | .15 | .13 | .10 |
| | | | 7 | .32 | .25 | .20 | .29 | .23 | .18 | .25 | .20 | .16 | .21 | .16 | .13 | .17 | .13 | .11 | .09 |
| | | | 8 | .29 | .22 | .17 | .27 | .20 | .16 | .23 | .17 | .14 | .19 | .15 | .12 | .15 | .12 | .09 | .07 |
| | | | 9 | .26 | .19 | .15 | .24 | .18 | .14 | .20 | .15 | .12 | .17 | .13 | .10 | .14 | .11 | .08 | .06 |
| | | | 10 | .23 | .17 | .13 | .22 | .16 | .12 | .19 | .14 | .10 | .16 | .12 | .09 | .13 | .09 | .07 | .05 |
| RECESSED R-40 FLOOD WITH REFLECTOR SKIRT | IV — 0% 85% | 0.7 | 1 | .96 | .94 | .92 | .94 | .92 | .91 | .90 | .89 | .88 | .87 | .86 | .85 | .84 | .84 | .83 | .82 |
| | | | 2 | .91 | .88 | .86 | .90 | .87 | .85 | .87 | .85 | .83 | .84 | .83 | .82 | .82 | .81 | .80 | .79 |
| | | | 3 | .87 | .84 | .81 | .86 | .83 | .81 | .84 | .81 | .79 | .82 | .80 | .78 | .80 | .78 | .77 | .76 |
| | | | 4 | .83 | .80 | .77 | .82 | .79 | .77 | .81 | .78 | .76 | .79 | .77 | .75 | .78 | .76 | .74 | .73 |
| | | | 5 | .79 | .76 | .73 | .79 | .75 | .73 | .77 | .74 | .72 | .76 | .73 | .71 | .75 | .73 | .71 | .70 |
| | | | 6 | .76 | .73 | .70 | .76 | .72 | .70 | .75 | .72 | .69 | .74 | .71 | .69 | .73 | .70 | .68 | .67 |
| | | | 7 | .73 | .69 | .66 | .73 | .69 | .66 | .72 | .68 | .66 | .71 | .68 | .66 | .70 | .67 | .65 | .64 |
| | | | 8 | .70 | .66 | .63 | .70 | .66 | .63 | .69 | .65 | .63 | .68 | .65 | .63 | .67 | .65 | .63 | .62 |
| | | | 9 | .67 | .63 | .60 | .67 | .63 | .60 | .66 | .62 | .60 | .65 | .62 | .60 | .65 | .62 | .60 | .59 |
| | | | 10 | .64 | .60 | .58 | .64 | .60 | .58 | .63 | .60 | .58 | .63 | .60 | .57 | .62 | .59 | .57 | .56 |
| 2 LAMP FLUORESCENT WITH WRAPAROUND PRISMATIC LENS | V — 24%↑ 50%↓ | 1.2 | 1 | .71 | .68 | .65 | .67 | .65 | .62 | .60 | .58 | .56 | .53 | .51 | .50 | .47 | .45 | .44 | .41 |
| | | | 2 | .63 | .58 | .54 | .59 | .55 | .52 | .53 | .50 | .47 | .47 | .45 | .42 | .42 | .40 | .38 | .35 |
| | | | 3 | .56 | .50 | .46 | .53 | .48 | .44 | .47 | .44 | .40 | .42 | .39 | .37 | .38 | .35 | .33 | .31 |
| | | | 4 | .50 | .44 | .40 | .48 | .42 | .38 | .43 | .39 | .35 | .38 | .35 | .32 | .34 | .32 | .29 | .27 |
| | | | 5 | .45 | .39 | .34 | .43 | .37 | .33 | .38 | .34 | .31 | .35 | .31 | .28 | .31 | .28 | .26 | .24 |
| | | | 6 | .41 | .35 | .30 | .39 | .33 | .29 | .35 | .30 | .27 | .32 | .28 | .25 | .28 | .25 | .23 | .21 |
| | | | 7 | .37 | .31 | .27 | .35 | .30 | .26 | .32 | .27 | .24 | .29 | .25 | .22 | .26 | .23 | .20 | .19 |
| | | | 8 | .33 | .27 | .23 | .32 | .26 | .23 | .29 | .24 | .21 | .26 | .22 | .20 | .23 | .20 | .18 | .16 |
| | | | 9 | .30 | .24 | .20 | .29 | .23 | .20 | .26 | .22 | .18 | .24 | .20 | .17 | .21 | .18 | .16 | .14 |
| | | | 10 | .27 | .22 | .18 | .26 | .21 | .18 | .24 | .19 | .16 | .22 | .18 | .15 | .19 | .16 | .14 | .13 |

# TYPES OF LUMINAIRE DISTRIBUTION

Luminaires may be classified according to how they distribute the light emitted by their lamps, and the characteristic spread of their beams. This information, along with the S/MH ratio, is normally supplied by the fixture manufacturer for each luminaire.

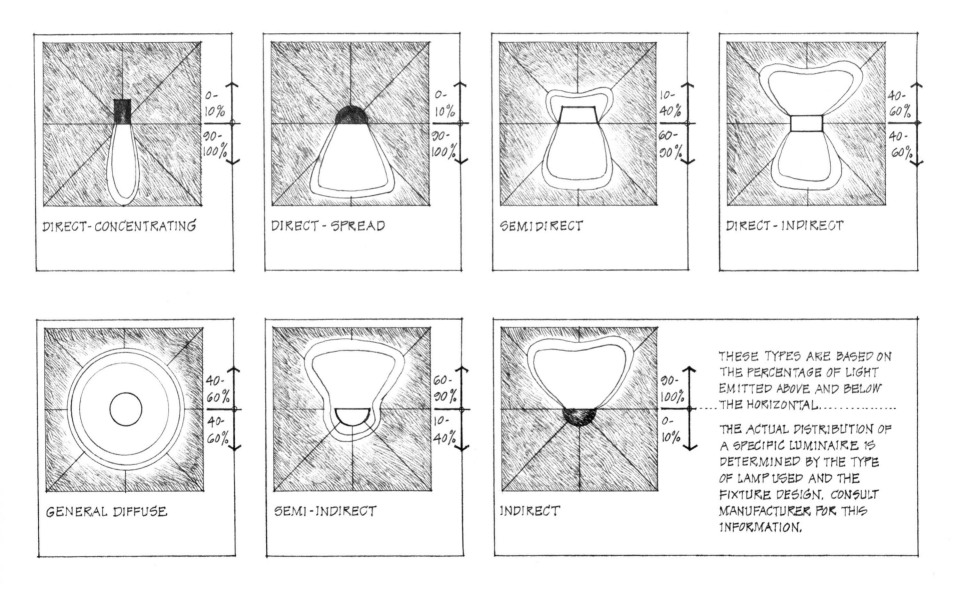

**DIRECT-CONCENTRATING**
0-10%
90-100%

**DIRECT-SPREAD**
0-10%
90-100%

**SEMIDIRECT**
10-40%
60-90%

**DIRECT-INDIRECT**
40-60%
40-60%

**GENERAL DIFFUSE**
40-60%
40-60%

**SEMI-INDIRECT**
60-90%
10-40%

**INDIRECT**
90-100%
0-10%

THESE TYPES ARE BASED ON THE PERCENTAGE OF LIGHT EMITTED ABOVE AND BELOW THE HORIZONTAL.

THE ACTUAL DISTRIBUTION OF A SPECIFIC LUMINAIRE IS DETERMINED BY THE TYPE OF LAMP USED AND THE FIXTURE DESIGN. CONSULT MANUFACTURER FOR THIS INFORMATION.

The S/MH guideline specifies the ratio of maximum luminaire spacing to mounting height in order to achieve an acceptable uniformity of illumination. For most luminaires, the mounting height is measured from the luminaire to an assumed work plane. For semi-indirect and indirect lighting systems that utilize the ceiling plane as a reflector, the mounting height is measured from the ceiling to the work plane.

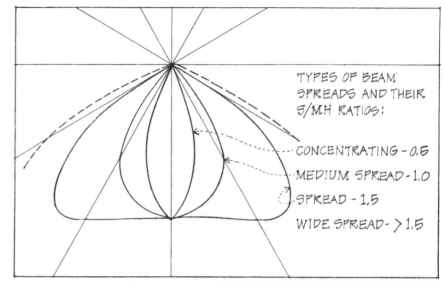

TYPES OF BEAM SPREADS AND THEIR S/MH RATIOS:

CONCENTRATING - 0.5

MEDIUM SPREAD - 1.0

SPREAD - 1.5

WIDE SPREAD - > 1.5

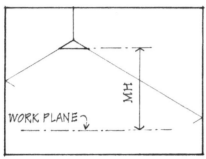

DIRECT LIGHTING OF THE WORK OR VISUAL TASK PLANE.

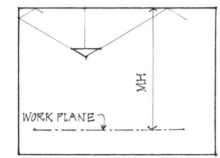

INDIRECT LIGHTING, USING THE CEILING PLANE AS A REFLECTOR.

MAXIMUM-SPACING-TO-MOUNTING-HEIGHT (S/MH) RATIOS ARE CALCULATED AND SUPPLIED BY THE FIXTURE MANUFACTURER.

PLACING LUMINAIRES TOO FAR FROM WALL REDUCES WALL BRIGHTNESS AND MAY RESULT IN LOWER LEVEL OF ILLUMINATION.

FOR INCREASED WALL BRIGHTNESS AND GENERALLY HIGHER LEVEL OF ILLUMINATION, SPACE LUMINAIRES AWAY FROM WALL 1/3 TO 1/2 OF (S).

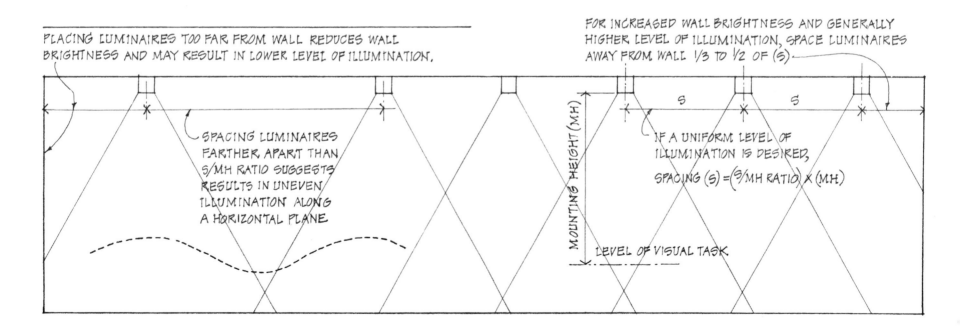

SPACING LUMINAIRES FARTHER APART THAN S/MH RATIO SUGGESTS RESULTS IN UNEVEN ILLUMINATION ALONG A HORIZONTAL PLANE

MOUNTING HEIGHT (MH)

IF A UNIFORM LEVEL OF ILLUMINATION IS DESIRED,

SPACING (S) = (S/MH RATIO) X (MH)

LEVEL OF VISUAL TASK

# ACOUSTICS

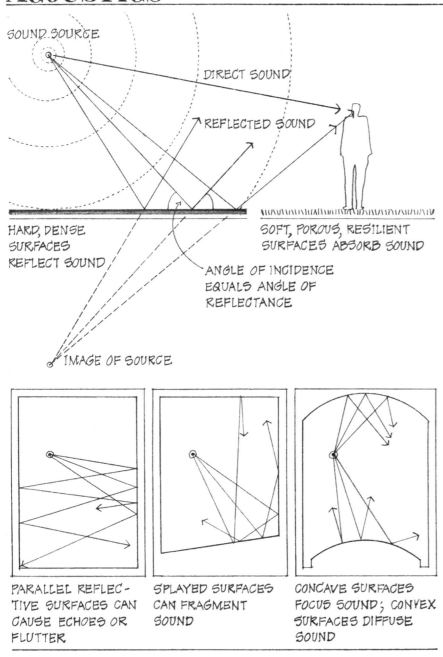

SOUND SOURCE

DIRECT SOUND

REFLECTED SOUND

HARD, DENSE
SURFACES
REFLECT SOUND

SOFT, POROUS, RESILIENT
SURFACES ABSORB SOUND

ANGLE OF INCIDENCE
EQUALS ANGLE OF
REFLECTANCE

IMAGE OF SOURCE

PARALLEL REFLEC-
TIVE SURFACES CAN
CAUSE ECHOES OR
FLUTTER

SPLAYED SURFACES
CAN FRAGMENT
SOUND

CONCAVE SURFACES
FOCUS SOUND; CONVEX
SURFACES DIFFUSE
SOUND

In interior design, we are concerned with the control of sound in interior spaces. More specifically, we want to preserve and enhance desired sounds and reduce or eliminate sounds which would interfere with our activities.

Sound is a form of kinetic energy caused by vibration. The resulting wave motion travels outward spherically from its source until it encounters an obstacle or surface in its path. Hard, dense, rigid materials reflect sound while soft, porous, resilient materials absorb and dissipate sound energy.

When a sound wave reaches our ears, it vibrates our ear drums, resulting in the sensation of hearing. In a room, we first hear a sound directly from its source and then a series of reflections of that sound. Reflective surfaces are useful when they reinforce desirable sounds by directing and distributing their paths in a room. The continued presence of reflected sounds, however, can also cause problems of echo, flutter, or reverberation.

Echoes can occur in large spaces when parallel reflective surfaces spaced more than 60 feet (18 m) apart cause the interval between direct and reflected sounds to be more than 1/15 th of a second. In smaller rooms, parallel reflective surfaces can cause mini-echoes or flutter. Reverberation refers to the continued presence of a sound in a space. While some music is enhanced with long reverberation times, speech can become muddled in such an acoustic environment. To correct these situations, it may be necessary to alter the shape and orientation of a room's surfaces or install more sound-absorbing materials.

The requirements for sound level, reverberation time, and resonance vary with the nature of the activity and the types of sounds generated. An acoustical engineer, given stated criteria, can determine the acoustical require-ments for a space. The interior designer should be aware of how the selection and disposition of reflective and absorbent materials affect the acoustical qualities of a room.

Unwanted noise generated outside a room can be controlled in three ways. The first is to control and isolate the noise at its source. The second is to organize the building plan such that noisy areas are located as far away as possible from quiet areas. The third is to eliminate possible paths - through the air or through a building's structure - that the noise can take from its source to the space.

Sound can be transmitted through the solid materials of a building's structure. Since structure-borne sounds are difficult to control, they should be isolated at their source. Using quiet equipment, resilient mountings, and flexible connections can help reduce structure-borne sound.

Sound can be transmitted through any clear air path, even the tiniest cracks around doors, windows, and electrical outlets. Careful weatherstripping to block these openings can help prevent airborne noise from entering a room.

Sound can also penetrate a room's wall, floor, or ceiling construction. This transmission can be reduced by introducing discontinuity in the construction assembly and using heavy, rigid materials that resist sound vibration. As a guide to designers, various construction assemblies have been tested for their theoretical insulation value and assigned an STC (Sound Transmission Class) rating.

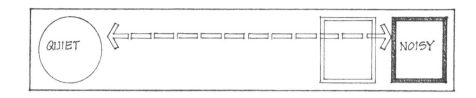

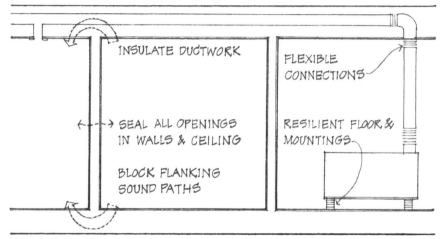

CONTROLLING AIR-BORNE AND STRUCTURE-BORNE SOUND

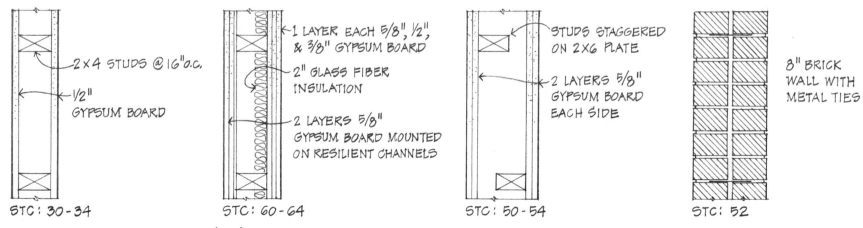

2×4 STUDS @ 16"o.c.

1/2" GYPSUM BOARD

STC: 30-34

1 LAYER EACH 5/8", 1/2", & 3/8" GYPSUM BOARD

2" GLASS FIBER INSULATION

2 LAYERS 5/8" GYPSUM BOARD MOUNTED ON RESILIENT CHANNELS

STC: 60-64

STUDS STAGGERED ON 2×6 PLATE

2 LAYERS 5/8" GYPSUM BOARD EACH SIDE

STC: 50-54

8" BRICK WALL WITH METAL TIES

STC: 52

SOUND TRANSMISSION CLASS (STC) RATINGS OF SEVERAL WALL ASSEMBLIES

# STANDARDS & CODES

This final section outlines some considerations of a system which, while not immediately visible, affects the design of a building and its interior spaces. This system consists of a variety of laws and regulations enacted by federal, state, and local governments in an effort to protect the public health, safety, and general welfare.

Zoning regulations control the size, location, and use of buildings. Building codes regulate how a building is constructed and occupied. Many of these regulations incorporate standards established by governmental or independent testing agencies. (See page 312 for a listing of model codes and standards.)

While architects and engineers bear the primary responsibility for complying with code requirements, the interior designer should be aware of these regulatory devices and be sensitive to how they might affect the design of interior spaces. It should also be remembered that codes often set minimum standards, and mere compliance will not ensure that a building will be efficient, comfortable, or well designed.

The following are some specific areas of concern which affect the work of the interior designer. For further detailed requirements, always check the applicable codes.

The applicable building code usually specifies minimum standards for the structural stability of a building and the quality and design of its materials and construction. When planning the interior of a new building or the remodeling of an existing one, an architect or engineer should be consulted if any alterations to a building's structural elements are anticipated.

Fire safety is a prime area of concern of building codes. Requirements for the noncombustibility or fire-resistance of a building's structural elements and exterior walls are specified according to the building's occupancy, floor area, height, and location. In addition, fire-resistant walls and doors may be required to subdivide a building into separate areas and prevent a fire in one area from spreading to others.

Even when a building's structure would not support combustion, a fire can occur because of its finish materials and contents. This is of particular significance for interior designers when specifying such materials as carpet, draperies, upholstery, and furniture finishes. Regulations may prohibit the use of materials with a low flash point or set standards for the degree of flame spread and smoke emission allowed.

Sprinkler systems are increasingly being relied on to control a fire that does start. In addition, a type of fire/smoke detector and alarm system is usually required to warn of fire.

The means-of-egress requirements of fire codes provide for the safe and efficient evacuation of a building in case of fire. These requirements are usually based on a building's size, construction, and type of occupancy. In principle, there should be at least two alternative ways of exiting a building from any space within in case one route is cut off by fire or smoke. Exit passages, stairs, ramps, and doorways should be clearly marked, well lit, and wide enough to accommodate the number of occupants. Exit doors should swing outward in the direction of travel and, in places of public assembly, be equipped with panic hardware that will unlatch under pressure.

In addition to structural and fire safety, general areas of health and safety are dealt with in building codes. These include the design of stairways in terms of allowable riser-to-tread ratios, minimum widths based on occupancy, the use of landings, and requirements for handrails.

For habitable spaces, natural light must be provided by exterior glazed openings, and natural ventilation by means of exterior openings. These requirements are usually based on a percentage of a room's floor area. For some types of occupancy, artificial light and a mechanically operated ventilating system can be substituted.

Increased attention is being paid to making buildings, particularly government and other public facilities, accessible to the physically handicapped - to the blind, the deaf, or those confined to a wheelchair. Specific concerns include the use of ramps and elevators for access to the various levels of a building, adequate space and uncluttered layouts for ease of movement, provision of usable restrooms and other facilities, accessibility of hardware such as door handles, light switches, and elevator controls, and non-visual means of orientation for the sight-impaired.

## MODEL CODES AND SPONSORING ORGANIZATIONS

Basic Building Code
Basic Fire Protection Code
Basic Plumbing Code

- Building Officials and Code Administrators International, Inc.

National Building Code
Fire Prevention Code

- American Insurance Association
  (formerly National Board of Fire Underwriters)

Uniform Building Code

- International Conference of Building Officials

National Electrical Code
Life Safety Code

- National Fire Protection Association

National Plumbing Code

- American Society of Mechanical Engineers

Uniform Plumbing Code

- International Association of Plumbing and Mechanical Officials


## ORGANIZATIONS THAT ISSUE STANDARDS

ANSI    American National Standards Institute
ASTM    American Society for Testing and Materials
FHA    Federal Housing Administration
GSA    General Services Administration
HUD    Department of Housing and Urban Development
NBS    National Bureau of Standards
NFPA    National Fire Protection Association
UL    Underwriters' Laboratories Inc.